GUIDEBOOKS

DEVON

AND EXMOOR

WILLIAM FRICKER

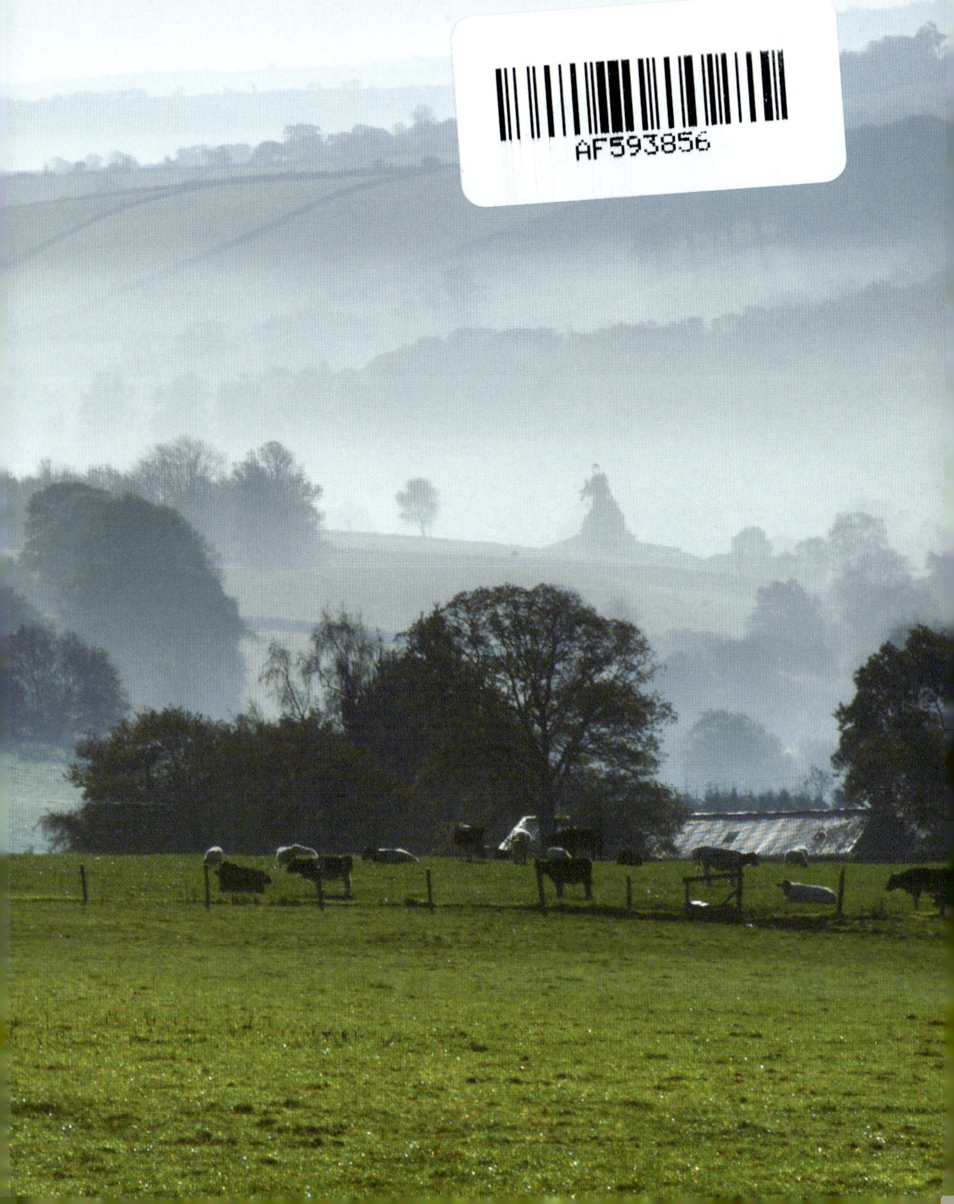

To Isabella, Harry, Flora and Alice, fellow habitués of Devon

Research & Text: William Fricker

Photography: William Fricker (unless as credited with an initial- see page 204)

First published in the United Kingdom, in 2007, by Goldeneye, Unit 10, Chivenor Business Park, Barnstaple, North Devon EX31 4AY

www.goldeneyeguides.co.uk

Cartographic Consultants: Cox Cartographic Ltd

Maps taken from Goldeneye's Digital Database

Book design and layout: Chris Dyer Design

A CIP catalogue record for this book is available from the British Library.

ISBN Number 1-85965 173 9

EAN Number 978185965173 5

Printed in England

Abbreviations in Text

C14	14th Century
Mar-Oct	1 March to 31 October (inclusive)
NT	National Trust property
EH	English Heritage property
BHs	Bank Holidays
W/Es	Weekends
East	Easter
E/C	Early Closing
TIC	Tourist Information Centre
M	Monday
Tu	Tuesday
W	Wednesday
Th	Thursday
F	Friday
Sa	Saturday
Su	Sunday
SS	Supplied by Subject (reference illustrations)
WL	Wolsey Lodges

Beach & Surfing Abbreviations

HT	High Tide
HZ	Hazardous/Dangerous
Ls	Lefts (left turns)
LG	Lifeguard
LT	Low Tide
N	North
P	Parking
Rs	Rights (right turns)
S	South
S-B	Surfboard
SW	Southwest
WC	Toilets

With special thanks to the guys at Atlantic Surfboards, and Surf South West, for checking our surfing details.

English Heritage Opening Times

The general rule is: Good F or 1 Apr (whichever is earlier) to 30 Sept, daily 10-6, (from 9 in July/Aug). 1 Oct to Maundy Th or 31 Mar (whichever is earlier), Tu-Su 10-4, closed 24-26 Dec & 1 Jan.

B&B and Hotel Prices

£	Up to £35
££	£36 - £50
£££	£51 - £80
££££	£81 - £100
£££££	£101 - £150
££££££	Over £150

Correct Information

The contents of this publication were believed to be correct and accurate at the time of printing. However, Goldeneye accepts no responsibility for any errors, omissions or changes in the details given, or for the consequences arising thereto, from the use of this book. However, the publishers would greatly appreciate your time in notifying us of any changes or new attractions (or places to eat, drink and stay) that you consider merit inclusion in the next edition. Your comments are most welcome, for we value the views and suggestions of our readers. Please write to: The Editor, Goldeneye, 10 Chivenor Business Park, Barnstaple EX31 4AY, Great Britain.

"Hail thou, my native soil! Thou blessed plot,
Whose equal all the world affordeth not!
Show me who can so many crystal rills,
Such sweet clothed valleys, or aspiring hills;
Such woods, grand pastures, quarries, wealthy mines,
Such rocks in which the diamond fairly shines;
And, if the earth can show the like again,
Yet, will she fail in her sea-ruling men.
Time never can produce men to o'ertake
The fames of Grenville, Davies, Gilbert, Drake,
Or worthy Hawkins, or of thousands more,
That by their power made the Devonian shore
Mock the proud Tagus; for whose richest spoil
The boasting Spaniard left the Indian soil
Bankrupt of store, knowing it would quit cost
By winning this, though all the rest were lost."

William Brown of Tavistock 1590-1645

Saunton Sands

When I started on this Odyssey I gave myself *so many* months to do the research, photography and final copy. I had the advantage of having collected, over many years, a vast database of information and images, but my task was continually extended. First, by the enormity of my subject, and second, by my own search for perfection, and my endless self-criticism, which at times, left me floundering. Would I ever finish this book? My poor wife, Caroline, has had to put up with my constant soul searching and remonstrations. But it is to her credit that she believed the task would eventually be finished. I must also thank my book designer, Chris Dyer, for persuading me to expand the pages to let the book breath with a varying tempo. On my travels across this great county I met many Devonians (and Blow-Ins) who generously gave me their time, friendship, and refreshment, when most needed, and who urged me to get the job done. I hope I haven't disappointed them.

I may well have infuriated many by missing out a favourite village or church, or country pub. I can only apologise. But be assured, as soon as this book is printed I will be considering ways of improving the next edition. But Dear Reader, I would like to hear from you, and I value your suggestions, and with a little luck the first edition will sell out, and I can swiftly make amends with the second edition.

William Fricker

Buckland Barton, April 2007

Buckland Wood

Overbecks Gardens

PAX

Devon is a big county, England's third largest after Yorkshire and Lincolnshire. It has been described as the most beautiful county in England. A land of rich pastures; green fields, rivers and woodland encompassing two National Parks, and a coastline diverse in its ruggedness and endless charm. A landscape so achingly beautiful that one wonders what the hedgerows and meadows were like before the arrival of carbon emissions and pesticides.

It is a county with a long and chequered history, producing men with big ideas; Drake, Hawkins, Raleigh who sailed the seas in tiny craft, in the name of Elizabeth 1, and England. These men were Soldiers, Privateers, Men of Letters, Scientists, Navigators, brave beyond measure. They brought great pride to Devon, and wealth to the merchants of Dartmouth, Plymouth and London, and power, to England.

It is a sobering thought to ponder, that in this Bicentenary Year, of the, Abolition of the Slave Trade, that Devon and England's wealth originated from this horrific business. Although, most of the commercial underwriting came from Bristol and London, it was to the Devon Privateers that these merchants looked to do their dastardly deeds.

Devon was on the Front Line against the Spanish, Dutch and the Portugese. It was indeed the Wild West of its day, and it was to Devon Men that England sort to defend our trade routes and protect us from marauding Spaniards.

Life in the countryside was spare and unforgiving. The peasant's lot was not to be envied. The land was owned by a small number of families who came over from Normandy with William the Conqueror. Town life saw the upheavals of plague and fires. One-half of the clergy were wiped out in the plague of 1348.

It was not until the Railway Age that tourism took a foothold in the economy of the region. Shipbuilding has been a constant provider of work, precarious at times, for the yards of Devonport and Appledore.

Devon is now England's greenest county. The County Council is championing Sustainable Tourism to combat global warning. There are more green businesses and organic food producers here than anywhere in the UK. We have included many of the best farm shops, restaurants, hotels and gastro-pubs. Our selection has been severe. We expect them to use local produce, for Devon's larder is so abundant, there should be no excuses for providing less than excellent fare. We expect top quality. So look to feast on this green and pleasant land. Bon Appetit.

Devon has long been a favourite family holiday destination, and many who come, year on year, have second homes. South and East Devon has long been a last Port-of-Call for the genteel retired. North Devon has a growing reputation as Devon's surfing centre. The M5 stops at Exeter, and this creates two westbound routes that strike to the north, and south, of Dartmoor. Those Cornwall bound press their foot down and leave behind a Devon foolishly unexplored and ignored. But, before you, too, head off on a fast-flowing A-road, consider branching off onto an unbeaten track. Dispose of your Sat-Nav and take time to wander aimlessly across the back reaches of Exmoor and Dartmoor, into the unbidden depths of mid-Devon, and beyond. You may well find your Shangrila.

St Boniface, see page 85

These recommendations are in no order of preference.

1. Exmoor pony trip – there are many riding schools who organize daily or weekend rides. See the Exmoor Visitor newspaper.
2. Take a surf lesson in Croyde, Saunton or Woolacombe – two hour, or half-day lessons.
3. Hire a Yawl (small boat with motor) from Salcombe and explore the estuary, or fish for bass and mackerel (tackle provided).
4. Evensong Exeter Cathedral.
5. Dartmoor Tors Walk – bag five tors in a morning or afternoon.
6. Tour the Blue Plaque buildings in Sidmouth.
7. Cycle the Tarka Trail, from Torrington to Meeth, and back.
8. Take an Exmoor Safari in a Land Rover Defender and spy the wild deer.
9. Take a trip to Lundy, and swim with the seals.
10. Treat yourself to a Dry Martini (007's Cocktail) in the Art Deco setting of the Burgh Island Hotel.
11. Catch the Dart Valley Railway from Paignton to Kingswear.
12. Take a boat trip up the River Dart from Dartmouth to Totnes, or vice versa.
13. Descend to the Teign Gorge from Castle Drogo.
14. Drive the coastal road from Porlock to Lynmouth.
15. Treat yourself to a Devon Cream Tea.
16. Lunch at an English Country House hotel; Combe House Hotel, Blagdon Manor, Lewtrenchard Manor or Hotel Endsleigh.
17. Fish n Chips at Babbacombe.
18. The fan vaulting, St Mary's, Ottery St Mary.
19. The Devon Guild of Craftsmen, Bovey Tracey followed by a visit to see the Rood Screen in the Parish church. An opportunity to compare old and new craftsmanship.
20. Widecombe in the Moor. To reach it you will have had to cross the Moor. You must decide whether to go North, South, East or West.
21. Aimlessly follow a South Hams country lane in Late May/Early June and marvel at the wild hedgerows.
22. Family bucket and spade beaches; Putsborough (North Devon), Hope Cove (South Hams), Blackpool Sands (South Hams).
23. Retail Therapy; Dart Farm Village, Topsham.
24. Festival Fever; Literary or Music Festivals at Dartington.
25. Surf Festival (Ocean Fest) Croyde.
26. Food Festivals at Dartmouth and Exeter.
27. Visit a Castle, Country House or Garden.

Powderham Castle ss

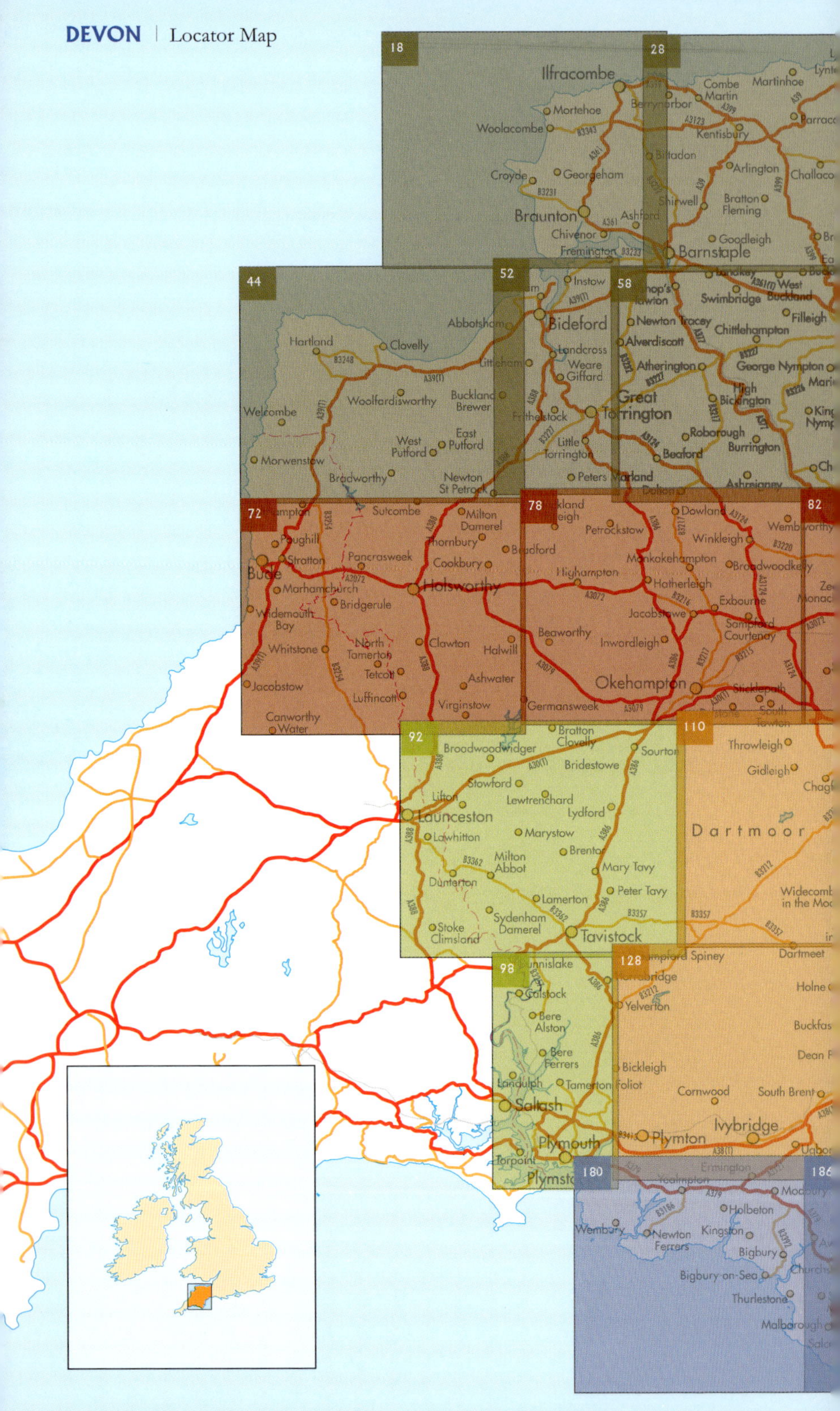
18
28
44
52
58
72
78
82
92
98
110
128
180
186
Ilfracombe
Mortehoe
Woolacombe
Croyde
Georgeham
Braunton
Chivenor
Fremington
Combe Martin
Martinhoe
Berrynarbor
Kentisbury
Bittadon
Arlington
Shirwell
Bratton Fleming
Goodleigh
Barnstaple
Instow
Bideford
Abbotsham
Hartland
Clovelly
Landcross
Weare Giffard
Woolfardisworthy
Buckland Brewer
Welcombe
West Putford
East Putford
Morwenstow
Bradworthy
Newton St Petrock
Little Torrington
Great Torrington
Peters Marland
Newton Tracey
Alverdiscott
Swimbridge
Chittlehampton
Filleigh
Atherington
George Nympton
High Bickington
Roborough
Beaford
Burrington
Sutcombe
Milton Damerel
Thornbury
Bradford
Poughill
Stratton
Bude
Pancrasweek
Cookbury
Holsworthy
Marhamchurch
Bridgerule
Widemouth Bay
Whitstone
North Tamerton
Clawton
Halwill
Tetcott
Ashwater
Jacobstow
Luffincott
Virginstow
Canworthy Water
Petrockstow
Dowland
Winkleigh
Monkokehampton
Broadwoodkelly
Highampton
Hatherleigh
Exbourne
Jacobstowe
Sampford Courtenay
Beaworthy
Inwardleigh
Okehampton
Germansweek
Broadwoodwidger
Bratton Clovelly
Sourton
Bridestowe
Stowford
Lifton
Lewtrenchard
Launceston
Lydford
Lawhitton
Marystow
Brentor
Milton Abbot
Mary Tavy
Dunterton
Peter Tavy
Lamerton
Stoke Climsland
Sydenham Damerel
Tavistock
Throwleigh
Gidleigh
Dartmoor
Calstock
Bere Alston
Bere Ferrers
Landulph
Tamerton Foliot
Saltash
Plymouth
Torpoint
Yelverton
Bickleigh
Cornwood
South Brent
Plympton
Ivybridge
Dartmeet
Buckfast
Yealmpton
Holbeton
Wembury
Newton Ferrers
Kingston
Bigbury
Bigbury-on-Sea
Thurlestone

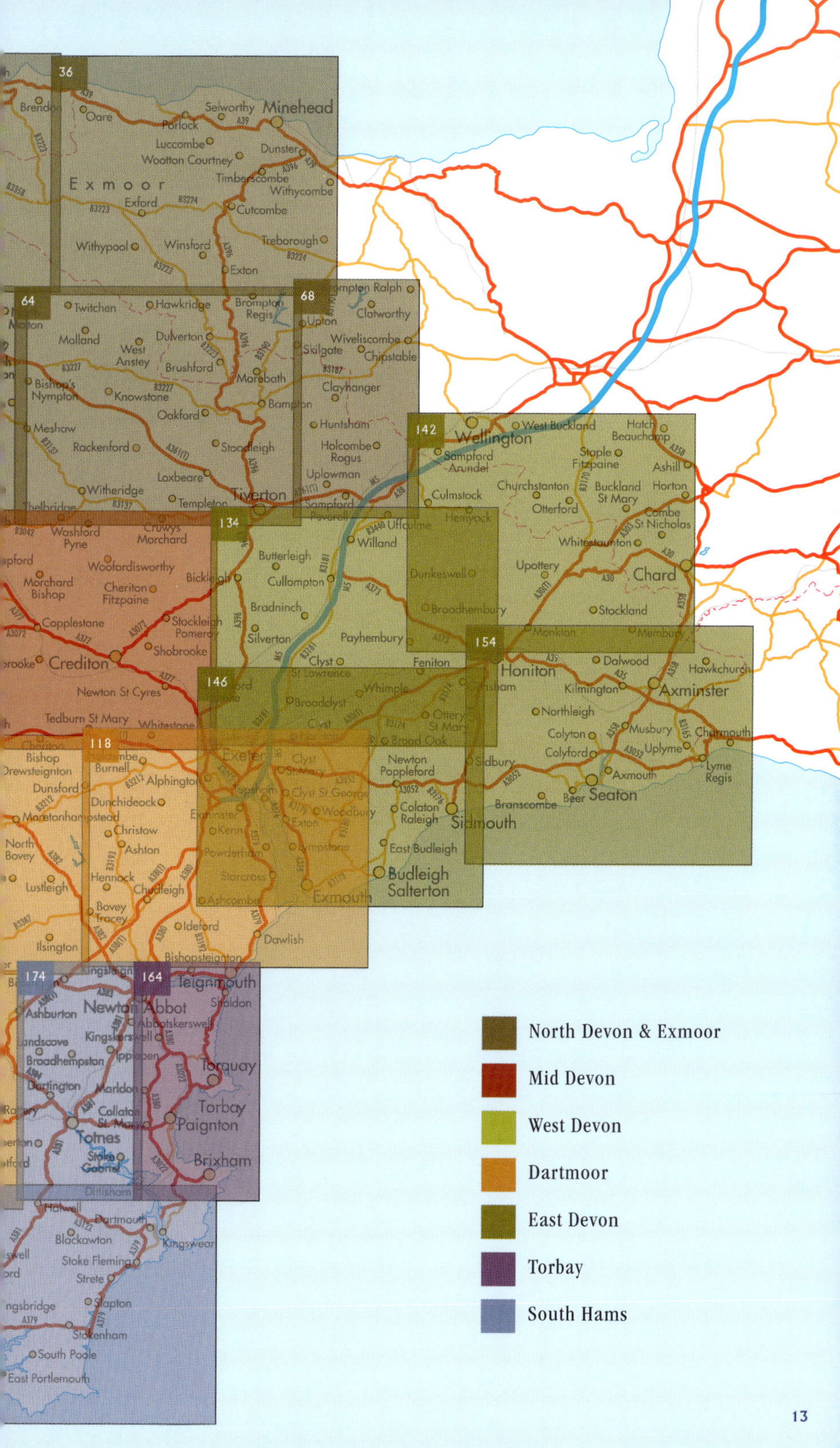

North Devon & Exmoor
Mid Devon
West Devon
Dartmoor
East Devon
Torbay
South Hams

A Breif Nott of ye places of Descent in ye County of Devon yt are most dangerous, & require greatest regard, & assistance. /
In ye South Division.
Plymouth. /
Salcum haven. /
The long Sandes in ye pishes of Stokenham Slapton, & Stokefleming being 4 myles in length
Blackpoole in ye pishes of Stokefleming being betweene the haven of Dartmouth, & long Sands. /
The Haven, & Port of Dartmouth. /
Torribay wth ye pishes of Brixham Paington Cockington, & Tormoham contayning in length 4 myles.
In ye East division.
Saltrton in ye pish of Budleigh cont a myle & halfe in length
In ye North Division
Wollacomb Sands in ye pishes of Georgham & Morrthoe cont in length 2 myles. /
PART OF CORNWALE
DERT MORE
Barnestable
Okehampton
Plimpton
Plymouth
Lanceston
Chimleigh
Modbury
Hather ley
Bediford
Lyfton
OCCIDENS

PARTE OF SOMERSET SHIRE
Duluerton
Wellington
Tenerton
Columbton
Charde
PARTE OF DORSET SHIRE
Lyme
Excester
OCEANVS
BRITANNICVS
Tor bay
Dartmouth hauen
Chidley
Culliton
DEVONIÆ COMITAT RERVMQVE omnium in eodem memorabilium re: cens, vera pticularisq descriptio
Anno Dni 1575
Scala Miliarum

North Devon is a rural landscape of small villages, rich pastures, secluded coves and long sandy beaches. The two ancient ports of Barnstaple and Bideford have grown up beside the wide estuary of the Taw and Torridge rivers.

Stretching southwards from these ports is the gentle pastoral countryside known as 'The Land of the Two Rivers' so vividly brought to life in the works of Henry Williamson. The warm equable climate, together with the nature of the countryside provides excellent recreational opportunities, particularly for the walker, fisherman and surfer, and remains a favourite destination for family beach holidays.

The Hartland Peninsula on the western tip is Devon's Land's End, and a place tempered by the punishing seas and dramatic coastline. Often overlooked because of its isolation, a visit should be planned in with it's neighbour, Clovelly. The coast is in sharp contrast to the pastoral, inland country that runs in an Easterly direction from Great Torrington to Tiverton.

The Exmoor National Park is largely in Somerset, with a small portion lying in Devon. At times the climate is harsh with mist, cloud and rain, and is reminiscent of Scotland. When the skies clear, the wild, wide beauty is unsurpassed. The landscape is undulating, full of rolling hills, marshland, bracken, heather and gorse, and divided by swift flowing streams which cut through the steep-sided valleys, known as combes. The rolling moorland provides splendid views seawards across the Bristol Channel to Wales. In places the coast is crowned with high cliffs that fall precipitously to the sea.

The Exmoor sheep and wild ponies are seen everywhere, as can be found buzzard and raven. The roaming red deer is rarely seen close to, they feed at night and by day lie hidden in the woods or bracken. But, if startled (although unlikely, for they will hear and smell you coming) they can be a dangerous animal.

Of a somewhat gentler aspect than Dartmoor, and formerly a royal hunting forest. Exmoor is the only highland area of England to overlook the sea. Like Dartmoor, it provides contrasting landscapes of remote moorland and snug villages, but also a fine rugged coastline. It is noted for its ponies, somewhat smaller than the Dartmoor variety, and is the only place in England where red deer can still be seen. Less than half the National Park lies within the Devon boundary, but this includes the towns of Lynton and Lynmouth, the Doone Valley with its romantic associations, the beautiful Heddon Valley and over 20 miles of truly magnificent coastline.

Hoar Oak Water, Watersmeet

A
B
C
D
E
F
1
2
3
4
5
6
7
8
9
10
Tunnel Beaches
Tourist Information Centre
Ilfracombe Museum
Car Park
Church of St Philip and St James
Post Office
Aquarium
St Nicholas Chapel
Car Park
Ilfracombe Princess
No. 11
The Quay
Bristol Channel Cruises
Toilets
Car Park
Cinema
HIGH ST
Westwood
TORRS PARK
All Saints Church
CHURCH ST
HIGHFIELD ROAD
Church of St Peter
HILLSBOROUGH ROAD
BARNSTAPLE ROAD
CHAMBERCOMBE RD
Torrs Park
ST BRANNOCK'S RD
MARLBOROUGH ROAD
Chambercombe
Ilfracombe
LUNDY ISLAND
North West Point
North East Point
North End
Gannet's Rock
Gannet's Bay
Half Wall
Frenchman's Landing
St James's Stone
Brazen Ward
Long House and Farm (Widows Tenement rems)
Threequarter Wall
Tibbett's Point
Tibbett's Hill
Halfway Wall
Jenny's Cove
Needle Rock
Quarter Wall
Quarterwall Cottages (rems)
Beacon Hill
Old Lighthouse
Shop
Halftide Rock
Milcombe House
Marisco Tavern
Jetty
Goat Island
Castle
Rat Island
Surf Point
Shutter Point
Seal's Hole
ILFRACOMBE (summer only)
BIDEFORD
CLOVELLY (summer only)
Baggy Point
Croyde Hoe
Middlebor
Hi
Croyde Bay
Downend
St Brannock's Church
CHALONER'S RD
Lemon Grass
SAUNTON ROAD
CAEN ST
Museum
Toilets
Car Park
Tourist Information Centre
Westone Deli
Squires Fish Restaurant
Post Office
EXETER RD
Braunton Great Field
Braunton
Lundy
0
1
2 miles
0
1
2
3 kilometres

G
H
J
K
L
M
1
2
3
4
5
6
7
8
9
10
Bristol Channel Cruises
Aquarium
Dovetail's Gallery
No. 11 The Quay
Tunnel Beaches
The Old Corn Mill
Ilfracombe Museum
Ilfracombe Princess
Westwood
La Gendamerie
Lundy
Rillage Point
Samson's Bay
Widmouth Head
Cupstone Point
Beacon Point
Hele Bay
ILFRACOMBE
Brandy Cove Point
ST PHILIP & ST JAMES
ST NICHOLAS
Hele
Watermouth Castle
Widmouth Hill
Goosewell
A399
Flat Point
ALL SAINTS
Torrs Park
ST PETER
Chambercombe
Chambercombe Manor
Hagginton Hill
Berrynarbor
Pensport Rock
Shag Point
Bull Point
Tarka Trail
Lee Bay
Grey Cottage
Lee
Southcliffe Hall
Lincombe
Slade
A361
Shield Tor
Kitstone Hill
Hill Barton
Rockham Bay
Higher Warcombe
Windcutter Hill
Slade Res.
B3232
Warmscombe
Sterridge Valley
ST MARY MAGDALENE
Mortehoe
Town Farm House
Shellfish
Borough Farm
Shaftesborough
Oakridge
Francis
Twitchen
Watersmeet Hotel
Borough Cross
Mullacott Cross
Two Pots
A3123
Woolscott Barton
Seymour Villas
B3343
Ettiford
Farm Shop
Twitchen
Tumuli
The Boardwalk
Beachcomber
Woolacombe
Osaborough
Trimstone
Hore Down Gate
Narracott
Tumulus
West Beach
Red Barn
Potter's Hill
Willingcott
Cheglinch
West Stowford Barton
Woolacombe Sands
Roadway
Bradwell
Dean
Tumuli
Colam Stream
Woolacombe Down
Higher Spreacombe
Buttercombe
ST CALIXTUS
West Down
28
Pickwell Down
Tarka Trail
ST PETER
Bittadon
North Downs
Snow Ball
Fullabrook Down
Hartnoll Barton
Bar
Pickwell
Ox's Cross
North Buckland
Metcombe Down
Putsborough
Little Comfort
Little Silver
The Lower House
ST GEORGE
Woodcrafts
Metcombe
Georgeham
Ora Hill
Crowborough Farm
Halsinger Down
Beara Down
Patsford
Swindon Down
B3232
Croyde
Forda
Darracott
Gipsy Corner
Thatch
Groove
Cross
Upcott
Nethercott
Winsham
Halsinger
Milltown
South Hole
Knowle
Middle Marwood
Whiddon
Saunton Down
North Lobb
The Castle
Beer Charter
Saunton
Lobb
Buckland
Boode
Marwood
B3231
ST MICHAEL
Walking on Waves
Surf South West
Ash Barton
Whitehall
Guineaford
Marwood Hill
Kingsheanton
ST BRANNOCK
Braunton Down
Pippacott
Saunton Sands
Braunton
Lemon Grass
Squires Fish Restaurant
Westone Deli
Luscott Barton
Prixford
Mainstone
Braunton Great Field
Velator
Heanton Punchardon
Windy Cross
Fishery
Blakewell
Danger Area
ST AUGUSTINE
West Ashford
ST PETER
Ashford
Tutshill
Braunton Burrows
Wrafton
A361
Toll
Braunton Marsh
River Caen
RMB Chivenor
A361
Tarka Trail
Chivenor Business Park
Penhill Point
ST MARY
Bradiford
Pilton
Pottington
Danger Area
Tarka Trail
Horsey Island
Fremington Quay Café & Heritage Centre
Penhill
New Bridge
Sticklepath
Point
Danger Area
River Taw
Tarka Trail
ST PAUL
Muddlebridge
B3233
ST MARY
The Neck
Yelland
B3233
Fremington
Combrew
Bickington
Hele

52

BRAUNTON

Bustling village, and one of the oldest in Devon. An early Celtic settlement developed by the legendary St Brannock who arrived by sail in a stone coffin from Brittany! In Devon, considered to be the West Country's centre for the surf and board industry. At the last count there were twelve surf (and factory) shops in the village. Not to be missed, the charming church of St Brannock. Velator is the former shipping centre and harbour for the village. The village has a number of pubs and coffee shops serving light meals. There are no gastro-foodie pubs to encounter. The White Lion is popular with surfers, and has a good Indian Restaurant/Takeaway, the London Inn is for hard drinkers and TV sports, the Mariners for sailors and seafarers, and the Black Lion behind the church is small, and the local's Local, serving Doom Bar. For a family style pub, the Tarka Inn at Chivenor serves average fare, and on a clear day has a spectacular view across the Estuary. (J8)

Velator Creek, Braunton

Special Places to Visit...

Braunton Museum, Caen Street Car Park. Super little museum illustrating local life, village crafts, strip-farming and coastal sailing ships. TIC. Open daily all year. (J8) 01271 816688

Braunton Burrows. 2,400 acre National Nature Reserve extending three miles along the estuary and coast. Important for the study of evolution of sand dunes and associated plant ecology (400 species). Abounds in wildlife; foxes, rabbits, hedgehogs, moles, weasels, mink, shrews, lizards and voles. Also butterflies, birds and rare plants. Free public access except for an area sometimes closed for military training. Recently categorised by UNESCO as a Biosphere Reserve to accord it international protection. Nearby is Braunton Great Field (best seen from the hill above), a rare survival of the ancient strip tenure system of farming. Originally divided into one acre strips (on Edward 1's ruling) - the Chief (Lord of the Manor) would have at least 500 acres, the Freeman 100 acres and the peasants rented strips from their Chief. Families would share their ploughs and oxen. Today, five farmers work this land. (G9)

Braunton Marsh

Braunton Marsh. Former wild, tidal salt marsh now tamed into lush pastureland inhabited by cattle, wild flowers and bountiful birdlife. Protected by the Great Sea Bank stretching from Velator to Broadsands (White House) built in 1808. (G9)

Crow Point. Naturally formed in 1809 and sticks out like a hook. It's 30 feet high in places topped with (protected) Marram grass. Not as accessible as it used to be due to the placement of some hideous lumps of rock. Apparently, to stop overnight campers. (H10)

Saunton Sands. Extensive 4-mile stretch of compact sands cleansed by the rolling Atlantic waves. Overlooked by the giant rabbit warren, Braunton Burrows. Immortalised in the 1920s works of Henry Williamson: "The Dream of Fair Women", "The Pathway", "Tarka the Otter" and "Salar the Salmon". Film location in WW11 for Vivien Leigh's Cleopatra, then subsequently mined (Chivenor was an anti U-Boat base), to be later used as a practice venue for the US Normandy Landings of June 1944. Superb situation for water sports; sand-yachting, beach casting, surfing and windsurfing. Lifeguards in summer. Surf and sea survival school and shops at north end. Beach huts (bungalows) for rent: 01271 892002. Sands Cafe Bar open for food (and drink) only; breakfast, light lunches and dinner. In superb position overlooking the car park (!), and at an excruciating angle for one's neck, the beach. Apparently the local residents blocked the architect's

400,000 bce Acheulean hand axes deposited in Kent's Cavern.

250,000 bce Hand axes deposited in Axe Valley.

Saunton Sands and Braunton Burrows

original plans to provide a view. Open from 10 in seasons. For a really superb view, and a light lunch on the balcony or comfortable sofas, the Saunton Sands Hotel is recommended. (G8)

St Brannock's Church. Norman tower and recently restored lead spire. Noted for its superb medieval bench ends. (J8)

Tarka Trail. A 180 mile trail (280km) follows the route taken by Tarka the Otter on his travels through "The Land of the Two Rivers", the Taw and Torridge, as depicted in Henry Williamson's classic novel "Tarka the Otter" written in the 1920s. The trail can be walked but also offers on and off-road cycling. The trail becomes a dual purpose walkway-cycleway allowing for relatively easy and safe cycling starting at Braunton. The route runs on tarmac beside the Taw Estuary to Barnstaple and can be enjoyed depending on the wind direction. Just hope it follows you. There is however abundant birdlife to hold your interest. From Barnstaple along the south side of the Taw Estuary to Instow with refreshments to be had at Fremington Quay, or John's Deli in Instow. The route now becomes more interesting beside the Torridge to the Puffing Billy pub below Great Torrington, to cross the river to Watergate Bridge, the trail joins a bridle path and what follows is arguably the most interesting section of this trail. It is cyclable on a hybrid, touring or folding bike all the way to Meeth. Look out for the excellent little cafe at Yard, the Railway summit. So you have 32 miles (51km) of traffic-free cycling. There is bike hire at Braunton, Fremington Quay (also bike shop), Bideford and the Puffing Billy, Torrington.

Velator. Former shipping centre and port to Braunton that traded with South Wales and the Bristol Channel ports in coal, salt, manure and flour. The trade was dictated to by tide and weather, and eventually proved too difficult after the channels silted up. (J8)

Where to Eat, Drink & Be Merry...

The Lemon Grass, Caen St.
Popular thai restaurant. Booking essential. (J8) 01271 813663

Squires Fish Restaurant, Exeter Road.
A popular meeting place for locals, and extremely popular with holidaymakers. Always busy. Restaurant and Take-Away facility. Licensed. (J8)

CROYDE

A popular holiday and surfing centre with pretty thatched cottages, camp-sites and (too few) pubs and restaurants. The village can become unduly hectic and rowdy. There are limited places to eat and drink. They say "If you can surf Croyde, you can surf anywhere". The rips and currents are like no other. The Oyster Fall (just off Downend Point) sets the Bar (see Surfing details). Brazing walks to Baggy Point. (G7)

Places to Visit...

Baggy Point. Given to the National in 1939 by Constance and Florence Hyde. A brazing circular 40-minute walk can be had up to the Point where you may see rock climbers traversing the wall, and fisherman longing for bass and conger. Inspired Henry Williamson to write many of his nature stories. Note the unusual plaque at entrance. Access possible for wheelchairs but be prepared for a steep push. NT car park. (F6)

Surf the Hill Mountain Board Centre, Ruda Holiday Village. Learn to mountain board; it's skateboarding, surfing and snowboarding, all rolled into one. Open Su 9-6 weather permitting. (G7) 07816320830 www.surfthehill.co.uk

Where to Eat, Drink & Be Merry...

Blue Groove. Cafe/restaurant and bar serving breakfast, light lunches and evening meals, baguettes, salads and burgers plus cocktails. Artwork on display. Sit outside and admire the cool surfers. (G7) 01271 890111

The Thatch. Pub beloved by surfers (and hangers-on) and their surf chicks. Can be busy in summer. Real Ales. Variety of lagers. Excellent salads and thick-cut sandwiches. B & B. Next door, Billy Budds, more surfy but same ownership. (G7) 01271 890349

Where to Stay...

Combas Farm. Isolated at the end of a long bridle path. Quaint old-fashioned cottage offers homespun comforts. Large kitchen garden and farm produce delivers fab breakfasts. (G6) 01271 890398

Skir Cottage, Georgeham

Ilfracombe Harbour

Painting of Ilfracombe by Unknown Artist, Ilfracombe Museum

Croyde Bay Cottages. Oyster Falls bungalow overlooks Downend and The Oyster Reef, the ultimate break, the Farmhouse is hidden away in downtown Croyde. Both sleep 6. No pets. (F7) 01271 345039 www.croydebaycottages.co.uk

GEORGEHAM

Largely unspoilt village with thatched cottages. Henry Williamson, author of Tarka the Otter, lived much of his life here, settling in Skir Cottage on his return from the First World War. In 1928 he was awarded the Hawthornden Prize for writing Tarka, and with the money he bought some land at Ox's Cross. He's buried in the churchyard. Much expansion and building of new homes. Village store, pub (The Rock) and new dining pub, The Lower House on 01271 890240. (H7)

Places to Stay...

Crowborough Farm B & B. Just a stroll from the pubs of Georgeham. A simply furnished farmhouse, secluded and peaceful. 3 bedrooms. No pets. Open all year. £. (H7) 01271 891005 www.crowboroughfarm.co.uk

8,500-5,500 bce Later Mesolithic deposits in Devon.

3,500-2,500 bce Late Neolithic cultures in Devon.

ILFRACOMBE

A popular holiday centre developed by the Victorians in the Railway Age. A place of high cliffs and rocky beaches bordered by the sweeping Exmoor hills. Well situated for fine coastal walks and trips to Exmoor. The ancient harbour is a great attraction and has recently been refurbished. The town gets a mixed press. It has seen better days but is on the up and is a popular place to live and property is exceptional value for money. New restaurants and galleries are opening, as are contemporary places to stay. It is also close to the beaches of Woolacombe and Croyde and must be considered a place to stay. St Nicholas Chapel and Lighthouse surmount Lantern Hill. Hillsborough Iron Age Fort (a fine walk). Torrs walks. Trips from the quay on Paddle Steamer Waverley and Queen of Cornwall. Landmark Theatre. Cinema. Victorian Fair in July. Lundy Island office. E/C Th.(K3)

Places of Interest…

Aquarium, The Pier. Award-winning, all-weather, family attraction provides a fascinating journey into the aquatic life of North Devon. Follow a unique-zoned journey from an Exmoor stream to Lundy and its marine reserve. Shop and café with outside seating. Open daily Feb-Oct 10-4. (L3) 01271 864533 www.ilfracombeaquarium.co.uk

Bristol Channel Cruises. On board the paddle steamer Waverley (the last ocean-going paddle steamer in the world) and motor cruiser M.V. Balmoral from Minehead and Ilfracombe July-Oct 1/2 term, timetable from TICs. (K3) 01446 721221

Chambercombe Manor, Chambercombe Lane. Attractive small manor house with C16-C17 additions. Period furnished rooms, armour and porcelain. Haunted chamber. 4 acres of Herb and water garden. Teas. Murder Mystery evenings. Open East-Oct Su-F. (L3) 01271 862624

Dovetails Gallery, 60 High Street. Run by enthusiastic Art lecturer who promotes the local art scene; paintings, ceramics, sculpture, glass, jewellery, textiles and prints. Open 9-5. Closed Th & Su. (L3) 01271 864769

Keypits Quads. Adventure and Trekking Centre. Quad bikes, Karting, paint Ball Battles, Thunderball and Off Road Drives. Open East to Oct 10-5. Winter opening by appointment. (M3) 01271 862247 www.keypitts.com

Ilfracombe Museum, Wilder Rd. Fascinating collections of natural history, minerals, Victoriana, maritime and local history. 'Blue Peter Award'. Open daily Apr-Oct 10-5, Nov-Mar M-F 10-1. (L3)

Ilfracombe Princess, The Harbour. Wildlife and coastal cruises to view seals, porpoises and dolphins, and sea birds. Take binoculars. (L2) 01271 979727 wwww.ilfracombeprincess.co.uk

The Old Corn Mill & Pottery, Watermouth Road. Restored C16 watermill with 18ft overshot wheel produces stone ground flour. Pottery made and for sale. Cream teas. Open East or Apr-Oct M-Sa 10-5, Su in Aug. (L3) 01271 863185 www.oldcornmillandpottery.co.uk

Tunnel Beaches. Established in 1823; four unique tunnels were carved through the rocks to create a sheltered beach with tidal seawater pool. It's ideal family bathing with swimming and paddling pool. Café Blue Bar. Open Easter, then daily May-Oct, 10-5 (July-Aug 9-7). Small fee. (K3) 01271 879882 www.tunnelbeaches.co.uk

Twitchen Farm Shop, West Down. Organic Red Ruby Devon beef and lamb from their farm shop; steaks, joints, chops/cutlets and shoulders. Open daily. (K5) 01271 867844

Places to Stay…

Westwood, Torrs Park. Helen and John Vowles have transformed a large Victorian house into a chic, luxurious B & B by using contemporary fabrics and furnishings. The bedrooms are spacious and full of the latest mod cons. Open all year. ££. (K3) 01271 867443 www.west-wood.co.uk

Where to Eat, Drink & Be Merry…

La Gendarmerie, 63 Fore Street. A quality bistro serving fresh produce with a touch of Mediterranean flair. Comfy leather sofas, stripped floors and modern art provide a youthful flourish. (K3) 01271 865984

No 11, The Quay. Damien Hirst's much lauded restaurant and bar has finally opened. Let's hope it does a Rick Stein to rejuvenate the town's prosperity. Laid back Tapas for lunch downstairs, whilst Dinner is served overlooking the harbour, upstairs. Fish is naturally, a speciality, as is local Devon beef. (K3) 01271 868090 www.11thequay.com

LEE

Set in a sheltered combe known as Fuschia Valley, for fuchsias grow wild in the hedgerows and stone banks. The lane leads to Lee Bay, a beach of special marine biological interest overlooked by the Lee Bay Hotel, an eyesore in a spectacular position that requires millions to bring it back to its former (if ever) glory. C14 Grampus Inn. Low tide provides sand and rock pools, and steps to Sandy Cove. Beware of getting stranded from inrushing tide on left sided beach. Note the special patterns of slate made by the swirling currents. Park opposite the church. (J3)

Places to Stay…

Grey Cottage. Julia Waghorn's slate clad cottage will charm you. The views from the steep hillside garden are stupendous. The bedrooms are bright and comfortable; Egyptian cotton sheets and deep baths. Julia is a professional chef. Dinner is not to be missed, and a half bottle of wine is always to hand, so beware of increasing waistlines. Ideal for house parties. (J3) 01271 864360 www.greycottage.co.uk

Woolacombe Sands

Southcliffe Hall.
Imposing building in superb position provides spectacular views down the valley to the sea and Lee Bay. An eclectic mix of architectural and interior design; stained glass, wood carvings and family portraits. The bedrooms are spacious and comfortable with new bathrooms. Evening meals an option. (J3)
01271 867068
www.southcliffehall.co.uk

Morte Point

MORTEHOE

Pretty, isolated hilltop village overlooking Woolacombe and Morte Bay. Surrounded by four campsites. Local beaches are either Rockham Bay reached by a footpath on the North Morte road, or Grunta, below the Old Chapel. A lovely circular family walk out to Morte Point and back via the Cemetery. Two Inns. Fish restaurants. (H4)

Places of Interest...

Borough Farm.
Working Sheepdog Demonstration and Falconry Display by Jonathon Marshall from the North Devon Birds of Prey Centre. (G4)
01271 870056
www.marshallfalcons.co.uk

Bull Point Lighthouse. Built in 1879 to protect shipping from the dangers of Morte Point. Now an automatic station. Self-catering cottages to rent. (H3)

Morte Point. Scene of many shipwrecks and loss of life. Beware of the Morte Race, a notorious and treacherous current. In full flow, an amazing site. An exhilarating spot on windy days. Look out for the razor-sharp rocks, sculptured by wind, rain and the sea. (G4)

Mortehoe Heritage Centre.
Maritime history, local flora and fauna, farming and country skills. 'Hands on' games and puzzles for children. Tractor and trailer rides in July & Aug. Open daily East-Oct. (H4)
01271 870028

St Mary Magdalene, Mortehoe. Founded in 1170 by William de Tracey. Superb Norman doorway. 48 magnificent bench ends. (G4)

Where to Eat, Drink & Be Merry...

Mortehoe Shellfish. The Huelin family run a Lobster-Crabber boat, The Walrus, out of Ilfracombe, and supply various restaurants in the North Devon area. They have also opened their simple home as a restaurant from Easter to the end of September. You won't find fresher lobster or crab anywhere better than this. And, for the beach, they provide Seafood Barbecue's. Lunch; 11.30-3, Supper from 7.00 pm. (H4) North Morte Road 01271 870633

55 Roman occupation of Exeter area.

80 Exeter becomes capital of the Dumnonian tribe as Isca Dumnoniorum.

Mortehoe Shellfish

Where to Stay...

Town Farmhouse. Listed building belonging to the National Trust converted into a comfortably furnished and centrally heated B & B close to Morte Point and Coastal Footpath. Cream teas in summer. Ample parking. (H4) 01271 870204 www.townfarmhouse.co.uk

Watersmeet Hotel. Seaside hotel overlooks one of Britain's finest beaches. Relaxed, informal atmosphere pervades this bright and colourful hotel. Sea views. Swimming pool. Restaurant (open to non-residents). No pets. (G4) 01271 870333 www.watersmeethotel.co.uk

WOOLACOMBE

One of the purist beach resorts in the UK, and the world. For the coast is untouched by campsite and bungalow. All about you is National Trust land protecting it from unsavoury development. A busy family holiday village with a two-mile long sandy beach extending to Putsborough Sands. Excellent for swimming, surfing and sandcastles. Invigorating coastal path to Baggy Point (popular with rock climbers) and Ilfracombe. (G5)

Where to Eat, Dink & Be Merry...

Beachcomber Cafe, The Esplanade. Access through main car park. The view straight up the beach will provide the heartiest appetite for their burgers, pizzas and stuffed jacket potatoes. (G5) www.beachcombercafe.co.uk

Red Barn. The heart and soul of Woolacombe welcomes surfers and families alike. Friendly atmosphere, a full range of beers and lagers, and solid, good value food to fill up your tummies, but don't expect nouvelle cuisine. Longboards are displayed like Old Masters in the V & A. Live music nights. Open all year. (H5)

The Boardwalk Bar & Restaurant, The Esplanade. One of the great views in England can be had whilst you sip your drink or tuck into your lunch or dinner. Freshly prepared meals. Open daily in season. (G5) 01271 871115 www.theboardwalkwoolacombe.co.uk

Westbeach Restaurant & Bar. Fashionable, lively restaurant described by The Guardian as "Retro-Chic". A welcome addition to North Devon's food emporia. Specialises in locally caught fish (bass and lobster) and Devon steaks (recommended). The bar is a notable meeting place in the evenings and can be noisy. (G5) 01271 870877 www.westbeachbar.com

Where to Stay...

Woolacombe Bay Hotel. One of the great family holiday hotels run by the Lancaster family for the past 20 + years. Spacious and suitable for children and grandparents of all ages. Squash, tennis and pools. Grounds lead down to beach. Special Autumn and Spring Breaks (2 nights for price of 1). Apartments. (G5) 01271 870388 www.woolacombe-bay-hotel.co.uk

Hele Bay. Shingle and rocks. R/WC/D. (L2)

Rapparree Cove. Shingle, sand and rocks. R/D. (L3)

Lee Bay. Shingle. Rock pools. A marine biologists' delight. Cut out steps at low tide to Sandy Cove. P/WC/Hotel Bistro in summer. (J3)

Grunta Beach, Mortehoe. Named after pigs landing. Sand at low tide. Rock pools. Access via coast path. (G4)

Taw Estuary

Special Places to Visit...

Fremington Quay Heritage Centre. Free entry to Visitors' Centre, featuring exhibitions plus permanent displays of Fremington's past. The Lookout; Wildlife Reference Gallery with Field Guides. Cafe and restaurant. Open Tu-Su all year. (K10) 01271 378 783 www.fremingtonquaycafe.co.uk

Marwood Hill Gardens. 18 acre garden with many rare trees and shrubs. Rock and alpine garden, lakes, large bog garden, famous collection of camellias (largest in country), clematis, Australian plants. Nursery with plant sales. Garden open daily dawn-dusk, Nursery open daily 11-5. (M8) 01271 342528 www.marwoodhillgarden.co.uk

Mike Taffinder Woodcrafts. Wood-framed mirrors, candle-holders and original items crafted from ancient oak by a man with a passion for wood and an eye for the unusual. Best phone before visit, he may be walking his dog. (J6) 07974 391228

Marwood Hill Gardens

Mike Taffinder Woodcrafts

Beaches & Surfing...

Rockham Bay. Sand at low tide. Isolated. Rock pools. Interesting rock formations and wreck remains. 3/4 miles walk from North Morte campsite. (G3)

Combesgate, Woolacombe. New steep steps descend to expansive sandy (wet) beach at low tide. Rock and sand pools. Good surfing with nice peaks at low tide. Protected from north winds. Beware of strong tidal flow/undercurrents. No dogs May-Sept. P on road. (G4)

Barricane, Woolacombe. Sand at low tide. Safe family beach. Good for shells and rock poolsKeep an eye out for children. Natural swimming pool at high tide. Cafe (evening meals in summer). Short walk from P. (G4)

Woolacombe Sands. Two miles of flat sand. Popular family beach. Water sports all year; surfing, windsurfing, kayaking. Life Savers School. Former Longboard centre - northern end produces Rights at half-tide. Beach casting for bass. R/WC/D/LG/P. (G5)

Putsborough Sand (Vention). Superb, flat family beach with spacious sand and dunes. Popular with young families. Water sports. Beach casting for bass. Short walk from P (charge). Dogs allowed on R side. Cafe/WC/Camping (advised to pre-book). Narrow lanes leading to beach best avoided during bank holidays. (G6)

Croyde. Flat sand at LT. Sand dunes and rocks at north and south sides. Surfing for experienced only - can be crowded. Rated as one of England's best beach Breaks, especially "Oyster", off Downend. Surf School. R/LG/WC/P. (F7)

Saunton Sands. Sand dunes (Braunton Burrows), rocks, water sports, brazing walks. Surf popular with longboarders and beginners - slow breaks. At extreme low tides it's possible to see rock forms that came down from Scotland in the Ice Age. Sands Cafe Bar/LG/Surf Survival Club/Board hire/P. (G8)

614 Battle at "Beandum", Bindon near Axmouth. Between the Saxons and Dumnonia.

680 St Boniface born in Crediton (approximate date).

Busy Day at Croyde

Saunton Surf Schools...

Surf South West. Surf school on Croyde Bay and Saunton Sands. Surf lessons, surf courses and surf holidays. Normal sessions 10.30-12.30 and 1.30-3.30. Open daily Apr-Oct. (F7) Croyde Burrows Beach Car Park Moor Lane 01271 890400 www.surfsouthwest.com

Walking On Waves. Sarah Whiteley's school is based at Saunton Sands and holds individual, group and family lessons. BSA registered. (G8) 01598 710961 www.walkingonwaves.co.uk

Croyde Surf Schools...

Surfing Croyde Bay, 8 Hobbs Hill. Courses for all abilities, from two hours, equipment supplied; wetsuits etc. (F7) 01271 891200 www.surfingcroydebay.co.uk

Coastal Footpath...

Combe Martin to Ilfracombe (5 miles). Much of this section inevitably follows the main road, but there are interesting diversions around Napps Hill, Widmouth Heath and Rillage Point, and a final climb over Hillsborough with its prehistoric fort and fine views.

Ilfracombe to Woolacombe (8 miles). The path ascends through Torrs Walk and continues along an easy level track and down to the village of Lee. From here the going becomes more difficult, keeping close to the cliff edge past Bull Point Lighthouse, and to the promontory of Morte Point, notorious for its wrecks - then past the shell beach of Barricane and down to the wider sands of Woolacombe.

Woolacombe to Braunton (12 miles). From Woolacombe the path traverses 2 miles of sand dunes, though some may prefer the easier going along the beach. From Vention the path rounds Baggy Point, famed for rock climbing and sea birds, and descends to the main road as far as Saunton. From here the path crosses Braunton Burrows Nature Reserve along the Tarka Trail towards Crow Point, then strikes north east beside the estuary to Velator, and follows the old railway line to Barnstaple which has been renamed as the Tarka Trail. It's now possible to follow the Tarka Trail on foot, or by bicycle all the way to Bideford without the encumbrance of the motorcar.

Surfers, Saunton Sands

LUNDY ISLAND (NT).

Romantic and historic island, and one-time fortress and home to pirates. A place of great contrast and beauty, lies nineteen miles west of Morte Point.

Just three miles long and half a mile wide, Lundy's western cliffs, popular with rock climbers, rise to 400 ft, whilst in the east there are small valleys filled with woodland, bracken, rhododendrons and hydrangeas.

The footpath running between these shrubs can be difficult, and it is easy to trip up over their roots. So beware. Soft walking boots or trainers are advised.

The small community includes a Victorian church, a pub - the Marisco Tavern, the Marisco Castle and two lighthouses plus a shop. Campsite for 40 people and 23 holiday cottages.

A short break or holiday here will contrast sharply with your average city lifestyle. The peace and solitude, the exposure to weather and the lack of cars apart from the farmer's Land Rover will appeal to many. It may take a day or two to get used to the slow pace of life.

Those who find it difficult to adjust may gravitate to the Marisco Tavern. A splendid place; Great jollity and friendships to be made here. The home made pies and fine ales are difficult to refuse. Not a bad place to be stuck in foul weather. A return trip on the Oldenburg in a Force 6 is not to be recommended.

Basking sharks can be seen during the months, July to September, Puffins May to mid July, and Seals all the year, and the best places to see them; Landing Bay, Frenchman's Landing, Gannets Bay, Rat Island and the North End, or always away from rough water.

Visitors can take a day trip aboard the MS Oldenburg from Bideford, or Ilfracombe. Herewith some telephone numbers detailing more information. Sailings: 01237 470422, and accommodation from the Landmark Trust: 01628 825925, or call Lundy on: 01237 431831. Lundy Booking Office: 01271 863636. www.lundyisland.co.uk

A
B
C
D
E
F
0
1
2 miles
0
1
2
3 kilometres
Widmouth Head
Samson's Bay
Water Mouth
Combe Martin Bay
Hangman Point
Rawn's Rocks
Blackstone Point
The Mare and Colt
Elwill Bay
Ramsey Beach
Heddon's Mouth
East Cleave
Trentishoe
Watermouth Castle
Widmouth Hill
Goosewell
Sandy Bay
Wild Pear Beach
Challacombe
Tarka Trail
Great Hangman
Sherrycombe
Red Cleave
North Cleave
ST PETER
Holdstone Down
Girt Down
Knap Down
Trentishoe Down
Millltown
River Heddon
Hagginton Hill
ST PETER
A399
Lee
Pack of Cards Inn
Combe Martin Museum
Combe Martin
Flowerpot Men
Berrynarbor
Clorridge Hill
ST PETER & ST VINCULA
Silver Dale Nurseries
Verwill
Stony Corner
Walner
Heale
Heale Down
Voley Castle
Hill Barton
Sterridge Valley
A399
Nutcombe
Dean
Voley
Bodstone Barton
Bowden
Woolscott Barton
Stoneditch Hill
Wildlife & Dinosaur Park
Coulsworthy
Henstridge
Cowley Wood Conservation Centre
Ettiford
Tumuli
A3123
Standing Stone
A3123
Tumuli
South Ley
Silkenworthy Knap
A399
Kentisbury
ST THOMAS
Hollacombe
Tumulus
Tumuli
Berry Down Cross
Berry Down
Tumulus
Mattocks Down
Stonecombe
B3239
Kentisbury Down
Tumuli
A39
Narracott
Colam Stream
Bugford
Week
Tumuli
Patchole
Westland
East Stowford Barton
Beachborough Country House
Ford
Kentisbury Ford
Arlington Beccott
Wigmoor
East Down
A39
Wistlandpound
ST PETER
Indicott
ST JOHN BAPTIST
18
Bittadon
Clifton
Winford Bridge
Wistlandpound Reservoir
Hewish Down
Bowden Corner
Arlington
Stowford
Hartnoll Barton
Lock Lane Cross
Churchill
ST JAMES
Whitefield Down
Churchill Down
Arlington Court (NT)
White Cawsey
Exmoor Zoological Park
Little Silver
Bowden
Okewill Cross
Okewill
Coombshead
Swindon Down
B3232
Garman's Down
North Woolley
River Yeo
Loxhore
Viveham
Milltown
ST MICHAEL
A39
Whiddon
Muddiford
Smythapark
Inn
Upcott
Loxhore Cott
Beara
Marwood
Higher Muddiford
Camp
Roborough Castle
ST MICHAEL
Bratton Mill
ST PETER
Guineaford
Broomhill Hotel & Sculpture Garden
Youlston
ST PETER
Bratton Fleming
Marwood Hill
Lower Loxhore
Shirwell
Shirwell Cross
Chumhill
Kingsheanton
Sloley Barton
Prixford
Haxton
Bratton Cross
Youlston Wood
Chelfham Barton
B3232
Waytown
Camp
Blakewell
Hartpiece
Birch
ST BARTHOLEMEW
Tutshill
Brightlycott
Bradiford Water
Hakeford
Orswell
Burridge
Snapper
Stoke Rivers
A39
River Yeo
Roborough
Northleigh
Pitt
Bradiford
ST MARY
Middle Dean
Great Beccott
ST GREGORY
Pilton
Raleigh
Pottington
Pannier Market
Chambers Brasserie
Goodleigh
Yarde
Heritage Centre
Derby
Parish Church
Willesleigh
Gunn
Waytown
River Front Café
Zena's Café
Fort Hill
ST PETER & ST PAUL
Farm Shop
Stone Cross
BARNSTAPLE
Sticklepath
Hutcherton Down
Bradninch
The Tawstock, N.Devon College
Birch
ST MARY
North Devon Leisure & Tarka Tennis Centre
ST JOHN BAPTIST
Westacott
Tarka Trail
Accott
Bickington
Acland Barton
East Acland
Harford
Hele
Newport
A361(T)
Hurscott
Sandick Cross
Taddiport
A39(T)
Lake
1
2
3
4
5
6
7
8
9
10

58

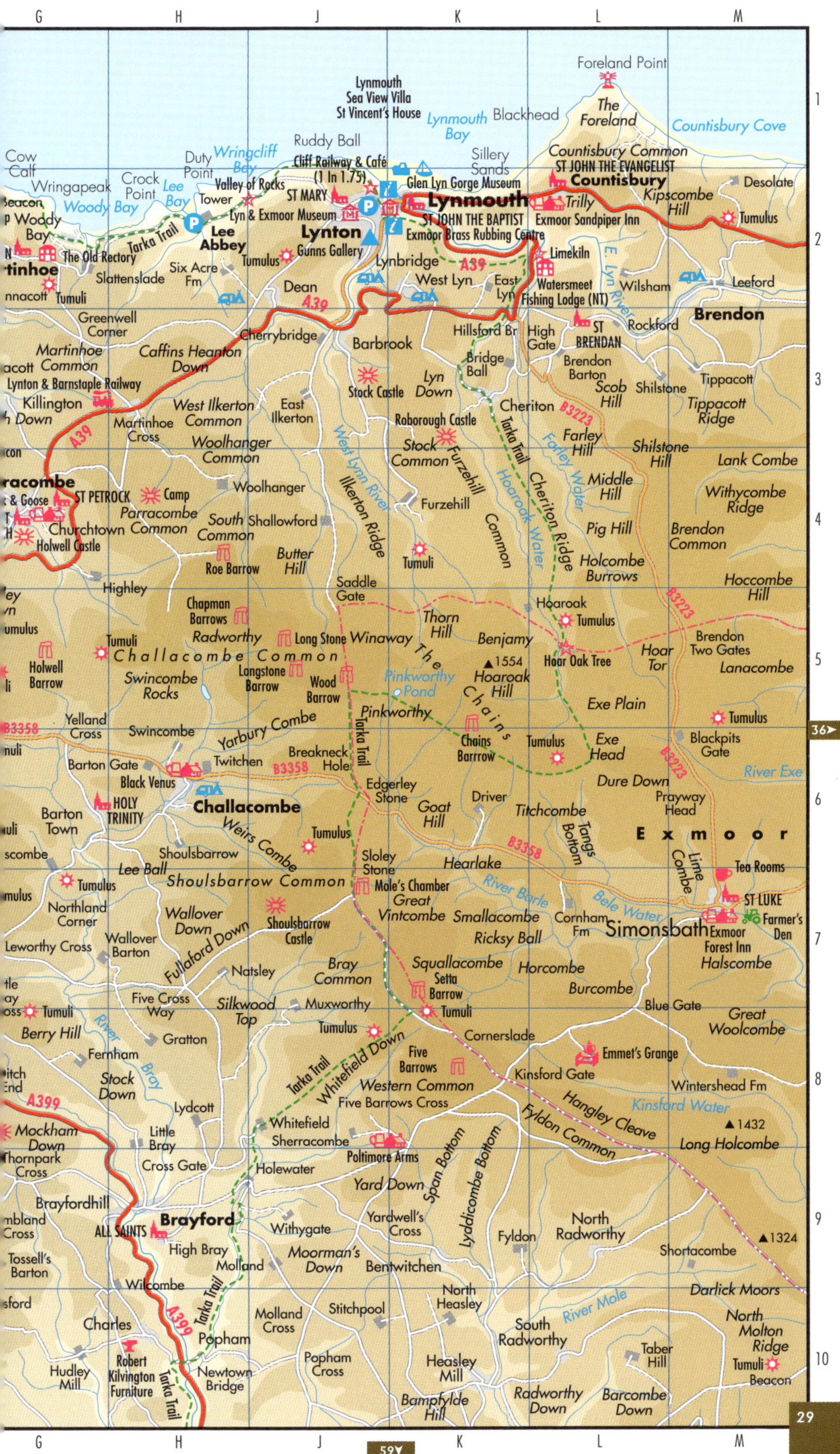
G
H
J
K
L
M
Foreland Point
The Foreland
Countisbury Cove
Lynmouth Sea View Villa
St Vincent's House
Lynmouth Bay
Blackhead
Ruddy Ball
Sillery Sands
Countisbury Common
ST JOHN THE EVANGELIST
Countisbury
Desolate
Kipscombe Hill
Tumulus
Cow Calf
Wringapeak
Crock Point
Duty Point
Wringcliff Bay
Lee Bay
Woody Bay
Cliff Railway & Café (1 In 1.75)
Valley of Rocks
Glen Lyn Gorge Museum
Tower
ST MARY
Lyn & Exmoor Museum
Lynmouth
Trilly
Exmoor Sandpiper Inn
ST JOHN THE BAPTIST
Exmoor Brass Rubbing Centre
Lynton
Lee Abbey
Tarka Trail
The Old Rectory
Gunns Gallery
Tumulus
Lynbridge
A39
Limekiln
E. Lyn River
Six Acre Fm
Slattenslade
Dean
West Lyn
East Lyn
Watersmeet Fishing Lodge (NT)
Wilsham
Leeford
Tumuli
A39
Brendon
Greenwell Corner
Hillsford Br
High Gate
ST BRENDAN
Rockford
Martinhoe Common
Caffins Heanton Down
Cherrybridge
Barbrook
Bridge Ball
Brendon Barton
Lynton & Barnstaple Railway
Scob Hill
Shilstone
Tippacott
Killington
Stock Castle
Lyn Down
Cheriton
B3223
Tippacott Ridge
West Ilkerton Common
East Ilkerton
Roborough Castle
A39
Martinhoe Cross
Woolhanger Common
Stock Common
Furzehill
Tarka Trail
Farley Hill
Farley Water
Shilstone Hill
Lank Combe
West Lyn River
Ilkerton Ridge
Hoaroak Water
Cheriton Ridge
Middle Hill
ST PETROCK
Camp
Woolhanger
Withycombe Ridge
Parracombe Common
Furzehill
Churchtown
South Common
Shallowford
Pig Hill
Brendon Common
Holwell Castle
Common
Roe Barrow
Butter Hill
Tumuli
Holcombe Burrows
Hoccombe Hill
Highley
Saddle Gate
Chapman Barrows
Thorn Hill
Hoaroak
Tumulus
B3223
Radworthy
Long Stone
Winaway
Benjamy
Brendon Two Gates
Tumuli
Challacombe Common
The Chains
1554
Hoar Oak Tree
Hoar Tor
Lanacombe
Holwell Barrow
Longstone Barrow
Wood Barrow
Pinkworthy Pond
Hoaroak Hill
Swincombe Rocks
Exe Plain
Pinkworthy
Tumulus
Yelland Cross
B3358
Swincombe
Yarbury Combe
Chains Barrow
Tumulus
Exe Head
Blackpits Gate
36➤
Tarka Trail
Breakneck Hole
B3223
Barton Gate
Twitchen
B3358
River Exe
Black Venus
Edgerley Stone
Dure Down
HOLY TRINITY
Driver
Prayway Head
Barton Town
Challacombe
Goat Hill
Titchcombe
Tangs Bottom
Weirs Combe
Tumulus
Exmoor
Shoulsbarrow
B3358
Lime Combe
Tea Rooms
Lee Ball
Sloley Stone
Hearlake
Tumulus
Shoulsbarrow Common
Mole's Chamber
River Barle
ST LUKE
Great Vintcombe
Bele Water
Farmer's Den
Northland Corner
Wallover Down
Shoulsbarrow Castle
Smallacombe
Cornham Fm
Simonsbath
Exmoor Forest Inn
Wallover Barton
Ricksy Ball
Halscombe
Lewworthy Cross
Fullaford Down
Natsley
Bray Common
Squallacombe
Horcombe
Setta Barrow
Burcombe
Five Cross Way
Silkwood Top
Muxworthy
Blue Gate
Tumuli
Tumuli
Great Woolcombe
Berry Hill
River Bray
Tumulus
Cornerslade
Gratton
Fernham
Five Barrows
Emmet's Grange
Stock Down
Tarka Trail
Whitefield Down
Kinsford Gate
Western Common
Five Barrows Cross
Wintershead Fm
A399
Lydcott
Hangley Cleave
Kinsford Water
Fyldon Common
Whitefield
1432
Mockham Down
Little Bray
Sherracombe
Poltimore Arms
Span Bottom
Lyddicombe Bottom
Long Holcombe
Thornpark Cross
Cross Gate
Holewater
Yard Down
Brayfordhill
North Radworthy
ALL SAINTS
Brayford
Withygate
Yardwell's Cross
Fyldon
1324
Tossell's Barton
High Bray
Moorman's Down
Shortacombe
Molland
Benwitchen
Wilcombe
Darlick Moors
North Heasley
A399
River Mole
North Molton Ridge
Charles
Tarka Trail
Molland Cross
Stitchpool
South Radworthy
Popham
Taber Hill
Robert Kilvington Furniture
Hudley Mill
Popham Cross
Heasley Mill
Tumuli
Beacon
Tarka Trail
Newtown Bridge
Radworthy Down
Barcombe Down
Bampfylde Hill
1
2
3
4
5
6
7
8
9
10
59▼

BARNSTAPLE

Principal town (and former busy port) of North Devon is undergoing a transformation from sleepy market town to busy route centre. Major new regeneration of Shapland's warehousing site beside the River Taw and the new bridge crossing from Sticklepath to Pottington will ease the bottleneck of traffic. C16 bridge, crook-spired church. Pannier Market (Friday farmer's market). Queen Anne's Walk (C16 colonnaded arcade). Guildhall. Remains of Castle beside Market car park. Queens Theatre. Cinema. Fair in Sept. Guided Town walks from TIC. Tarka Tennis & Leisure Centre. E/C W. (B10)

Places to Visit...

Barnstaple Heritage Centre, The Strand. Discover the rich past of this ancient town with hands-on activities and tableaux. Gift shop. Wheelchair access. Open all year M-Sa from 10. (B10) 01271 373003

Museum of Barnstaple & North Devon, The Square. Victorian gothic building, housing this local museum; history, geology, archaeology, local pottery and militaria. Tarka Gallery. Undersea World. TIC. Open all year M-Sa 9.30-5. (B10) 01271 346747 www.devonmuseums.net/barnstaple

Where to Eat, Drink & Be Merry...

Chambers Brasserie, 1 Lloyd Chambers. Mediterranean style dining on two floors. Steaks and fresh fish in season. Open M-Th 11.30am-11pm, F & Sa (-12pm). (B10) 0845 241 0599

Lillico's 1844, The Strand. Mediterranean bistro and bar split over two floors. Try lunch, brunch or high teas. Dinner is from 6.30. (B10) 01271 372933

Zenas CafeBarRestaurant, 1 Market Street. Inspired by a molting pot of ideas, from the Mediterranean to the Caribbean. A chic place for a quick coffee, or a longer stay; lunch or dinner is recommended. (B10) 01271 378844

Barnstaple Painting, Museum of Barnstaple

Spire, St Peter & St Paul, Barnstaple

Pannier Market, Barnstaple

BERRYNARBOR

Beautiful, ancient village with a history going way back to the Bronze Age. The Domesday Book (1085) listed four other manors in the vicinity. St Peter's church, Ye Olde Globe Inn (improving) and tea rooms to visit. A web of footpaths and walks connects the village; see Post Office for details, run by volunteers. (B3)

COMBE MARTIN

A long, straggling village bordered by some of the most beautiful countryside in England; rich, undulating pastures that lead down to a small harbour, and beach. Nearby, Trentishoe Downs and the Heddon Valley, and beyond the wild combes of Exmoor. Former silver mining centre. Fine Parish Church of St Peter ad Vincula. Wildlife Park and Dinosaur Park up the hill, south of the village. Curious C18 inn; 'Pack of Cards'. Aug carnival. E/C W. (C3)

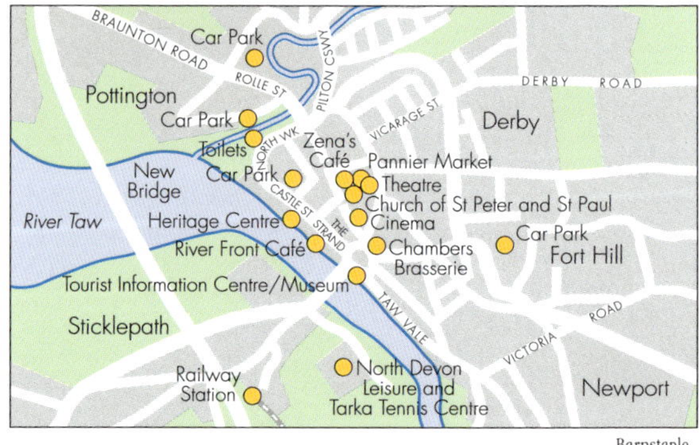

Barnstaple

780 Saxons reach the Tamar.

825 Saxon Devonians defeated the Cornish at Galford on the Lew.

Places of Interest...

Combe Martin Museum, The Parade. Illustrates old village industries. Newly designed displays. Disabled access. Shop. Open East to mid-July & school hols, 1.30-4. (C3) 01271 882920

Silver Dale Nurseries, Shute Lane. National Collection of Hardy Fuchsias with over 300 varieties. Shrubs, alpine, perrenials, herbs and bedding plants. Worth visiting for the stupendous views. Open daily 10-6 (Tea Gardens East-Oct). (D4) 01271 882539

Above Heddon Valley

St Peter Ad Vincula, Combe Martin. A magnificent Perpendicular church with fine C12 medieval Tower decorated with pinnacled battlements and a superb collection of gargoyles. It stands at over 100 ft and was built from the wealth of the silver industry. A typical Devon wagon roof, carved English rood screen, medieval windows, C14 paintings on the wainscotting and C15 font. Sunday services. Open afternoons. (C3)

Watermouth Castle. C19 castellated house with the accent on family entertainment; mechanical music, 'Granny kitchen', Explore the Dungeon Labyrinths and Adventure Land. Open daily Apr-Oct except Sa. (A2) 01271 867474 www.watermouthcastle.com

Wildlife & Dinosaur Park. Set in 26 acres of a Subtropical paradise. Home to Snow Leopards, Timber Wolves, Sea Lions, Primates and Meerkats, to name a few. Of special interest for children are the many dinosaurs, some are animated and appear to be alive! Open daily mid-Mar to early Nov 10-3 (last adm). (D4) 01271 882486 www.dinosaur-park.com

LYNTON & LYNMOUTH

Twin villages in a spectacular setting; Lynton on its cliff edge overhangs the small port of Lynmouth. The two are linked by a steep, wooded hill connected by footpath, road and funicular railway powered by water tanks. The rivers East and West Lyn fall rapidly to the sea through picturesque wooded gorges.

On the night of the 15th August, 1952 a freak cloudburst on Exmoor turned the East and West Lyn rivers into raging torrents destroying all that lay before them; 31 died, 93 houses were destroyed, power lines, bridges, cars and caravans were swept into the sea (similar to Boscastle's recent tragedy). Amazingly the Rhenish Tower c.1860 overlooking the harbour survived.

The area is proud of its literary connections; Percy Bysche Shelley honeymooned here in 1812, and Samuel Taylor Coleridge conceived the idea of "The Ancient Mariner" whilst on a walking tour with Dorothy and William Wordsworth.

These valleys, and the surrounding country provided the setting for Blackmore's Lorna Doone. Popular walking centre with easy, waymarked trails up to Watersmeet and Countisbury Hill. The steep, coastal road up to Countisbury, and on to Minehead, which overlooks the Bristol Channel and South Wales, is not to be missed and is arguably one of the most scenic drives in England. (J2)

Places to Visit...

Cliff Railway. Built by the publisher of the Strand Magazine, Sir George Newnes. He wanted to create a little Switzerland, an Alpine-style village in North Devon. This Victorian invention is operated by water ballast tanks and it connects the two villages. You can't visit these two villages without a ride on this extraordinary contraption. Superb sea views and woodland walks. Open daily in summer. (J2) 01598 753486 www.cliffrailwaylynton.co.uk

Lynmouth Harbour & Rhenish Tower

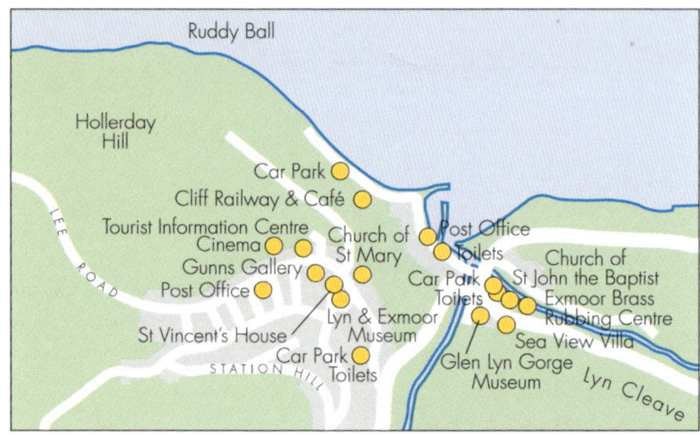

Lynton and Lynmouth

sided hillsides. Waymarked trails with two fine high-level walks up Myrtleberry Cleave and Lyn Cleave (easiest ascent from Hillsford Bridge). Easy riverside walk up from Lynmouth. (L2) www.nationaltrust.org.uk

Valley of Rocks. A place of legend and dramatic scenery tempered by a micro-climate of swirling mists and brazen winds. The geologist will tell you it's a rock-strewn elevated valley created in the Ice Age, a mere collection of massive sandstone outcrops inhabited by Cheviot goats imported from Northumberland. They have become quite an attraction and a talking point in the local press when yet another tourist has her handbag snatched. A great place to scramble on the rocks, the more refined walker will follow the coastal path. Below the rocks, nestling in a bowl, the local Cricket Ground, and just along the road, Mother Meldrum's Tea Gardens. (H2)

Exmoor Brass Rubbing, Watersmeet Road. Over 200 facsimile brasses and rubbing plates. Open East-Sept, Half terms M-F, W/Es school & BHs 10.30-5. (K2) 01598 752529 www.exmoorbrassrubbing.co.uk

Glen Lyn Gorge. Dramatic ravine that carried much of the flood water during the 1952 disaster. Hydro-Electric plant and exhibition on water-power. Open daily East-Oct 10-5 (-6 July/Aug). (K2) 01598 753207

Gunns Gallery, 11 Lee Road. Established in 1893, sells originals and prints of many leading artists. (J2) 01598 753352 www.gunnsgallery.co.uk

Lee Abbey. Christian Centre for holidays, retreats and conferences. The house was built in 1859 and stands on the site of the old Manor of the de Wichelhalse family. A small natural history museum is open displaying the work of Ursula Kay. There's an Honesty Box toll on the road through the estate leading to the picturesque coastal road to Woody Bay.

Lee Abbey Nature Trail. Passes through the private estate down a wooded valley to cliff girt beaches with rock pools. (H2)

Lyn & Exmoor Museum, Market Street. Old Exmoor crafts, implements and way of life. Open Apr-Oct M-F 10-12.30, 2-5. Su 2-5. (J2) 01598 752225

Middleham Gardens. Rose and fuchsia gardens, Californian redwoods and evergreen oaks. Albeit, somewhat overgrown, but charming. Open daily, all year. (K2)

Hoar Oak Water, Watersmeet

Watersmeet Fishing Lodge (NT). Built in 1832 and set in a picturesque valley at the confluence of the East Lyn and Hoar Oak Water. Focal point for many lovely walks. NT shop and tearoom. Open daily mid March to Oct 10.30-dusk. (L2) 01598 753348

Watersmeet (NT). Five miles of wooded valleys of the East Lyn River and its tributary, the Hoar Oak. A spectacular landscape of fast-flowing rivers, ancient woodland and steep-

878 Hubba landed at Appledore, to fight battle at Kenwith Castle before retreating to their ships off Northam.

893 Danes attack Exeter and north Devon.

Lynton & Barnstaple Railway. Train rides along the first mile re-opened of Former Woody Bay Station, closed in 1935. Open daily Apr-Oct 11-4, W/Es & Su in winter. Steam W/Es, Sch Hols & Christmas. (G3) 01598 763487 www.lynton-rail.co.uk

Places to Stay…

Sea View Villa, 6 Summerhouse Path. A Grade 11 Georgian house affording splendid sea views. This is sheer luxury, par excellence. Lavishly decorated, I loved the Dining Room with its mass of wine bottles. Bedrooms with bath and all the trimmings. Now under new ownership. Evening meal Tu-Sa. (K2) 01598 753460 www.seaviewvilla.co.uk

River Heddon, Heddon Valley

St Vincent House Hotel & Restaurant, Castle Hill. Belgian chef Jean Paul and his wife Linda have created a comfortable haven of Gallic and English charm in their C19 house. Breakfast and Dinner served with produce from the local fishing boats and Exmoor farms. (K2) 01598 752244 www.st-vincent-hotel.co.uk

Eat, Drink & Be Merry…

Cliff Top Cafe, Lee Road. Child friendly cafe at the top of the Cliff Railway. Child portions, al fresco dining and colouring books to hand. Open in season 9-7. (J2) 01598 753366

SIMONSBATH

Situated in the very heart of Exmoor in a sheltered valley beside the River Barle. Popular angling and walking centre. Two hotels. Farmer's Den for riding and outdoor gear. Exmoor Forest Inn (recently refurbished) to assuage your thirst following a walk beside the River Barle to Cow Castle. Free parking. (M7)

Boeveys Tea Rooms. We hear mixed reports of this little Tea Room serving snacks and light lunches, and afternoon teas. Open daily in season. (M7) 01643 831622

Natural Places of Interest…

Foreland Point, Countisbury & Watersmeet. 13,000 acres of National Trust land, including the East Lyn River up to Rockford Bridge, and several miles of coast and cliffs to the east of Lynmouth. Many footpaths (details from excellent National Trust leaflets). Foreland Point Lighthouse is open weekday afternoons. Footpaths ascend to Watersmeet from Lynmouth and continue in many directions. (L1)

Great Hangman. Imposing hill rising to 1044 feet which drops precipitously to the sea. An impressive coastal landmark. Remote place inhabited by skylark, wheatear, raven and stonechat. On coastal footpath. Named after a sheep rustler who mistakenly hanged himself. (D2)

Heddon Valley and Mouth. A beautiful, thickly wooded valley sided by steep hillsides. Arguably one of the most enchanting valleys in England. A path leads from behind the right side of the Inn down a tricky slope to the riverbank and follows the river to Heddon Mouth, a rock strewn beach with a massive old limekiln. The river is only fordable in dry months. The valley has numerous walks in all directions. National Trust shop opposite car park.

Hoar Oak Tree. Ancient boundary mark of Exmoor Forest. The present tree was planted in 1917, and is the third in more than three centuries. To reach it, follow the wall westwards from Brendon Two Gates for two miles across rough country. (L5)

River Barle. The source begins in the north-west corner of Exmoor beside the man-made Pinkworthy Pond. The Barle winds a diagonal course in a south-easterly direction meeting the River Exe just to the north of Exebridge. A walk beside this river provides a key insight into the magic of Exmoor. (K5)

Simonsbath Walk to Cow Castle

Illustration of the Poltimore Hunt, Poltimore Arms

Rockford Bridge. Popular beauty spot on the East Lyn River. (L3)

Shoulsbarrow Castle. Iron Age fort on remote moorland. (J7)

The Chains. Central area of Exmoor; the source of the rivers Barle, Exe and West Lyn. Remote, desolate and waterlogged. (K5)

Trentishoe. A strategic hamlet with farmstead, church and mill overlooking the Heddon Valley. The church mainly dates from 1861, yet there's documentary evidence of Rectors back to 1260! Worth a detour.

Wistlandpound Reservoir. Fishing available for natural brown trout and larger rainbows. Season 15 Mar - 12 Oct. Permits from Post Office, Challacombe, The Kingfisher, Barnstaple and Fishing Tackle, Combe Martin. (F6)

Special Places to Stay…

Beachborough Country House B & B, Kentisbury. Lovely rambling Grade 11 rectory offers style and comfort. Flagstone floors, log fires and huge sash windows shelter you from the outside world. Tennis court. Private dinner parties. (E5) 01271 882487 www.beachboroughcountryhouse.co.uk

Bratton Mill B & B, Bratton Fleming. You'll be intrigued by the track leading down to the Mill, and stirred by the splendour and isolation of it. You will be offered a welcome drink, or tea by the river. Tasteful and comfortable furniture decorates the house. Your hostess is charming, too. Nearby, pubs with excellent reataurants. ££. (E7) 01598 710026 www.brattonmill.co.uk

Tack Room, Emmetts Grange

Emmetts Grange B & B (WL), Simonsbath. A small, isolated hamlet amidst a stunning Exmoor landscape. For those who enjoy country pursuits (riding, fishing, hunting), antiques and a luxurious lifestyle coupled with gourmet cuisine. This is for you. Stabling available. Dog friendly. Your hostess is a Master of Foxhounds and mother of young children. Tennis court. (L8) 01643 831138 www.emmettsgrange.co.uk

The Old Rectory, Martinhoe. Small C19 Country House hotel set in three acres of mature, tranquil gardens. Rooms are cosy and tastefully furnished. Candlelit dinners from local organic produce. In superb walking country. No children under 14. Dog friendly. (G2) 01598 763368 www.oldrectoryhotel.co.uk

Pubs Serving Food…

Exmoor Sandpiper Inn, Countisbury. In spectacular position with stupendous views to be held in summer from their outside seating area. Log fires, comfy sofas and a changing selection of dishes. Real Ales. Friendly towards walkers and their dogs. Accomodation. Start off point for many circular walks. (L2) 01598 741263

Fox & Goose, Parracombe. Fresh fish in season supplied by local boats, and on the menu the day I visited; bass, fish stew, tiger prawns, red mullet fillets, and Game in season....all the walls are covered in bric-a-brac; lobster pots, badger and fox heads, hunting prints and paraphenalia. A good time feel factor. Local Exmoor brews. Foremost a dining pub rather than a local inn. (G4)

Hunters Inn, Heddon Valley. An imposing (chalet-style) hostelry set in a valley of great beauty. With some nouse and design flair (and a good deal of money) this could be one of the great Inns of England. Sadly, the interior is a great disappointment, an opportunity sorely missed. Heddon Valley is a centre for walking and riding. Home cooked fare and real ales. B & B. Open daily. (F2) 01598 763230 www.huntersinn.net

Poltimore Arms, Yard Down. Isolated little country pub popular with Exmoor folk. Serves real ales and good, honest fare at a reasonable

937 Victory for Athelstan, the First King of All Britain over the Danes at Brunanburh.

945 King Edmund's council held at Colyton.

price. Open daily in summer, limited hours in winter. The views and the drive westwards via the Five Barrows is sensational. (K9)

The Exmoor Forest Inn, Simonsbath. Recently refurbished after many sad years in disrepair. Welcome hostelry after walking or fishing the Barle. Restaurant/pub food uses local produce. Accommodation; Prices ££. Non-Smoking. Dog friendly. (M7) 01643 831341 www.exmoorforestinn.co.uk

Special Places to Visit...

Arlington Court (NT). Elegant house built in 1822 by Thomas Lee. Home of the Chichester family; the present contents consist largely of the collections of Rosalie Chichester (aunt of Sir Francis), who died in 1949. Fascinating medly of objects d'art, model ships, pewter, costumes and furniture. Watercolours by William Blake. Costume displays. Famous collection of horse carriages (rides available), including Queen Victoria's pony bath chair. Victorian formal garden. Extensive park and nature trail. Garden open daily mid-march to Oct & BHs 10.30-5 (House 11-5) except Sa. Footpaths through Park and woodland open all year. NT shop and licensed restaurant. (D6) Arlington, 01271 850296 www.nationaltrust.org.uk

Arlington Court. Two-mile nature trail through the park. Lakeside and woodland scenery, Shetland ponies, Jacob's sheep, botanical and ornithological interest. Buzzards and ravens. Heronry and bird hide. Open daily 11-6. Small admission charge to Park. (D6) 01271 850296

Blakewell Fishery. Trout fishery. Family fun, catch your own trout. Farm shop, tackle room, ornamental fish and water garden. Tea room/Cafe - open 11-5, East/May until September. Fishery and Visitor Centre open daily 9-5. (A8) 01271 344533 www.blakewellfisheries.co.uk

Broomhill Hotel & Sculpture Garden. 300 sculptures set in 10 acres of gardens (charge) in a most glorious valley. Contemporary Art Gallery (free), restaurant and hotel. Open May-Oct, W-Su 11-4, Nov-Apr Th-Su 12-6. (B8) 01271 850262 www.broomhillart.co.uk

Chapman Barrows. Eleven Bronze Age burial mounds on Challacombe Common. Fine views towards North Devon. (H5

Robert Kilvington Furniture Design. Bespoke furniture and sculpture for domestic and public spaces. Open by arrangement only. (H10) Charles Bottom Cross 01598 760356

Exmoor Zoological Park. Over twelve acres of landscaped gardens on the edge of the National Park with exotic birds and animals. Open daily; summer 10-6, winter 10-4. (F6) 01598 763 352 www.exmoorzoo.co.uk

Short Walks on Exmoor...

1. Lynmouth to Countisbury and Foreland Point Lighthouse. (H1)

2. Lynmouth to Watersmeet via Lyn Cleave and Myrtleberry Cleave. (H1)

3. Watersmeet to Rockford Bridge beside the East Lyn River. (H1)

4. Arlington Court Nature Trail. (D6)

Beaches...

Lynmouth. Shingle, sand and rocks. Boating pool. Breaks for experienced surfers only. R/WC/D. (K1)

Lee Abbey. Sand and rocks. Short walk from P/R/WC. Toll. (H2)

Carriage Ride, Arlington Court NT

Combe Martin. Pebbles, rocks and pools. Some sand at LT. Boating pool. R/WC/D. (B3)

Watermouth Castle. Protected inlet popular for mooring light craft. Sand at LT/P. (A2)

Two Moors Way. This is a Long Distance footpath, although not officially designated as one, which runs from Lynton to Ivybridge, linking the Exmoor and Dartmoor National Parks. The Way makes the use of footpaths, bridleways and public roads. From Lynton to watersmeet then southwards along the Cheriton Ridge to Hoar Oak Tree and Exe Head, crossing the B3358 at Cornham Farm. Then striking south-east to meet the River Barle below Pickedstones Farm. Cross country to Withypool, the Way proceeds down-stream beside the Barle to Tarr Steps. Then south towards West Anstey

Coastal Footpath...

County Gate to Lynmouth. (8 miles). Follow the path back to Glenthorne House where it continues along the coast towards Foreland Point, above some of the highest cliffs in England. After a steep climb to Countisbury Common there are two alternative routes; one following the coast, with fine seaviews towards Lynmouth, and the longer route crossing over to the wooded valley of the East Lyn.

Lynmouth to Combe Martin (13 Miles) The path starts with the beautiful North Walk leading to the Valley of the Rocks. From here to Woody Bay the route runs along a minor road, but there is an alternative way through the woods higher up. From Woody Bay the path follows a level elevated track with fine views, then descends to the River Heddon and zig-zags its way up Heddon Mouth Cleave. The path ascends to Trentishoe Down and follows a course over open grassland, culminating the ascent of Great Hangman and the final descent past Little Hangman into Combe Martin.

974 Benedictine Abbey of Tavistock founded. 1001 Danes landed at Exmouth.

Porlock Bay
Hurtstone
Gore Point
Submarine Forest
Porlock Beach
Worthy
Exmoor Glass
Porlock Weir
Porlockford
Andrew's on the Weir
West Porlock
Porlock
ST DUBRICUS
Greencombe Garden
Toll
Porlock Hill (1 In 4)
Old Barrow Hill
The Guildhall
Yenworthy
Embelle Wood
Broomstreet
Ashton
A39
County Gate
Yenworthy Common
Lorna Doone Farm
Malmsmead
CULBONE CHAPEL
Culbone
Silcombe
Quarter Barrow
Ash
Culbone Hill
ST MARY
Oare
Oare Water
Lillycombe
North Common
Culbone Stables Inn
Smalla Combe
Pitt
Birchanger
Malmsmead Hill
Cloud Fm
1196
Oare Common
Oareford
Oare Post
Weirwood Common
Whit Stones
Black Hill
Lank Combe
1283
Hawkcombe Head
Porlock Common
Hawk Combe
Hawkcombe
Doverhay Down
Lucott
Badgworthy Lees
Badgworthy Water
Doone Valley
1335
South Common
Black Hill
Mill Hill
Weir Water
Berry Castle
Nutscale Water
1041
Ley Hill
Holnicote Estate
Hoccombe Combe
Hoccombe Hill
Badgworthy Hill
Kittuck
Chalk Water
Stone Circle
Black Barrow
Tarr Ball Hill
Pool Fm
Babe Hill
Hoccombe Water
Manor Allotment
Meads
Lucott Moor
Lucott Cross
Stoke Pero
Lanacombe
Trout Hill
Larkbarrow
Madacombe
1518
Long Combe
Stoke Ridge
Stoke Pero Common
Long Combe
East Pinford
Swap Hill
Alderman's Barrow
Almsworthy Common
Wilmersham Common
West Pinford
Beckham
Stone Circle
1457
Elsworthy
Rowbarrows
Dunkery Beacon
Wellshead Allotment
Exford Common
1675
Tumuli
E X M O O
Warren Fm
Codsend Moors
1500
Ravens' Nest
Dry Hill
Rams Combe
Allcombe Water
Pitsworthy
Hoar Moor
Ware Ball
Clovenrocks Bridge
Exe Cleave
Westermill Fm
Wellshead
Hillhead Cross
River Quarme
B3223
Red Stone Hill
Sharcott
Kitnor Heath
Codsend
Riscombe
Downscombe
Ashott Barton
River Exe
Edgcott
ST MARY MAGDALENE
Hereliving
Stetfold Rocks
Winstitchen Fm
White Water
White Cross
Crown Hotel
B3224
Newland House
Ley
Exford
Combe
Flexbarrow
Pennycombe Water
Great Woolcombe
Chibbet Post
Camp
Cow Castle
Road Castle
Lyncombe
1266
Staddon Hill
Horsen Fm
River Barle
Pickedstones Fm
Tumulus
Buckworthy
Staddon
Road Hill
Blackland
Landacre
Halsgrove
Weatherslade
Nethercote
Ferny Ball
Landacre Bridge
Hillway
Roam Hill
River Exe
Sherdon
Tumulus
1455
Dillacombe
ST ANDREW
Withypool
Comer's Cross
Bye Combe
Brightworthy Barrows
Waterhouse
The Royal Oak Inn
Uppington
Comer's Gate
Great Ashe
Sherdon Water
Sherdon Fm
Withypool Common
Green Barrow
Woolcombe Allotment
Withypool Hill
River Barle
1324
Barcombe
Stone Circle
Winsford Hill
North Batsom
Barkham
Withypool Cross
Halscombe Allotment
West Water
Worth Hill
Porchester's Post
Caratacus Roman Stone
Willingford
Worth
Sandyway Cross
Sportsman's Inn
Westwater Allotment
Knaplock
Litton Water
Humber's Ball
Beacon
Twitchen Ridge
Hawkridge Plain
Old Barrow
Parsonage Down
Liscombe
Twitchen Barrows
Tarr Farm Inn
Tarr Steps
Wheatclose Cross
Blindwell
White Post
Cloggs Down
Parsonage Farm
Ashway Side
Varle Hill
B3223

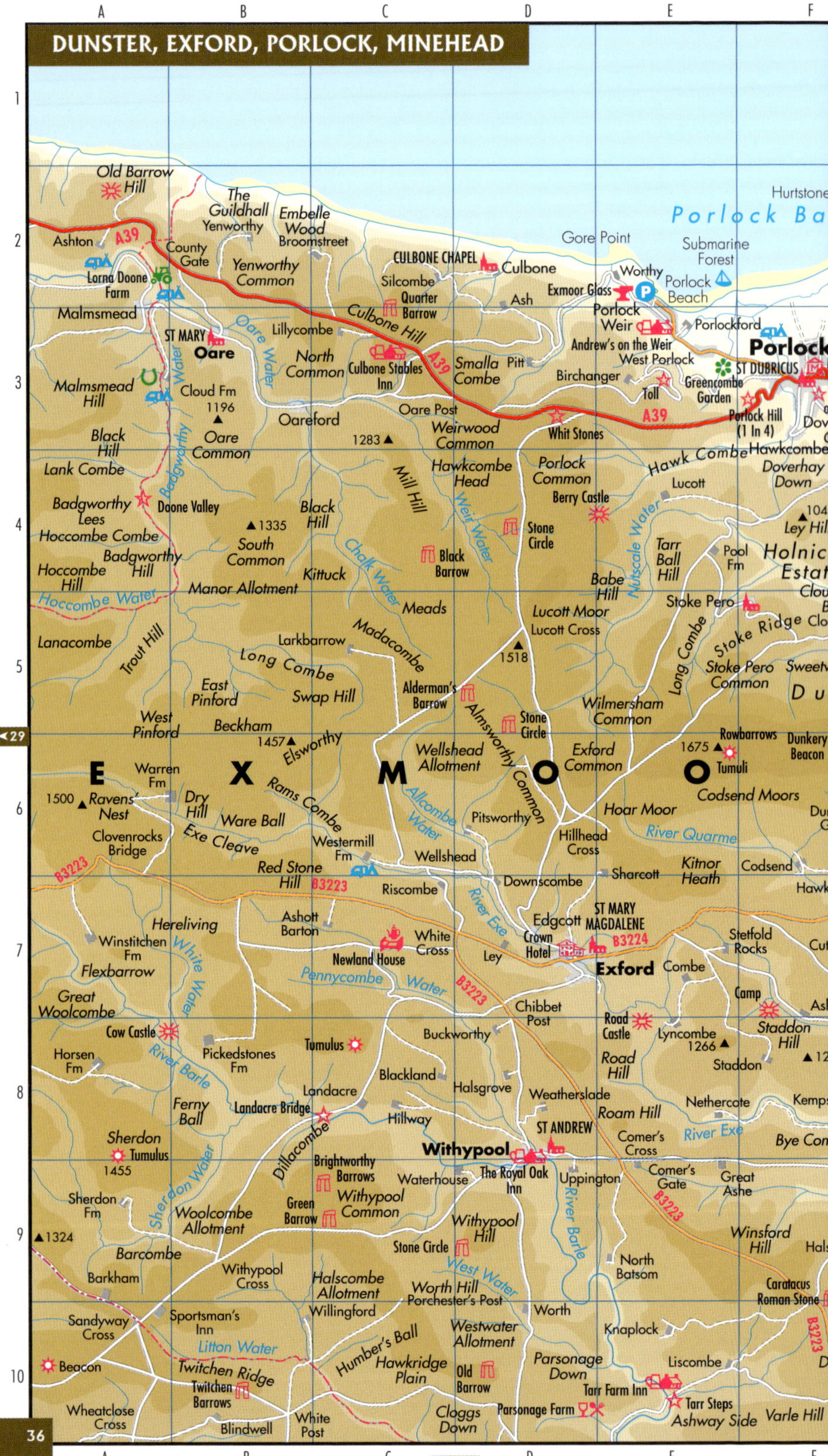

29
64

MINEHEAD
Dunster
Selworthy
Minehead Without
Alcombe
Carhampton
Timberscombe
Wootton Courtney
Luccombe
Cutcombe
Luxborough
Withycombe
Treborough
Exton
Brompton Regis
Brendon Hills
A39
A396
B3224
B3190
2 miles
3 kilometres

65
68

Dunster Castle

DUNSTER

Arguably the most picturesque of Exmoor villages overlooked, and dominated, by the Castle. You can park on the north, and south end, of the village, or on the High Street, next to the C17 Yarn Market. Do explore on foot and visit the Gallox bridge, the Water Mill and admire some of the 200 listed buildings. The beautiful Parish Church is quite outstanding. Always a popular centre from whence to explore Exmoor and the coast. Hobby Horse Dance, 1st May. It is becoming a centre for fine cuisine, and there are a number of tearooms. Waymarked circular walks lead off into Vinegar Hill, to Bat's Castle, but the more adventurous climb up Knowle Hill which can on a clear day provide expansive views. (L5)

Special Places to Visit...

Dunster Castle (NT). Imposing C13 building with many additions through the years, and major remodelling from 1868-72. Home of the Luttrell family for 600 years. Notable staircase, ceilings and family portraits. Terrace walk with sub-tropical plants. Garden and park open daily March-December, from 11 to dusk except 23 Mar-Oct 10-5. Castle open 23 Mar-31 Oct daily 11-5, Oct 11-4 except Th. (L5) 01643 821314 www.nationaltrust.org.uk

Dunster Dolls Museum, 17 High St. Home to over 900 dolls from all over the world. Open Easter to end Sept M-F 10.30-4.30. W/Es 2-5. (L4) 01643 821220

Parish Church of St George. Priory church built in the C14 shared by the monks and parishioners. Bell tower is open on Th evenings during bell ringing practice. (L4)

Jano Clarke Pottery, 1 Castle Hill. Distinctive hand thrown stoneware pots in the anglo-oriental tradition. Local materials used. Open Tu-Su 10-5. (L4) 01643 821836

Where to Eat, Drink & Be Merry...

Cobblestones Restaurant & Café, 24a High Street. Friendly café serving light lunches, coffee and cakes. Also open Saturday evenings, and for Sunday lunch. (L5) 01643 821595

Reeves, 20-22 High Street. New restaurant gaining a well deserved reputation. Cosy and intimate, with a flair for interior design, the food is prepared by Justin who trained in Oxford and at country house hotels in the Cotswolds. Open Tu-Sa for dinner, and lunch weekends 12-2 pm. (L5) 01643 821414 www.reevesrestaurantdunster.co.uk

Where to Stay...

Dunkery Beacon Hotel, Wootton Courtenay. In a breathtaking position overlooking spectacular country. Former hunting lodge recently developed into a small, intimate, family hotel. Comfortable rooms and home cooked cuisine.(H5) 01643 841241 www.dunkerybeaconhotel.co.uk

The Luttrell Arms. Small, C15 hotel used in medieval times as a guesthouse for the Abbots of Cleeve. 4-poster beds and high ceilings, log fires and the choice of bar snacks or the more formal restaurant with al fresco dining. (L5) 01643 821555 www.luttrellarms.co.uk

Spears Cross Hotel, 1 West Street. Award-winning B & B in much demand. Fabulous oak door leads into a lounge with Inglenook fireplace. The bedrooms are top notch with contemporary fittings, and massive beds. No dogs. (L5) 01643 821439 www.spearcross.co.uk

1003 Exeter sacked by the Danes.

1018 Benedictine abbey of Buckfast founded by Danish king, Cnut.

MINEHEAD

Seaside resort on the Bristol Channel developed in the C19 from an old fishing port sheltered by high cliffs to the west. The sandy beach is extensive at low tide but the grey Bristol Channel does not invite a leisurely bathe, better to drive west to Woolacombe. The town has some fine Georgian houses and the picturesque Old Town with its fine church is not to be missed. The town's situation makes for a convenient centre from which to explore Exmoor, the Quantocks and Brendon Hills. It is possible to walk up to North Hill through the Old Town, and onto Selworthy via the coastal footpath. On May 1st, the Minehead Sailors' Hobby Horse parades through the streets in commemoration of a phantom wreck that entered the harbour without Captain or crew, and has done so for years. (J3)

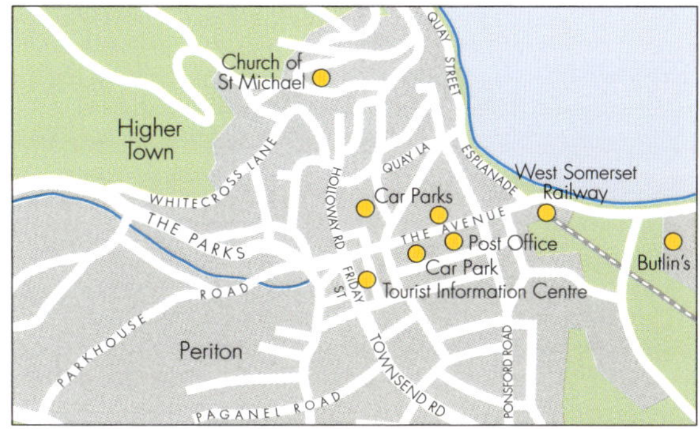

Minehead

Andrew's On The Weir ss

Special Places to Visit...

Butlins Minehead, Seafront. Sub-Tropical sunsplash waterworld; funfair, family fun and daytime entertainment, Odeon cinema and bowling alley. Quite an experience. Open daily. (L3) 0870 242 0870 www.butlinsonline.co.uk

Exmoor Classic Car Collection, Parkhouse Road. Private collection of road-going old cars and motorbikes with 1000s of exhibits. Open East-Sept Th-Su 11-4. (J4) 01643 841476

West Somerset Railway. One of the major railway preservation schemes - 20 miles from Bishops Lydeard to Minehead. Trains (steam but sometimes diesel) run daily May-Oct, and some days in April. Connecting buses between Bishops Lydeard and Taunton. All trains steam-hauled from mid-July to end Aug & BHs. Ten restored stations along the line. (K4) 01643 704996 www.West-Somerset-Railway.co.uk

PORLOCK

Picturesque village set back from the coast in a beautiful Exmoor valley protected on three sides by heather covered moors. An abundance of flora and fauna, and pure air plus a temperate climate makes for a relaxing ambience. Fine church with interesting tombstones. A popular and purposeful walking centre with many shops selling gear. It's just off the coastal footpath, and close to many fine Exmoor walks.

The small hamlet at **Porlock Weir**, 2 miles north-west has a charming harbour overlooked by fisherman's cottages. Much of this area is owned by the National Trust and the Blathwaite Estate (Owners of Dyrham Park, Bath) who have thankfully retained a continuity of lifestyle by renting to the same families over many generations. E/C W. (F3)

Andrew's on the Weir. A small, dog friendly Restaurant With Rooms owned by Andrew Dixon and his wife Sarah, both madly passionate about food, and Exmoor produce. Five bedrooms with bath. A great destination for lunch, or dinner. Open W-Su, lunch 12-2.30 pm, Dinner 6.30-9.30 pm. (E3) 01643 863300 www.andrewsontheweir.co.uk

Exmoor Glass. Glassblowers create top quality decanters, goblets, vases and jugs. Regular demos. Gallery open daily 10-5, Studio M-F 9-4. (E3) Harbour Studios 01643 863141 www.exmoorglass.co.uk

Greencombe Gardens. Enchanting old garden on the edge of woodland overlooking Porlock Bay. Choice rhododendrons, azaleas, camellias, maples, roses, hydrangeas, ferns and small woodland plants. Completely organic with compost heaps on show. Plant sales. Open W/Es, M, Tu & W 2-6 Apr-July. (E3) 01643 862363

Porlock Museum, Doverhay. Quaint little museum displaying the history of the locality. Open daily in summer. (F3) 01643 862645 www.doverymanor-musuem.co.uk

Packhorse Bridge, Allerford

Villages of Interest...

Allerford.
Pretty village noted for the Packhorse Bridge and thatched cottages. Fine walks to Selworthy, Bossington Hill and Porlock Bay. (G3)

Culbone. Hamlet with the smallest church in England. Once home to charcoal burners and a leper colony. Reached via car, or the coastal footpath from Porlock Weir, or County Gate. (D2)

Exford. Bright, attractive village astride the River Exe with a Village Green, and two sportsman's inns. Exmoor's fox and stag hunting centre now in decline following the recent hunting ban. (E7)

Luccombe. Quiet little village with white-washed thatched cottages which overlook a peaceful churchyard. Amidst superb walking and trekking country. (G4)

Oare. Scattered village in steep wooded country. The church was immortalised in R D Blackmore's novel Lorna Doone as the setting for Lorna's wedding. (B3)

Selworthy. National Trust village with many picture-postcard thatched cottages. Superb views across the Holnicote Estate towards Dunkery Beacon. Fine wagon roof to church. Short, easy waymarked walks lead into the woods. (H3) Periwinkle Cottage Tea Rooms. Home-made cakes and soups, light lunches and cream teas. Open daily in season. (H3) 01643 862769

Selworthy

Horner. Quaint hamlet of thatched cottages and running water. A steep ascent leads off into the woods. Walking centre. Tea shops. (G4)

Luccombe

Winsford. One of Exmoor's prettiest villages and well known for the thatched Royal Oak Inn, and as the birthplace of Ernest Bevin in 1881, the Labour Statesman. (G9)

Withypool.
Unspoilt village in the centre of Exmoor spanned by a beautiful five-arched bridge. R D Blackmore wrote much of Lorna Doone while staying at the Royal Oak Inn. Fine country to the south-west, and riverside walk beside the Barle to Tarr Steps. (D8)

Natural Places of Interest...

Badgworthy Water. A beautiful little valley associated with the Lorna Doone story. Convenient parking at Malmsmead for the easy-going walk, or pony trek beside the riverbank to Badgworthy Wood, an ancient place with tangled oaks, moss and lichen. (A4)

Brendon Hills.
Rolling hills of patchwork fields and woodland in varying shades of greens and brown. Often overlooked as a place of great beauty because of their close proximity to Exmoor and the Quantocks. The walk across Exmoor through these fields to the Quantock Hills were considered by John Hillaby, the great long distance walker and author, to be "the most beautiful part of England". (K9)

Caratacus Stone.
Inscribed ancient stone of the Dark Ages set in a shelter on Winsford Hill. (F9)

Clatworthy Reservoir.
Artificial lake of 130 acres created in 1960. trout fishing. Viewing area and nature trail.

Coastal Road; Porlock to Lynmouth. One of the most spectacular and awe-inspiring coastal drives in England. It begins, or ends, with a warning more reminiscent of the "Golden Age of Motoring" when cars were not given to good brakes and trenchant tyres: "Stay in First Gear". It remains a steep, and hazardous ascent (for an under-powered vehicle) up Porlock Hill, a 1 in 4 gradient. There is an alternative route: the toll road through the Blathwaite Estate, a less dramatic route, but blessed with the buzzard and raven, and wild flowers. Once up on the brow of the hill, there are superb views seawards and inland across the rolling patchwork landscape. On a clear day you can spy the South Wales coast all the way to Worms Head on the Gower Peninsula. It is worth turning around and driving back the route you came, for it will look very different.

1086 Domesday Book compiled. About 20,000 persons out of a total Devon population of some 70,000 accounted for.

1137 Exeter Castle besieged by King Stephen.

River Barle, Cow Castle

Landacre Bridge. Medieval bridge in excellent condition. Popular picnic spot beside the River Barle. Walks beside Barle to Cow Castle, a fine viewpoint. (B8)

North Hill. Lovely scenic drive from Minehead to Selworthy Beacon. Nature trail. Campsite. (J3)

Tarr Steps. Ancient clapper bridge crossing the River Barle, and one of Exmoor's most visited attractions so beware of large crowds on weekends and bank holidays. Walks up riverbank. It's possible to cross the river in a 4 x 4, or on horseback but not in a saloon car. Car park and toilets in close proximity. Best approached from the B3223 on Winsford Hill. Tarr Farm Inn provides teas and refreshments. (E10)

Cow Castle. Iron Age stronghold in commanding position. Fine viewpoint overlooking the River Barle. Reached via a flat, easy walk from Simonsbath running parallel with the Barle. (A8)

Dunkery Beacon.
Rises to 1,704 feet, and is the highest place on Exmoor. Formerly the site of a fire beacon. Wonderful views in all directions. Short-easy walk from road. (F6)

Tarr Steps

Webber's Post.
Popular spot below Dunkery Hill with fine views over Stoke Pero Common and Selworthy Beacon. Nature trails and bridleways lead off in all directions, and can cause havoc with your map reading skills. Paths to Stoke Pero church and Dunkery Beacon. Car park. (G5)

Badgworthy Water

Holnicote Estate (NT). Over 12,000 acres given over to the National Trust by Sir Richard Acland. Extends from the coast to the summit of Dunkery Beacon, including the picturesque villages of Allerford, Bossington, Selworthy, Tivington and Luccombe. Three packhorse bridges and several prehistoric sites plus Selworthy Tithe Barn, the Horner Valley, Selworthy Beacon, Hurlstone Point and North Hill. The footpaths criss-cross in all directions and can be quite mind boggling to navigate around. They have crazy names based on Acland's children and grandchildren. Booklets of walks available from the National Park. (F4)

Horner Wood.
Ancient and secluded woodland below Dunkery Hill. The little stream, the Snorer (Hwrnwr), saxon named because of its gurgling sound, winds its way around the knobbly oaks. Now one of Britain's National Nature Reserves. (G4)

Lorna Doone Painting, Poltimore Arms

Special Places to Visit...

Exmoor Falconry & Animal Farm, Allerford. Flying displays; owls to eagles. Feed the animals. Hawk walk. Falconry tuition. Shop and tea garden. Open Mar-Oct Su-F 10.30-4.30, & BH Sa. (G3) 01643 862816 www.exmoorfalconry.co.uk

Discovery Safaris of Porlock, c/o Visitor Centre. This Exmoor safari views the National Park in a specially designed Land Rover Defender to explore the stunning scenery of Exmoor by using off-road routes. Available all year. Trips last 2-3 hours. (K3) 01643 863444 wwww.discoverysafaris.com

Lorna Doone Farm, Malmsmead. C14 farmhouse known as Plovers Barrow Farm in Blackmore's Lorna Doone, the home of John Ridd. Now an artsncrafts and gift shop, next door The Buttery tea rooms. Open daily late Mar-Oct 10-6, Nov-Christmas 11-4.30. (A2) 01598 741278

Mill Pottery, Wootton Courtenay. Michael Gaitskell is one of the West Country's most respected ceramicists producing a fine selection of handmade stoneware (pots and jugs). Working waterwheel. Open Tu-Sa 10-1, 2-5.30. Jan-Mar & Su & M, by appointment. (H5)01643 841297 www.millpottery.co.uk

West Somerset Rural Life Museum, Allerford. Victorian schoolroom, laundry and dairy. Craft worker's tools. Croquet lawn. Picnic area. Open East & school hols, then May-Oct 10.30-1, 2-4.30. (G3) 01643 862529

Pubs Serving Food...

Royal Oak Inn at Luxborough. Hidden away in the Brendon Hills, this little cosy, flagstoned pub has built a reputation for good, honest fare and real ales. Cottage-style accommodation with bathrooms. (L7) 01984 640319 www.theroyaloakinnluxborough.co.uk

Culbone Stables Inn. The David Family have just taken over this old roadside inn. There's not much they don't know about meat - they own butchers shops aplenty, and judge livestock at Country Fairs. So expect superb steaks. Bedrooms are of contemporary design. Close to Coastal footpath. (C3) 01643 702843 www.geralddavid.co.uk

Tarr Farm Inn. C16 farm set in its own 40 acres overlooking Tarr Steps and the River Barle. Modern bedrooms with all mod cons. Restaurant provides meals from local farms. Activities organised. (E10) 01643 851507 www.tarrfarm.co.uk

Special Places to Stay...

Crown Hotel. Exmoor Coaching Inn and sporting hotel under new ownership delivers a warm welcome to you, your dogs and horses. Log fires and luxurious bedrooms. Impressive food in Restaurant. Cosy country bar and meals. (D7) 01643 831554 www.crownhotelexmoor.co.uk

Gloucester Old Spot (weaners), Hindon Organic Farm

Mill Pottery, Wootton Courtenay ss

Hindon Organic Farm. Lovely old creaking farmhouse at the end of a long, long lane. Be prepared to reverse! An organic farm for many years producing fresh organic meats; Aberdeen Angus beef, Gloucester Old Spot pork, Hindon hams, sausages and pies. (H3)01643 705244 www.hindonfarm.co.uk

Newland House. Small and peaceful home decorated with antiques. Log fires. Cream teas. Stables and paddocks for horses. Dog friendly. A short 1 1/2 miles from Exford. (C7) 01643 831199 www.newlandhouse-exmoor.co.uk

1205 First mayor of Exeter recorded - second only to Winchester in provincial cities.

1205 Totnes issued with a Charter. Possibly the oldest Municipal Borough in England.

Walking on Exmoor...

Walking is the most satisfying way to experience Exmoor's many virtuous delights. Her charms will seduce you into returning again, and again, and whether your sins are as a naturalist, geologist, botanist, fresh air fiend, or just a keen horseman. You will always be in her debt. We are privileged to walk her beautiful paths.

The National Park is dissected by scores of footpaths and bridleways (about 650 miles in total). Most signposted and waymarked. There are many publications available giving detailed plans for walks, including some excellent leaflets published by the Exmoor National Park, the National Trust and local tourist offices. Guided, and special interest walks can also be arranged throughout the season through several Tourist Information Centres. The recommended walks listed below are only a small indication of some of the areas, and routes worthwhile exploring. All start within easy reach of a car park.

1. Bossington to Selworthy, either via Hurlstone Point or Selworthy Beacon. (G2)

2. North Hill 3-mile trail. (J3)

3. Webber's Post to Stoke Pero Church and Dunkery Beacon. (G4)

4. Cloutsham Woodland Trail. (F5)

5. Horner to Webber's Post via Horner Wood. (G4)

Beaches & Surfing...

Blue Anchor.
Sand and shingle. R/WC/P. (M4)

Dunster Beach.
Shingle and sand. R/WC/P. (M4)

Minehead.
Shingly sand. R/P/WC. (K3)

Porlock Weir.
Pebbles. HZ swimming. Fast waves for experienced surfers. P/WC/R. (E2)

Stoke Pero Trees

Dunkery Beacon from Stoke Pero

Coastal Footpath...

Minehead to County Gate
(9 miles). The path begins fairly easily from the end of Minehead Quay, passing gently through woodland onto North Hill. For about three miles there is wonderful high level walking towards Selworthy Beacon, a fine viewpoint at 1013 feet, and worth a slight detour. Then down the hill to Bossington, a pretty village, and a short length of road work before following the beach to Porlock Weir, a delightful little harbour overlooked by a row of fisherman's cottages. The path then climbs up beside Yeanor Wood towards Culbone Church, set secluded in a wooded glade. The path continues with slight elevations to Glenthorne House. From here the path ascends to County Gate where there is a car park and National Park Centre.

THE HARTLAND PENINSULA
0 1 2 miles
0 1 2 3 kilometres
Hartland Point
Shipload Bay
Eldern Point
Chapman Rock
West Titchberry Farm
Cow & Calf
Blagdon
Titchberry
Gawlish Cliff
Exmansworthy Cliff
Fatacott
Beckland Bay
Windbury Point
Blackchurch
Upright Cliff
Damehole Point
Exmansworthy
Mouthmill
Gallant Down
Blegberry
Pitt
Brownsham
Snacksland
Dyer's Lookout
Broad Beach
Markadon
Lavender Farm
Berry
The Warren
Pattard Cross
Yapham
ALL SAINTS
Hartland Abbey
Cheristow
Norton
Hescott
Clovelly Court
Hartland Quay
ST NECTAN
Hartland Pottery
Ballhill
Wrinkle
Hartland Quay Museum
Stoke
Hartland
B3248
Velly
Slerra
St Catherine's Tor
2 Harton Manor
Springfield Pottery
Millthorne Chairs
Mettaford
Hugglepit
Little Barton
Rosedown
Speke's Mill Mouth
Kernstone
Natcott
Highford
Clovelly Dykes
Docton Mill
Leigh
Longpeak
Trellick
Farford
Warmleigh
Milford
Lymebridge
Philham
Baxworthy Corner
A39(T)
Mansley Cliff
Eddistone
Elmscott
Staddon
Burford
High
Welsford
Tosberry
Seckington
Tosberry Moor
Docton
Tumuli
Welsford Moor
Seckington Water
Sandhole Cliff
Bursdon Moor
Nabor Point
South Hole
Hardisworthy
Tumulus
Gorvin
Ramtor Rock
Lutsford
Summerwell
Putshole
Embury Beach
Embury Beacon
Wembsworthy
Huddisford
Bursdon
Knap Head
Henaford
Biteford
Marsh
Welcombe
Pottery
Tredown
Welcombe Cross
Deptford
Horton Bridge
Welcombe Mouth
Inn
Mead
Upcott
Greadon
Darracott
Meddon
Marsland Mouth
Marsland Cliff
Gull Rock
Gooseham Mill
Shorstone
Brimford Bridge
North
Marsland
Woolley
Yeol Mouth
Cornakey Cliff
Gooseham
Hardsworthy
Eastcott
Woolley Barrow
Westcott
East Youlstone
Henna Cliff
Crimp
Dinworthy
ST JOHN BAPTIST
Tea Rooms
Morwenstow
West Youlstone
Bush Inn
Rule Cross
Killarney Springs
Higher Sharpnose Point
River Tamar
Ryall
Tonacombe
Shop
Wrasford Moor
Berridon
Milton
Woodford Cross
Uppacott
Stanbury
Blatchborough
Stowford
CORNWALL
Sturdson Cross
Eastaway
Stanbury Mouth
Sturdson
Woodford
Broxwater
Upper Tamar Lake
Kimworthy
Lower Sharpnose Point
Hollamoor
Taylor's Cross
Lamberal Water
Coombe
Aldercombe
Darracott
Newland
Steeple Point
Coombe Valley Nature Trail
Brocklands Adventure Park
Kilkhampton
Alfardisworthy
A B C D E F
1 2 3 4 5 6 7 8 9 10

72

Westward Ho!
Rock Nose
Mermaid's Pool
Buckleigh
Cornborough Range
Cornborough
Rickard's Down
Abbotsham Court
Greencliff Rock
Greencliff
Abbotsham
ST HELEN
The Big Sheep
Winsford
Handy Cross
Cockington
Bowood
Atlantic Village
Abbotsham Cross
Babbacombe Mouth
Babbacombe
A39(T)
Higher Rowden
Knotty Corner
Lundy Island
Lion Hotel
Clovelly
Bight a Doubleyou
Lower Bight of Fernham
The Gore
Gauter Point
Peppercombe Castle
Portledge
Fairy Cross
Ford
Littleham Court
Winscott
The Hobby
Hobby Drive
Burnstone
Hobby Lodge
Walland Cary
Buck's Mills
Northway
Gilscott
Woodtown
Yeo Vale
Hoops Inn
Hoops
Milky Way Adventure Park
ST ANDREW
Alwington
Thornery
Slade
Bitworthy
Buck's Cross
Waytown
Horns Cross
Foxdown
Goldworthy
Bulland
Tuckingmill
Kennerland Cross
Broadparkham
ST JAMES
Newhaven
Halsbury
West Town
Cranford
River Yeo
Sedborough
Bocombe
Parkham
Stone
Cabbacott
ST MARY & ST BENEDICT
Buckland Brewer
Woolfardisworthy
Coach & Horses
Ash
Hordland
Bableigh
Alminston Cross
Gorwood
Beara Farmhouse
Venn
Melbury
Melbury Reservoir
Stroxworthy
Melbury Bridge
Melbury Hill
Thorne
Duerdon
Leworthy
Winslade
Bilsford
River Duntz
Clew Cross
Lower Twitchen
Craneham
Powler's Piece
Hole
Ashmansworthy
Tumulus
Rush Barrow
Hembury Castle
Eckworthy
Wrangsworthy Cross
Narracott
Common Moor
Tythecott
Ashbury
Hele
Dipple
Tumuli
Tumulus
River Torridge
Collingsdown
Milford
East Ash
Kismeldon Bridge
East Putford
Venn
Thornehill Head
Challash
Ash
Mambury
Galsworthy
Thorne Moor
Cory
Ley
Volehouse
Tumulus
Wonders Corner
West Putford
Field Irish
Silworthy Cross
Withecott
The Gnome Reserve & Wild Flower Garden
Bradworthy Common
Hankford
Bower
Colscott
Haytown Pottery
Stibb Cross
Silworthy
Doves Moor
Haytown
ST MICHAEL
ST JOHN BAPTIST
Bradworthy
Wheelers Cross
Thriverton
Chollaton
Bulkworthy
Downmoor
Cleverdon
Roseland Cross
ST JAMES
Binworthy
Abbots Bickington
Eastbridge
A388
Little Ford
Durpley
Five Lanes
Northcott
Brendon
Camp
Woodford Bridge
Durpley Castle
Great Derworthy
Bradworthy Cross
South Lane
Worden
Billhole
ST PETROCK
Newton St Petrock
ST ANDREW
Shop
Forestreet
Instaple
Matcott
Sutcombe
52
73

Clovelly Harbour

BUCK'S MILLS

Name derived from the Saxon "Bussac Hewise", meaning homestead. An isolated hamlet of romantic cottages (most are second homes, and are usually empty) at the bottom of a steep combe protected by high cliffs to either side, and from behind, thick woodland. In times gone by, the villagers made a living from fishing; herring, mackerel, lobster and prawn, as well as coastal lime burning needed for the fertilising of inland farms, so as to neutralise the acid soil. The steep, wide road from the beach was built to transport lime shipped in from South Wales. Hence, the massive lime kilns above the beach. As the fishing declined, the villagers sought new employment in the quarries on Lundy, sailing daily to and from work. Bygod, they were tough, in them, thar days. (J4)

CLOVELLY

A timeless village of cobbled streets and quaint cottages descend steeply to a harbour and backdrop of rich blue sea. Set in a superb position amidst beautiful scenery Clovelly belongs to the Rouse family who take great care to maintain the buildings in traditional materials. It's a former fishing port whose major wealth came from catching mackerel and herring. Today, it's a centre for small fishing trips, and visiting day-trippers.

When the fishing dried up Clovelly men would seek employment digging the quarries on Lundy. Clovelly folk were a hardy breed. It was not just the men who worked their socks off, the women got stuck in, too. With the quarrying, and the making of fishing nets.

Visiting Clovelly is an unforgettable experience and loved by children and folk of all ages. Take sensible shoes, the descent on cobble stones can be slippery. It is also steep, and the unfit or elderly would be wise to either take a ride on a donkey, or seek a lift in the Land Rover to the harbour.

On arrival, park in the parking area provided and enter via the Visitor Centre where there is a charge which helps maintain the village for future generations. Open daily. (G4) 01237 431781 www.clovelly.co.uk

Clovelly Harbour

1303 First recorded mayor of Barnstaple.

1307 Introduction of Stannary Towns for the administration of tin mines; Tavistock, Ashburton, and Chagford. Later, Plympton was added in 1327.

What to see, and Whom to Visit in Clovelly...

Ann Jarvis Designs. Scarves, ties, cushions and accessories designed and handprinted onto silks, velvets and fine wools. Commissions and day courses undertaken at workshop. Open Summer, daily 10-5. Winter, M-F 10.30-3.30. (G4) 01237 431033

Clovelly Court Garden. These are undergoing a major restoration programme. A classic example of a Victorian kitchen garden with magnificent greenhouses. The unique maritime microclimate provides exotic flower borders and fruit. Open daily Mar-Oct 10-4. (F4) 01237 431200

Clovelly Pottery. Variety of exhibits from different ceramicists. Resident Caroline Curtis hand throws slip decorated earthenware pots. Open summer M-Sa 10-6, Su 12-5.30. (G4) 01237 431042

Hobby Drive Walk. Follow the signs from Clovelly. This was laid out between 1811-29 by Sir James Hamlyn Williams, as a celebration of nature. One of the schemes that came to mirror the Romantic Movement of the early C19. The pathway was designed to accomodate carriages, and it features four gently curving bridges. The panoramic views peer down on Clovelly, and westwards towards Lundy and West Wales. They are unforgettable. There are a number of caves just off this drive that were used to store the C19 smuggler's contraband. But, beware of ghostly forms. (G4)

Visit Lundy Island, Clovelly Harbour. Visit Lundy by an alternative route on the fast "Jessica Heettie", and see the abundant wildlife and swim with the seals. Spend one hour sailing and six hours ashore. Sails Apr-Oct inclusive. (G4) 01237 431042 www.clovelly-charters.ukf.net

HARTLAND PENINSULA

An isolated corner of Devon full of interest. The village of Hartland is a popular centre for the arts and crafts and has a number of pubs and tearooms. The church is strangely two miles westwards at Stoke.

Visit Lundy Island on the Jessica Hettie ss

Special Places to Visit in and around Hartland...

Darville Gallery, 97 West St. Emporium with a range of antiques, collectibles and decorative goods. The ground floor showroom is arranged as a museum. Open W-Sa 10.30-5. (D4) 01237 441984

Hartland Abbey & Gardens. Founded in 1157, the current building has been an historic family home since 1539. Furnished in Queen Anne, Georgian and Regency splendour; pictures, murals, furniture, porcelain. Beautiful informal gardens designed by Gertrude Jekyll with a woodland walk to the Atlantic Ocean. Cream teas. Open Apr to first Su in Oct. W, Th , Su & BHs, plus Tu in July-Aug, 2-5.30. Gardens also open Su-F. (C4) 01237 441264 www.hartlandabbey.com

Mural, Hartland Abbey

Drawing Room, Hartand Abbey

Millthorne Chairs

Hartland Pottery, North St. Established in 1981 to produce many items of stoneware using Chun (deep blue) and copper red glaze. Many processes (e.g. throwing pots) on view. Open in summer M-F 10-6, Sa 10-4. (D4) 01237 441693

Rood Screen, St Nectan's

Roof, St Nectan's

Hartland Quay. A wild and windswept corner of England forever associated with smugglers of contraband, and a favourite landing for Sir Francis Drake and Sir Richard Grenville, Devon men. It's set on a treacherous coastline, and little wonder that the quay was swept away in 1841, 1887 and 1896. The present quay was rebuilt in 1979. The former harbour master's house is now the hotel and inn. A wide road leads down to the slipway built for the transport of lime imported from South Wales. (B4)

Hartland Quay Museum. Features four centuries of local shipwrecks, old coastal occupations, shipping, smuggling and fishing. A wonderful introduction to this corner of Britain. Gift shop. Open daily. (B4) 01237 441371

Millthorne Chairs, 10 Fore St. Windsor Chairs (full-size and children's) handmade in Beech, Ash and Elm based on traditional designs. Bob Seymour also produces photos of seascapes and forms in large prints. Open daily. (D4) 01237 441590

Springfield Pottery. Established in 1979 by Philip Leach, grandson of Bernard Leach. Earthenware pottery hand-made from local clays; tiles, garden pots, domestic ware and individual pots. Open M-Sa 9-5. (D4) 01237 441506 www.springfield-pottery.com

St Nectan's Church, Stoke. A sailor's landmark for miles around, and one of the finest churches in Devon and the West Country. The 128 foot tower is the tallest in North Devon. Perpendicular, and largely built in the mid C14. The tower is in four stages with buttresses and massive gargoyles. The interior is large and lofty, indeed spacious with Early Jacobean pulpit, C15 Rood Screen, C20 stained glass by Christopher Webb. A simple plaque to Sir Allen Lane, the founder of Penguin Books whose family have a long association with Hartland. There's a little museum with all manner of pieces that gives this church that extra wow factor.

Stained Glass, St Nectan's

Places to Stay…

2 Harton Manor B & B, The Square. C16 building set in the heart of the village. Comfortable bedrooms and lounge are decorated with original art. Your hostess, Merlyn Chesterman runs printmaking Woodcut Workshops. Open all year. £. (D4) 01237 441670 www.twohartonmanor.co.uk

Hartland Quay Hotel. Without doubt one of the most spectacularly sited hotels in Britain. Set on dramatic, rugged cliffs overlooking the Atlantic. Book in when a Force 8 is forecast. Experience some real weather, and if the wind and drama doesn't blow you away, get stuck into some fine food and beer in the Wrecker's Retreat (and hopefully, you'll sleep through the storm). Simple, pine furniture in bedrooms with bathrooms, and stupendous views. (B4) 01237 441218 www.hartlandquayhotel.com

1340 Teignmouth attacked by French privateers.

1342 Dartmouth made a Corporate Borough.

2 Harton Manor B & B

MORWENSTOW

No visit to this area will be complete without a visit to this historic village. The village is only made up of a few farms and cottages, but it is to the church, pub and tearoom that one is drawn to.

Church of St John the Baptist. Famous for Richard Stephen Hawker, 1803-75, the eccentric and original vicar-poet, and originator of harvest festivals. A compassionate man, he would stalk the wild coast in beaver hat, fisherman's long boots and yellow cloak in search of shipwrecked sailors. Many of whom he failed to save, he laid to rest in his churchyard. To stimulate and awaken his congregation he sometimes dressed as a mermaid! His original hut made of driftwood clings to the cliffs. Opposite, the Rectory Tea Rooms, open daily in season. (A9)

The Bush Inn. C13 freehouse revitalised into a contemporary gastro-pub on the Devon-Cornish border. Cosy, authentic snug bars plus a more spacious, modern dining area. Local fish and steaks, a speciality. Accommodation. (A9) 01288 331242 www.bushinn-morwenstow.co.uk

Bush Inn, Morwenstow

Special Places to Visit...

Cheristow Lavender Farm. Grows over 100 varieties of lavender and many English roses. Soaps and oils. Tearoom. Open East-Sept Th-M 10.30-4.30. (C4) 01237 440078

Docton Mill & Gardens. Historic site of former flour mill now a flourishing and captivating garden with water features; leat, head weir and tailrace. 8 acres encompass bog garden, orchard and woodland. Walk to coastal waterfall and beach at Spekes Mill Mouth. B & B. Plant sales and tea room. Open daily Mar-Oct 10-6. (C6) 01237 441369 www.doctonmill.co.uk

Haytown Pottery. Domestic earthenwares and humorous individual animals made by David Cleverly. Open East-Sept, Tu-Th 11-7 but call beforehand 01409 261476 www.david-cleverlyceramics.co.uk (K9)

Killarney Springs. Family fun park; twisters, drop slides, bumper boats, playgrounds and much more. Open daily Apr-Oct 10-6, & W/Es, school holidays Nov-East 11-4. (D9)

Milky Way Adventure Park, Nr Clovelly. Rides, large indoor adventure play area, sports hall, narrow gauge railway, collection of farming and agricultural equipment and Birds of Prey. Open daily Mar-Nov, W/Es & 1/2 terms Nov-East. (G5) 01237 431255 www.themilkyway.co.uk

The Gnome Reserve & Wild Flower Garden, West Putford. Set in a 4 acre reserve of woodland, stream, pond, meadow and garden is the home of more than 1,000 gnomes and pixies! Approx. 250 labelled species of wild flowers, herbs, grasses and ferns. Open daily mid-Mar to Oct, 10-6. (H9) 0870 845 9012 www.gnomereserve.co.uk

Welcome Pottery. Handthrown and decorated earthenware pottery and Raku animal sculpture. Open Mar-Oct, M-Sa 10-5. (B7) 01288 331361

Beara Farmhouse

Special Places to Stay...

Beara Farmhouse. The Dorsett's know a thing or too about the comforts of home, interior design and building skills. Their fabulous home has been converted from a ruin into a rural idyll at the bottom of a rough track. Self-catering cottages, too. (L6) 01237 451666 www.bearafarmhouse.co.uk

Red Lion Hotel, Clovelly. Waking up to the sounds of an ancient harbour is a blissful experience. The rooms are all modern and comfortable with nautical themes, and have superb harbour or sea views. All with bathrooms and mod cons. The restaurant serves fish directly off the local boats. (G4) 01237 431237 www.clovelly.co.uk

West Titchberry Farm. A traditional farmhouse B & B. Clean and comfortable, a little old fashioned. Don't expect "Country Living" decor. All rooms have their own bathroom. Packed lunches and pick-up off the Coast Path can be arranged. Self-catering, too. (C3) 01237 441287

Pubs/Places Serving Food...

Cheristow Country Kitchen. Farmhouse kitchen restaurant open for evening meals and Sunday lunch. Freshly cooked meals from their own

1346 Devon ports provide 88 ships for Crecy and Calais campaign.

1348 Black Death reaches Devon, about one third of population dies. Nearly half the clergy die.

Hartland Quay

livestock of Dexter cattle, Gloucester Old Spots and Wiltshire Horn sheep. Open daily. Booking advised. Self catering. (C3) 01237 441522 www.cheristow-cottages.co.uk

Coach & Horses, Buckland Brewer. Popular "local" providing fine ales and excellent grub; skate, bass, monkfish, and local vegetables in season. Themed nights. 01237 451393 (M6)

Hoops Inn. Thatched inn dating from the C13. Log fires, real ales and huge portions have made this a popular hostelry down the years. Accommodation and dogs welcome. In former times, a meeting place for smugglers and seafarers, Sir Richard Grenville, Drake, Raleigh and Hawkins all met here. 01237 451222 www.hoopsinn.co.uk (J5)

Natural Places of Interest...

Coombe Valley Nature Trail. Start from Combe Cottages and follow a green and peaceful wooded valley rich in oak woods, honeysuckle and birdlife; buzzards, woodpeckers, dippers. Nearby, Stowe Barton, home of Sir Richard Grenville who was immortalised in Tennyson's poem, "The Revenge". (B10)

Peppercombe. The section of the coastal path from this hamlet to Buck's Mills is wonderful, and a detour to the beach is worth considering for its geological interest; triassic marl colours in reds, browns and bright yellow. The castle was demolished by fierce storms and eroding cliffs around 1900. (K4)

Shipload Bay. If you have the legs for it, descend the 260+ steps to a beach of grey shingle, and if your luck is in you can watch Grey seals laze here in early summer. (C3)

Coastal Footpath...

Westward Ho! to Clovelly (12 miles). For the first mile the path makes use of the old railway track beneath the Kipling Tors, but soon becomes more arduous with many ups and downs following the rock coast to the tiny fishing village of Bucks Mills. A few miles further the path joins the 'Hobby Drive', and by an easy twisting route through beautiful woodlands it reaches Clovelly. (M2-G4)

Peppercombe

Clovelly to Hartland Quay (10 miles). Probably the finest section of the whole path. From Clovelly the route ascends the windswept headland of Gallantry Bower, then drops down to the little rocky cove of Mouth Mill. There follows some 4 miles of fine walking along the cliff tops to Shipload Bay, one of the rare sandy beaches of this coast, and onward to Hartland Point. The coastline now turns sharply to the south and the seascapes increase in magnificence with their fantastically contorted geological formations. There is some hard but rewarding walking over these last few miles to Hartland Quay. (G4)

Hartland Quay to Marsland Mouth (6 miles). The spectacular scenery continues with some fairly stiff walking. At Spekes Mill Mouth there is a fine waterfall, from which the path ascends once again to the cliff tops. From here the path maintains a fairly steady altitude until descending to the small beach at Welcombe Mouth. A further half-mile leads the traveller, at last, to the Cornish border. (H4)

Beaches & Surfing...

Bucks Mills. Small harbour with sand and rocks. 1/2 mile from P (J4).

Clovelly. Shingle and pebbles. Boating pool. R/WC, 1/2 mile walk from P (G4).

Shipload Bay. Shingly sand and rocks 1/2 mile from P (C3). Hartland Point. Shingle, rocks, cliffs. Short walk from P.R (B3).

Welcombe Mouth. Haunt of Cruel Coppinger, an C18 smuggler. Pebbles, rocks and a sandy beach at LT. Short walk from P/R. (A7)

Marsland Mouth. Rocky. Not conducive to bathing unless you are a hardy surfer. Poet's hut on north hillside set up by the late Ronald Duncan, playwright and novelist.

Forest Trails. The Forestry Commission have organised waymarked trails scattered throughout the county. Most have information centres where detailed booklets can be obtained. Locations include Eggesford, Hartland Forest, Holsworthy, and Melbury in the north west. www.forestry.gov.uk

1356 Watercourse, or leat (clean water for cleanliness and health) provided for the inhabitants of Cullompton by the Abbot of "Bokland".

1390 Exeter Cathedral's great East Window is rebuilt by Robert Lyen.

Images from The Mortehoe Heritage Centre and The Hartland Quay Museum

1403 Plymouth burned by Breton raiders.

1404 Breton raiders land on Slapton Sands prior to invading Dartmouth.

TORRIDGE & ESTUARY
Northam Burrows
Northam Burrows Country Park
Beaver Inn
Royal George
Appledore
The Neck
Crow Rock
Instow Sands
Instow
Decks
Sail Cats
ST JOHN BAPTIST
Waterside Gallery
John's Deli
Yelland
Fremington
Bickleton
North Devon Maritime Museum
West Farm
Diddywell
Appledore Crafts
Bensons
Gallerie Marin
Tarka Cruises
Quay Gallerie
Marshford Organic Produce
Westward Ho!
Skern Lodge
Rock Nose
Mermaid's Pool
ST MARGARET
Northam
Buckleigh
Worlington
Knightacott
Instow Signal Box
Huish
Tapeley Park
ST PETER
Westleigh
Combe
Holmacott
Cornborough
Rickard's Down
Silford
Raleigh Hill
Orchard Hill
Southcott
Horwood
East Barton
Eastleigh
Abbotsham Court
Abbotsham
Burton Art Gallery
LAVINGTON CHAPEL
ST MARY
Capecino Plus
Dunstable Farm Dairy Ices
Salterns
Pillhead
Kathleen & May
East-the-Water
Bideford Railway Heritage Centre
Weach Barton
Ashridge
Little Pillhead
ST HELEN
The Big Sheep
Winsford
Handy Cross
BIDEFORD
Woodtown
Bullworthy
Warmington
Bowood
Knotty Corner
Abbotsham Cross
Atlantic Village
Upcott
Tarka Trail
Gammaton
Stony Cross
Alverdiscott
Tennacott
Reservoir
Ashridge
Winscott
Littleham Court
Pillmouth
Landcross
HOLY TRINITY
Oldiscleave
Gammaton Moor
Haddacott
Woodtown
Yeo Vale
ST SWITHIN
Littleham
Hallspill
Huxhill
Huntshaw Water
Huntshaw
ST MARY MAGDALENE
Edge Mill
River Yeo
Annery
Park
Huntshaw Bridge
Bulland
Saltrens
Weare Giffard
HOLY TRINITY
Foxes' Cross
Halsbury
Looseham
Berry Castle
Higher Darracott
Darracott Moor
Priestacott Moor
Darracott Reservoir
ST MARY & ST BENEDICT
Buckland Brewer
Coach & Horses
Upcott
ST GEORGE
Monkleigh
Furze
Beam Viaduct
Furzebeam Hill
Gorwood
ST MARY & ST GREGORY
Rothern Bridge
Crowbear
Moortown
Great Torrington
Frithelstock Priory
Frithelstock
Thorne
River Duntz
ST MICHAEL
Torrington 1646
Dartington Crystal
Frithelstock Stone
ST MARY MAGDALENE
Torrington Museum
Castle Hill
Taddiport
Plough Arts Centre
RHS Garden
Craneham
Hembury Castle
Smithacott
Priestacott
Stretchacott
Bowden
Rosemoor
South Healand
Tythecott
Tumulus
Ashbury
Clements Hill
Watergate Bridge
Cross
Little Torrington
ST GILES
Undercleave
Southcott
West Ford
Thornehill Head
Challash
Bibbear
Langtree Common
Smytham
Hollam
Thorne Moor
Wonders Corner
Langtree
Withecott
Langtree Week
Collacott
Bagbear
Huntshaw
Stowford
Great Potheridge
Doves Moor
Stibb Cross
Burstone
Berry Cross
Yard
Potheridge Gate
Lambert
Browns
Rivaton
Suddon
Peters Marland
Willeswell Moor
Dunsbear
Binworthy
R Mere
Stapleton
Winswell
Durpley
Badworthy
Woollaton
Eastwood
Moorhill
Newton St Petrock
Durpley Castle
Week
Merton Moor
0 1 2 miles
0 1 2 3 kilometres
A39(T)
B3236
A386
B3233
A388
B3227
B3232
A3124

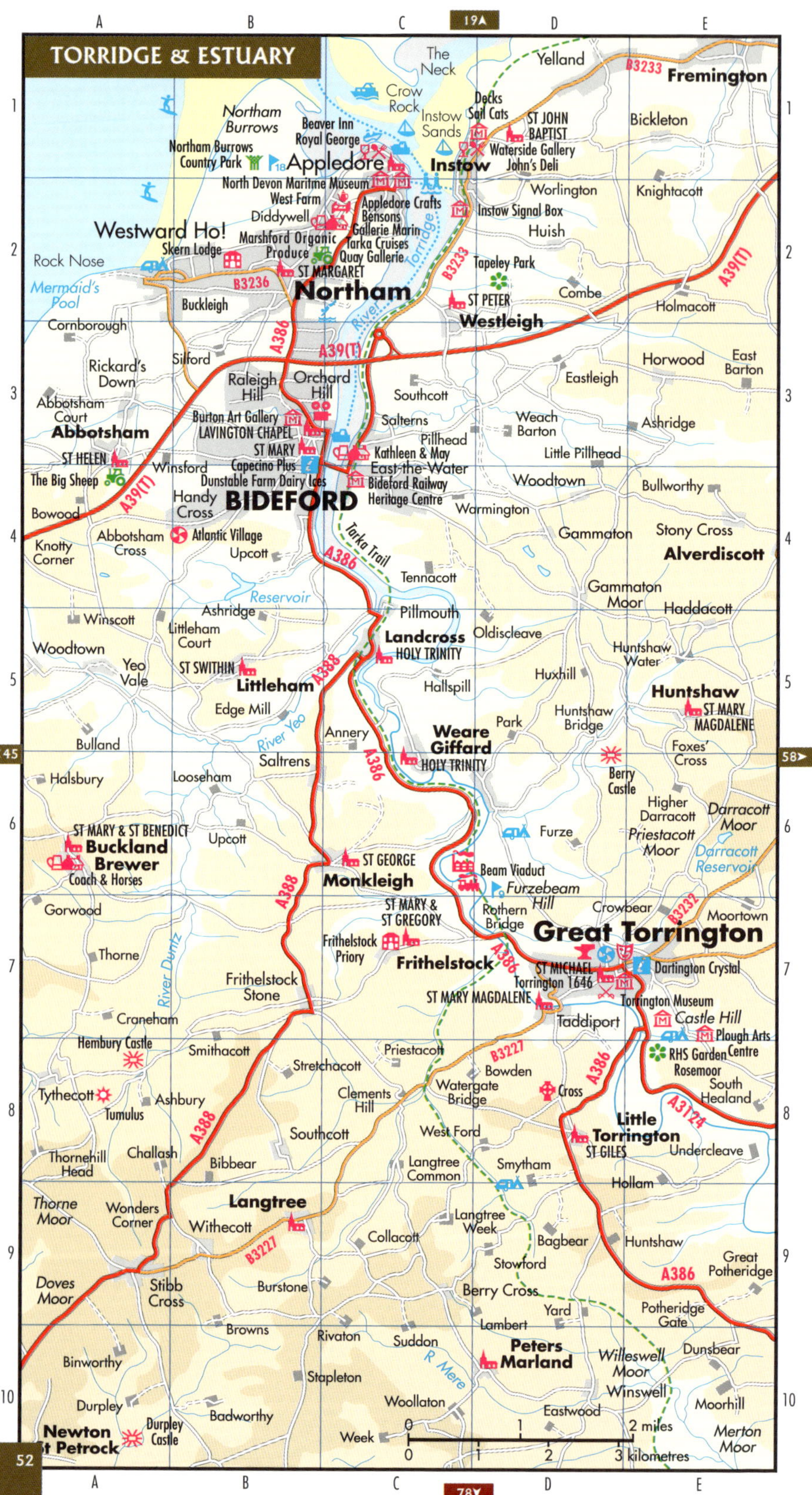

19▲
◄45
58►
78▼

BIDEFORD

A lively and busy town on the Torridge Estuary, and to this day, cargo ships load and unload on the quay. In the C16 and C17, one of Britain's major seaports, handling cargoes from, and to, the New World. A favourite haunt of Drake, Grenville, Hawkins and Sir Walter Raleigh, who it is claimed brought his first cargo of tobacco to Bideford. Furthermore, in the late C17, local merchants traded wool with Newfoundland sending out more ships than any other apart from London and Topsham.

The fine 24-arch C15 bridge is one of the longest (677 ft) in the country, but now overshadowed by the new bridge down river. New Year's Eve attracts over 20,000 revellers to celebrate the New Year who dress up in all manner of garb. Pannier Market on Tuesdays and Saturdays. Trips to Lundy Island. Regatta in Sept. E/C W. (B4)

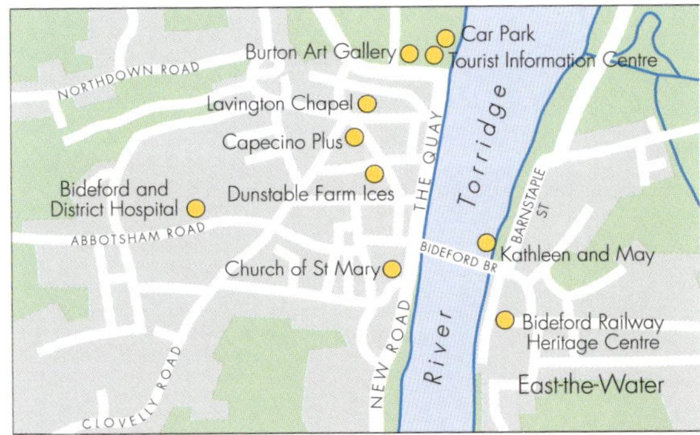

Bideford

The Old & New Bridges, Bideford

Special Places to Visit...

Bideford Railway Heritage Centre, Former Railway Station. Visitor Centre in restored railway carriage. Refreshments. Hibberd 0-4-0 "Planet" Diesel loco No. 3832 built in 1957. Open East-Oct Su & BHs 2-5. Nov-East Su 2-4. (C4) 01237 423585

Burton Art Gallery & Museum, Kingsley Road. The Museum of Bideford; with three exhibition spaces, museum, craft gallery, shop, workshop and lecture theatre and coffee shop. Open all year Tu-Sa & BH Ms 10-5, Su 2-5 (4 winter). (B3) 01237 471455 www.burtonartgallery.co.uk

Kathleen & May off Clovelly pj

Burton Art Gallery

Kathleen & May Preservation Trust, Brunswick Wharf. Guided tours of the fully restored, last remaining wooden hull, top-sail, 3-masted schooner in Britain. Due to a hectic fundraising schedule it is worth contacting them well ahead of time to ensure seeing this impressive ship.
Open in season W & W/Es 1-4.
(C4) 01237 476375
www.kathleen-and-may.co.uk

The mouth of the Taw and Torridge Estuary

Where to Eat, Drink & Be Merry...

Cafecino Plus, 25 Mill Street. Bustling bistro open for coffee and light meals. Evening meals include fresh fish; sea bass and cod suplied by Clovelly Fish. Take-Aways, too. (C3) 01237 473007 www.cafecinoplus.com

Dunstable Farm Dairy's Ice Cream Parlour, 14a Mill St. A full treat of flavours to assuage your thirst and hunger. (C3)

APPLEDORE

One of the most attractive villages in North Devon. It's set on the Torridge Estuary, and has ancient inter-connecting streets with rows of colour-washed cottages reminiscent of the Greek, Cycladean islands. A thriving fishing and trading village since the C14. Many of the fisherman's cottages date back to the Elizabethan period. The centuries old shipbuilding tradition has had a precarious existence. Many pubs, craft shops, and home to many artists. The view out to sea from the RNLI Station & Museum is memorable. It is worth exploring the little streets and watching the boats come and go. Like a lot of holiday places the cottages are often sadly empty but for a few months of the year. (C2)

Special Places to Visit...

Appledore Crafts Co, 5 Bude Street. Co-operative run gallery founded by 14 local craftsmen who produce fine furniture, lighting, paintings, ceramics, glass, textiles and jewellery. Open: Summer 10-6 daily. Winter 10-4 W-Su. (C2) 01237 423547 www.appledorecraftscompany.co.uk

Appledore Crafts Co

Gallerie Marin, 31 Market St., Specialises in Marine Art, landscapes and wildlife. Displays 20 well-known artists. Open daily. (C2) 01237 473679

North Devon Maritime Museum, Odun Road. North Devon's nautical history displayed with paintings, models, tools and photos. Shipbuilding through the ages. Wrecks and rescues. World War 11. Fishing and navigational exhibits. Open East-Oct 2-5, also from May-Sept M-F 11-1. (C2) 01237 422064

Skern Lodge. Adventure activities for all ages and abilities. Climbing, powerboats, abseiling, surfing, archery, rafting. canoeing and tunnels. (B2) Appledore 01237 475992 www.skernlodge.co.uk

Tarka Cruises, Schooners Tea Shop. Scenic pleasure cruises up the Torridge. Fishing trips. May to Oct. (C2) 01237 477505 www.appledore-letting.co.uk

Where to Stay...

West Farm, Irsha Street (WL). A delightful B & B with a magical garden hidden behind high walls. Large bedrooms with bathrooms. Your hostess, Gail Sparkes has a great sense of humour and a rebellious nature. (C2) 01237 425269 www.appledore-devon.co.uk

Where to Eat, Drink & Be Merry...

Beaver Inn, Irsha Street. Popular, unpretentious Freehouse provides seafood and meat dishes. Superb panoramic views of the Estuary. Jazz nights. Dogs welcome. (C2) 01237 474822

Royal George, Irsha Street. Cosy pub with separate restaurant supplying fantastic views across the Estuary, too. Fish a speciality. Bermudan connections. (C2) 01237 474335

Bensons Restaurant, 20 The Quay. Small diner offering seafood directly off the local boats. Home made puds. Light lunches and dinner. (C2) 01237 424093

Quay Gallery & Restaurant, 9 The Quay. A family business provides the perfect antidote to our frenetic lives; a laid-back ambience from which to enjoy light lunches and cream teas, surrounded by art; paintings and ceramics. Evening Restaurant upstairs 7-9 pm. (C2) 01237 473355 www.9thequay.co.uk

INSTOW

Popular holiday village with sandy beach, pedestrian ferry to Appledore and fine views of the Torridge Estuary. Sailing Club. Home of the famous Test Match umpire, David Shepherd. Unique thatched cricket score box and pavilion. Stopping off point for riding the Tarka Trail. The Commodore Hotel is a civilised destination, popular with golfers and the Retired. A number of pubs and restaurants, and the Deli (Johns) within the post office. (C2)

1494 Great Court of tinners meets at Crockern Tor.

1496 Devon and Cornwall men rebel against taxes. Defeated at Blackheath.

What to See & do...

Instow Signal Box, Level Crossing. Built in 1873, now restored to its former glory with levers, gate wheel and instruments. Open East-Oct Su & BHs 2-5, Nov-East Su 2-4. (D2) 01237 423585

Sail Cats, The Beach. Learn to sail amazingly quick catamarans. Equipment and expert tuition provided. (D2) 01805 624489 www.sailcats.co.uk

Waterside Gallery, Marine Terrace. Paintings, sculpture, pottery, picture framing and a selection of gifts. Open Tu-Sa 10-1, 2-5. (D2)01271 860786

Westerly View from Torrington Car Park

Torridge Valley, Nr Rosemoor

Where to Eat...

Decks, Marine Parade. In sensational position overlooking the Taw/Torridge Estuary and Appledore. Local fish predominate the delectable dinner menu; Sea Bass, Skate and Lemon Sole. Luncheon a delight. Book in advance for prime table positions (beside window upstairs). (D2) 01271 860671 www.decksrestaurant.co.uk

GREAT TORRINGTON

An ancient hilltop town set in a strategic position overlooking the River Torridge and rolling, green countryside. The English Civil War's Battle of Torrington in 1646 ended the Royalist's resistance to the Parliamentarian cause in the West Country. The TV series "Down To Earth" was shot around the town and vicinity. Note the fine Market Square with Town Hall and other interesting buildings. Twenty miles of footpaths on The Commons, a public area of 365 acres with flora and fauna. The town is the centre for many Sealed Knot re-enactments of the Civil War. Pannier Market on Thursdays and Saturdays. May Fair, first Th. (E7)

Dartington Crystal. Handmade lead crystal ware. Viewing galleries and guided tours. Historic glass exhibition. Family Activity Centre. Open daily; tours M-F 9-3.15, Shop/Restaurant daily from 10. (D7) 01805 626242

Great Torrington Museum, Town Hall. Collection of local historic interest including the Coronation Coronets and robes of the last Earl and Countess Orford of Torrington. Open May-Sept M-F 11-4, Sa 11-1. (E7) 01805 626146 www.great-torrington.com

Plough Arts Centre, 9-11 Fore St., Lively centre with special workshops, galleries, live events, film shows and more. Open daily. (E7) 01805 622552 www.plough-arts.org

Torrington 1646, Castle Hill. Celebrates the last battle of the Civil War fought between the Prince of Wales' Army and the New Model Army led by Oliver Cromwell and Sir Thomas Fairfax. Physic Garden. Coffee shop with home-made soups and cakes. Open M-Sa all year. (D7) 01805 626146

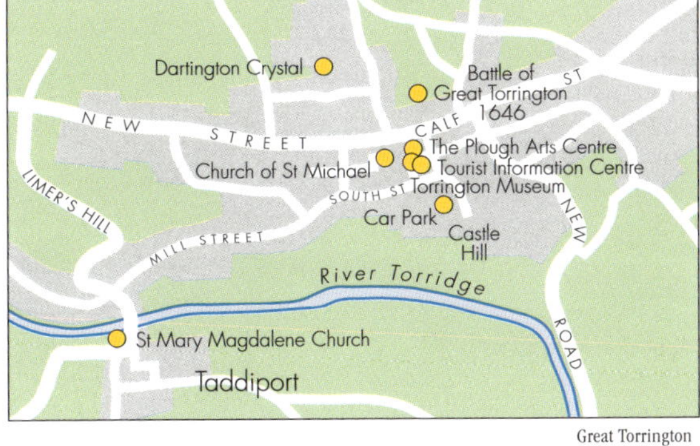

Great Torrington

. Cottage Garden, RHS Rosemoor ss

Dairy. Health & Harmony Festive Weekends Open daily late Mar to early Nov except Sa, 10-5. (D2) 01271 342558 www.tapeleypark.com

The Big Sheep. Sheep in all shapes, sizes and disguises, combining to create the bizarre, the entertaining and the unexpected. Sheep dairy and sheep milking. Mountain Boarding. Open daily Apr-Oct & winter W/Es, 10-6. (M3) 01237 472366 www.thebigsheep.co.uk

High Seas, Westward Ho!

Special Places to Visit...

Frithelstock Priory. Commanding ruin of C13 Augustinian priory with adjoining church. (C7)

Kenwith Nursery. Specialists in dwarf and rare conifers. Mail order. Open Mar-Oct Tu-Sa, Nov-Feb W-Sa, 10-4.30. (E8) 01805 603274 www.kenwithnursery.co.uk

Marshford Organic Produce, Churchill Way. Specialise in varieties of mixed salads and greens; oakleaf, spinach and rocket, plus little gems, caesars and more. Open daily. (C2)

Northam Burrows Country Park. 640 acres of grassy plain, saltmarsh, dunes and a notable pebble ridge. Access to two miles of safe, sandy beach. Walks and trails. Burrows Centre has exhibitions and displays. Shop. Toilets for disabled. Centre open daily East-Sept 10-5, Park open all year. (B2) 01237 479708

RHS Garden Rosemoor, Nr Great Torrington. An enchanting 65 acres of gardens and woodland, including 2,000 roses in 200 different varieties, colour theme gardens, herb garden and potager, stream and bog garden, cottage garden, fruit and vegetable garden, and semi-tropical areas. Plant Centre, Restaurant and shop. Picnic area. Open daily Apr-Sept 10-6 (-5 winter). (E7) 01805 624067 www.rhs.org.uk

Tapeley Park Gardens, Nr Instow. With magnificent views out to sea, these fascinating gardens offer a variety of exciting terrains; wooded lakes, pleasure grounds, new Organic Permaculture garden, traditional walled kitchen garden, and beside the unique Italian terraces rare plants flourish in the warm Devon climate. Home since 1700 to the Christie family who built the Opera House at Glyndebourne. Also pigs and pets, pug's graves, ilex tunnel, grotto, croquet, bowls, plant sales, lunches and cream teas in the Queen Anne

WESTWARD HO!

Unusually, a seaside resort named after a book - it was established in 1863 in recognition of Charles Kingsley. Rudyard Kipling was educated at United Services College (some buildings survive as guest houses), and set 'Stalky & Co' in the hills to south, now named 'Kipling Tors'. Interesting pebble beach to north. A quieter beach to surf becoming increasingly popular, away from the hordes of Croyde and Saunton. Fine bass fishing, and excellent fishing tackle shop. Major tennis club in North Devon. E/C W. Pot Wollopers is gaining a reputation as a place to eat. (B2)

Beaches & Surfing...

Westward Ho! Wide expanse of sand. Pebble ridge behind. Water sports. R/WC/LG (B2).

Instow. Flat, estuary sand, fine for sun bathing and ball games, but not conducive for bathing. R/P. (C1)

1538 Dissolution of the monasteries begins in Devon with priories in Barnstaple, Cornworthy, Exeter, Frithelstock and Pilton.

1549 Crediton occupied by 10,000 Catholic insurgents demonstrating against The Reformation.

Images from The North Devon Maritime Museum in Appledore

1563 Exeter Ship Canal opened, the first canal with locks in England.

1568 Drake and Hawkins attacked at San Juan de Ulua in the Spanish West Indies.

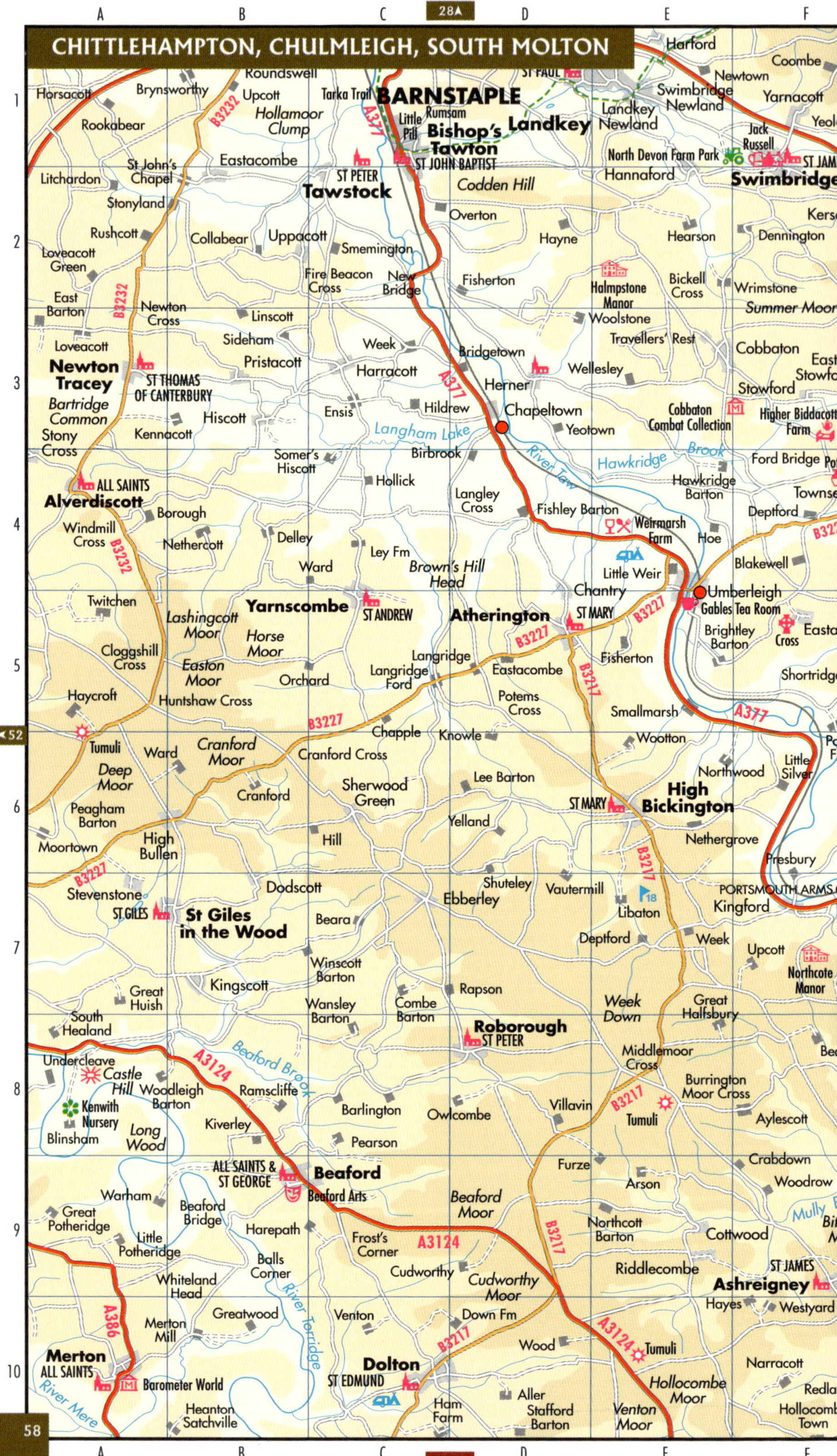
CHITTLEHAMPTON, CHULMLEIGH, SOUTH MOLTON
28▲
78▼
◄52
A B C D E F
1 2 3 4 5 6 7 8 9 10
Harford
Coombe
Newtown
Horsacott
Brynsworthy
Roundswell
Upcott
Hollamoor Clump
Tarka Trail
BARNSTAPLE
ST PAUL
Swimbridge Newland
Yarnacott
Rookabear
B3232
A377
Little Pill
Rumsam
Bishop's Tawton
Landkey
Landkey Newland
Jack Russell
Eastacombe
ST JOHN BAPTIST
North Devon Farm Park
Swimbridge
Litchardon
St John's Chapel
ST PETER
Tawstock
Codden Hill
Hannaford
Stonyland
Overton
Kerse
Rushcott
Collabear
Uppacott
Hayne
Hearson
Dennington
Loveacott Green
Smemington
Fire Beacon Cross
New Bridge
Fisherton
Halmpstone Manor
Bickell Cross
Wrimstone
Summer Moor
East Barton
Newton Cross
Linscott
Woolstone
Sideham
Week
Travellers' Rest
Cobbaton
Loveacott
Bridgetown
East Stowford
Newton Tracey
ST THOMAS OF CANTERBURY
Pristacott
Harracott
Herner
Wellesley
Stowford
Bartridge Common
Hiscott
Ensis
Hildrew
Chapeltown
Cobbaton Combat Collection
Higher Biddacott Farm
Stony Cross
Kennacott
Langham Lake
Yeotown
Somer's Hiscott
Birbrook
River Taw
Hawkridge Brook
Ford Bridge
ALL SAINTS
Hollick
Hawkridge Barton
Alverdiscott
Langley Cross
Townsend
Borough
Fishley Barton
Deptford
Windmill Cross
Nethercott
Delley
Weirmarsh Farm
Hoe
B3227
Ley Fm
Brown's Hill Head
Little Weir
Blakewell
Ward
Twitchen
Chantry
Umberleigh
Yarnscombe
ST ANDREW
Gables Tea Room
Lashingcott Moor
Atherington
ST MARY
Brightley Barton
Easter Cross
Horse Moor
Cloggshill Cross
Langridge
Fisherton
Easton Moor
Langridge Ford
Eastacombe
Shortridge
Orchard
B3217
Haycroft
Huntshaw Cross
Potems Cross
Smallmarsh
A377
Chapple
Knowle
Wootton
Tumuli
Ward
Cranford Moor
Cranford Cross
Little Silver
Deep Moor
Northwood
Lee Barton
Cranford
Sherwood Green
High Bickington
Peagham Barton
Yelland
High Bullen
Hill
Nethergrove
Moortown
Presbury
Stevenstone
Dodscott
Shuteley
Vautermill
PORTSMOUTH ARMS
ST GILES
St Giles in the Wood
Ebberley
Libaton
Kingford
Beara
Deptford
Week
Upcott
Winscott Barton
Northcote Manor
Kingscott
Rapson
Great Huish
Wansley Barton
Combe Barton
Week Down
Great Halfsbury
South Healand
Roborough
ST PETER
Middlemoor Cross
Undercleave
A3124
Beaford Brook
Castle Hill
Woodleigh Barton
Ramscliffe
Burrington Moor Cross
Kenwith Nursery
Barlington
Owlcombe
Villavin
Tumuli
Aylescott
Long Wood
Kiverley
Blinsham
Pearson
Crabdown
ALL SAINTS & ST GEORGE
Beaford
Furze
Arson
Woodrow
Warham
Beaford Arts
Beaford Moor
Mully Brook
Great Potheridge
Beaford Bridge
Harepath
Northcott Barton
Cottwood
Little Potheridge
Frost's Corner
Balls Corner
Riddlecombe
ST JAMES
Cudworthy
Cudworthy Moor
Ashreigney
Whiteland Head
Hayes
Westyard
A386
Greatwood
Venton
Down Fm
Merton Mill
River Torridge
Wood
Tumulus
Narracott
Merton
ALL SAINTS
Dolton
ST EDMUND
Hollocombe Moor
Redland
Barometer World
Aller
Hollocombe Town
River Mere
Heanton Satchville
Ham Farm
Stafford Barton
Venton Moor

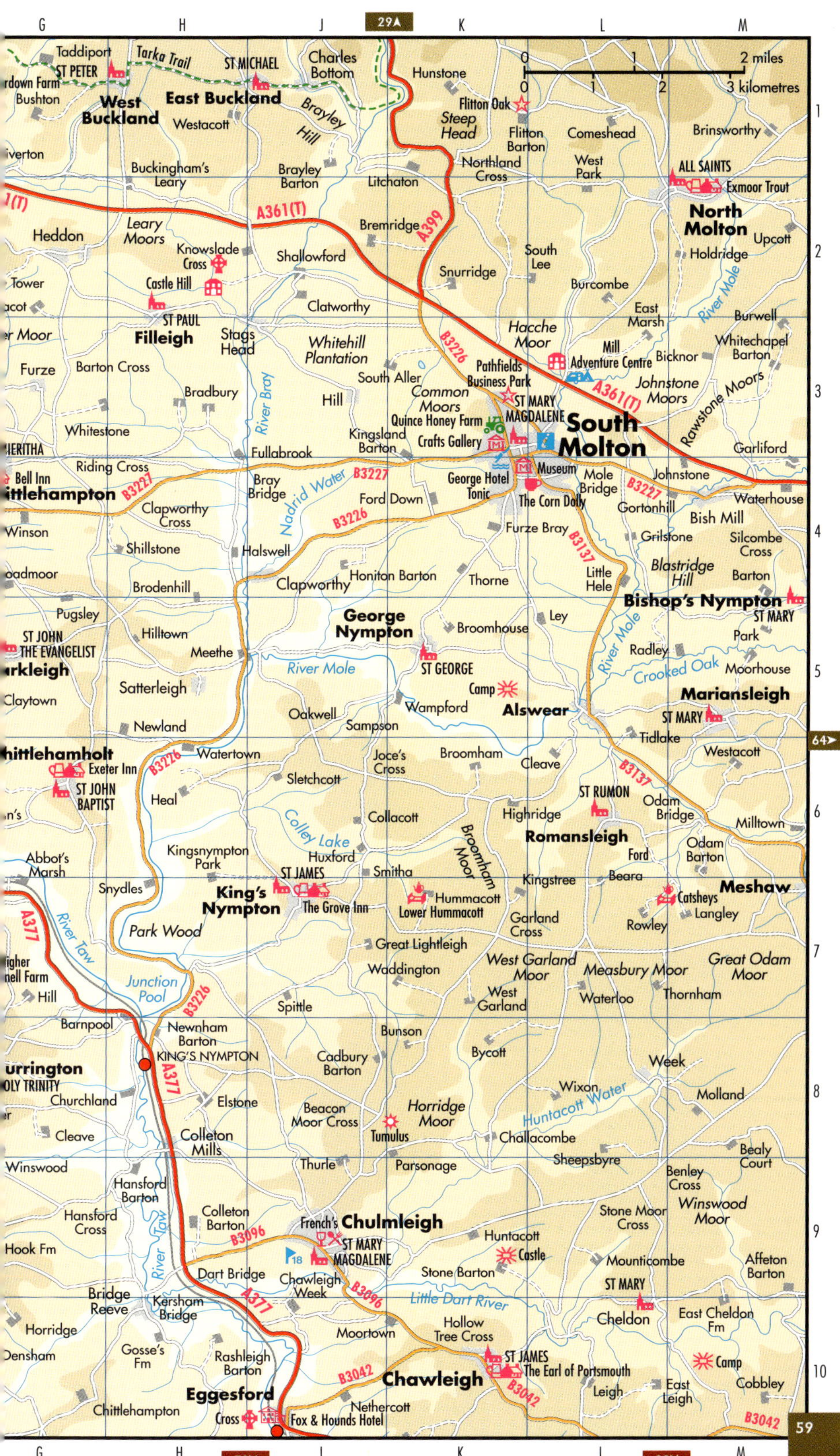

29▲
64►
79▼
82▼
Taddiport
ST PETER
Tarka Trail
ST MICHAEL
Charles Bottom
Hunstone
West Buckland
East Buckland
Westacott
Brayley Hill
Flitton Oak
Steep Head
Flitton Barton
Comeshead
Brinsworthy
Buckingham's Leary
Brayley Barton
Litchaton
Northland Cross
West Park
ALL SAINTS
Exmoor Trout
North Molton
Upcott
Holdridge
Heddon
Leary Moors
A361(T)
Bremridge
A399
Knowslade Cross
Shallowford
South Lee
Castle Hill
Snurridge
Burcombe
River Mole
ST PAUL
Filleigh
Clatworthy
East Marsh
Burwell
Stags Head
Whitehill Plantation
Hacche Moor
Whitechapel Barton
Furze
Barton Cross
B3226
Mill
Adventure Centre
Bicknor
Pathfields Business Park
South Aller
Johnstone Moors
Bradbury
Common Moors
ST MARY MAGDALENE
Rawstone Moors
River Bray
Hill
Quince Honey Farm
South Molton
Whitestone
Kingsland Barton
Crafts Gallery
Garliford
Fullabrook
Museum
Bell Inn
Riding Cross
Bray Bridge
Nadrid Water
B3227
George Hotel
Tonic
Mole Bridge
Johnstone
Waterhouse
Ford Down
The Corn Dolly
Gortonhill
Clapworthy Cross
Bish Mill
Winson
Furze Bray
Grilstone
Silcombe Cross
Shillstone
Halswell
B3137
Blastridge Hill
Brodenhill
Clapworthy
Honiton Barton
Thorne
Little Hele
Barton
Bishop's Nympton
ST MARY
Pugsley
George Nympton
Ley
ST JOHN THE EVANGELIST
Hilltown
Broomhouse
Park
Meethe
Radley
Satterleigh
River Mole
ST GEORGE
Crooked Oak
Moorhouse
Camp
Mariansleigh
Claytown
Oakwell
Wampford
Alswear
ST MARY
Newland
Sampson
Tidlake
Watertown
Joce's Cross
Broomham
Westacott
Exeter Inn
Cleave
Sletchcott
ST RUMON
ST JOHN BAPTIST
Heal
Odam Bridge
Collacott
Highridge
Milltown
Colley Lake
Romansleigh
Abbot's Marsh
Kingsnympton Park
Huxford
Broomham Moor
Ford
Odam Barton
ST JAMES
Smitha
Beara
Snydles
King's Nympton
The Grove Inn
Hummacott
Lower Hummacott
Kingstree
Catsheys
Meshaw
Langley
A377
Garland Cross
Rowley
River Taw
Park Wood
Great Lightleigh
Waddington
West Garland Moor
Measbury Moor
Great Odam Moor
Junction Pool
West Garland
Waterloo
Thornham
Hill
Spittle
Barnpool
Newnham Barton
Bunson
Bycott
KING'S NYMPTON
Cadbury Barton
Week
Churchland
Elstone
Wixon
Molland
Beacon Moor Cross
Horridge Moor
Huntacott Water
Cleave
Colleton Mills
Tumulus
Challacombe
Winswood
Thurle
Parsonage
Sheepsbyre
Bealy Court
Benley Cross
Hansford Barton
Winswood Moor
Hansford Cross
Colleton Barton
French's
Chulmleigh
Stone Moor Cross
Hook Fm
B3096
ST MARY MAGDALENE
Huntacott
Castle
Affeton Barton
Dart Bridge
Mounticombe
Stone Barton
Chawleigh Week
ST MARY
Bridge Reeve
Kersham Bridge
Little Dart River
Cheldon
East Cheldon Fm
Horridge
Hollow Tree Cross
Moortown
Densham
Gosse's Fm
Rashleigh Barton
ST JAMES
Camp
The Earl of Portsmouth
B3042
Chawleigh
Leigh
East Leigh
Cobbley
Eggesford
Chittlehampton
Cross
Nethercott
Fox & Hounds Hotel
0 1 2 miles
0 1 2 3 kilometres

SOUTH MOLTON

Busy Market town for North East Devon, and route centre for Exmoor. Wide main street. C18 Guildhall and Museum. As the town's prosperity grew from the wool and cloth trade in the C17, and as several of the mills were powered by the River Mole, processing wool and corn, the town became an important thoroughfare for merchants, gaining a riotous reputation employing some 500 Ladies of Ill Repute (see Museum). Sheep Fair - end Aug. E/C W. (L3)

Crafts Gallery, Griffin's Yard, North St.
One of the few craft galleries in North Devon and a development of the organic natural foods emporium selling Jenny Wilkinson's woven textiles and work from many West Country craftsmen. Cafe. Parking. Open daily. (K3) 01769 574284 www.craftsgallerygriffinsyard.co.uk

Quince Honey Farm, North Rd.
Britain's largest honey farm and home to a million bees. Unique exhibition of observation hives. Honey and beeswax products for sale. Open daily Apr-Oct 9-5. (K3) 01769 572401 www.quincehoney.co.uk

South Molton Museum, The Guidhall.
Glimpses into the domestic life, trades, industry, mining and farming of the town and district's past. Open Mar-Nov M Tu & Th 10.30-4. W & Sa 10.30-12.30. (L3) 01769 572951 www.northdevonlink.co.uk/south-molton-museum

Where to Eat, Drink & Be Merry…

Corn Dolly, 115a East Street.
Real tea shop providing breakfast, light lunches and cream teas. Home baked fare. Gifts. Open daily. (K4)

Tonic, High Street.
Chic Cafe/Bar run by four enthusiastic women. Food and drink for most occasions; range of coffees, pizzas, salads, sandwiches. Open daily from 11 (9 on Th & Sa) until 11pm (Closed 3-6pm). (K3) 01769 574440 www.tonic-uk.com

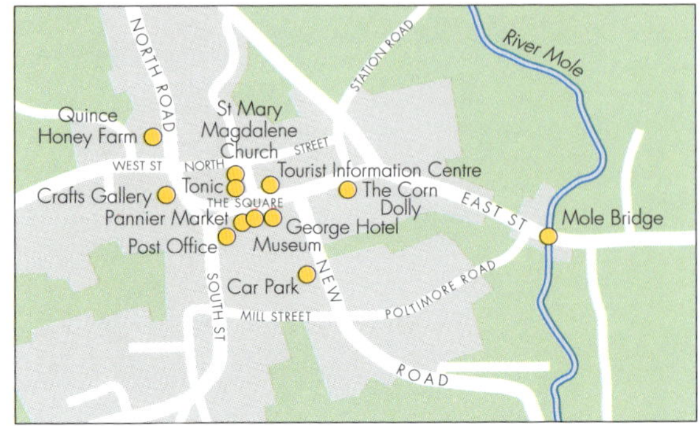

South Molton

Castle Hill Estate

Special Places to Visit…

Castle Hill. Grade 1 Palladian mansion built in 1730 by Hugh Fortescue, Lord Clinton, as his family home is set in 5,500 acres of prime agricultural land. Home of the late Sir John Fortescue, historian and the Queen's Librarian at Windsor Castle and good friend to Henry Williamson who lived for seven years at Shallowford where he wrote Salar the Salmon and raised many children. Now the home of Lord and Lady Arran. House open by appointment only, Garden April-August inclusive, or by appointment. An impressive sight from the road. Public access is permitted along two paths from Feb-Sept inclusive, starting from Filleigh Village Hall (3/4 hour) and Filleigh Sawmill (1/2 hour). (H2)

Cobbaton Combat Collection. British and Canadian fighting vehicles of World War 11. Field guns, radios and other equipment. Home Front section, Women's Land Army. Children's play area. Militaria shop. Open Su-F Apr-Oct & Su July-Aug, Nov-Mar M-F, 10-5. (E3) 01769 540740 www.cobbatoncombat.co.uk

Stained Glass Window, Atherington

1570 Start of Devon fisherman seeking cod off the Grand Banks of Newfoundland.

1571 Crediton hit by the Plague with 540 deaths.

Catsheys ss

Lower Hummacott, Nr Kings Nympton. Charming Georgian farmhouse set in 6 acres of formal gardens with streams, ponds, woodland and ever present wildlife overlooking a pastoral landscape so typical of North Devon. The King size bed is enormous and inviting. The house is decorated with antiques, and figurative oil paintings, by the award-winning artist. Organic breakfasts and evening meals on Su & M. £. (K7) 01769 581177 www.tonywilliamsart.co.uk

Special Places to Stay...

Catsheys, Nr Romansleigh. A quite stunning rural hideaway brimming with artwork; sculptures, ceramics and paintings, overlook eleven acres of gardens and woodland. Massive beds with modern bathrooms. Light, airy spaces furnished with pieces handcrafted by your host. Bookings by prior arrangement only. (L7) 01769 550580 www.catsheys.co.uk

Fox & Hounds Hotel, Eggesford. Former Victorian Coaching Inn set amidst the beautiful Taw Valley. Roaring fires and comfy leather sofas will relax you. Bedrooms are being refurbished. Fishing rights on five beats; Ghillie services and fly fishing tuition available. Day tickets available to non-residents. Bar foods and restaurant. (J10) 01769 580345 www.foxandhoundshotel.co.uk

George Hotel, 1 Broad Street. South Molton's venue for Country, bluegrass and folk music gigs, film societies and carol services. Dinner specials at Live Events. Nine guest bedrooms. (L3) 01769 572514 www.georgehotelsouthmolton.co.uk

Halmpstone Manor. Set in isolated and idyllic countryside, the Manor House dates back to the C12. Romantic 4-poster beds, large bathrooms, large sofas and good food provide a welcome retreat from today's hurly-burly lifestyle. Dinner by arrangement. (E2) 01271 830321 www.halmpstonemanor.co.uk

Heavy Horses, Higher Biddacott Farm

Tony Williams Painting, Lower Hummacott ss

Higher Biddacott Farm, Chittlehampton. B&B in C12 farm house. Large bedroom with 1680 pargetted ceiling by the famous Abbot Brothers. Jonathan Waterer is a Devon-style Horse Whisperer, training Heavy and Light Horses. Wagon tours. Pre-arranged Dinner available. Also, a Self-catering cottage and a Wildlife Trail. (F3) 01769 540222 www.heavy-horses.net

Northcote Manor, Nr Burrington. C18 manor house set in 20 acres of mature woodland with outstanding views overlooking the Taw Valley. Classic English Country House hotel provides luxury and comfort at a relaxed pace. Great bathrooms and big beds. Boasts one of North Devon's finest restaurants (open to non-residents for lunch and dinner). If your conversation is at a loss then admire the Murals of monks past. (F7)01769 560501 www.northcotemanor.co.uk

1575 The first county map of Devon produced by Christopher Saxton.

1578. Queen Elizabeth 1 grants Sir Humphrey Gilbert Letters Patent to found an English Colony – Wth Sir Francis Drake and Thomas Carew they amass seven vessels. This scheme fails, too.

Hoar Frost, River Taw, Umberleigh

Rood Screen, Atherington

Arts & Craft Interests...

Beaford Arts. The rural arts organisation for North Devon creates opportunities to enjoy and experience a wide range of arts activities. Live performances, touring exhibitions, Touring Cinema and community arts projects. Residential Centre created by the Dartington Hall Trust for workshops and courses. (C9) Greenwarren House 01805 603201 www.beaford-arts.co.uk

Chittlehampton Pottery. Roger Cockram creates handmade pots and jars based on a Natural World theme. Open M-F 10-5.30 & some W/Es. (F4) 01769 540420 www.rogercockram-ceramics.co.uk

Countryside Interests...

Exmoor Trout, North Molton. Trout farm displaying the growth of trout from eggs to giant brood stock. Spectacular feeding time. Farm shop. Open daily 8.30-5. (M2) 01598 740321

Higher Hacknell Farm. Award-wining organic food supplier farming organicaly since 1988; South Devon beef, Lleyn and Lenx Texel lamb, pork sausages. See website for more details. (F7) 01769 560909 www.higherhacknell.co.uk

Marshall Falcons. A chance to have a go at flying hawks and falcons. Lunch, equipment, tuition and transport all included. Meet at the Hoops Inn and fly birds above the cliffs. Flies from Apr-Oct. 01271 373309/07866 748977 (C1) www.marshallfalcons.co.uk

North Devon Farm Park. Miss Piggland and Rabbit World. Indoor Jungle World. Rare breeds of cattle, goats, poultry, wildfowl and many breeds of sheep. Nature trail. Picnic area. Open daily Apr-Oct 10-5. (E1) 01271 830255 www.farmpark.co.uk

Mill Adventure Centre, South Molton. Indoor climbing wall and outdoor activities galore; rock climbing, coasteering, swimming, caving, jumping, survival training and more, all with qualified instructors. Cafe. Outdoor gear/hire shop. Open daily 10 til late. (L3) 01769 579600 www.milladventure.co.uk

Tordown Farm. Traditional Devon farm of 130 acres with C16 and C17 buildings in rolling countryside. Hedges, wildflower pastures, woodland and wildlife reserve. Barn and Tawny owls, cattle and sheep. Cream teas. Open all year, Sa-Th 10-5. (G1) 01271 830265

Where to Eat, Drink & Be Merry...

French's of Chulmleigh, Fore Street. A friendly, family run restaurant where you can enjoy a quality home-cooked meal in a relaxed atmosphere. Traditional and Cosmopolitan meals at affordable prices. Smoke-free. Vegetarian friendly. Open M-Sa 9.30-3, Eves W-Sa from 6.30. (J9) 01769 580023 www.frenchsofchulmleigh.co.uk

The Earl of Portsmouth, Chawleigh. Leading foodie pub who pioneered sourcing its materials from local farms. Soups and bread made on premises. Specials may include Aberdeen Angus braised steaks, lambs liver and bacon. (K10) 01769 580204 www.earlofportsmouth-pub.co.uk

The Grove Inn, Kings Nympton. Gracious and friendly hospitality awaits you in this traditional country pub serving fine Devon cuisine and real ales. No wonder we keep hearing encouraging reports about this new foodie-pub. Winner of North Devon's Food & Drinks Award in 2005/6. (J7) 01769 580406 www.thegroveinn.co.uk

Weirmarsh Farm Restaurant, Nr Umberleigh. Popular and amazing value-for-money restaurant. 5 course dinner for around £25.00 per person. Advance booking essential (by at least two weeks). Special room for parties of 8 or more. Licensed. Open Th, F & Sa. (E4) 01769 560338

Chittlehampton

BAMPTON, DULVERTON, TIVERTON
Holywell Cross
Holy Well
Brinsworthy
Reservoir
Headgate
West Twitchen Ball
ST PETER
Twitchen
Cussacombe Common
Round Hill
White Post
Cussacombe Gate
Moorhouse Ridge
Cloggs Down
Cloggs
Lyshwell
Parsonage Farm
Hawkridge Common
Hawkridge
Hollowcombe
Zeal
Danes Brook
Millbrook
Pitt
Pulham
Twitchen Mill
Tumulus
Molland Common
Tumulus
White Moor
Anstey Gate
West Anstey Common
Burch
Kerswell
Luckworthy
Upcott
Smallcombe
West Anstey Barrows
Whitcott
Bickingcott
Molland
ST MARY
West Mollard Barton
Stone
Ringcombe
990
Bremley
Netherwill
West Anstey
ST PETROCK
Burwell
Sundercombe
Whitechapel Barton
Reach
Sheepwash
Pulworthy
Beer
Waddicon
Whitechapel Moors
Veraby
Abbots Park
Hill
East Anst
Camp
River Yeo
Hilltown
Kipscott Barton
Bottreaux Mill
New Park
River Yeo
Dunsley
Garliford
North Hayne
Yeo Mill
Higher Radnidge Moor
B3227
Bullaford
Cuckoo
Waterhouse
Kerscott
Wester Bullaford Moor
Wester New Moor
Easter New Moor
Tumulus
Newtown
Smallacombe Moors
Silcombe Cross
A361(T)
Port
Muckford
B3227
Tumuli
Little Hill
Paul's Moor
Luckett Moor
Blackerton
Barton
Broadhill
Bishop's Nympton
ST MARY
Welland
Wadham
Owlaborough
Crooked Oak
Park
East Knowstone
Avercombe
Ash Mill
Cross Side
Castle
ST PETER
Woodburn
Moorhouse
Yeo Barton
Rodsworthy
Ford
Masons Arms Inn
Knowstone
A361(T)
Bowden
Roachill
Swineh
Westacott
Harpson
Side Moor
Tumulus
Knowstone Inner Moor
Hares Down
Rose Ash
ST PETER
Beaple's Moor
Rackenford Moor
Trittencott
Whippenscott
Nethercott
Nutcombe
Moortown
Knowstone Outer Moor
A361(T)
Milltown
Catkill
Tumulus
Great Ash Moor
North Backstone
Fox Brake
ST JOHN BAPTIST
Meshaw
Burcombe
Venhay Down
Tumuli
Batsworthy
The Lodge
Frankhill
Meshaw Barton
Whitestone
Ash Moor
Creacombe
Backstone
Little Rackenford
B3137
Great Odam Moor
Nettlefield
Parsonage Cross
Rackenford
ALL SAINTS
Bulworth
Meshaw Moor
Irishcombe Fm
Grendon
Thorn
River Dart
Tumulus
Tumuli
Burrow Cross
Wilson
Berry Castle
Blagrove
West Yeo Moor
Queen Dart
Little Dart
Mogworthy
Mouseberry
Rowden
Sturcombe River
Bradford Barton
Leat Down
Newland
Hilltown
Tumuli
Dart Raffe Moor
Lutworthy
Long Stone
Hellinghayes
Rose Moor
Elworthy
Betham
Witheridge Moor
Adworthy
B3137
Newhouse
Cuddenhay
Tumuli
Pilliven
Affeton Moor
ST JOHN BAPTIST
West Yeo
New Bridge
Foxdon
Five Crosses
East Worlingham
Witheridge
Affeton Barton
Combe Ho
Chapner
B3137
Edgeworthy
ST MARY
ST MARY
Drayford
Eastway
No Man's Land
Woodford
Stretch Down
West Worlingham
Stockham
Gogland
River Dalch
Woodhouse Villa
Upcott
Mudford Gate
Crandle
Mill Barton
Stubborn
Thelbridge
ST PETER
Washford Pyne
Henceford Moor
B3042
Furze
0 1 2 miles
0 1 2 3 kilometres
A B C D E F
1 2 3 4 5 6 7 8 9 10

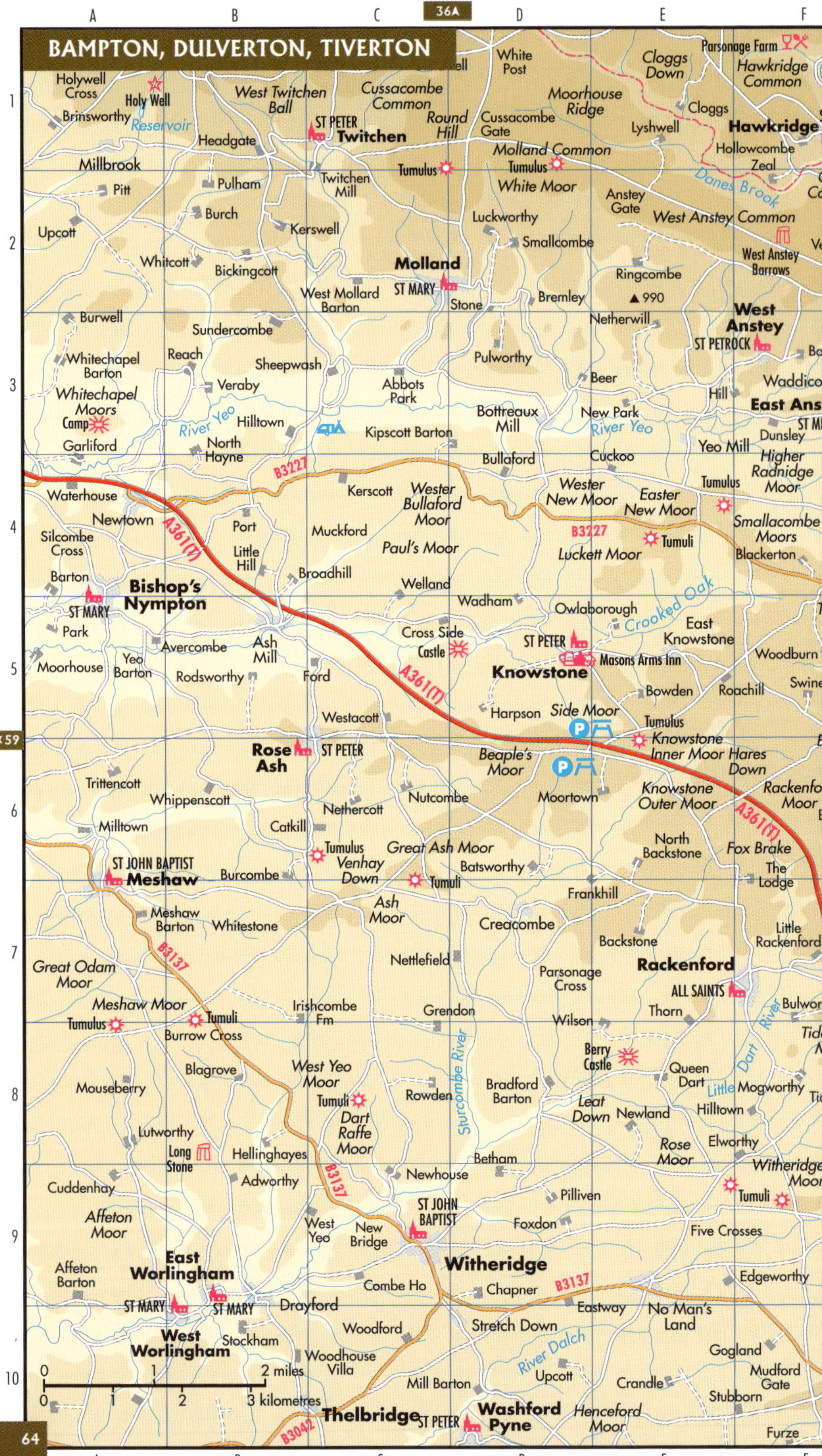

36A
59
79

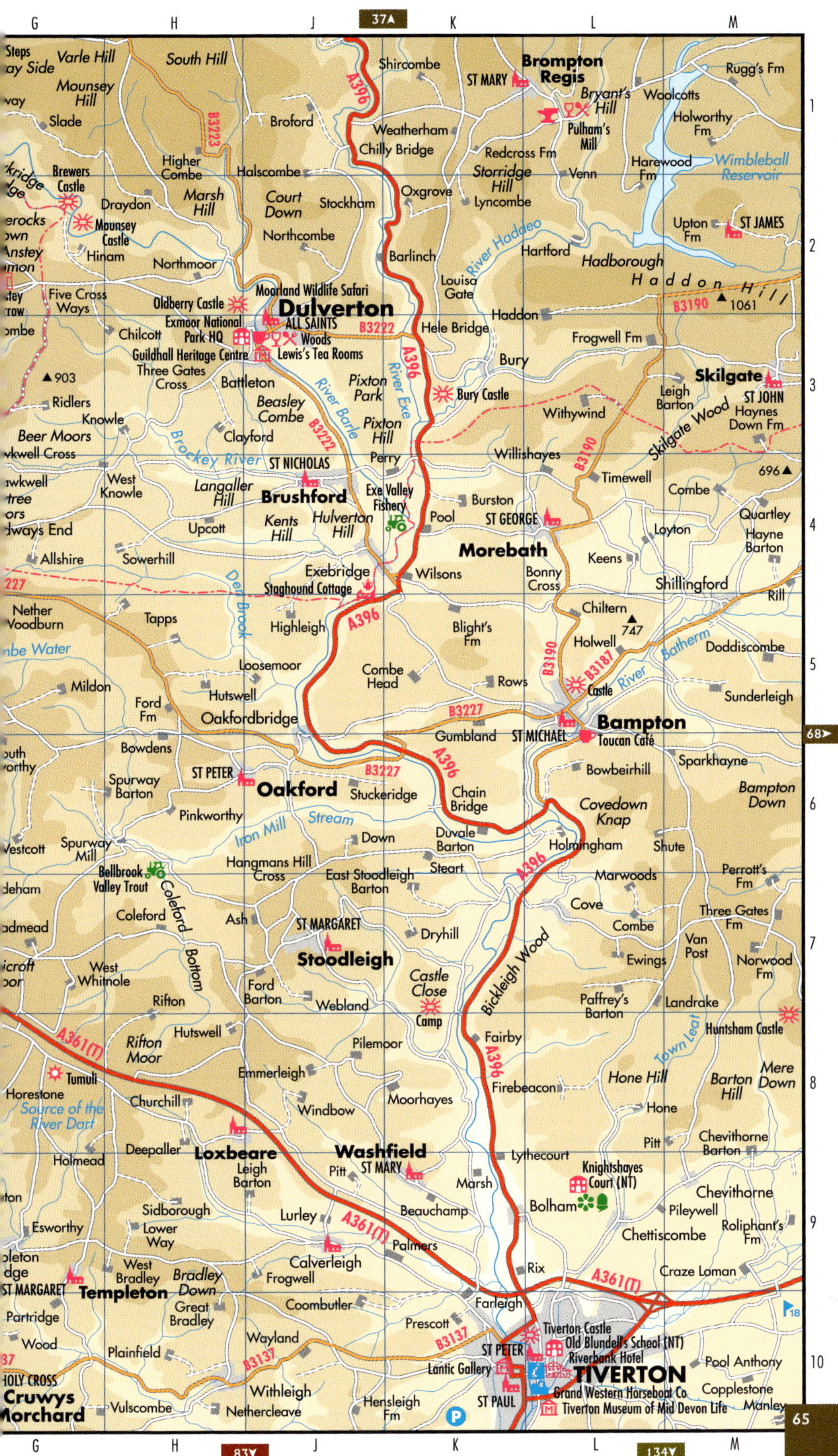

Dulverton
Brompton Regis
Brushford
Morebath
Bampton
Oakford
Stoodleigh
Loxbeare
Washfield
Templeton
TIVERTON
Cruwys Morchard
Skilgate
Wimbleball Reservoir
Haddon Hill
River Exe
River Barle
River Haddeo
A396
A361(T)
B3222
B3227
B3190
B3137
B3223
B3187

BAMPTON

A natural route centre set in a sheltered wooded valley. Fine C13 and C16 church with Saxon Cross.

A thriving wool centre in the C18 and by the 1800s the largest sheepfair in the South West, for over 14,000 sheep were sold at Bampton Fair. Today, the town is famous for the annual October Fair, on the last Thursday.

In the 1880s it became, for the next one hundred years, the famous Bampton Pony Fair trading in Exmoor ponies. The locality is rich in wildlife encouraged by the conservation policy in the town.

For a light lunch the Toucan Café on pretty, Brook Street, is recommended. (L5)

Where to Eat, Drink & Be Merry...

Back of Beyond Restaurant, Parsonage Farm. The Boyces just love to cook, especially flavoursome meat reared from their rare breeds stock. They are also proud of their home-made ice cream. All for just £25.00 per head. (F1) 01643 831197 www.back-of-beyond.com

Lewis's Tea Rooms, High Street. Traditional tearoom serving all-day breakfast, light lunches and cream teas. Always busy. (J3)

Woods Bar & Dining Room. Fast becoming a talking point amongst food afficianados. They serve healthy portions of classic British food. No preciousness here. (J3) 01398 324007

River Exe below Bye Common

DULVERTON

Often described as the gateway to southern Exmoor but it is much more than that. It's a thriving community with all sorts of buildings and interesting shops, plus galleries, tearooms, pubs and restaurants. An old-fashioned country town happy with its lot. The National Park have their HQ here, and there are easy riverside walks beside the River Barle. It has the best shooting and fishing on Exmoor, the Barle is well stocked with Brown Trout and Salmon. The church tower dates from the C12, and inside are memorials to the colourful Sydenham family, and stained glass provided by the founded of the YMCA, George Williams. (J3)

Guildhall Heritage & Arts Centre, Off Fore St. Exhibitions of local artists and craftsmen, plus Touring Exhibitions. Open daily East-Oct 10-4.30. (J3) 01398 323818

Special Places to Stay...

Staghound Cottages, Exebridge. Former 500 year old Inn has character in abundance and a homely feel. Comfortable accommodation, organic breakfasts and the opportunity to buy ceramic pieces direct from Penny the Potter, your hostess. (J4) 01398 324453 www.staghound.co.uk

Pottery, Staghound Cottages ss

Arts & Crafts Interest...

Lantic Gallery, 38 Gold Street. New Tiverton gallery displaying a variety of artists and craftsmen. (L10) 01884 259888 www.lanticgallery.co.uk

Pulhams Mill, Nr Brompton Regis. Solid timber furniture in English hardwoods, and hand painted English china and tiles with rural scenes. Open in summer M-F & BHs 10-6, Sa 10-5 & most Su, in winter M-Sa 10-5. (L1) 01398 371366

Countryside Interests

Bellbrook Valley Trout Fishery. Consists of 7 lakes fed from 2 streams in 40 acre valley. Fly fishing for Rainbows. Day fishing. Tuition available. Open all year. (H6) 01398 351292 www.bellbrookfishery.com

Exe Valley Fishery, Exebridge. Farm shop and fly fishing lakes. Open daily 9-5. (K4) 01398 323328

Wimbleball Lake. 370 acre reservoir. Fishing, sailing, campsites. Waymarked walks. Nature reserve and trail. A quiet place for relaxation. Refreshments. Open daily, all year. (M1) 01837 871565

Where to Eat, Drink & Be Merry...

Masons Arms Inn, Knowstone. Thatched village inn with small, cosy rooms and log fires. Tastefully decorated with old family paintings. Food is superb, and chef recently awarded Michelin Star. Dining room extension has interesting murals on the ceilings, and fine countryside views. Booking advised. Just off the Two Moors Way. Open Tu-Sa 12-3, 6-11 pm. Su 12-3 pm. (E5) 01398 341231 www.masonsarmsdevon.co.uk

Riverbank Hotel & Restaurant, 45 Gold Street, Tiverton. Serves freshly made vegetarian and organic food and cakes. Open for lunch and teas. B & B. Bike shed. Aromatherapy available. (L10) 01884 254911 www.riverbankhotel.co.uk

1583 June. The Golden Hind sails from Plymouth with five vessels for the New World. Sir Humphrey Gilbert lands at St John's Newfoundland and founds the first British colony. Later to drown on return voyage aboard the Squirrel off the Azores.

1585 War with Spain declared. Plymouth became Naval Base.

TIVERTON

Market town for the Exe Valley, and main centre for the north east corner of Devon. The major attractions are the imposing Castle, Old Blundell's School and the notable Parish Church next to the Castle. There is a Town Trail leading you to the most interesting aspects of this small, industrial town. The major employer, the Heathcoat lace factory, in operation since 1816. The Luddites had forced John Heathcoat, inventor of the bobbinet lace machine, to leave Loughborough. (L10)

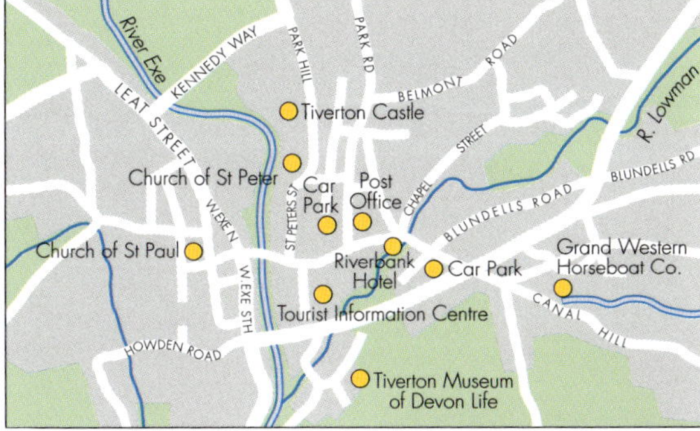

Tiverton

Special Places to Visit...

Grand Western Canal Country Park, Canal Hill. The canal meanders through eleven miles of beautiful Devon countryside. On either side a rich diversity of wildlife; wildflowers, plants, hedgerows, fields and small woodland. The towpath provides easy walking with good car parking and picnic sites available. The Canal today (Tiverton-Lowdeswells) is a remnant section of the intended route between Bristol and the English Channel. Work began in 1810, was completed in 1814, with the northern section completed in 1838. However, it was unprofitable and closed in 1869. (L10) 01884 254072

Grand Western Horseboat Co., The Wharf. The enchantment and tranquility of travel, at a slow pace; a painted barge pulled by heavy horses mingles with nature. Boat hire. Picnics. Open East-Oct. Reservations advised: (L10) 01884 253345 www.horseboat.co.uk

Knightshayes Court (NT). Victorian Gothic house designed by two contrasting architects. Richly decorated interior. Paintings. Garden of interest at all seasons; specimen trees, formal terraces, unique topiary, rare shrubs, 'Garden in the Wood'. Plant sales. Restaurant and NT shop. Garden open 2 Mar-4 Nov, House open daily 17 Mar-4 Nov 11-5 except F. (L9)01884 254661 www.nationaltrust.org.uk

Parish Church of St Peter. A grand building built from the proceeds of the wool trade. The intricate detail of sailing ships cut into the white limestone of the South Porch was the gift of the wool merchant, John Greenway in 1517. Inside, Tomb Memorials to the rich burgers of the town; George Slee and John Waldron. (L10)

Tiverton Castle. Historic fortress of Henry 1 built in 1106. Fine medieval gatehouse and tower. Romantic ruins of chapel, solar and curtain walls. Fine Civil War armoury, old wall and new gardens. Open East Su to end June & Sept, Su, Th & BH Ms, plus Su-Th in July/Aug, 2.30-5.30. Other times for parties of 12 or more. (L10) 01884 253200 www.tivertoncastle.com

St Peter, Tiverton

Tiverton Museum of Mid Devon Life, Beck's Square. Local industries, railway gallery, Victorian laundry. Great Western Canal relics, wartime history, model aircraft. Open Feb-Dec 21 M-F 10.30-4.30, Sa 10-1. (L10) 01884 256295 www.tivertonmuseum.org.uk

Knightshayes Court ss/nt

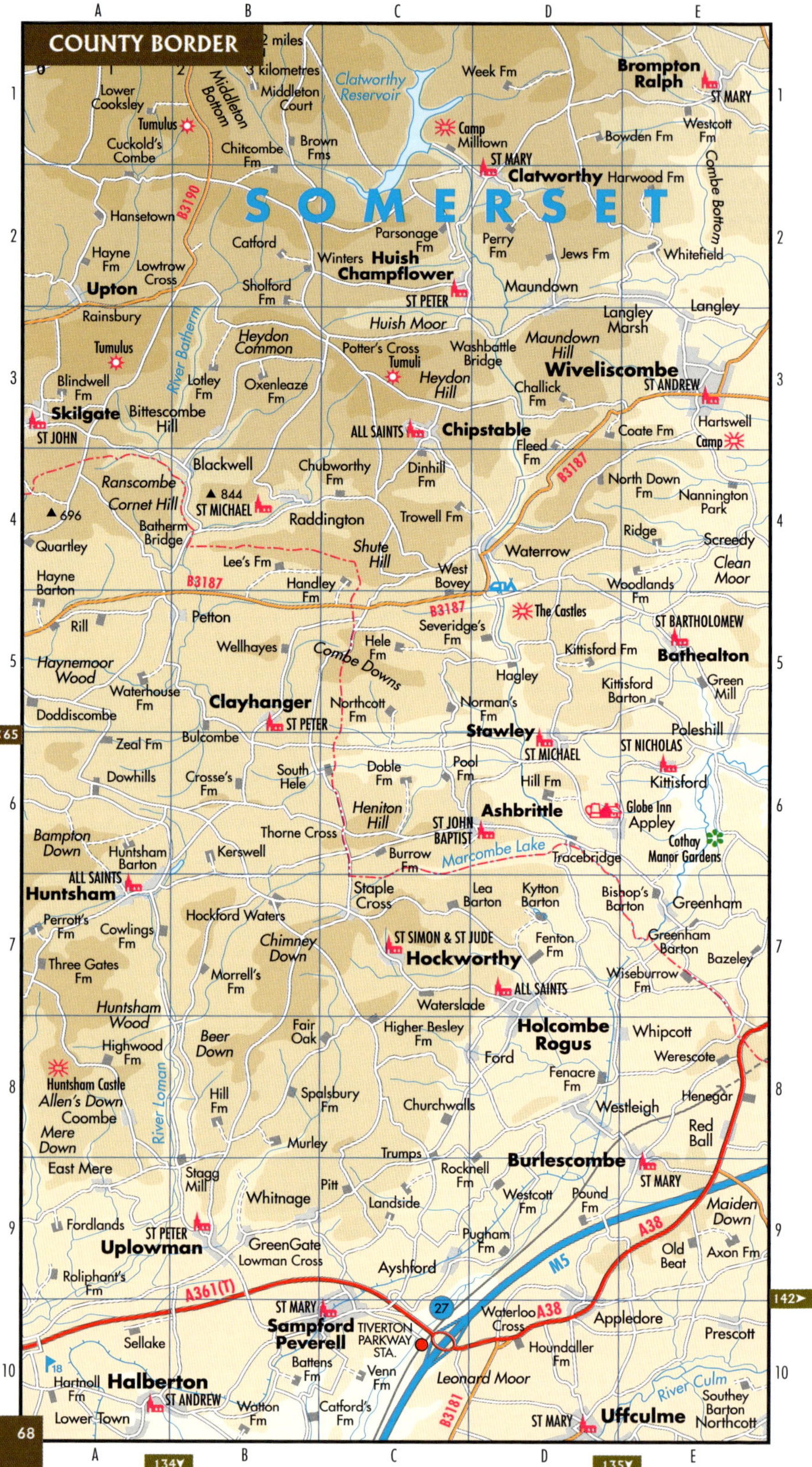

65
142
134
135

Places to Visit...

Cothay Manor Gardens. Magical garden laid out in the 1920s has been redesigned and replanted within original framework of yew hedges. The Manor built in 1480 has remained virtually untouched. Open May-Sept W, Th, Su & BHs 2-6. House by appoint. (E6) 01823 672283

Villages of Interest...

Sampford Peverell. Fine church built by Sir Hugh Peverell, Lord of the Manor from 1241 to 1296. His monument lies on the north side of the Chancel. Restored in the mid C19.

Where to Eat, Drink & Be Merry...

Globe Inn, Appley. Hidden away down narrow Somerset lanes is this popular C16 Freehouse with cosy, little rooms. Superb prints of ships. No dogs. Open Tu-Su. (D6)

Cothay Manor Gardens al/ss

This stretch of country belongs to a Devon often neglected and forgotten. An undulating, pastoral landscape lying between the coastal resorts and medieval trade routes of North Devon, and to the south, the great expanse of Dartmoor.

Here are isolated villages and hamlets, sometimes made up of a single or secondary homestead originally built from the local earth, commonly known as cob. Connected by narrow country lanes set between high hedgerows, that with time, have grown in height and width. Built up by peasant farmers long since dead, who cleared the stone from the fields, a tapestry of a thousand natural colours; greens, reds, oranges and mauves.

Is this the rural idyll of an England long forgotten, and sort for, in glossy magazines? Not if you live and work here. The 45 parishes that surround Holsworthy and Hatherleigh have created the brand "Ruby Country" to market their towns following the disastrous foot n' mouth epidemic of 2001. The name is taken from the indigenous breed of cattle, Ruby Red Devon; a handsome beast, given to fine cuts of meat.

It was this Devon, in isolation, that so attracted the poet, Ted Hughes. He lived the last third of his life in the parish of North Tawton. Close to nature, he wrote about the natural world, as he saw it, and fished the upper reaches of the Taw and Torridge, for salmon and sea trout.

These communities have witnessed a great change since the development of the A30 and A36, now largely inhabited by commuters from Exeter and Taunton. Yet, despite this, there are still those whose lifestyle remains unchanged, where the major social event of the week is Market Day, or the village cricket match. The church, pub and village store continue to be the focal points of village life.

Mid Devon can be a charming place to visit. You will find that people have more time for you. Just watch the locals of Hatherleigh walk about their daily business, forever stopping to talk with their friends and acquaintances. You, too, will come across friendly pubs and churches offering solitude and fine craftsmanship.

Torridge Valley, Sheepwash

44A
A
B
C
D
E
F
Kilkhampton
ST JAMES
Penstowe
Houndapit
Stibb
Tumulus
Camp
Thurdon
Alfardisworthy
Lower Tamar Lake
Lutson
Sandy Mouth
Scadghill
Lymsworthy
Aldercott
Dunsmouth
Killock
Hassaford
Lopthorne
Higher Pigsdon
Bude Aqueduct
Menachurch Point
Camp
Rhude Cross
Dexbeer
Northcott
Camp
Norton
Venn
Moreton Pound
Dunsdon
Poughill
Puckland
Maer
Hersham
ST OLAF
Bush
Flexbury
Colebrook
Bude & North Cornwall Golf Club
Bude-Stratton Museum
Battle of Stamford Hill 1643
Leigh
CAMP
Grimscott
Lana
Brendon
Bude Haven
Big Blue Surf School
The Bude Light
ST ANDREW
Burmsdon
Small Brook
A3073
Cross Lanes
Launcells Cross
Kingford
Ebbingford Manor
ST MICHAEL AND ALL ANGELS
Bude
Stratton
Tamarstone Bridge
ST SWITHIN
Launcells
Anderton
ST PANCRAS
Pancrasweek
Lynstone
Howard
A39(T)
A3072
Red Post
A3072
Upton
Thorne
Pitworthy
The Bude Canal
Cann Orchard
Thorn
River Tamar
Burnard's Ho.
Buttsbear Cross
Whalesborough
Hobbacott
Norton
Scotland
Helebridge
ST MARWENNA
Marhamchurch
B3254
Derril
Dux
Jewell's Cross
ST BRIDGET
Salthouse
Rattenbury
Helscott
Bridgerule
Hopworthy
ST SWITHUN
Widemouth Bay
Woolston
Borough Cross
Newacott
Monks
Kennicott
Titson
Tackbear
Bounds Cross
Trelana
Derrill Water
Wanson
Box's Shop
Merrifield
Langford
Milton
Bevill's Hill
Outdoor Adventure
Burracott
Bakesdown
Worthen
Penhalt
Coppathorne
Langaton
Bowdah
Poundstock
Hoollafr
Bangors
ST NEOT
Keywood
Knowle
Leigh
Thorne
Tinney
Westcott
Trevolter
Newmill
ST ANNE
Whitstone
Penlean
Treskinnick Cross
NATIVITY OF ST MARY
Swannacott Wood
East Balsdon
Vacye
West Balsdon
Allisdon
Ashbury
Week St Mary
ST DENIS
Kerley
Penhallam Castle
Dimma
Week Green
Westcott
Dilland
Tumuli
Dinnicoombe
Tumuli
Sudcott
Foxhole
Semersdon
Wilsworthy Cross
Wilsworthy
ST JAMES
Jacobstow
Tumuli
Greena Moor
Ogbeare Hall
Greenamoor Bridge
Tumuli
Landhillick
Southcott
Creddacott
Westcott
Blagdon
CORNWALL
Slue
Higher Whiteleigh
Brendon
Villaton
Headon
Wilheven
West Curry
Kersworthy
Curry Lane
Beardon
Exemoor
South Wheatley
Maxworthy
River Ottery
Langdon
Canworthy
Clubworthy
Caudworthy
Canworthy Water
Pattacott
Copthorne
Bennacott
North Be
Troswell
Winston
South Beer
0
1
2 miles
1
2
3 kilometres
1
2
3
4
5
6
7
8
9
10

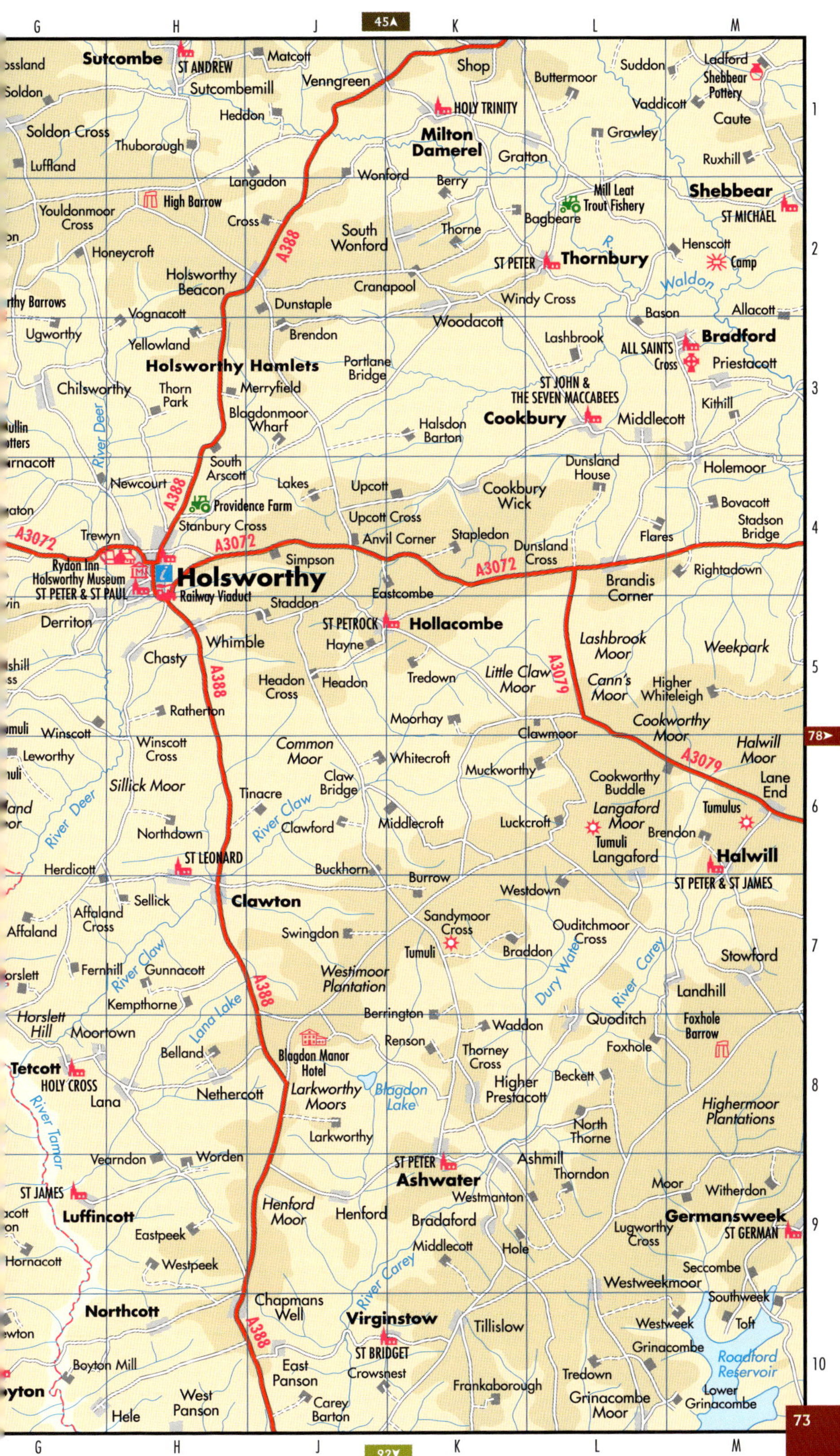

45
G
H
J
K
L
M
Sutcombe
ST ANDREW
Matcott
Sutcombemill
Venngreen
Shop
Buttermoor
Suddon
Ladford
Shebbear Pottery
Soldon
Heddon
HOLY TRINITY
Vaddicott
Caute
Soldon Cross
Thuborough
Milton Damerel
Grawley
Luffland
Gratton
Ruxhill
Langadon
Wonford
Berry
Mill Leat Trout Fishery
Shebbear
High Barrow
Youldonmoor Cross
Cross
Bagbeare
ST MICHAEL
A388
South Wonford
Thorne
Henscott
Honeycroft
ST PETER
Thornbury
Camp
Holsworthy Beacon
Cranapool
Waldon
R.
Dunstaple
Windy Cross
Allacott
Vognacott
Woodacott
Bason
Ugworthy
Brendon
Lashbrook
Bradford
Yellowland
ALL SAINTS
Cross
Priestacott
Holsworthy Hamlets
Portlane Bridge
Chilsworthy
Thorn Park
Merryfield
ST JOHN & THE SEVEN MACCABEES
Kithill
River Deer
Blagdonmoor Wharf
Halsdon Barton
Cookbury
Middlecott
South Arscott
Dunsland House
Holemoor
Newcourt
Lakes
Upcott
Cookbury Wick
A388
Providence Farm
Bovacott
Stanbury Cross
Upcott Cross
Stadson Bridge
A3072
Trewyn
A3072
Anvil Corner
Stapledon
Flares
Dunsland Cross
Rydon Inn
Simpson
A3072
Rightadown
Holsworthy Museum
Holsworthy
Brandis Corner
ST PETER & ST PAUL
Railway Viaduct
Staddon
Eastcombe
Derriton
ST PETROCK
Hollacombe
Whimble
Lashbrook Moor
Weekpark
Hayne
Chasty
A3079
Headon Cross
Headon
Tredown
Little Claw Moor
Cann's Moor
Higher Whiteleigh
A388
Ratherton
Moorhay
Cookworthy Moor
Winscott
Clawmoor
Halwill Moor
Winscott Cross
Common Moor
78
Leworthy
Whitecroft
A3079
Muckworthy
Claw Bridge
Cookworthy Buddle
Lane End
Sillick Moor
Tinacre
River Deer
River Claw
Langaford Moor
Tumulus
Clawford
Middlecroft
Luckcroft
Northdown
Brendon
Tumuli
Langaford
Halwill
ST LEONARD
Herdicott
Buckhorn
Burrow
ST PETER & ST JAMES
Westdown
Sellick
Clawton
Affaland Cross
Sandymoor Cross
Affaland
Swingdon
Ouditchmoor Cross
Tumuli
Braddon
Stowford
River Claw
Westimoor Plantation
Dury Water
River Carey
Fernhill
Gunnacott
A388
Landhill
Kempthorne
Horslett Hill
Lana Lake
Berrington
Waddon
Quoditch
Foxhole Barrow
Moortown
Renson
Foxhole
Thorney Cross
Belland
Blagdon Manor Hotel
Beckett
Tetcott
Higher Prestacott
HOLY CROSS
Larkworthy Moors
Blagdon Lake
Highermoor Plantations
Lana
Nethercott
River Tamar
North Thorne
Larkworthy
Vearndon
Worden
Ashmill
ST PETER
Thorndon
Ashwater
Moor
ST JAMES
Westmanton
Witherdon
Henford Moor
Luffincott
Henford
Bradaford
Germansweek
Lugworthy Cross
ST GERMAN
Eastpeek
Middlecott
Hole
Hornacott
Westpeek
River Carey
Seccombe
Westweekmoor
Chapmans Well
Southweek
Northcott
Virginstow
Tillislow
Westweek
Toft
A388
ST BRIDGET
Grinacombe
Roadford Reservoir
Boyton Mill
East Panson
Crowsnest
Frankaborough
Tredown
West Panson
Carey Barton
Grinacombe Moor
Lower Grinacombe
Hele
92

BUDE

Cornish seaside resort developed by the Victorians. Now very much the centre for surfing in North Cornwall. There are long, extensive beaches bestowed with three miles of sand at low tide. The top end of town is the major shopping area with an abundance of surf shops, an excellent bookshop and some small restaurants. Not to be missed, the Old Canal, built in 1826 at a length of 43 miles. For 60 years it transported coal and lime inland, and exported grain and slate. Eventually, to be killed off by the Railways. Best sections to be seen at Marhamchurch, Hobbacott Down and Werrington. The coastline has been the scene for many shipwrecks; 80 ships foundered between 1824-74. Carnival and fete, third week of August. "Blessing of the Sea" in August. E/C Th. (A3)

Stratton Museum, The Canal. History of the Bude Canal, shipwrecks, lifeboats and railways. Heritage Trail. Open daily Good F-Sept, Th & Su in Oct, 11-5. (A3)

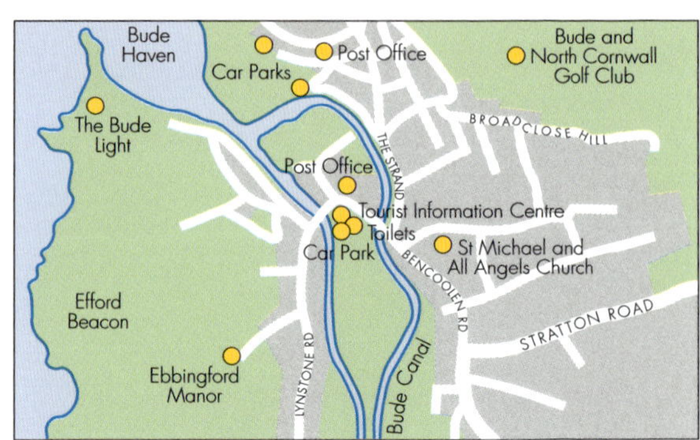

Bude

Holsworthy

HOLSWORTHY

Market town with a thriving cattle market, and Pannier Market every Wednesday in the Market Square. Be sure to visit "St Peter's Fair" in early July to catch the crowning of the "Pretty Maid". The centre of a rural idyll; scattered farms and hamlets, rolling, green pastures unintimidated by our crazy world. Hereabouts is real Devon for you. Unsophisticated, quiet, miles from the nearest motorway. A haven of peace. (H4)

Holsworthy Museum, Manor Offices. Housed in a C17 Parsonage. Themed rooms feature the area's heritage, traditions and bygones of rural life. Open M-F 11-1, (W to 3.30). (H4) 01409 259337

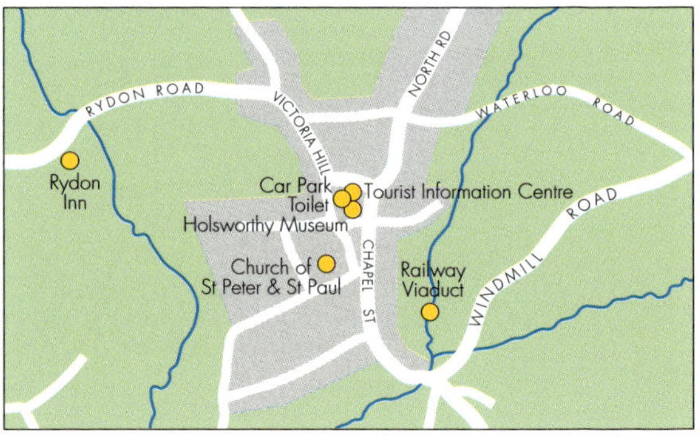

Holsworthy

Countryside Interests...

Mill Leat Trout Fishery. Fresh and smoked trout. Children's fishing ('Catch your own') in two lakes and 1/2 mile of River Waldron 9-5.30, (dusk fly fishing). Three self-catering cottages. (L2) 01409 261426 www.millleat.co.uk

Providence Farm Organic Meats, Crosspark Cross. Farm shop and mail order service selling their range of poultry, pork, beef and lamb produce. Open W-Sa 9-5.30. Tavistock Pannier Market every F 9-4. (H4) 01409 254421 www.providencefarm.co.uk

Tamar Lakes. Reservoirs in remote country near Tamar's source. Sailing, canoeing, lakeside walks. Fly fishing in upper lake. Lower lake has coarse fishing, bird sanctuary and hide. Shop and refreshments. (F1)

1593 Sir Richard Hawkins departs Plymouth for South America, and ultimate disaster off Chile.

1604 Tiverton clothier Peter Blundell founds Blundell's School.

Blagdon Manor Hotel & Restaurant.

Comfortable, relaxed and laid-back is how the Moreys would describe their C17 Manor hotel. Liz provides the warm hospitality and attention to detail whilst Steve provides the superb cuisine from the South West's rich larder of local farms and fishing grounds. Children over 12. Dogs welcome. Bedrooms all facilities. (J8) 01409 211224 www.blagdon.com

Waldon Valley, Thornbury

Arts & Craft Interest...

Mullin Potters.
Studio and gallery showing variety of handmade ceramics. Open daily, 10-6. (G3) 01409 253589

Churches of Interest...

Kilkhampton Church. Norman S. doorway with superb collection of bench ends. Grenville tombs. (D1)

Launcells Church.
Fortunate to be the only Cornish church not tampered with by the Victorians. Wall painting and 60 carved bench ends. (C3)

Poughill Church.
Bench ends and large wall painting of St Christopher. (B2)

Where to Eat, Drink & Be Merry...

Life's A Beach, Summerleaze Beach, Bude. Bistro restaurant offers all types of food from locally caught Bass to burgers and pizzas. A fantastic spot to watch the sunset, and to relax after a day's surf. Open daily in season. (A3)

The Bay View Inn, Marine Drive, Bude. Surfer's hangout overlooking the roaring Atlantic. Currently being refurbished with chic, modern bedrooms. Wholesome tasty menu using local farms for hungry surfers. (A5) 01288 361273

Shebbear Pottery

The Rydon Inn, Rydon Hill.
Take the Bude Road out of Holsworthy. Inside, the barn-like wood construction based on a Devon longhouse glows with warmth. You can lunch or dine overlooking the lake and nourish yourself with better than average pub grub. They claim it's a gastro-pub. It's certainly the place to eat, hereabouts. (G4) 01409 259444 www.rydon-inn.com

Beaches & Surfing...

Duckpool. Rocky with strong currents. Footpath leads to Coombe Valley Nature Trail. P. Surfing – LT R breaks off the rocks. (A1)

Sandy Mouth. Expansive beach, rocky at HT, swift currents, HZ at LT, Bass fishing, P/cafe. Surfing – Clean with good beach breaks. Fine, small swell off banks. Beware rip tides. (A1)

Northcott Mouth. Extensive sand, pebbles and rocks. Bathing HZ two hours either side of LT. P. Surfing – Banks at LT create heavy hollow

1607 The first Puritan Pilgrims depart Plymouth for the New World.

1615 Tiverton made a Municipal Borough.

Sandy Mouth

Outdoor Adventure ss

waves backing off at HT except on big swells. Good R hander at N side. Beware rip tides. (A2)

Bude - Crooklets Beach.
Spacious firm sands at LT, bathing HZ at LT. S-B hire, cafe, LG. Surfing – Fine, short breaks for body boarders. With hollow sandbanks waves flow at all stages of tide. At HT Tower Rock produces a good shallow wave. Try Wrangles Rocks to N at LT. (A3)

Bude - Summerleaze Beach.
Popular surfing beach, roomy firm sands and bathing pool at LT. S-B hire. Access. Surfing – HT sheltered from SW wind. R breaks into harbour. Take-oo can be steep. Beware strong rips. Ls at LT. Hollow fast wave off The Barrels. (A3)

Bude – Middle Beach.
Surfing – Good Ls and Rs with swells up to 6ft. Popular with locals. (A3)

Bude – Upton.
Surfing – Good Rs and Ls on the N and S side. Difficult access down cliff. (A3)

Widemouth Sand.
Large sandy beach, rock pools, HZ at LT. Tent and S-B hire/WC/P/cafe. Surfing – A popular break for all abilities, at all stages of the tide. Best up to 6ft. (A5)

Coastal Footpath...

From Duckpool the path leads up to the Coombe Valley Nature Trail. At low tide one can follow the sands to Bude, or take the clifftop path. Ascend to Compass Point for extensive views northwards. The path overlooks reefs, buttresses and pinnacles. Then easy going onto Widemouth Sands.

Xtreme Sports...

Big Blue Surf School, Summerleaze Beach. Learn, improve, excel at one of Europe's top schools with National Team coach Jon Price. Open Apr-Oct. 01288 331764. (A3)

Outdoor Adventure, Atlantic Court. Activity centre for the ultimate coastal experience; coasteering, surfing, coastal traversing, sea cliff abseils, rock climbing, sea kayaking. Activity Weekends. Accomodation. Tuition. 01288 362900. (A6)

1618 Sir Walter Raleigh arrested by fellow Devonian, Sir Lewis Stucley on orders of Elizabeth 1.

1620 Sep 16. The Pilgrim Fathers set sail in the Mayflower from Plymouth for New England.

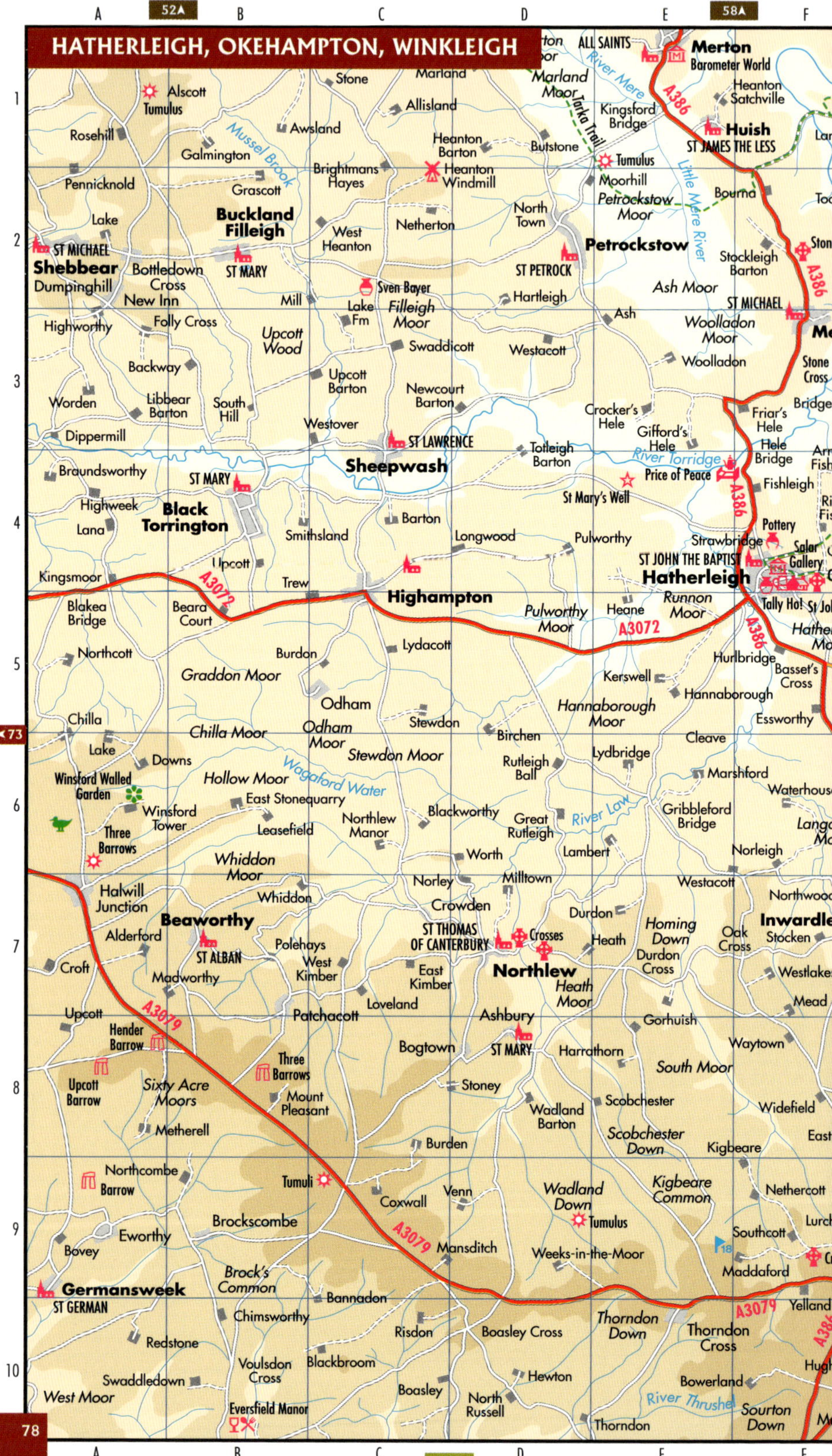

HATHERLEIGH, OKEHAMPTON, WINKLEIGH
52A
58A
A
B
C
D
E
F
1
2
3
4
5
6
7
8
9
10
73
93
Alscott Tumulus
Stone
Marland
Marland Moor
ALL SAINTS
Merton
Barometer World
River Mere
Tarka Trail
Heanton Satchville
Kingsford Bridge
A386
Huish
ST JAMES THE LESS
Rosehill
Mussel Brook
Awsland
Allisland
Heanton Barton
Butstone
Tumulus
Galmington
Brightmans Hayes
Heanton Windmill
Moorhill
Little Mere River
Pennicknold
Grascott
Petrockstow Moor
Bourna
Lake
Buckland Filleigh
North Town
West Heanton
Netherton
ST MICHAEL
Shebbear
Dumpinghill
Bottledown Cross
New Inn
ST MARY
Petrockstow
ST PETROCK
Stockleigh Barton
Stone
Mill
Sven Bayer
Lake Fm
Filleigh Moor
Hartleigh
Ash Moor
Highworthy
Folly Cross
Upcott Wood
Ash
ST MICHAEL
Woolladon Moor
Swaddicott
Westacott
Woolladon
Backway
Upcott Barton
Newcourt Barton
Stone Cross
Worden
Libbear Barton
South Hill
Crocker's Hele
Friar's Hele
Bridge
Dippermill
Westover
Gifford's Hele
Hele Bridge
ST LAWRENCE
Totleigh Barton
Braundsworthy
Sheepwash
River Torridge
Price of Peace
Fishleigh
ST MARY
St Mary's Well
Highweek
Black Torrington
Barton
Pottery
Lana
Smithsland
Longwood
Pulworthy
Strawbridge
Salar Gallery
Upcott
ST JOHN THE BAPTIST
Hatherleigh
Kingsmoor
A3072
Trew
Highampton
Blakea Bridge
Beara Court
Pulworthy Moor
Heane
Runnon Moor
Tally Ho!
A3072
Northcott
Burdon
Lydacott
Hurlbridge
Basset's Cross
Graddon Moor
Kerswell
Hannaborough
Odham
Hannaborough Moor
Chilla
Chilla Moor
Odham Moor
Stewdon
Birchen
Essworthy
Lake
Stewdon Moor
Cleave
Downs
Wagaford Water
Rutleigh Ball
Lydbridge
Winsford Walled Garden
Hollow Moor
Marshford
East Stonequarry
Waterhouse
Winsford Tower
Northlew Manor
Blackworthy
Great Rutleigh
River Lew
Gribbleford Bridge
Three Barrows
Leasefield
Worth
Lambert
Norleigh
Whiddon Moor
Norley
Milltown
Westacott
Halwill Junction
Whiddon
Crowden
Northwood
Beaworthy
Durdon
Inwardleigh
Alderford
ST ALBAN
Polehays
ST THOMAS OF CANTERBURY
Crosses
Heath
Homing Down
Oak Cross
Stocken
West Kimber
Durdon Cross
Croft
Madworthy
East Kimber
Northlew
Westlake
Heath Moor
Upcott
Loveland
Ashbury
Mead
A3079
Patchacott
Gorhuish
Hender Barrow
ST MARY
Waytown
Bogtown
Harrathorn
Three Barrows
South Moor
Upcott Barrow
Sixty Acre Moors
Stoney
Mount Pleasant
Scobchester
Widefield
Wadland Barton
Metherell
Scobchester Down
Burden
Kigbeare
Northcombe Barrow
Tumuli
Wadland Down
Kigbeare Common
Coxwall
Venn
Nethercott
Brockscombe
Tumulus
Eworthy
A3079
Mansditch
Southcott
Bovey
Weeks-in-the-Moor
Brock's Common
Maddaford
Germansweek
Bannadon
ST GERMAN
Yelland
Chimsworthy
Thorndon Down
A3079
Risdon
Boasley Cross
Thorndon Cross
Redstone
Voulsdon Cross
Blackbroom
Hewton
Swaddledown
Boasley
Bowerland
North Russell
West Moor
River Thrushel
Eversfield Manor
Sourton Down
Thorndon

59
G H J K L M

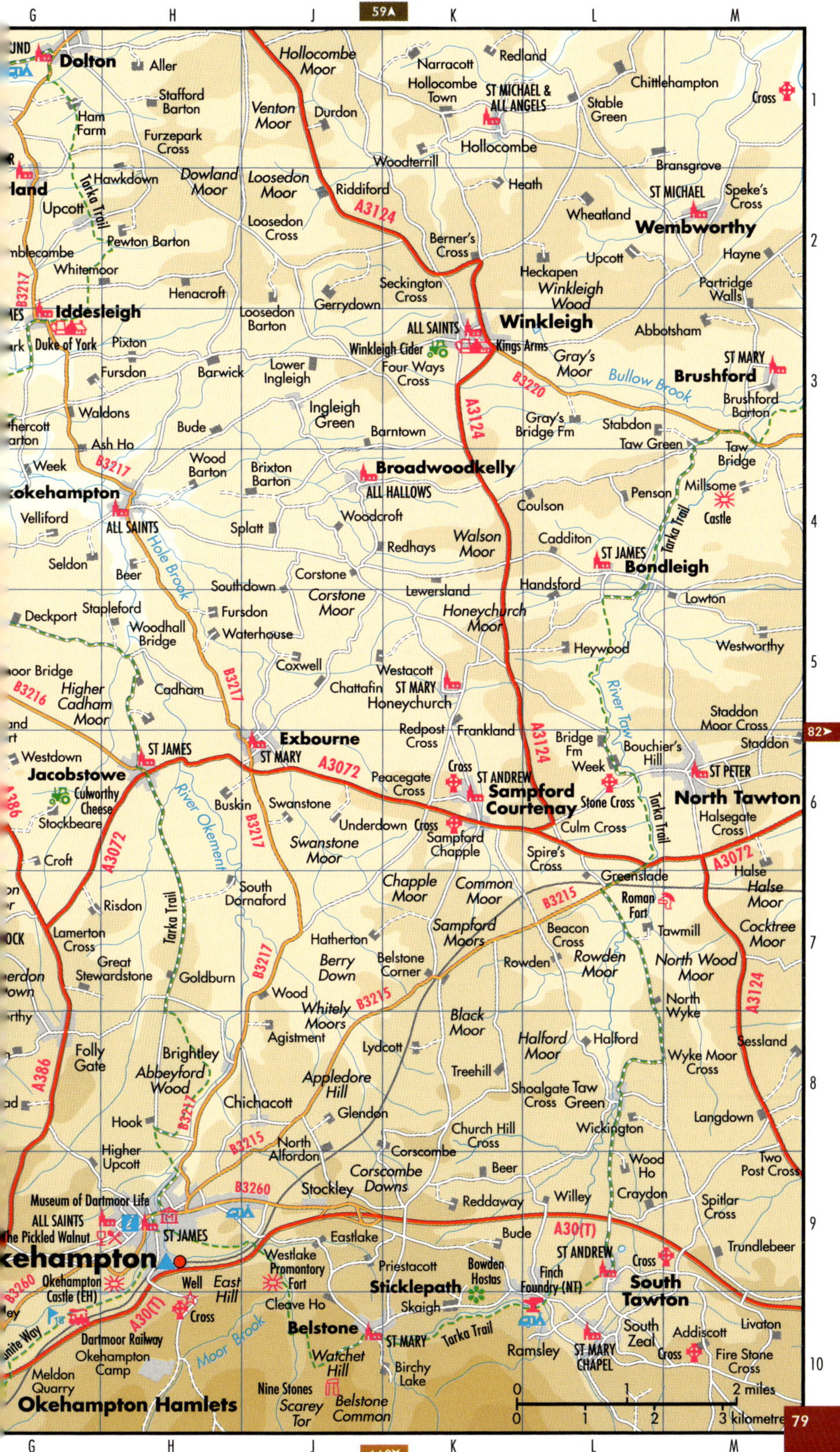

1 2 3 4 5 6 7 8 9 10

82

110

G H J K L M

HATHERLEIGH

Ancient market town of thatched and cob cottages nestling in a rural landscape shaped by a thousand years of settlers and farming. This must be one of the most delightful little towns in Devon. The local community realize the privilege of living here and are always active in promoting regular events, from the Arts Festival in July to the Carnival in November. Artwork is exhibited about the town. The Livestock Market is famous. (E4) www.hatherleigh.net

Special Places to Visit...

Hatherleigh Market. This is quite an attraction, from the Monday auction of ewes and lambs to the sales of live poultry on Tuesdays. Monthly horse sales. Café. Phone for details: 01837 810496 (E4)

Hatherleigh Methodist Chapel, High St. The beautiful stained glass was suppliedby the monks of Buckfast Abbey. (F4)

Hatherleigh Pottery

Hatherleigh Pottery, 20 Market Street. A working pottery with showroom displaying the work of Jane Payne and Michael Taylor plus textiles and original prints from local craftsmen. Open Easter to New Year M-Sa 10-5. (F4) 01837 810624 www.hatherleighpottery.co.uk

Salar Gallery, 20 Bridge St. The Devon landscape and its occupants provide a never-ending source of inspiration for the painters, sculptors, photographers and craftspeople who show their work here. Regular exhibitions. Open Tu-Sa 10-1,2-5. Closed W. (F4) 01837 819940 www.salargallery.co.uk

Hatherleigh

St John the Baptist. Built at the top of the High Street it's fine position provides splendid views. Early Norman church with C15 additions. In 1990 the medieval wooden spire collapsed during a great storm causing extensive damage and gaining national press coverage. Some interesting churchyard monuments. (F4)

Where to Eat, Drink & Be Merry...

Tally Ho! Country Inn, 14 Market Street. Traditional pub with oak beams and log fires serving home cooked food and real ales. Beer garden. Open all day. B & B. (F4) 01837 810306

The George Hotel, Market St. Medieval Inn that has been a sanctuary for monks, a brewery, law court and coaching inn. Open for breakfast, cream teas and Dinner. Quality of food and service is sadly not guaranteed. Accommodation. (F4) 01837 810454 www.georgehoteldevon.co.uk

Salar Gallery ss

NORTH TAWTON

Interesting little town formerly the home of the poet, the late Ted Hughes where he had a farm nearby. More recently it's claim to fame, as the setting for the TV series "Jam and Jerusalem". An elaborate clock stands in the Town Square to mark the 1877 jubilee. Interesting church, closed when I visited but there are remains of a Saxon or Roman cross, lovely bench ends and some C15 stained glass to look at if you have the opportunity. (M6)

Special Places to Stay...

Price of Peace B & B. Sits peacefully on the banks of the River Torridge abundant with wildlife. Luxury accommodation with bathrooms in the heart of Devon, and an ideal touring destination, or perfect for a peaceful break. Open all year. (F4) 01837 810781 www.priceofpeace.co.uk

Price of Peace ss

Duke of York

Where to Eat, Drink & Be Merry...

Duke of York, Iddesleigh. A friendly welcome awaits you in this old Devon Longhouse. Old photos, bank notes, low ceilings, small rooms and a large fireplace provide a fine ambience. Simple, honest food can be eaten in the bar but we recommend the Dining Room, and a selection of real ales to succour the palate. B & B. (G3) 01837 810253

1625 The Earl of Totnes created by Charles 1, and awarded to George Carew.

1628 Sir Ferdinando Gorges establishes colony of New Plymouth.

OKEHAMPTON

Finely situated town on the northern edge of Dartmoor, and well situated for exploring the "High Tors" and West Devon but has no distinguished places to stay (or eat). The gastronome will journey a few miles south-west to a veritable feast of choice, although you can get a simple, value-for-money meal at the Pickled Walnut. Of late, has become a centre for family cycling and mountain biking on Dartmoor. The Granite Way starts off from the former Railway Station. The arrival of Waitrose (that must surely serve a vaste hinterland) brought amazement and great joy to the local chattering classes. (H9)

Places to Visit...

Museum of Dartmoor Life, 3 West St.
Recently refurbished; Illustrates the lives, work and beliefs of Dartmoor's people across time. Tearoom, gift and craft shops. Open all year M-F, & Sa Apr-Oct, daily July-Sept. (H9) 01837 52295

Okehampton Castle
(EH). Ruins of the largest castle in Devon built in the C11. The square Norman Keep is all that remains of a seat of once great power in the hands of the Courtenays, Lords of Devon before Henry Courtenay upset Henry V111, and subsequently lost his head. It's strategic position is in effect, questionable. Open daily Apr-Oct 10-dusk. (G9) 01837 52844 www.english-heritage.org.uk

The Granite Way.
A family cycling trail for 11 miles/18 klms, otherwise known as National Cycle Network Route 27. The trail follows the former Okehampton to Lydford railway line and affords superb views of Dartmoor and the West Devon countryside. It crosses two spectacular viaducts at Meldon and Lake. There is a short, on-road section via Bridestowe, continuing to Lydford (& café) along the former railway line. Cycle hire is available at Okehampton's former station where there is ample parking space.

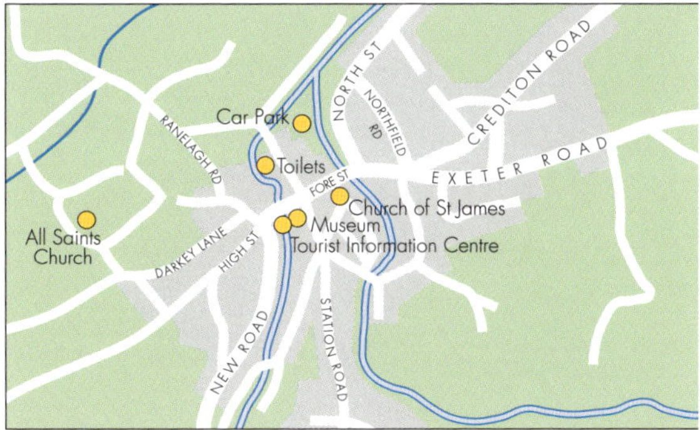

Okehampton

Where to Eat, Drink & Be Merry...

The Pickled Walnut, Fore Street. Excellent value little restaurant just off the High Street. All is prepared on the premises. Vegetarians catered for, as are those wishing for a light, simple meal. Coffee and cakes. Artwork adorns the walls. Open from 10 am. (H9) 01837 54242

Winkleigh Cider Co., Hatherleigh Rd. Traditional cider pressed here since 1916. Apples from local orchards are fermented and matured in giant oak vats. Shop sells range of ciders. Open M-Sa 9-5. (K3) 01837 835560

Winsford Walled Garden. A Victorian garden now the subject of private restoration. A must-see for all garden enthusiasts. Covered exhibition details work to date. B & B. Open daily except Tu May-Oct, 9.30-6. Car park. Disabled access. (A6) 01409 221477 www.winsfordwalledgarden.co.uk

Okehampton Castle

Special Places to Visit...

Bowden Hostas. The National Collection of over 1,000 hybrid Hostas in a 1 acre garden. Plant sales. Open Days. Visitors welcome. (K10) Cleave House, Sticklepath 01837 840481 www.hostas-uk.com

Finch Foundry (NT). C19 water powered edge tool works. 3 working water wheels. Giant trip hammer and shears. Demos of working machinery. Open daily 17 Mar-Oct except Tu, 11-5. (L9) 01837 840046 www.nationaltrust.org.uk

Svend Bayer. Much respected by his fellow Ceramicists. He produces large pots, and many are Anagama inspired. Open daily in summer season. (C2) 01409 231282

Countryside Interests...

Culworthy Cheese, Stockbeare Farm. Hand made cheeses in many varieties. Beware of rough pot-holed track. (G6) 01837 810587

Eversfield Manor. 850 acre organic estate producing Aberdeen Angus beef, lamb, pork and chicken plus wild venison and game reared in the woods. See website for details. (B10) 01837 871400 www.eversfieldorganic.co.uk

1638 Lighting strike over Widecombe church kills four of the congregation.

1643 Sep 5. Articles of surrender were signed and the Royalists took control of Exeter after a siege.

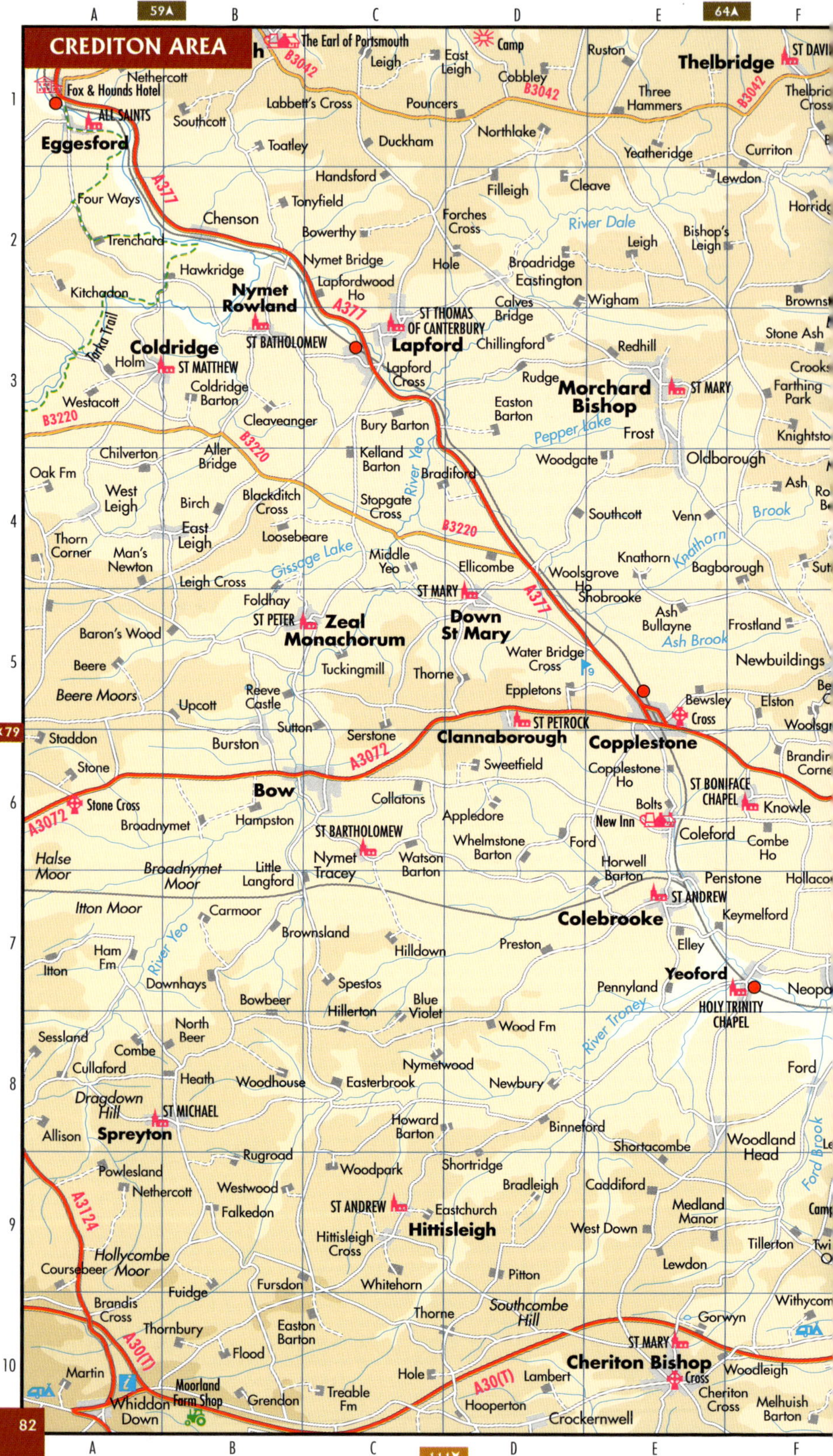

CREDITON AREA
A
B
C
D
E
F
59
64
The Earl of Portsmouth
Camp
Ruston
Thelbridge
ST DAVID
Fox & Hounds Hotel
Nethercott
Leigh
East Leigh
Cobbley
B3042
Three Hammers
Thelbridge Cross
ALL SAINTS
Southcott
Labbett's Cross
Pouncers
Eggesford
Toatley
Duckham
Northlake
Yeatheridge
Curriton
Handsford
Lewdon
Filleigh
Cleave
Four Ways
Tonyfield
Chenson
Forches Cross
River Dale
Horridge
Bowerthy
Bishop's Leigh
Trenchard
Nymet Bridge
Leigh
Hawkridge
Hole
Broadridge
Lapfordwood Ho
Eastington
Kitchadon
Nymet Rowland
A377
Calves Bridge
Wigham
Brownstone
Tarka Trail
ST THOMAS OF CANTERBURY
Stone Ash
Coldridge
ST BATHOLOMEW
Lapford
Chillingford
Redhill
Holm
ST MATTHEW
Lapford Cross
Rudge
Morchard Bishop
ST MARY
Crooks
Farthing Park
Westacott
Coldridge Barton
Easton Barton
B3220
Cleaveanger
Bury Barton
Pepper Lake
Frost
Knightstone
Chilverton
Aller Bridge
Kelland Barton
River Yeo
Woodgate
Oldborough
Oak Fm
Bradiford
Ash
West Leigh
Birch
Blackditch Cross
Stopgate Cross
Southcott
Venn
Brook
Thorn Corner
East Leigh
Loosebeare
Man's Newton
Middle Yeo
Knathorn
Knathorn
Bagborough
Gissage Lake
Ellicombe
Woolsgrove Ho
Leigh Cross
ST MARY
Shobrooke
Foldhay
Ash Bullayne
ST PETER
Zeal Monachorum
Down St Mary
Frostland
Baron's Wood
Ash Brook
Water Bridge Cross
Beere
Tuckingmill
Thorne
Newbuildings
Beere Moors
Reeve Castle
Eppletons
Upcott
Bewsley
Elston
Sutton
ST PETROCK
Cross
79
Staddon
Burston
Serstone
Clannaborough
Copplestone
A3072
Sweetfield
Stone
Copplestone Ho
Stone Cross
Bow
Collatons
ST BONIFACE CHAPEL
Knowle
Broadnymet
Hampston
Appledore
Bolts
New Inn
Coleford
ST BARTHOLOMEW
Whelmstone Barton
Ford
Combe Ho
Halse Moor
Nymet Tracey
Watson Barton
Horwell Barton
Broadnymet Moor
Little Langford
Penstone
ST ANDREW
Itton Moor
Carmoor
Colebrooke
Keymelford
Brownsland
Preston
Elley
Ham Fm
Hilldown
Itton
Yeoford
Downhays
Spestos
Pennyland
HOLY TRINITY CHAPEL
Bowbeer
Hillerton
Blue Violet
Wood Fm
River Troney
Sessland
North Beer
Combe
Cullaford
Nymetwood
Ford
Heath
Woodhouse
Easterbrook
Newbury
Dragdown Hill
ST MICHAEL
Howard Barton
Binneford
Allison
Spreyton
Shortacombe
Woodland Head
Ford Brook
Rugroad
Powlesland
Woodpark
Shortridge
Nethercott
Bradleigh
Caddiford
A3124
Westwood
Medland Manor
Falkedon
ST ANDREW
Eastchurch
Hittisleigh Cross
Hittisleigh
West Down
Tillerton
Hollycombe Moor
Coursebeer
Lewdon
Fuidge
Fursdon
Whitehorn
Pitton
Brandis Cross
Thorne
Southcombe Hill
Withycombe
Thornbury
Easton Barton
Gorwyn
A30(T)
Flood
ST MARY
Martin
Hole
Lambert
Cheriton Bishop
Woodleigh
Moorland Farm Shop
Treable Fm
Cross
Whiddon Down
Grendon
A30(T)
Hooperton
Crockernwell
Cheriton Cross
Melhuish Barton
111

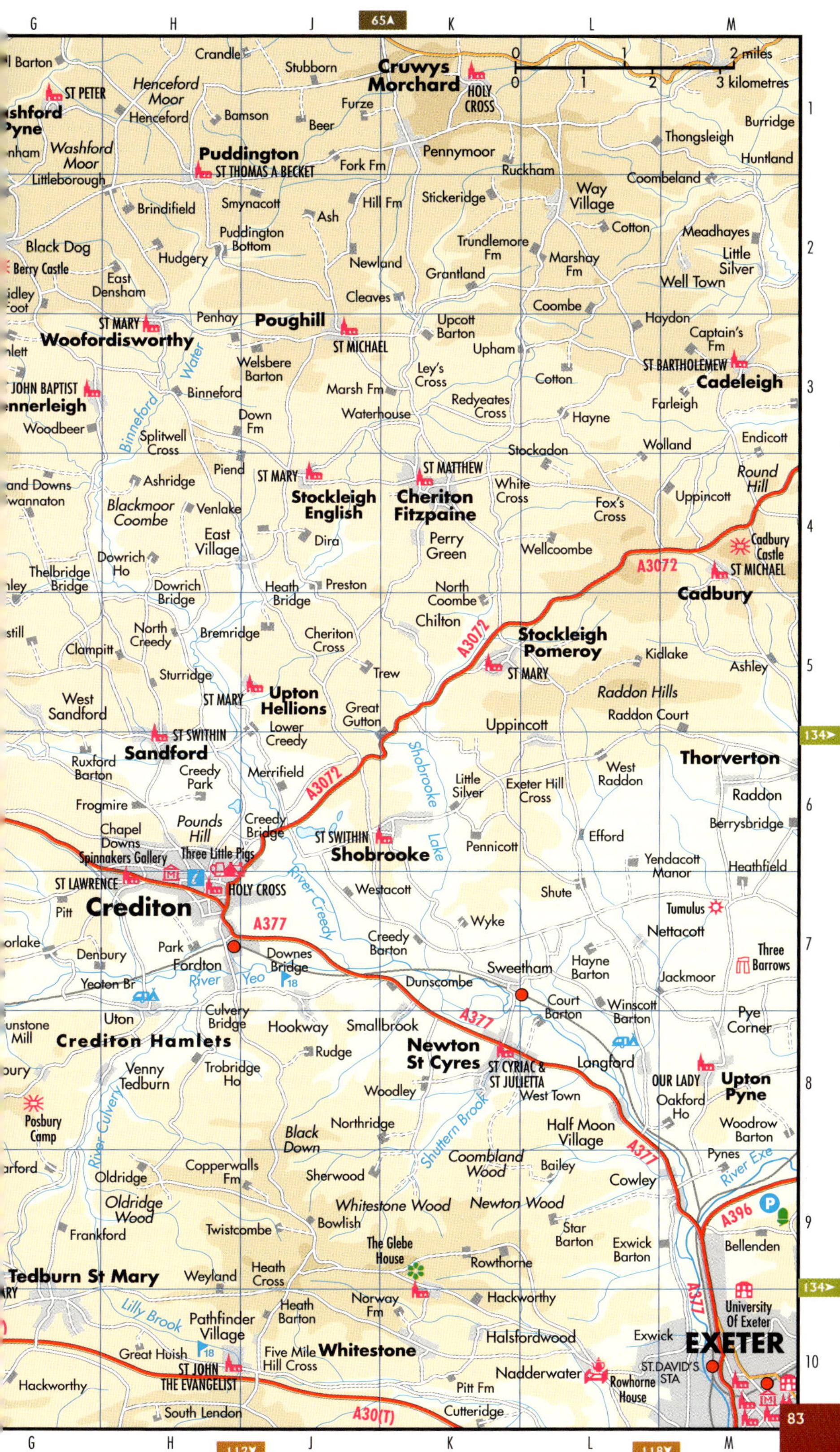

G
H
J
65
K
L
M
0
1
2 miles
0
1
2
3 kilometres
Barton
Crandle
Stubborn
Cruwys Morchard
HOLY CROSS
ST PETER
Henceford Moor
Henceford
Bamson
Furze
Beer
Burridge
Thongsleigh
Huntland
Washford Moor
Littleborough
Puddington
ST THOMAS A BECKET
Fork Fm
Pennymoor
Ruckham
Coombeland
Brindifield
Smynacott
Ash
Hill Fm
Stickeridge
Way Village
Cotton
Meadhayes
Black Dog
Berry Castle
Puddington Bottom
Hudgery
East Densham
Newland
Trundlemore Fm
Grantland
Marshay Fm
Little Silver
Well Town
Cleaves
Coombe
Haydon
ST MARY
Woofordisworthy
Penhay
Poughill
ST MICHAEL
Upcott Barton
Upham
Captain's Fm
ST BARTHOLEMEW
Cadeleigh
JOHN BAPTIST
Welsbere Barton
Binneford
Binneford Water
Ley's Cross
Marsh Fm
Cotton
Redyeates Cross
Farleigh
Woodbeer
Down Fm
Waterhouse
Hayne
Endicott
Splitwell Cross
Stockadon
Wolland
Piend
ST MARY
ST MATTHEW
Round Hill
Ashridge
Stockleigh English
Cheriton Fitzpaine
White Cross
Uppincott
Blackmoor Coombe
Venlake
Fox's Cross
East Village
Dira
Perry Green
Wellcoombe
Cadbury Castle
ST MICHAEL
Dowrich Ho
A3072
Thelbridge Bridge
Dowrich Bridge
Heath Bridge
Preston
North Coombe
Cadbury
North Creedy
Bremridge
Cheriton Cross
Chilton
Stockleigh Pomeroy
Clampitt
A3072
Kidlake
Ashley
Sturridge
Trew
ST MARY
West Sandford
ST MARY
Upton Hellions
Great Gutton
Raddon Hills
Raddon Court
ST SWITHIN
Lower Creedy
Uppincott
Sandford
Thorverton
Ruxford Barton
Creedy Park
Merrifield
Shobrooke Lake
Little Silver
Exeter Hill Cross
West Raddon
Raddon
Frogmire
A3072
Berrysbridge
Chapel Downs
Pounds Hill
Creedy Bridge
ST SWITHIN
Shobrooke
Pennicott
Efford
Spinnakers Gallery
Three Little Pigs
Yendacott Manor
Heathfield
ST LAWRENCE
HOLY CROSS
Westacott
Shute
Crediton
River Creedy
Tumulus
Pitt
A377
Wyke
Nettacott
Denbury
Park
Downes Bridge
Creedy Barton
Three Barrows
Fordton
Sweetham
Hayne Barton
Jackmoor
Yeoton Br
River Yeo
Dunscombe
Court Barton
Winscott Barton
Uton
Culvery Bridge
Hookway
Smallbrook
A377
Pye Corner
Mill
Crediton Hamlets
Rudge
Newton St Cyres
ST CYRIAC & ST JULIETTA
Langford
Venny Tedburn
Trobridge Ho
Woodley
West Town
OUR LADY
Upton Pyne
Oakford Ho
Posbury Camp
River Culvery
Northridge
Shuttern Brook
Half Moon Village
Woodrow Barton
Black Down
A377
Pynes
Oldridge
Copperwalls Fm
Sherwood
Coombland Wood
Bailey
River Exe
Cowley
Oldridge Wood
Whitestone Wood
Newton Wood
Bowlish
A396
Frankford
Twistcombe
Star Barton
Exwick Barton
Bellenden
The Glebe House
Rowthorne
Tedburn St Mary
Weyland
Heath Cross
Lilly Brook
Heath Barton
Norway Fm
Hackworthy
A377
University Of Exeter
Pathfinder Village
Halsfordwood
Exwick
EXETER
Great Huish
Five Mile Hill Cross
Whitestone
ST JOHN THE EVANGELIST
Nadderwater
Rowhorne House
ST.DAVID'S STA
Hackworthy
Pitt Fm
South Lendon
A30(T)
Cutteridge
112
118
134
1
2
3
4
5
6
7
8
9
10

CREDITON

Ecclesiastical capital of the west before Exeter, and birthplace of St Boniface (Winfrith). Magnificent medieval church, but few other buildings survive due to disastrous fires in later times, 1743, when all but few of the C16 buildings were destroyed, also paying ruin to many of the cloth makers and their looms. The woollen cloth industry was the major employ in the C16. Crediton serge was exported worldwide, and was very much a family industry; the children combing and carding the cloth, the mother spinning and the father weaving. In the C19, the cloth industry declined, and tanning leather became the staple industry of the town. The fertile countryside has effected the commercial output of the town. Smaller industries have thrived, and a number of trading estates are to be found on the outskirts. The soil is red, at times, crimson, and the cob walls on the farms bears witness to this phenomena. A town trail is available to those seeking more information. (H7) www.crediton.co.uk

Crediton

New Inn, Coleford ss

Nymet Bridge, Nr Lapford

Places of Interest...

Spinnakers Gallery, 107 High Street.
Since opening in December 2005, this gallery has expanded rapidly and specialises in paintings, glass, ceramics, sculpture and contemporary jewellery by predominantly West Country artists, as well as national names such as John Yardley and Peter Leyton. Open 9.15-5 Tu-F and Sa 10-4 (H7) 01363 774885 www.spinnakersgallery.co.uk

Spinnakers Gallery ss

Pubs Serving Food...

Three Little Pigs, Parliament Square.
This is more a museum of bric-a-brac and an attic turn-out. Unbelievable collection of memorabilia. If at a loss for conversation, or a loss of appetite, just look and wonder. Real Ales and pub grub. (H6)

New Inn, Coleford.
C13 whitewashed cob pub in thatched village. Great ambience. (E6) 01363 84242 www.reallyreal-group.com

Countryside Interests...

Moorland Farm Shop.
Organic beef, lamb and pork, plus fowl, cheeses and delis f rom their award-winning farm. Open daily. (A10) 01647 231666 www.fishleighestate.com www.dartmoorhappyhogs.co.uk

1643 Tavistock a Royalist stronghold. 1645 Exeter besieged by Parliamentarians.

The Buller Memorial

St Petroc Window

Churches...

Church of the Holy Cross. The grandest feature of this country town. A red, sandstone building dating from the 1130s. There was a church here before but it would have been made of wood, and was probably some short distance from this site. The birth of St Boniface in 680 together with records dating back to the C10 proves that a monastery was built here. As a Norman Collegiate Church it was the ecclesiastical centre of Devon until the Bishop's throne was removed to Exeter in 1050 under the command of Leofric. Apparently Exeter was easier to defend against the marauding Danes. Fine monuments survive, Tuckfield, Periam and others, and notable stained glass. The Chancel Roof, restored by John Hayward over 40 years in the Victorian Era is very fine. Small museum.

The Sully Tomb

The Sun Dial

Sir William Peryam

St Boniface has been described as the first European. He took Christianity to Germany and the Netherlands, and is their Patron saint. He was martyred with 52 of his followers in 754 at Dokkum in Friesland which today is a place of pilgrimage and prosperity. (H7) www.creditonparishchurch.org.uk

Tuckfield Memorial

St Boniface (Winfrith) by Witold Kavalec

COB

Cob has been in existence for many hundreds of years and has been the staple building material in many parts of the world. For British and European domestic (and agricultural) architecture, as well as Africa and Asia, Canada and the United States of America.

It is undergoing a strong revival, not least because of its eco-friendly properties. It is a non-pollutant, far more environmentally friendly than bricks and mortar. Recyclable? Yes. An old cob wall can be taken down and remixed with the new matter.

What is Cob? A "ready mix" of sub-soil, sand, clay, straw and water. The ingredients are stirred, or stamped upon, like porridge. Its strengths are that it is an indigenous material, pliable, and can be sculpted and styled by hand or a spade. Its drawback, heavy and labour intensive. Walls are built on top of a plinth of stone, at least two feet in height, and two feet thick, to prevent rising damp. Preparation is slow; each handmade block (patties) is put in place, piece by piece with a pitchfork. Once a section is lumped on top of the section below it is left to dry for at least three days in summer before the next batch can be made up. Moulding can take place while the cob is still damp. Each layer is then compressed by a thwacker; a flat piece of wood. Cob is cool in summer, warm in winter. It can be protected with lime plaster and painted with a lime wash of at least six coats. This instils a breathable quality and an aesthetic appearance. Crucial to its survival is that the top, and bottom, of the wall are protected from the elements otherwise the building will, with time, wither away. Witness the many farm sheds and buildings left to disintegrate.

The natural roof covering was historically straw. Devon is a county with an abundance of cob buildings. Explore the villages to the north and west of Crediton and you will find some good examples. In some cases, the bare cob will differ in colour from red and yellow, to crimson, as per the indigenous material of its locale.

New 'cob & thatch', Cadhay Rise

Thatch is not unique to Devon. It may just appear to be. There can be few counties in England with such a vast panoply of thatch buildings. In the following pages, we have illustrated a cross section of thatch designs to be found across Devon and Exmoor.

Many are enchantingly beautiful and blend in perfectly with their surrounding landscape. Thatch, too, is undergoing a revival and many of our Master Thatchers are now in demand overseas.

The preparation of thatch is a labour intensive process. Thatchers prepare their own materials or they buy in from East Anglia or Eastern Europe, namely Romania.

The process is as follows:-

1. Cut the harvest with the reaper and binder.

2. Let the sheaves dry in stooks (bundles) for 5 days.

3. Form a rick (a large pile) out of the sheaves.

4. Feed the sheaves into a combing machine to dry and separate (see below for details).

5. On leaving the combing machine the sheaves are trussed (tied) up into bundles ready for the thatcher.

Thatch Materials

Combed Wheat Straw. In use since the 1880s, the time a comber machine was devised which was attached to the threshing machine, hence the name. The comber machine had four drums and their purpose was to knock the corn out of the ears, and the flag or leaf of the corn out of the butts, which is the lower end of the straw. The reed then passes through the comber to be threshed. This leaves the straw in one piece and is laid out in lines, then trussed. The thatcher lays out the straw on the roof with the butts facing outwards. This makes for a tight finish similar to water reed. A wire netting is then required to prevent birds from removing the straw. Expected lifetime is 40 years, although this may be reduced if nitrogen or fertisliser gets into the straw.

Long Straw (or Devon Reed). In use since early times. The harvesting process is similar to combed straw. The difference is that the straw does not leave the threshing machine organised in lines. It is threshed into its complete length, soaked in a bed and drawn out into yelms. Sparred to the rook like combed and water reed, it will last up to 20 years.

Water Reed. In use since the Iron Age and harvested in Norfolk and the New Forest. Recommended for use on new or refurbished properties. The life span can be 50 years and does not require netting.

Apron: Single sided section of ridge to protect thatch under chimney or window

Arris: Rail

Baby: see 'Roller'

Back Filling: Laid above battens and under main thatch, used to adjust the tilt of reed or straw

Band / Bond: Twist of straw, reed withy or bramble used to tie a bundle of thatch to roof

Barge: See 'Gable'

Barge Board: Solid board used as an alternative to turned gable

Batting / Bolting: Bundle of tied, threshed straw

Biddle: Working platform hooked into thatch

Binder: See 'Rod' and 'Sway'

Binder: Reaper for cutting standing corn

Bolder Reed: Norfolk Reed bundle containing mostly bulrush

Bottle: Tied yelm of straw for setting eave of gable

Box Gutter: Leaded gutter formed behind chimney

Brotch / Broach: See 'Spar'

Brow: The course after the eaves course

Bunch: Bundle of water reed 2' circumference, 1' above butt, usually at the tie

Butt: Thicker end of a bundle of reed or straw

Butting: Arranging the ends of the reed by dropping bundles or nitches onto board

Cheek: Side of window

Chimney Block: See 'Apron'

Coat: Layer of entire thatch

Cock Up / Cockscomb: Topmost bundle of straw turned to shed water back onto the ridge

Continental Bundle: Imported bundle of water reed 1m around circumference or butt, usually tied twice

Compty: Substandard materials or thatch

Combed Wheat Reed: Straw which has had the corn leaf and weed removed - varieties include Aquilla, Marris Wiggen and Marris Huntsman

Course: Layer of reed or straw laid across the roof

Crook: See 'Iron'

Dolly: See 'Roller' and 'Bottle'

Dressing: Pushing reed into final position

Drift: See 'Legget'

Dutchman: Type of Legget originating from the Netherlands

Eave: First course of thatch

Fathom: Six bundles of water reed

Flue: See 'Gable'

Fargle: A goodly handful of steel sways

Feather: Seed head on water reed

Flag: Leaf on straw

Fleaking: A weave of water reed laid over the rafters instead of timber battens

Gable End: The overhang of thatch at a gable of the roof

Gadd: Cut length of hazel between 1" and 3" in diameter

Gaddule: Bundle of gadds

Hazel: Corylus Aveliana (L) - used for spars, sways and rods - said to be hardier than withy

Hook: See 'Iron'

Iron: Thatching nail used to fix sway to rafter, trapping thatch

Knuckle: Handful of straw, bent double

Ladder: types Pole, Push-up and Hanger

Legget: Tool that grips the ends of the reeds and pushes them into position

Ligger: See 'Rod'

Long Straw: Straw thrashed but not combed. Varieties of wheat : Little Josh, Red Standard, Square Headed Master

Net: A ¾" galvanised wire or ¾" polythene used to protect thatch from bird damage

Needle: Used to stich on the thatch

Nitch: Bundle of combed reed of weight 28lb or 14lb

Northampton Roll: Rolled and rodded gable end

Peg: See 'Spar'

Pinacle: Topmost bundle of ridging material used to shed water back onto the ridge

Pricker: Length of gadd about a yard long, used to fix sways on rick thatches

Ridge: Covering of supple straw or sedge grass, laid along apex of roof to bind and protect the main thatch. Types include wrap-over, butt up, flush, straight cut and patterned. Patterns include dragons' teeth, diamond, scalloped, clubbed, herring-bone and crossed.

Reeding Pin: See 'Spragger'

Roller: Continuous parallel bundle of thatch used to build up ridge

Rod: Hazel or withy, used to hold down thatch on the surface. Types include split, unsplit, apex, kettle and muff.

Rutland Cap: Peaked end at gable

Rye: Type of soft straw used for thatching

Sedge: Marsh Grass (Cladius Mariscus) used for ridging

Server: Skilled labourer

Set: See 'Tilt'

Sheaf: Bundle of unthrashed straw - 8 sheaves make a stook, 16 make a stock

Slapping: First course of ridge

Skirt: See 'Slapping'

Spar: A split length of hazel or withy, pointed and twisted to form a staple

Spit: See 'Spar'

Spot Board: Board for 'butting up' of reed bundles

Spragger: Pointed length of steel used to temporarily hold materials

Springing: See ' Tilt'

Stalch: A strip of thatch worked from eave to ridge

Standing Crop: The thatching materials whilst growing

Stool: Clump of Hazel

Straw: All types of straw which may be used to thatch - wheat straw is considered most suitable

Sway: Steel or hazel rod used with irons to secure thatch

Thrashing: Method of removing grain from straw

Tilt: The angle formed by tightening the sway between the top and the butt of the reed

Tilting Fillet: A 'V' section of timber fixed to the rafter to set the tilt

Twisle: A crank for twisting straw for grass bonds

Verge: See 'Barge'

Wadd: See 'Bottle'

Wand: Length of unsplit willow or hazel, less than 1" diam

Water Reed: Phragmites Communis obtained traditionally from East Anglia now additionally from European countries

Wimble: See 'Twisle'

Withy: Willow used for rods and sways - it is said to be less prone to woodworm - varieties include Black bar, Dicky Medoes, Swallow tail and Whissender

Yelm: Drawn and wet straw ready for laying

Lying between the western reaches of Dartmoor, and the River Tamar of the Cornish border, and to the south, the urban expanse of Plymouth, to the north the fast-burning A30. Within this triangle, an enchanting artery of small rivers, wooded valleys, and a bevy of hamlets and villages connected by slow lanes.

Not a place to hurry. Be advised to carry a compass, for disorientation is the norm in the Lew and Lyd Valleys. Road signs are, at times, confusing, and you map skills will be sorely tested if you wish to take advantage of the many fine hostelries within this domain.

Often the edges of a county are the most interesting. It is our habit to rush to the centre, and then to explore outwards. But, if you look to the natural border, in this instance, the Tamar Valley, and its feeding lines there are sweet names to conjure with; Sydenham Damerel, Horsebridge, Bere Ferrers, Weir Quay, Lopwell…into these conduits great ships passed by with their tonnage. Visit Morwellham Quay, and you will experience our rich, industrial past.

Explore this area and you will be forgiven a hearty appetite. For it is here that Tavistock was judged a worthy centre of fine produce and cuisine. And, not too far distant are the hotels; Blagdon Manor, Hotel Endsleigh, Lewtrenchard Manor, and the hostelries, Dartmoor Inn, Elephant's Nest, Harris Arms and Peter Tavy Inn that will nourish and tender your gastronomic desires. So, Bon Appetit, and a safe journey home.

The Lenkiewicz Foundation Plymouth

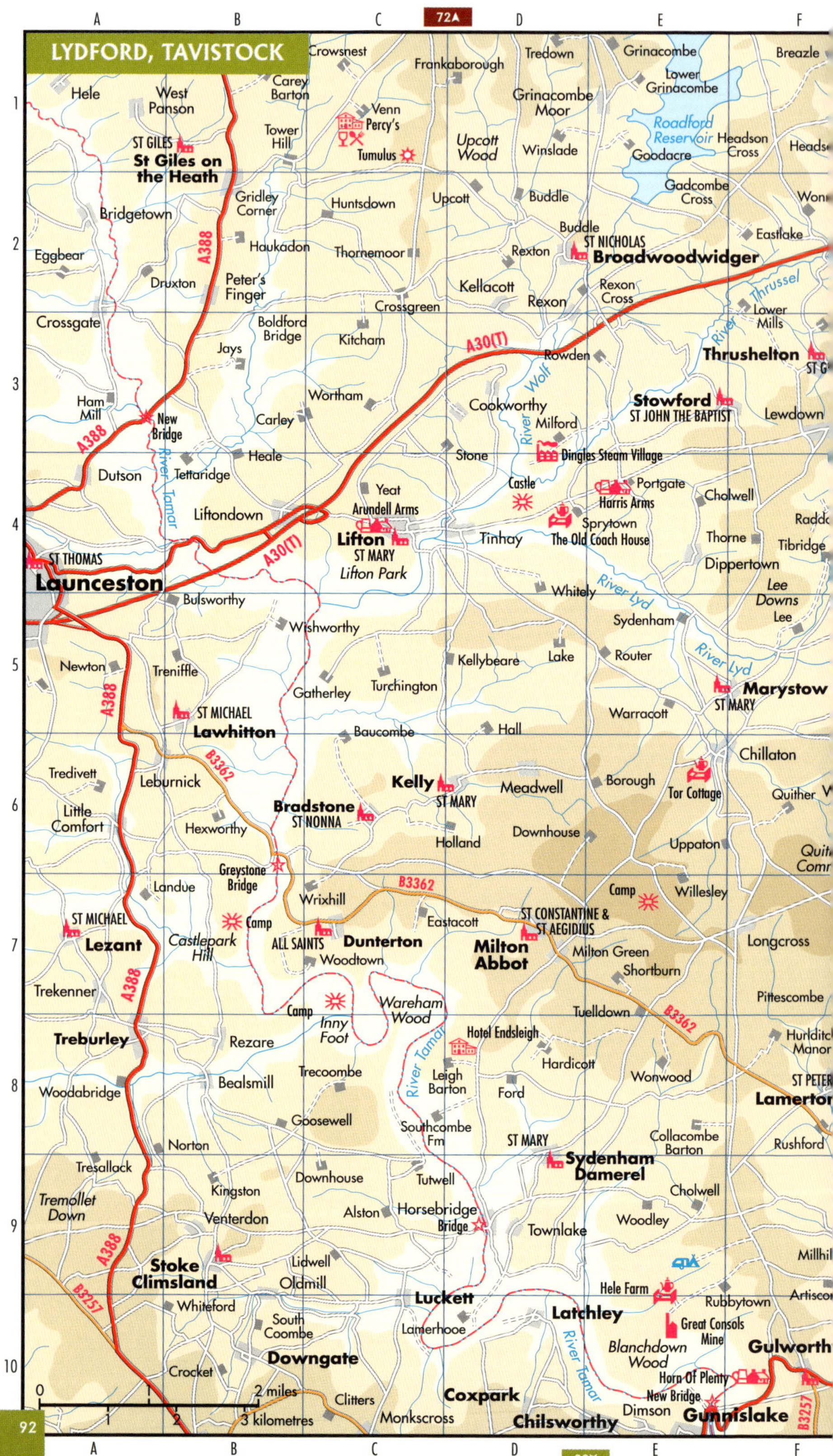

LYDFORD, TAVISTOCK
72▲
A
B
C
D
E
F
Hele
West Panson
Carey Barton
Crowsnest
Frankaborough
Tredown
Grinacombe
Lower Grinacombe
Breazle
Tower Hill
Venn
Percy's
Grinacombe Moor
Roadford Reservoir
ST GILES
St Giles on the Heath
Tumulus
Upcott Wood
Winslade
Goodacre
Headson Cross
Gadcombe Cross
Bridgetown
Gridley Corner
Huntsdown
Upcott
Buddle
Eggbear
Haukadon
Thornemoor
Rexton
Buddle
ST NICHOLAS
Broadwoodwidger
Eastlake
A388
Druxton
Peter's Finger
Kellacott
Rexon Cross
Rexon
River Thrussel
Lower Mills
Crossgate
Boldford Bridge
Crossgreen
Kitcham
Jays
A30(T)
Rowden
Thrushelton
Wortham
River Wolf
Stowford
ST JOHN THE BAPTIST
Lewdown
Ham Mill
New Bridge
Carley
Cookworthy
Milford
Heale
Stone
Dingles Steam Village
Dutson
Tettaridge
River Tamar
Yeat
Castle
Portgate
Harris Arms
Cholwell
Liftondown
Arundell Arms
Sprytown
Lifton
ST MARY
Lifton Park
Tinhay
The Old Coach House
Thorne
Tibridge
ST THOMAS
Launceston
Dippertown
Bulsworthy
Whitely
River Lyd
Lee Downs
Lee
Sydenham
Wishworthy
Newton
Treniffle
Kellybeare
Lake
Router
Gatherley
Turchington
Marystow
ST MARY
ST MICHAEL
Lawhitton
Warracott
Baucombe
Hall
Chillaton
Tredivett
Leburnick
B3362
Kelly
ST MARY
Meadwell
Borough
Tor Cottage
Quither
Little Comfort
Bradstone
ST NONNA
Hexworthy
Holland
Downhouse
Uppaton
Greystone Bridge
Landue
Wrixhill
Camp
Willesley
ST MICHAEL
Lezant
Camp
Castlepark Hill
ALL SAINTS
Dunterton
Eastacott
ST CONSTANTINE & ST AEGIDIUS
Milton Abbot
Milton Green
Longcross
Woodtown
Shortburn
Trekenner
Camp
Inny Foot
Wareham Wood
Tuelldown
Pittescombe
Treburley
Rezare
Hotel Endsleigh
Hardicott
Hurditch Manor
Trecoombe
Leigh Barton
Ford
Wonwood
ST PETER
Woodabridge
Bealsmill
Lamerton
Goosewell
Southcombe Fm
ST MARY
Sydenham Damerel
Collacombe Barton
Rushford
Norton
Tresallack
Kingston
Downhouse
Tutwell
Cholwell
Tremollet Down
Venterdon
Alston
Horsebridge Bridge
Townlake
Woodley
Lidwell
Millhill
Stoke Climsland
Oldmill
Hele Farm
Rubbytown
Artiscombe
Luckett
B3257
Whiteford
South Coombe
Latchley
Great Consols Mine
Lamerhooe
Blanchdown Wood
Gulworth
Downgate
Crocket
Horn Of Plenty
New Bridge
Clitters
Coxpark
Dimson
Monkscross
Chilsworthy
Gunnislake
0 1 2 miles
1 2 3 kilometres
98▼

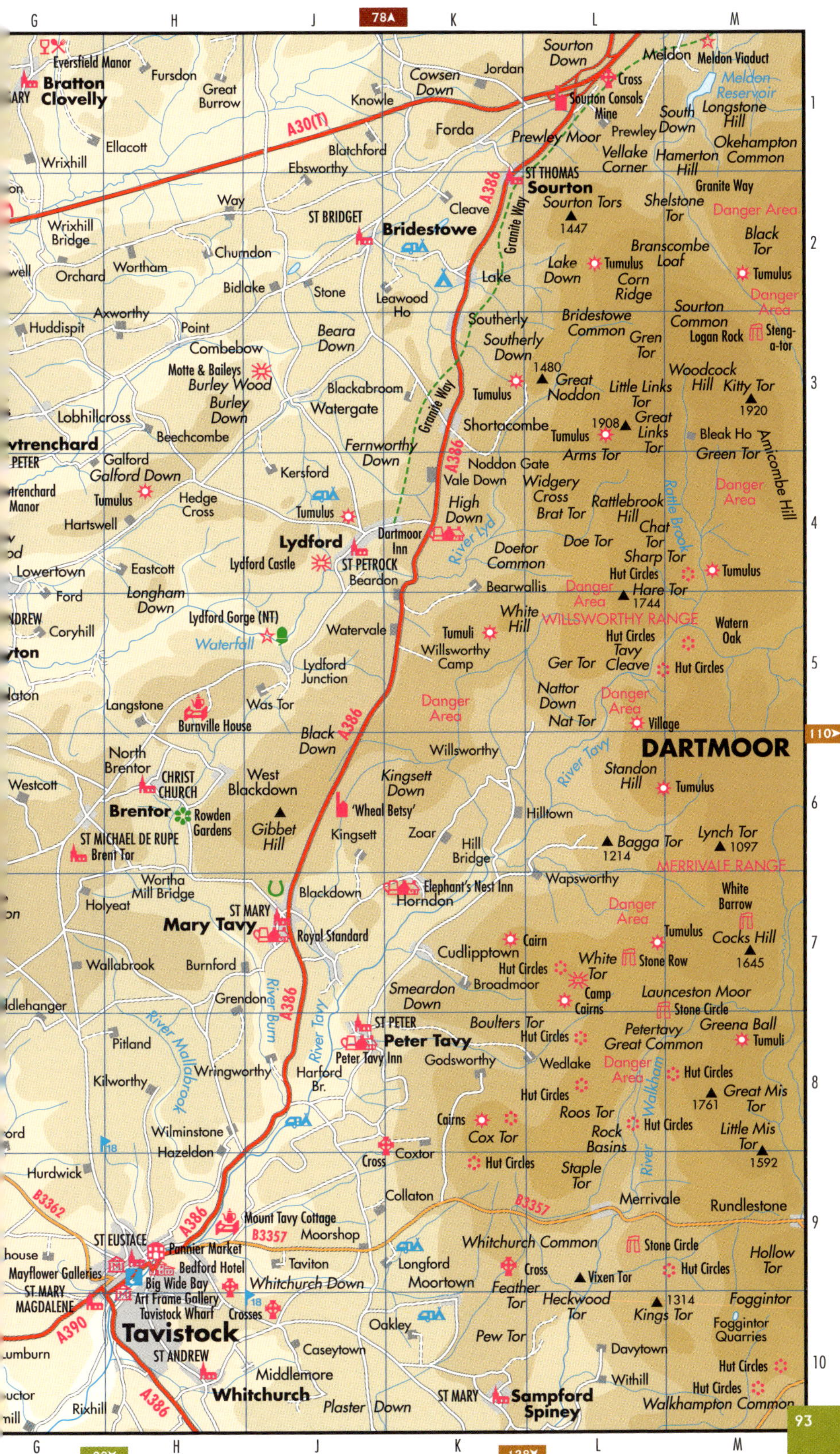

78
110
128
98
G
H
J
K
L
M
1
2
3
4
5
6
7
8
9
10
Eversfield Manor
Fursdon
Bratton Clovelly
Great Burrow
Cowsen Down
Jordan
Sourton Down
Meldon
Meldon Viaduct
Meldon Reservoir
Knowle
Cross
Sourton Consols Mine
South Down
Longstone Hill
A30(T)
Forda
Ellacott
Wrixhill
Blatchford
Prewley Moor
Prewley
Vellake Corner
Hamerton Hill
Okehampton Common
Ebsworthy
ST THOMAS
Sourton
Sourton Tors
1447
Shelstone Tor
Granite Way
Danger Area
A386
Way
Cleave
Wrixhill Bridge
ST BRIDGET
Bridestowe
Black Tor
Churndon
Branscombe Loaf
Lake Down
Tumulus
Orchard
Wortham
Bidlake
Stone
Lake
Corn Ridge
Leawood Ho
Huddispit
Axworthy
Point
Beara Down
Southerly
Bridestowe Common
Sourton Common
Logan Rock
Steng-a-tor
Combebow
Southerly Down
Gren Tor
Motte & Baileys
Burley Wood
1480
Great Nodden
Little Links Tor
Woodcock Hill
Kitty Tor
Blackabroom
Burley Down
Watergate
1920
Lobhillcross
Shortacombe
Great Links Tor
1908
Beechcombe
Bleak Ho
Amicombe Hill
Fernworthy Down
Arms Tor
Green Tor
Galford
Galford Down
Noddon Gate
Vale Down
Widgery Cross
Rattlebrook Hill
Rattle Brook
Kersford
Hedge Cross
Hartswell
High Down
Brat Tor
Chat Tor
Lydford
Dartmoor Inn
River Lyd
Doe Tor
Lydford Castle
ST PETROCK
Beardon
Doetor Common
Sharp Tor
Lowertown
Eastcott
Hut Circles
Ford
Longham Down
Bearwallis
Hare Tor
1744
Coryhill
Lydford Gorge (NT)
White Hill
WILLSWORTHY RANGE
Watern Oak
Waterfall
Watervale
Tumuli
Tavy Cleave
Willsworthy Camp
Ger Tor
Lydford Junction
Nattor Down
Langstone
Was Tor
Village
Nat Tor
Burnville House
Black Down
Willsworthy
DARTMOOR
North Brentor
CHRIST CHURCH
West Blackdown
Kingsett Down
River Tavy
Standon Hill
Westcott
Brentor
Rowden Gardens
'Wheal Betsy'
Hilltown
Gibbet Hill
Kingsett
Zoar
ST MICHAEL DE RUPE
Brent Tor
Hill Bridge
Bagga Tor
1214
Lynch Tor
1097
MERRIVALE RANGE
Wortha Mill Bridge
Wapsworthy
Holyeat
Blackdown
Elephant's Nest Inn
Horndon
White Barrow
ST MARY
Mary Tavy
Royal Standard
Cocks Hill
1645
Cairn
Cudlipptown
White Tor
Stone Row
Wallabrook
Burnford
Broadmoor
Camp
Launceston Moor
Smeardon Down
Cairns
Stone Circle
Grendon
River Burn
ST PETER
Boulters Tor
Greena Ball
Petertavy Great Common
Pitland
River Mallabrook
Peter Tavy
Peter Tavy Inn
Godsworthy
Wedlake
Walkham
Wringworthy
Harford Br.
Great Mis Tor
1761
Kilworthy
Roos Tor
Little Mis Tor
Wilminstone
Cox Tor
Rock Basins
Hazeldon
Coxtor
Cross
1592
Hurdwick
Staple Tor
River
B3362
Collaton
Merrivale
Rundlestone
B3357
Mount Tavy Cottage
Moorshop
ST EUSTACE
Pannier Market
Whitchurch Common
Bedford Hotel
Taviton
Hollow Tor
Mayflower Galleries
Big Wide Bay
Longford
Whitchurch Down
Moortown
Vixen Tor
ST MARY MAGDALENE
Art Frame Gallery
Feather Tor
Heckwood Tor
1314
Foggintor
Tavistock Wharf
Crosses
Kings Tor
Foggintor Quarries
A390
Oakley
Tavistock
Pew Tor
ST ANDREW
Caseytown
Davytown
Middlemore
Withill
Rixhill
Whitchurch
ST MARY
Sampford Spiney
A386
Plaster Down
Walkhampton Common

TAVISTOCK

One of the four "Stannary Towns", established to control the production and distribution of tin from Dartmoor, and birthplace of Sir Francis Drake in 1542 at Crowndale Farm (now no more), south of the town. Later, developed by the Dukes of Bedford who lived in what is now the Bedford Hotel, and in the summer for six weeks at Endsleigh House near Milton Abbot. The Bedfords were formidable, forward thinking town planners of their day, the early C19, and the impressive buildings have great dignity; the Town Hall and Pannier Market, and the long avenues were to their choosing. Drake's statue stands at the west end of the town's entrance, whilst at the end of the same road, stands a statue of Bedford. The Parish Church of St Eustace is formidable, too, and the Abbey, founded in 974, destroyed by Henry V111 in 1539 has a few surviving walls beside the riverbank. Tavistock is an attractive town, and a popular one to live in. It has plenty of smart, independent shops, good schools and a lively food culture. The area is noted for its abundance of smart hotels, restaurants and gastro-pubs. To offset, your indulgences, Dartmoor is a few steps to the east. Plymouth is within commuting distance, and the Cornish border, not too distant, either. (H10)

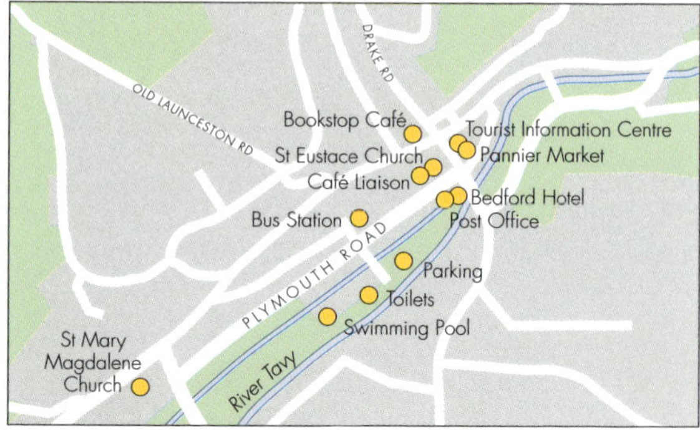

Tavistock

Dartmoor Ponies

Special Places to visit...

Artframe Gallery, 17 Duke St. Broad range of paintings, ceramics bronzes and studio glass. Original art, limited editions. Open M-Sa 9.30-5. (H10) 01822 611091 www.artframegallery.co.uk

Big Wide Bay, 14b Market St. Range of affordable contemporary fine art. Open 10-5.30 (Sa 4.30) closes M & W 2. (H10) 01822 611124 www.bigwidebay.com

Mayflower Galleries, 21 West St. Original paintings of local scenes specialising in Dartmoor images, and a large selection of collectable limited edition prints. (H10) 01822 613665

Pannier Market. Purpose built in the 1850s. Markets held daily Tu-Sa 9-4. Crafts and antiques Tu, Mixed W, Food/clothing F, All sorts on Sa. Dukes Coffee House. (H10)

Parish Church of St Eustace. A fine, C15 construction with pinnacle tower and wide nave. A roof of carved beams and bosses, bench ends and C16 font. Tomb monuments to many local dignitaries; Sir John Glanville and John Fitz. William Morris stained glass in the north-east Chantry window and a clear reflection of the wealth created by the wool and tin merchants of west Devon. (H9)

Tavistock Wharf, The Wharf. Tavistock's art centre featuring cinema, live music, theatre and an art gallery. Bar and coffee shop. Open daily. (H9) 01822 611166 www.tavistockwharf.com

Teddy's Dolls House, Village Shopping Arcade, Brook St. Collection of dolls and teddies. Dolls & Teddies Hospital. (H10) 01822 612128

Where to Eat, Drink & Be Merry...

Bookstop Coffee Shop, 3 Market St. A visit to the local, independent bookstore is always on my "List" of things to do when I visit a country town. Higgledeepiggledee on many floors, there will be something for everyone. And they claim to serve the best coffee in town. (H9) 01822 617244

Cafe Liaison, 3 Church Lane. Popular meeting place, you can sit under the trees in summer. Vegetarian cafe provides home-cooked fare, teas and coffees. Th-Sa evenings Tapas nights. Licensed. (H10) 01822 612225

1646 Bideford besieged by the Plague.

1660 General George Monck (later Duke of Albermarle) of Great Potheridge, near Great Torrington organizes (The Restoration) the return of Charles ll from exile.

Special Places to Visit...

Dingles Steam Railway, Nr Lifton. All weather attraction with hands-on approach to machinery. Traction Engines. Cafe. River walks. Open Easter, then late May to end Sept M-Th (& W/Es school hols) 10.30-5.30. (D3) 01566 783425

Merrivale Stone Circle. Remains from one of the earliest settlements in Devon. Clearly visible are boulders from Hut Circles, square dwellings, and Stone Rows from funeral burials. Two of the standing stones have markings indicating an A and a T, as an early road sign for crossing the Moor. A stream of pure water crosses the area. Park in car park. (L9)

Lydford Gorge

Lydford Gorge (NT). The beautiful woodland walk leads you down the deep wooded ravine 1.5 miles long carved out by the River Lyd as it plunges into the 'Devil's Cauldron'. The White Lady Waterfall is quite spectacular at 90 ft high. Open daily Apr-Oct from 10. Refreshments. Admission charge. Waterfall only rest of year 10.30-3. Tea room. (J5) 01822 820320 www.nationaltrust.org.uk

Rowden Gardens, Brentor. World famous for range of rare aquatic plants. Plant sales. Gardens open Apr-Oct. Nursey open all year. (H6) 01822 810275 www.patio-prides.co.uk

Wheal Betsy. Former tin mine in the care of the National Trust. You can spy the mine from the main road. (J6)

Churches of Interest...

St Michael De Rupe, Brent Tor. Built by the monks of Tavistock Abbey in the C14, and romantically poised on an extinct volcano at 1130 feet. Like Glastonbury Tor, a favourite with children to clamber up, and witness the fine views across to Dartmoor, and west to Brown Willy, on Bodmin Moor. (G6)

Quality B & B...

April Cottage, 12 Mount Tavy Road, Tavistock. Friendly accommodation overlooks the River Tavy. All bedrooms with bathroom. Easy walking distance to town centre. (H10) 01822 613280

Lydford Castle

Burnville House, Nr Brentor. Large, comfortable Georgian house with views across to Dartmoor offers solitude and farmhouse cuisine. 4 self-catering cottages. (H5) 01822 820443 www.burnville.co.uk

Hele Farm, Nr Gulworthy. Grade 11 listed farmhouse with organic dairy dating back to 1780. Somewhat old fashioned décor. Steeped in history of mining – see Great Consols Mine. Nature walks down to Tamar. Self catering, too. (E9) 01822 833084 www.dartmoorbb.co.uk

Mount Tavy Cottage. Lovely old gardener's cottage just ten minutes walk from Tavistock. Family room and 4-poster bedroom with bathrooms. Organic breakfasts. All set with 10 acres of paradise. Self catering, too. (H9) 01822 614253 www.mounttavy.freeserve.co.uk

Merrival Stone Circle

Hotel Endsleigh, Nr Milton Abbot. Olga Polizzi's hotel blends a fusion of country house style with contemporary boutique. Former fishing lodge with beautiful, ornamental gardens; Dairy Dell, Rock Gardens and Grotto, and an Arboretum. After a long summer lunch there's bound to be a tree to rest under, to dream of Shangrilas, in this hideaway overlooking the Tamar. (D8) 01822 870000 www.hotelendsleigh.com

The Old Coach House, Sprytown. You have the choice of Letting Rooms in the Coach House where you can come and go at your leisure, or traditional rooms in the Thatched Cottage. Communal breakfast room. Large secluded with an abundance of wild life. (C4) 01566 784224 www.theoldcoach-house.co.uk

Tor Cottage, Chillaton. A rural retreat in their own private valley with over 18 acres of wildlife to explore and get lost in. Elegant and spacious rooms. Outdoor pool. (E6) 01822 860248 www.torcottage.co.uk

Fly Fishing Tuition, Arundell Arms ss

Special Places to Stay...

Arundell Arms, Lifton. One of England's premier fishing hotels for more than a century offering 20 miles of Salmon, Sea Trout and Brown Trout fishing in a valley with five rivers. Tuition and ghillieing. Comfortable and relaxed. Modern French and English cuisine. (C4) 01566 784666 www.arundellarms.com

Mural , Buckland Abbey formerly from Lewtrenchard Manor

Bedford Hotel, Tavistock. Large, conservative town hotel offers traditional comforts and elegant charm. Quite a pile. It's a former Benedictine Abbey and residence of the Dukes of Bedford. Special Breaks. Serves food all day (the best Minute Steak I have ever tasted!), and if you have been rushed off your feet, a large armchair awaits you. "A Scotch or Pot of Tea, Your Grace...". (H9) 01822 613221 www.bedford-hotel.co.uk

Dartmoor Inn. More Restaurant With Rooms than pub. The beautifully designed pieces of artwork set the scene for great cuisine and a genial atmosphere. Regular art exhibitions. Accommodation. Despite being a short distance from the Moor and Gorge, sadly walkers and their grubby boots, aren't encouraged to venture here. Lunch served Tu-Su 12-2.15, dinner Tu-Sa 6.30-9.30. (K4) 01822 820221 www.dartmoorinn.co.uk

Lewtrenchard Manor. There's nothing stuffy about the ambience in this Jacobean manor hidden beneath the wild Tors of Dartmoor. With a history going back to the Domesday Book and evidence of a host of colourful Lords of the Manor's, a taste of Olde England pervades this historic setting. Sheer luxury, intimate comfort and fabulous food will tempt you back time and again. (G4) 01566 783222 www.vonessenhotels.com

Dartmoor Inn

1685 The Devonshire Regiment raised in Bristol as t he Duke of Beaufort's Musketeers to help crush Monmouth's Rebellion.

1685 Judge Jeffreys Bloody Assizes sent many West Country men to horrific executions – their bodies quartered before family and friends.

Percy's Country House Hotel & Restaurant. Chic, stylish design meets C15 Devon Long Barn. Food of intense quality. Restaurant has won garlands galore. Ingredients from organic producers and their 130 acres. Cookery School. Riding holidays. No children under 12, no dogs in public rooms. (C1) 01409 211236 www.percys.co.uk

Percy's ss

River Walkham, Merrivale

The Horn of Plenty Country House Hotel & Restaurant. Set in five acres of spectacular gardens and wild orchards overlooking the Tamar Valley. Intimate hotel offering fine cuisine and sporting facilities. Award-winning restaurant. Cookery courses with Peter Gorton. (F10) 01822 832528 www.thehornofplenty.co.uk

Pubs Serving Food...

Elephant's Nest, Horndon. Always a favourite. Nothing better than sitting out in their garden on a summer's evening with pint in hand. Recently refurbished. Accommodation. (K7) 01822 810273 www.theelephantsnest.co.uk

Peter Tavy Inn. Popular with all the foodie guides, for you have low beams, slate floors and large cosy fireplaces, plus an ambience conducive to children and dogs. Fine start off point for Dartmoor walks. (J8) 01822 810348

The Harris Arms, Portgate. Multi-award-winning "foodies-pub" on the Devon and Cornwall border provides a warm and friendly atmosphere, great food, extensive and eclectic wines, and fine, local ales. Fresh ingredients are sourced locally with an ever-changing Specials Board. Vegetarians and children catered for, and dogs welcome, too. Closed M (& Su Evenings in winter). (E4) 01566 783331 www.theharrisarms.co.uk

The Royal Standard, Mary Tavy. Fine pub where all the food is cooked to order; seafood, steaks and vegetarian meals. Real ales to savour. Lunch 12-2.30 pm. OAPs specials on Th. (J7) 01822 810011

The Harris Arms ss

1686 James 11 visits the West Country and pardons the dissenters. Later to grant freedom of worship with his Declaration of Indulgence.

1688 Nov 11. Prince William of Orange entered Exeter with swords drawn, colours flying and drums beating.

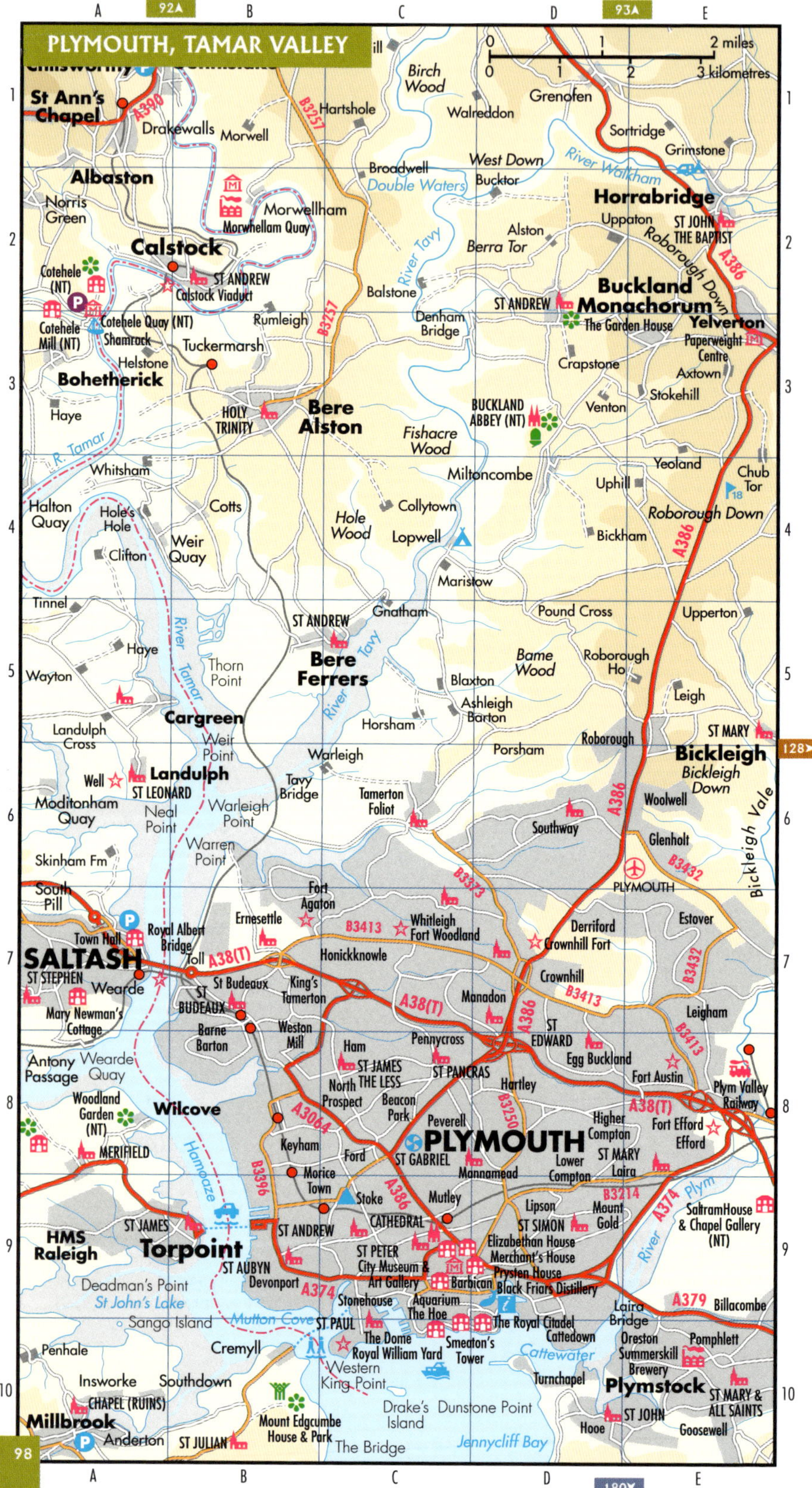
St Ann's Chapel
Drakewalls
Morwell
Hartshole
Birch Wood
Walreddon
Grenofen
Sortridge
Grimstone
Albaston
Norris Green
Broadwell
Double Waters
West Down
Bucktor
River Walkham
Horrabridge
Morwellham
Morwellham Quay
Calstock
Alston
Berra Tor
Uppaton
ST JOHN THE BAPTIST
Roborough Down
Cotehele (NT)
ST ANDREW
Calstock Viaduct
Balstone
River Tavy
Buckland Monachorum
ST ANDREW
The Garden House
Yelverton
Paperweight Centre
Rumleigh
Denham Bridge
Cotehele Mill (NT)
Cotehele Quay (NT)
Shamrock
Tuckermarsh
Helstone
Crapstone
Axtown
Bohetherick
Stokehill
HOLY TRINITY
Bere Alston
BUCKLAND ABBEY (NT)
Venton
Haye
Fishacre Wood
R. Tamar
Yeoland
Whitsham
Miltoncombe
Chub Tor
Uphill
Halton Quay
Hole's Hole
Cotts
Collytown
Roborough Down
Hole Wood
Lopwell
Bickham
Weir Quay
Clifton
Maristow
Tinnel
Gnatham
Pound Cross
Upperton
ST ANDREW
Haye
River Tamar
Thorn Point
Bere Ferrers
Bame Wood
Roborough Ho
Wayton
Blaxton
Leigh
River Tavy
Ashleigh Barton
Cargreen
Horsham
ST MARY
Landulph Cross
Weir Point
Porsham
Roborough
Bickleigh
Warleigh
Bickleigh Down
Well
Landulph
ST LEONARD
Tavy Bridge
Tamerton Foliot
Woolwell
Moditonham Quay
Neal Point
Warleigh Point
Southway
Glenholt
Bickleigh Vale
Warren Point
Skinham Fm
PLYMOUTH
South Pill
Fort Agaton
Ernesettle
Whitleigh
Derriford
Estover
Town Hall
Royal Albert Bridge
Fort Woodland
Crownhill Fort
SALTASH
Toll
Honicknowle
ST STEPHEN
Wearde
St Budeaux
King's Tamerton
Crownhill
Mary Newman's Cottage
ST BUDEAUX
Manadon
Leigham
Barne Barton
Weston Mill
Pennycross
ST EDWARD
Egg Buckland
Antony Passage
Wearde Quay
Ham
ST JAMES THE LESS
ST PANCRAS
Fort Austin
Plym Valley Railway
North Prospect
Beacon Park
Hartley
Woodland Garden (NT)
Wilcove
Peverell
Higher Compton
Fort Efford
Efford
PLYMOUTH
MERIFIELD
Keyham
Ford
ST GABRIEL
Mannamead
ST MARY
Laira
Lower Compton
Hamoaze
Morice Town
Stoke
Mutley
Lipson
Mount Gold
River Plym
SaltramHouse & Chapel Gallery (NT)
ST JAMES
CATHEDRAL
ST SIMON
HMS Raleigh
Torpoint
ST ANDREW
Elizabethan House
ST AUBYN
ST PETER
Merchant's House
Devonport
City Museum & Art Gallery
Prysten House
Barbican
Black Friars Distillery
Deadman's Point
St John's Lake
Stonehouse
Aquarium
Laira Bridge
Billacombe
The Hoe
The Royal Citadel
Sango Island
Mutton Cove
ST PAUL
Cattedown
Oreston
Pomphlett
Penhale
Cremyll
The Dome
Smeaton's Tower
Cattewater
Summerskill Brewery
Royal William Yard
Western King Point
Turnchapel
Insworke
Southdown
Plymstock
ST MARY & ALL SAINTS
CHAPEL (RUINS)
Drake's Island
Dunstone Point
ST JOHN
Millbrook
Mount Edgcumbe House & Park
Hooe
Goosewell
Anderton
ST JULIAN
The Bridge
Jennycliff Bay
A390
B3257
A386
A38(T)
B3413
B3373
B3432
A3064
B3250
B3396
A374
B3214
A379
0 1 2 miles
0 1 2 3 kilometres
92A
93A
128
180

PLYMOUTH

The largest city in Devon, and the most well known, for Plymouth men have exported their birthplace's name to forty other towns and cities across the world. It is the greatest city in the South West, and lies between the rivers Tamar and Plym which form the estuaries of the Hamoaze and Cattewater, making a fine natural harbour. It is a city of its own making with a swashbuckling, seafaring tradition, and although the men who made Plymouth great were Devon men; Drake, Frobisher, Gilbert and Raleigh, their initial loyalty was to their Queen, Elizabeth 1 and to England. They sailed under the Queen's flag, for England, and their own, self-interest, and were party to England's maritime supremacy in the Elizabethan era, and thereafter. In 1585, it became a Naval Base, and at the time of the Armada in 1588, Plymouth had superseded Dartmouth as the principal port of Devon. Sutton Pool was the location for the original port set beside the fishing quays of today's Barbican.

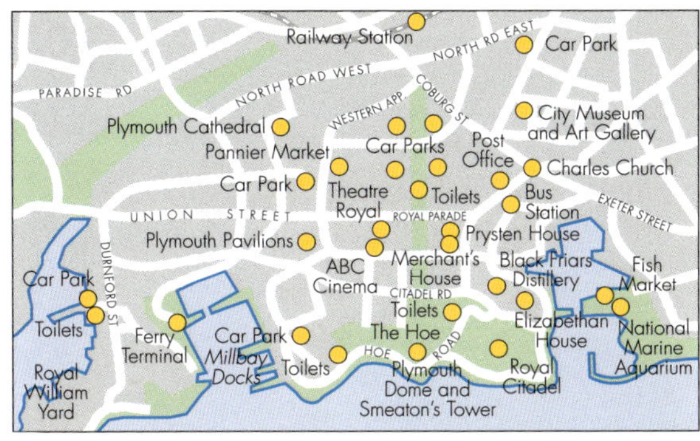

Plymouth

The city suffered terrible losses and destruction during the Second World War. The whole centre of the city was virtually obliterated with over 1,200 civilian mortalities, unknown service losses, 10,000 houses destroyed and more damaged. Utter destruction. These lost souls are remembered in the memorial, Charles Church, built 1641-1708 in the Gothic style. It, too, suffered untold destruction, now a mere shell of its former glory. So it is a fitting tribute that the Men of Plymouth saw fit to leave this "much talked about" monument in the centre of the Charles Cross roundabout, in front of the new shopping development, to be seen by all who drive into the city centre along the A374.

Sir Francis Drake's Statue, The Hoe

Sutton Pool, Plymouth

Following the Second World War, the rebuilding of the city centre was not considered a great success from an aesthetic or planning point of view, and the hideous Drake's Circus has been demolished to make way for the new £200 million Drakes Circus Shopping Centre, which opened to much fanfare on the 5th October, 2006. The City fathers and planners have drawn up ambitious plans for regenerating the City; "A Vision for Plymouth." This will be completed by 2020. We are already seeing progress. The Royal William Dockyard at Stonehouse, the former Victualling Yard (storage of food etc) has been developed into £1,000,000 apartments and prestigious offices, attended by art galleries and a coffee shop.

In 1691, William III established the Royal Naval Dockyard at Devonport in five acres, by 1765 it had expanded to a sprawling, 74 acres. Plymouth Dock was renamed Devonport in 1824. Much of the land is today in private hands, the remainder is known as the Plymouth Naval Base where one of their duties is to maintain and refuel the Vanguard Class of nuclear ballistic missile submarines.

Café on The Barbican

1688 Nov 5. Prince William of Orange lands at Brixham, and then makes a triumphant entrance into Exeter on November 9th.

1689 Dock, later to be known as Devonport, becomes the great western dockyard of the Channel Fleet.

Royal William Dockyard

The Barbican is where most visitors (who are not interested in shops) progress to. It is Plymouth's old harbour area, and luckily avoided the Luftwaffe's bombing raids. A place of character and activity, close to the fishing boats of the thriving fishing industry. The fish market trades from 4.00 am and supplies the great wholesale markets of Billingsgate and Birmingham, as well as the countless restaurants of the south-west, and beyond. There are ancient buildings, including Prysten House, the Elizabethan House, and the Merchant's House. Nearby is the Mayflower Stone from where the Pilgrim Fathers set forth aboard the Mayflower. All about you is life and activity, there are coffee shops, pubs and restaurants, and within view, the National Marine Aquarium.

With the sea to your left you ascend to the Hoe passing the Royal Citadel on your right. It is a fine, open space, given to kite flying and dog walking, and memories, dreams, reflections (apologies, dear Junge). There are impressive memorials; Armada Memorial, the Naval War Memorial, Soldiers of Plymouth, Royal Marines Memorial and the leaning, Smeaton's Tower, or so it appears.

Fish Sculpture, The Barbican

RAF Memorial, The Hoe

Plymouth is not the city to typify the characteristics of Devon; thatch, cream teas and pastoral bliss. It is out on its own. And like Venice, best approached from the sea. Although, today, most of us arrive by train, or car via unattractive ring roads cutting between dull housing and equally poor industrial estates. Don't let these negatives put you off. One feels tremendous energy emanating from all this activity and new birth. It is a city to explore and grow to like, if not love. It has a future, and if you tire of it, Dartmoor is but a stones throw away.

Special Places of Interest in Plymouth...

Black Friars Distillery, 60 Southside St.
"Spirit of Plymouth" exhibition - history of the city and its world famous gin. Open East-Dec M-Sa 10:30-4. Party bookings by arrangement. 01752 665292 www.plymouthgin.com

City Museum & Art Gallery, Drake Circus. Paintings and drawings, including some by Reynolds. Silver and porcelain. Natural history, archaeology, local history. Open Tu-F 10-5.30, Sa & BH Ms 10-5. 01752 304774

Crownhill Fort.
A quite extraordinary building situated on a hill on the northern outskirts of Plymouth, but well worth a visit to see it's unique design. It was a Victorian fort built in the 1860s to defend Plymouth, from what one may wonder, given its isolation. Open for visitors to explore the earth ramparts, gun emplacements and tunnels. Open Apr-Oct 10-5 Su-F. 01752 793754 ww.crownhillfort.co.uk

Merchant's House, St Andrew's St.
Built by William Parker, Mayor of Plymouth and a noted privateer, in early C17. Contains museum of early Plymouth history. Open Tu-F 10-5.30, (Apr-Sept Sa & BHs 10-5).

National Marine Aquarium, The Barbican.
Britain's biggest, Europe's deepest Aquarium; specimens mainly from local waters. Octopi, crabs, lobsters, starfish, conger eels. Open daily 10-6 (-5 in winter). 01752 220084 www.national-aquarium.co.uk

1690 Devonshire Regiment fight with King William 111 at the Battle of the Boyne.

1698 Samuel Darker sets up first permanent printing press in Exeter.

Smeaton's Tower, The Hoe

Plym Valley Railway, Coypool Road. 1 1/4 mile track under restoration from Marsh Mills station to Plym Bridge. 'Garratt' loco, largest in Europe. Steam and diesel operation on short length of track on selected weekends. Open all year 10-dusk. Shop and teas at W/E's.

Plymouth Arts Centre, 38 Looe Street. Three gallery spaces, independent cinema showing foreign, arthouse and independent film. Vegetarian restaurant. Open M-Sa 10-8.30, Su 6pm-8pm. 01752 206114 www.plymouthac.org.uk

Plymouth Boat Cruises. Cruises of Plymouth Naval Dockyards, 4 1/2 hours with on board commentary and landings. 8 Anderton Rise Millbrook 01752 822797 / 671166

Plymouth Dome, The Hoe. An award-winning visitor centre to experience the history, adventure and exploration of Plymouth, the sights and smells of an Elizabethan street, a man o' war, space age technology. Open daily from 9. 01752 603300

Prysten House, Finewell Street. Oldest building in Plymouth, probably C15, to house clergy visiting St Andrew's Church. Contains Plymouth Tapestry, and the "Finewell" and Courtyard. Open all year M-Sa 10-3.30 except BHs. 01752 661414

National Marine Aquarium

Smeaton's Tower, The Hoe. Famous lighthouse built in the 1750s recently restored. 93 stone steps. Open daily Mar-Oct 10-4, Oct-Mar Tu-Sa 10-4. 01752 603300

Summerskill's Brewery, Pompflett Farm Industrial Estate. Plymouth's oldest craft brewery. Brewers of prize-winning beers. 01752 481283

The Elizabethan House, New St., 400 year old timber framed house, managed by the National Trust as a shop and information centre. Open W-Su 10-5 & BH Ms. 01752 304774

The Green House, Chelson Meadow. Fun Hands-on sustainable waste exhibition centre, aimed at teaching about waste disposal in a fun way. Giant Hamster Wheel, Underground Cave, Colin the Can, enormous sorting machine. Riverside Cafe. Open Tu-Sa 10-5. 01752 482392 www.thegreenhouseplymouth.org.uk

The Royal Citadel. England's most important C17 fortress. Fine Baroque gateway with nearly a mile of massive ramparts. Historic guns. Royal Chapel of St Katherine. HQ of 29 Commando Regiment Royal Artillery. Access by guided tours only, daily May-Sept. Ticket sales from TIC.

1698 Thomas Newcomen of Dartmouth invents atmospheric steam pumping engine.

1698 Traveller and chronicler, Celia Fiennes visits Exeter, and marvels at the immense output of serge cloth. The most commercially productive area of Britain.

Plymouth Arts & Crafts...

Artframe Gallery, 61 Cornwall St. Features include paintings, limited edition prints, hand-made sculptures, ceramics and glass by local and international artists. Open M-Sa 9.30-5. 01752 227127

Barbican Gallery, 15 The Parade. Large selection of original oil and watercolour paintings. Resident artist Nicholas Lewis painting Th & F. Open M-Sa, 11-5, Su 11-4. Closed Tu. 15 The Parade 01752 661052 www.barbicangallery.com

Clayart, 57 Southside St., The Barbican. A creative cafe where customers paint their own designs on ceramics. Open daily. 01752 665565 www.clayart.co.uk

The Lenkiewicz Foundation, The Barbican

Lenkiewicz Foundation, The Barbican. Trust dedicated to the work of the late Robert Oscar Lenkiewicz (1941-2002); Artist and Plymouth personality of great verve and renown. Paintings and prints on show. Open office hours. 01752 668266 www.robertlenkiewicz.co.uk

New Street Gallery, 38 New Street. Paintings by leading contemporary artists; figurative and abstract work. Open M 12-4, Tu-Sa 10-4. 01752 221450

Somerville Gallery, 25 Mayflower St. One of the South West's larger galleries promoting original works from local artists especially Robert Lenkiewicz. Open 9.30-4. 01752 221600 www.somerville.com

Special Places to Visit...

Antony Woodland Gardens. Privately owned by the Carew Pole Garden Trust has 100 acres of woodland with 300 types of camellias bordering the Lynher River. Open Tu, W, Th & W/Es Mar-Oct 11-5.30. (A8)

Cotehele House ss/nt

Antony House & Gardens (NT). Built for Sir William Carew from 1711-1721 and considered the most distinguished example of early C18 architecture in Cornwall. Colonnades, panelled rooms and family portraits. Open 4 Apr-31 Oct Tu, W, Th & BH M's 1.30-5.30 (also Su June-Aug). (A8)

Buckland Abbey (NT) C13 Cistercian abbey bought by the grandfather of Sir Richard Grenville, and later the home of Sir Francis Drake. Now houses period rooms and museum of Drake relics including Drake's Drum, 3 1/2 acre shrub and herb garden and fine tithe barn. Estate walks. Craft workshops. Holiday family activities. Open daily Apr-Oct except Th 10.30-5.30. Nov-Mar W/Es 2-5. Shop and Refreshments. (D3) 01822 853607

Calstock Viaduct. 12 arch viaduct built to carry railway wagons from local mines to Calstock Quay where the wagons were raised and lowered in a lift. (B3)

Cotehele Gallery, The Quay. Showcasing professional artists and makers from the South West in seven exhibitions annually. Open daily Feb to Christmas - Summer 11.30-5, Winter 11.30-4.30. (A3)

Cotehele House (NT). Medieval house of grey granite (built 1485-1627) in romantic position overlooking the River Tamar and Devon beyond. For centuries, the Edgcumbe family home containing original furniture, C17 tapestries, armour and needlework. The gardens lie on several levels. Medieval dovecote. Ancient clock in chapel. Refreshment and shop. Open daily except F (house closed), 18 Mar-31 Oct 11-5 (4.30 in Oct). Gardens open all year 10.30-dusk. (A2)

Cotehele Quay (NT). Picturesque C18 and C19 buildings beside the River Tamar. A small outstation of the National Maritime Museum and berth for the restored Tamar sailing barge. 'Shamrock'. Museum and tea room. Open daily Apr-Oct. (A3)

Garden House, Buckland Monachorum. Breathtaking terraced walled garden surrounding ruins of medieval vicarage. Innovative with stunning colours. Tearoom and plant sales. Open daily Mar-Oct 10.30-5. 01822 854769 (D3) www.thegardenhouse.org.uk

Mary Newman's Cottage, 48 Culver St. C15 Cottage of Mary Newman, first wife of Sir Francis drake. Furniture supplied by the Victoria and Albert Museum. Open May-Sept Th 12-4 and BH M's 11-4. (A7)

1700 Exeter build a poor house and establish a Corporation for the Poor.

1700 At least 200 Devon ships trade with Newfoundland.

Royal Albert Bridge

Morwellham Quay.
Reconstruction of the busy C19 river port serving copper and arsenic mines, and its associated canals and railways. Workshops, 3 museums. C19 farm with animals, quays, raised railways. People in period costumes. Open daily 10-5.30 (closes 4.30 in winter). Last adm. 3.30, winter 2.30. Tearoom and shop. (B2) 01822 832766 www.morwellham-quay.co.uk

Mount Edgcumbe House & Park. Sensitively restored Tudor mansion in beautiful landscaped parkland. Formal English, French and Italian Gardens. National Camellia Collection. Park and gardens open daily all year. House and Earl's Garden open Apr-Sept W-Su & BH's 11-4.30. (B10)

Royal Albert Bridge. An iron single-track railway bridge built by I.K. Brunel in 1859, his last great feat of engineering. (B7)

Saltram House (NT). Largest country house in Devon, dating from the mid C18 with Tudor remnants. Mirror Room, Library, Chinese Chippendale bedroom. Furniture, plaster and woodwork. Pictures include 14 Reynolds portraits. Great Kitchen and stables. Garden with Orangery, shrubs and trees. Landscaped park. Open daily Apr-Oct except F 12-5. Garden open W/Es in winter 11-4. Park all year dawn til dusk. Restaurant, gallery (see below) and shop. (E9) 01752 336546

The Chapel Gallery, Saltram (NT). Contemporary works in Sculptural Ceramics, pottery, jewellery, prints, paintings, automata, glass and furniture. Events. Open W/Es Jan-Feb 11-4, Mar-Dec Sa-Th. (E9) 01752 347852

Tamar Valley Donkey Park.
Donkey sanctuary, Eeyore's Souvenir Store, woodland walk, cafe. Open daily Mar-Oct 10-5.30, W/Es Feb, Mar, Nov, Dec. Closed Christmas to end Jan. (A2) 01822 834072 www.donkeypark.com

Yelverton Paperweight Centre. Collection contains examples of the work of glass artists from studios of Saint Louis, Baccarat, Caithness, Strathearn, Whitefriars and individuals such as Paul Ysart and John Deacons. Free. Open daily Apr-Oct & 1-24 Dec, 10-5. Rest of the year, W/Es only or by appointment. (E3) 01822 854250 www.paperweightcentre.co.uk

Towns of Interest...

Calstock.
Attractive old river port on the Tamar. Steep wooded riverbank and the abundance of fruit growing provide a splendid site in spring, 12 arch viaduct. Numerous disused mining chimneys and engine houses haunt the landscape. (B3)

Saltash. Attractive river port with steep streets running down to Tamar estuary. C18 Guildhall. May Fair - 1st week. Regatta - June 3rd week. (A7)

The Great Kitchen, Saltram House ss/nt

1715 Construction of the Exeter Canal completed.

1727 John Gay's Beggar's Opera runs for 62 nights in London – a resounding success.

The Armada Memorial, The Hoe

Where to Eat & Drink in The City Centre...

Bistro-One, 68 Ebrington Street, Charles Cross. Run by Stephen Barrett, food and wine writer. Opens for breakfast, lunch and dinner. Special evenings dedicated to poetry, wine and Art. Expect an Interesting wine list. Fish from the Barbican, Game from Dartmoor. Open M-Sa 10-2.30, W-Sa 7-10pm. 01752 313315 www.bistro-one.co.uk

Chloe's, Gil Akaster House, Princess Street. Galllic and formal with crisp linen provides an air of class. Opens for coffee and pastries at 8 am Tu-F, Sa from 9. Ideal for lunch, or pre and post-theatre, dining. Cuisine is Classic with a touch of the New. Open 8-3, 5.30-Midnight. 01752 201523 www.chloesrestaurant.co.uk

Tanners Restaurant, Prysten House, Finewell Street. Opened by the Tanner Brothers in 1999 who have since reached celebrity TV status. Enjoy dining in Plymouth's oldest surviving building c.1498. Open Tu-Sa 12-2.30, 7-9.30. 01752 252001. www.tannersrestaurant.com

Fishing Boats, The Barbican

Where to Eat & Drink at The Barbican...

Monty's Coffee Shop, 13 The Barbican. All-day breakfasts, and a fine selection of coffees. A comfortable and friendly place to hang out. Open daily 9-7. 01752 252877

Piermasters Seafood Restaurant, 33 Southside Street. The original; the oldest seafood eatery in the City set opposite the old fish market. Full blackboard menu. Open daily for lunch, 12-2, and dinner 7-10. T 01752 229345 www.piermastersrestaurant.com

Yukisan, 51 Notte Street. The first Japanese restaurant in Devon! You can eat on three floors, on chairs or in the authentic manner, on cushions. Whichever, you chose, you are in for a Sushi feast. Open daily 11.30am-11.30pm. 01752 250240 www.yukisan.co.uk

Where to Eat & Drink in The Outer Reaches...

Seawings Restaurant, Lawrence Road, Mount Batten Pier, Plymouth. On the Eastern side of the City providing spectacular sea views. Cuisine is Modern English, fish a speciality, of course. Breakfasts from 8 am. Child friendly. Open Tu-Sa 8am-9.30pm, Su 10-5. 01752 402233.

The Brasserie, Mayflower Marina, Richmond Walk. On the Western side of the City overlooking a mass of sail and plastic (hulls). The scallop centre of the south-west. They have compiled 50 scallop dishes. Today, you may chose from 6. Nutritious "Slow Food" menus and light meals. Open daily 11-3, 7-11. 01752 500008

B&B's...

South Hooe Captain's House, Holes Hole, Nr Bere Alston. Quite a find. A rural idyll set in ten acres of woodland overlooking the Tamar. Free range eggs, home-grown vegetables and your own private jetty, and log fires in winter. Too much. Writer's workshops. 01822 840329. (A4)

The Basket Factory, Weir Quay. A comfortable house set within a large garden overlooks the Tamar. Children and dogs by arrangement.

The Barbican

1731 Great fire in Tiverton.

1741 Aug 27. Foundation stone of Devon and Exeter Hospital laid.

One of England's greater National Parks; the Forest of Dartmoor covers 365 square miles and contains the highest ground in England south of the Peak District. On its desolate moorland tracks the wanderer can believe they are further from a public road than anywhere in the country, but on the fringes lush valleys lead down on every side to thick woodland, green vegetation and picturesque villages.

Geologically, Dartmoor was formed by the up swelling millions of years ago of a vast mass of molten granite, bursting through the earth and forming a group of colossal and terrifying mountains. Softened and rounded through time, their summits cracked in pieces by the elements of snow and ice. All that remains are the "tors", piles of rock, often in uncanny shapes, which surmount the present day flattened landscape.

The main mass of Dartmoor is to a large extent a desolate peat bog, a challenge to the experienced walker, but to the east, where the rivers Teign and Dart carve their way tortuously through the rocks in deep gorges, is a more friendly landscape of grassy uplands with easily accessible viewpoints - Hound Tor, Haytor and Bonehill Down.

Dartmoor is well known for its attractive herds of ponies with their varied colouring - apparently wild but in fact individually owned. Every year they are rounded up and branded with the owner's mark. Feeding them is strictly prohibited, and in the interest of the animals who have plenty to eat, they must not be tempted to wander towards you across the roads.

Other wildlife includes foxes, badgers and otters - also the occasional adder. Fallow, roe and Sitka deer can often be seen, but the red deer of Exmoor have never penetrated the area. Buzzards, kestrels and various Birds of Prey are frequently seen, as well as the wheatear, while crows, ravens and the skylark are fairly commonplace. A variety of insects inhabit the Moor, and the interesting insect-eating sundew plant can often be identified. Heather, bracken and whortleberries grow in profusion in the drier areas, and in the woodland there is much to interest the student of mosses and lichens. These can often be seen covering the roadside stonewalls.

The Moor abounds in prehistoric remains. There are also many deserted medieval villages with remains of the traditional "longhouse" buildings. For centuries tin mining has been an important activity and there is much to interest the industrial archaeologist, including abandoned tramways and railways of more recent times - notably the Princetown Railway, once the highest railway line in England, now a moderately easy mountain bike track.

Many historic legends surround the Moor. Conan Doyle's "Hound of the Baskervilles" is based reputedly on Fox Tor. The macabre story of the man who killed his horse and unavailingly sought shelter within its carcase took place supposedly at Childe's Tomb nearby. A sadder tale is commemorated at Jay's Grave near Manaton where flowers grow mysteriously over the place of suicide of a betrayed sweetheart.

Saddle Tor

Bowerman's Nose

The Tors

Highest on the Moor are Yes Tor and High Willhays (2038 ft) in the north. To the east, are the fine viewpoints of Kes Tor and Hay Tor, the easily recognised shapes of Hound Tor and Bowerman's Nose, and Buckland Beacon with the Ten Commandments carved in the rock by a religious dissident. Near Tavistock are the westward-looking viewpoints of Pew Tor and Vixen Tor, and the isolated church-crowned summit of Brent Tor.

The Valleys

The River Dart rises in the Moor and crosses its centre. At Postbridge there is a fine clapper bridge, and lower down is Dartmeet, a famous beauty spot. On the eastern fringe the Teign flows for many miles through deep wooded valleys, while on the Tavistock side is the Tavy with its spectacular gorge. Smaller rivers draining the Moor are the Okement, and on the south side the Plym, Avon and Erme, each deeply cleaved into the landscape.

Crocken Tor

Once the meeting place of the Stannary Court, arbiters of the tin industry in the Middle Ages. Nearby is Wistman's Wood, a grove of gnarled and twisted trees, the surviving remains of primeval forest. Around here can also be seen parts of the Devonport Leat, an ancient water supply. In the most desolate part of the Moor is Cranmere Pool, a sinister bog and site of the first of the Dartmoor Postboxes (the custom being for visitors to leave a card and note the lapse of time before the next visitor came to collect and post it).

Walking on Dartmoor

Dartmoor offers opportunities for every kind of walker from the easy family stroll through woodland and over grassy hillsides to the long distance endurance test for those who prefer to make their own way across trackless country by map, compass and GPS. Most of the Moor is common land with free access to unfenced country, but there are restricted military training areas in the north-west. These are usually accessible at weekends and school holidays - enquiries should be made

locally. A comprehensive programme of guided walks, ranging from 1 1/2 to 6 hours duration is available, through summer starting from a variety of centres. For those who would rather go it alone there are many detailed books available - the following are just a few suggestions. The Ordnance Survey 1:25,000 Explorer series are recommended for use on the Moor.

The Moor is crossed by several ancient trackways which can still be traced. The Lych Way from Bellever to Lydford was used for funeral processions.

Short Walks - up to 3 hours

1. Sheepstor from Burrator Reservoir.
2. Black Tor & the Meavy Valley from the Princetown-Yelverton road.
3. Birch Tor & Vitifer Mine from Warren House.
4. Dr Blackall's Drive.
5. Vixen, Henwood & Pew Tors from Merrivale.
6. Bench Tor from Venford Reservoir.
7. Grimspound & Hamelton Tor.
8. Great Hound & Grae Tors.
9. Hay Tor & the Granite Tramway.
10. Belstone Tor from Belstone.
11. Bonehill & Honeybag Tors.

Longer Walks - up to 6 hours

1. Staldon from Cornwood.
2. Ditsworthy, Eylesburrow & Nuns Cross from Burrator.
3. Duckspool from Whiteworks.
4. Ryders Hill from Holne.
5. Cranmere Pool from Okehampton Military Rd
6. Shiel Top from Cornwood.
7. Doe & Great Links Tor from Lydford.

Walks for the experienced are better left for individual planning, but there are two historic routes which can be traced; the Abbot's Way (Buckfast-Princetown) and the Lych Way (Bellever-Lydford). A complete traverse of the Moor can be made up the Erme Valley from Ivybridge, past Childe's Tomb to Two Bridges, thence north via Cut Hill to Cranmere Pool and down to Okehampton.

The Two Moors Way provides a 100 mile walk from Ivybridge to Lynton, skirting the fringes of Dartmoor and continuing through pastoral mid-Devon, and across Exmoor.

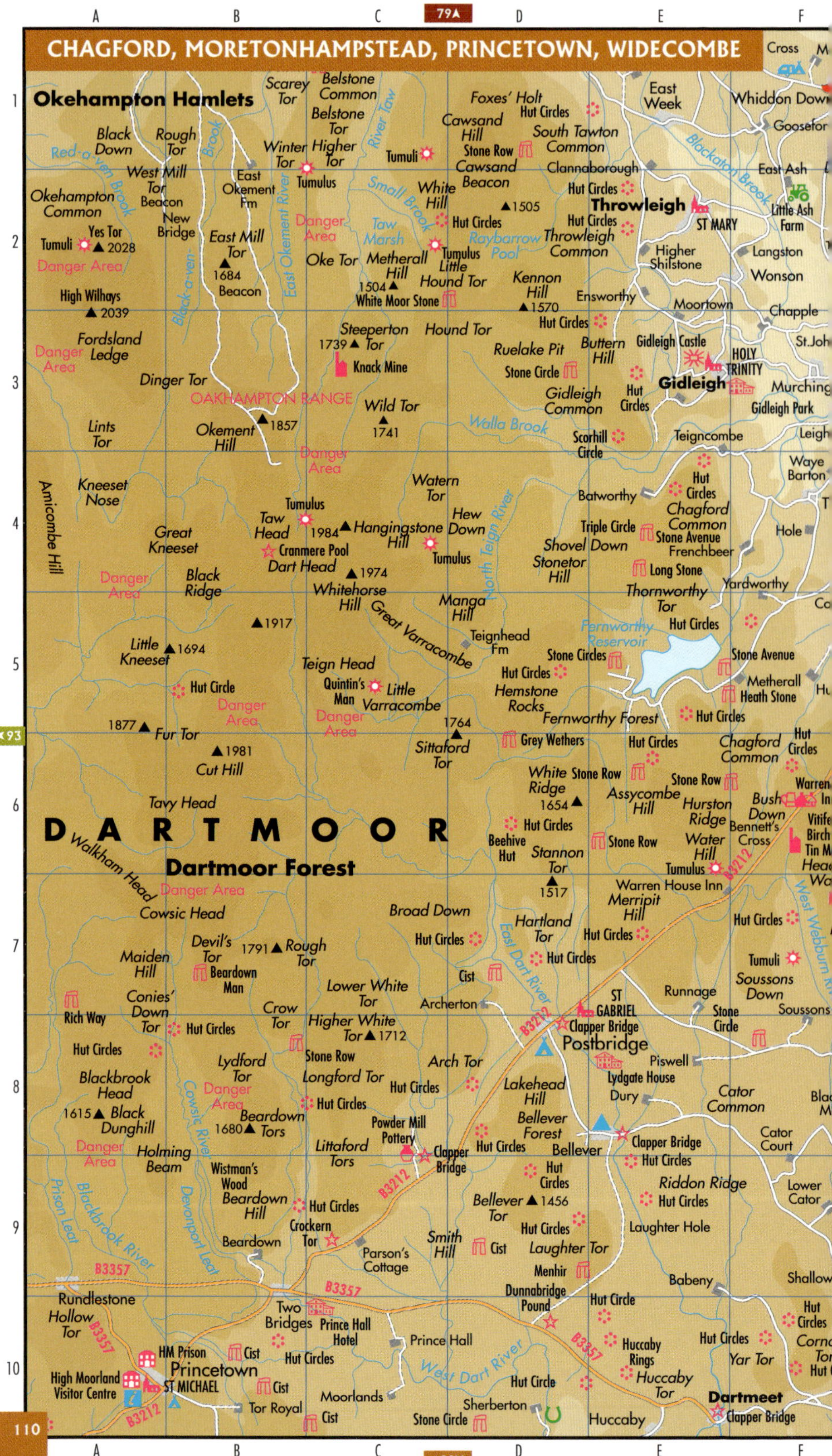
79
A
B
C
D
E
F
1
2
3
4
5
6
7
8
9
10
93
128
Okehampton Hamlets
Scarey Tor
Belstone Common
Belstone Tor
Higher Tor
Winter Tor
River Taw
Tumuli
Foxes' Holt
Hut Circles
Cawsand Hill
South Tawton Common
Stone Row
Cawsand Beacon
Clannaborough
East Week
Whiddon Down
Goosefor
Blackaton Brook
East Ash
Little Ash Farm
Cross
Black Down
Rough Tor
Red-a-ven Brook
West Mill Tor
Beacon
East Okement Fm
Tumulus
Small Brook
White Hill
1505
Hut Circles
Throwleigh
ST MARY
Okehampton Common
New Bridge
East Mill Tor
1684 Beacon
East Okement River
Danger Area
Taw Marsh
Raybarrow Pool
Throwleigh Common
Higher Shilstone
Langston
Wonson
Tumuli
2028
Yes Tor
Danger Area
Oke Tor
Metherall Hill
Little Hound Tor
Kennon Hill
1570
Ensworthy
Moortown
Chapple
High Willhays
2039
Black-a-ven Brook
1504
White Moor Stone
Fordsland Ledge
Danger Area
Steeperton Tor
1739
Hound Tor
Ruelake Pit
Buttern Hill
Gidleigh Castle
HOLY TRINITY
St. Joh
Knack Mine
Stone Circle
Gidleigh
Murching
Dinger Tor
OAKHAMPTON RANGE
Wild Tor
1741
Gidleigh Common
Hut Circles
Gidleigh Park
Lints Tor
Okement Hill
1857
Walla Brook
Scorhill Circle
Teigncombe
Leigh
Danger Area
Waye Barton
Kneeset Nose
Amicombe Hill
Tumulus
Waterm Tor
Batworthy
Hut Circles
Chagford Common
Taw Head
1984
Hangingstone Hill
Hew Down
North Teign River
Triple Circle
Stone Avenue
Frenchbeer
Hole
Great Kneeset
Cranmere Pool
Dart Head
Tumulus
Shovel Down
Stonetor Hill
Long Stone
Danger Area
Black Ridge
1974
Whitehorse Hill
Manga Hill
Thornworthy Tor
Yardworthy
1917
Great Varracombe
Fernworthy Reservoir
Hut Circles
Little Kneeset
1694
Teignhead Fm
Stone Circles
Stone Avenue
Teign Head
Hut Circles
Metherall
Hut Circle
Quintin's Man
Little Varracombe
Hemstone Rocks
Heath Stone
Danger Area
Danger Area
Fernworthy Forest
Hut Circles
1877
Fur Tor
1764
Grey Wethers
Hut Circles
Chagford Common
Hut Circles
1981
Cut Hill
Sittaford Tor
White Stone Row Ridge
Stone Row
Assycombe Hill
Warren
Tavy Head
1654
Hurston Ridge
Bush Down
Bennett's Cross
DARTMOOR
Hut Circles
Beehive Hut
Stone Row
Water Hill
Vitife
Birch
Tin M
Walkham Head
Dartmoor Forest
Stannon Tor
Tumulus
B3212
Head
Danger Area
1517
Warren House Inn
West Webburn River
Cowsic Head
Broad Down
Hartland Tor
Merripit Hill
Hut Circles
Maiden Hill
Devil's Tor
1791
Rough Tor
Hut Circles
East Dart River
Hut Circles
Hut Circles
Tumuli
Beardown Man
Cist
Soussons Down
Conies' Down Tor
Lower White Tor
Archerton
Runnage
Stone Circle
Soussons
Rich Way
Crow Tor
Higher White Tor
1712
ST GABRIEL
Hut Circles
B3212
Clapper Bridge
Postbridge
Hut Circles
Lydford Tor
Stone Row
Arch Tor
Piswell
Blackbrook Head
Longford Tor
Lydgate House
Danger Area
Hut Circles
Lakehead Hill
Dury
Cator Common
1615
Black Dunghill
Cowsic River
Beardown Tors
Hut Circles
Bellever Forest
1680
Powder Mill Pottery
Danger Area
Holming Beam
Littaford Tors
Clapper Bridge
Hut Circles
Bellever
Clapper Bridge
Cator Court
Hut Circles
Wistman's Wood
B3212
Hut Circles
Riddon Ridge
Lower Cator
Prison Leat
Blackbrook River
Beardown Hill
Hut Circles
Bellever Tor
1456
Hut Circles
Devonport Leat
Crockern Tor
Hut Circles
Laughter Hole
Beardown
Smith Hill
Parson's Cottage
Cist
Laughter Tor
B3357
Menhir
Babeny
Shallow
Rundlestone
B3357
Dunnabridge Pound
Hut Circle
Hollow Tor
Two Bridges
Prince Hall Hotel
Hut Circles
B3357
Prince Hall
Huccaby Rings
Hut Circles
Corn Tor
HM Prison
Cist
Hut Circles
West Dart River
Yar Tor
Princetown
Huccaby Tor
High Moorland Visitor Centre
ST MICHAEL
Cist
Moorlands
Hut Circle
Dartmeet
B3212
Tor Royal
Cist
Stone Circle
Sherberton
Huccaby
Clapper Bridge

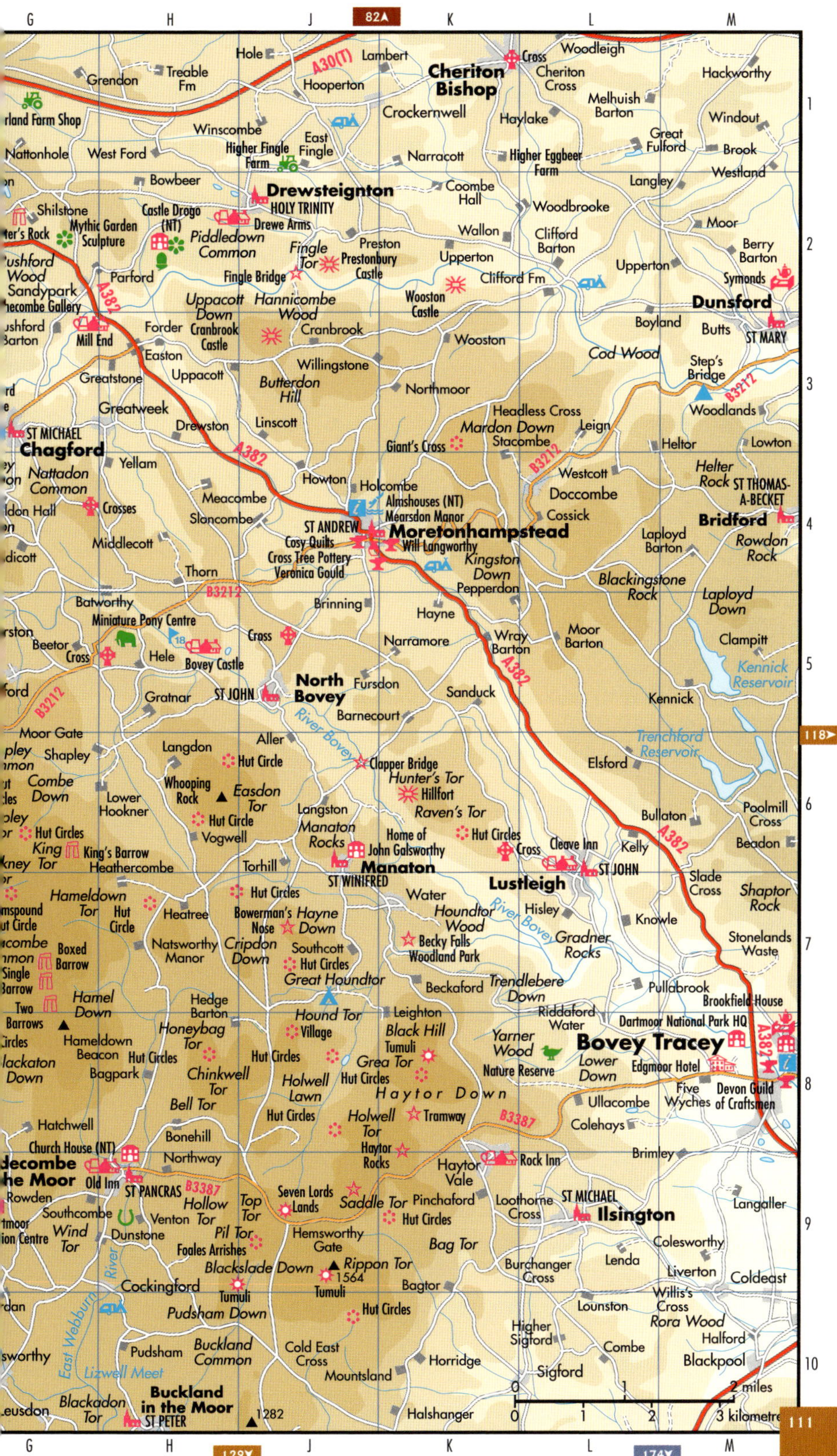

Cheriton Bishop
Drewsteignton
Chagford
Moretonhampstead
North Bovey
Manaton
Lustleigh
Bovey Tracey
Dunsford
Bridford
Ilsington
Buckland in the Moor
Haytor Down
Kennick Reservoir
Trenchford Reservoir
River Bovey

CHAGFORD

One of the four "Stannary Towns" given to manage the medieval tin industry, and thereafter an affluent little town for many years until the Agricultural Depressions of the 1870s and 80s. The far-thinking vicar of the time organised a modern sewage system to encourage tourism. This endeavour moved George Haynes to introduce electric lights, the first town west of London, to do so. The town, and surrounding hamlets are popular with the Retired, although there are always young persons enjoying the health shops and al fresco drinking. Has one of the few ironmongers (stores that sell every device known to man) left in the country. The surrounding hamlets and farms abound with sturdy, Dartmoor architecture. The Devon Longhouse is much in evidence; the vernacular design, of a long house usually built by a farmer in an L-shape within a courtyard. A comparable design would be a Cotswold house of similar proportions, and magnitude. Chagford is always a pleasant place to visit. It does lack a seriously good pub but makes up for this in other ways. You can buy a wet drink in the Three Crowns. Not a happy place in 1642 for the young poet Sydney Godolphin who was slaughtered in the porch by Cromwell's troops whilst defending the King's name. He returns to curse pub bores. The town has a number of delis/coffee houses, and health shops with cafes. And, an expensive restaurant, 22 Mill Street. (G3)

The Old Railway Track, Princetown

Spinster's Rock

Churchyard, Church of St Michael Archangel

Mythic Garden Sculpture ss

Special Places to Visit...

Church of St Michael the Archangel. A stone's throw from the aforementioned inn. For yet another poor soul met a sticky end; Mary Whiddon was shot dead by a jealous suitor beside the church steps, on her Wedding Day in 1641. Some scholars believe her sad end inspired the tale of Lorna Doone. Inside the church, some fine creations; a parclose screen, carved pulpit and roof bosses of rabbits and hares. (G3)

Monks Withecombe Gallery. Changing exhibitions of contemporary West Country artists in a light and airy studio overlooking the National Park. Open Tu-Sa 11-6. (G2) www.strategic-art.com

Mythic Garden Sculpture, Stone Lane. 5-acre arboretum presenting an annual sculpture exhibition. Collections of Birch and Alder trees in a landscaped water and woodland setting. Open daily mid-May to Sept 2-6. (G2) 01647 231311 www.mythicgarden.com

The Old (Bishop's) House , Chagford

1743 Aug 14. Fire destroys 450 homes in Crediton.

1750 10,000,000 gallons of cider were made for local consumption.

Sheep Pastures, Drewsteignton

MORETONHAMPSTEAD

A busy town, beware of the tricky road junction as you enter. Like many a Dartmoor town it profited from the medieval wool industry but has little to show for it save the church and the handsome almshouses built in 1637, for a great fire in 1845 destroyed all but a few of the medieval and Tudor buildings. Today, a centre for many craftsmen, and a convenient place from which to explore the Moor. Coffee shop with outside tables. (K4)

Arts & Crafts...

Contemporary Studio Pottery, Mill St. Co-operative run by six experienced potters. Holds 4 master classes per year. Open M & W-Sa 11-5. (G4)
www.contemporarystudiopottery.co.uk

Cosy Quilts, Underbow Cottage, Bow Lane. Traditional or contemporary quilts and wall hangings. (J4) 01647 440883

Cross Tree Pottery. Ceramic sculpture and murals. (J4) 01647 440782

Veronica Gould, The Unitarian Chapel. Hand painted silk wall hangings. Open M-Sa 10-6. (K4) The Unitarian Chapel Cross Street 01647 441199
www.veronicagould.com

Will Langworthy Pottery, 6 Ford St. Hand-thrown porcelain, crystalline glazes. Open M-Sa 10-5 and alternate Su. (K4) 01647 440993

PRINCETOWN

You may wish to visit this isolated village out of curiosity, and wonder at the poor, misguided souls who have thrown their lives away, to be incarcerated in this dark, and dismal place. It is eerie, and is penalised by the full force of weather, from the north and east. And, you may thank god for your good fortune, and freedom, and move on to warmer climes. The prison was built in 1808 by French and American prisoners of war. The officer's mess is an impressive building, now a Dartmoor National Park Centre. There are tearooms and gift shops. An easy off-road cycling route along the old railway tracks starts from here heading in an easterly direction. (A10)

Drawing Room, Castle Drogo

1755 Carpet manufacture begun by Thomas Whitty in Axminster at Court House.

1758 Death of Bampfylde Moore Carew at Bickleigh. King of the Gypsies and "Grand Master of the honourable fraternity of beggars".

WIDECOMBE IN THE MOOR

Set in a bowl of a valley surrounded by rugged country. Journey in from the Haytor road and what impresses is the perfect shape of the church, "The Cathedral of the Moor", and the isolation of the village, originally built by tin miners. The village is famous for the song about Widecombe Fair, held on the second Tuesday of September. Be advised, arrive early. And learn your lines, thus:

Tom Pearce, Tom Pearce, lend me thy grey mare,

All along, down along, out along, lee-

For I want to go to Widecombe Fair,

Wi' Bill Brewer, Jan Stewer, Peter Gurney, Peter Davy,

Dan'l Whiddon, Harry Hawk,

Old Uncle Tom Cobleigh and all,

Chorus - Old Uncle Cobleigh and all.

Special Places to Visit...

Parish Church of St Pancras.
The striking tower rises to 120 feet. It is a pinnacled battlement design. The interior shows two aisles with 6 bays and a painted screen. In 1638 a thunderstorm struck, killing four of the congregation, an event commemorated by a poem:- "Some had their skin all over scorcht, yet no harm in their cloaths." (H9)

Widecombe Church House (NT)
C16 brewhouse, later a village school. Incorporates Sexton's Cottage, now the National Trust shop. Open Spring BH to early Sept Tu Th 2-5. NT centre Good F-Oct daily 11-6. (H9) 01364 621321

Where to Eat, Drink & Be Merry...

Old Inn.
Cosy and traditional with flagstone floors. Popular so book! Large portions of food. Children and dogs welcomed. (H9) 01364 621207

Wayside Cafe.
Delicious home-made cakes cooked using traditional family recipes. Look out for the big teapot! (H9) 01364 621313

River Teign, Fingle Bridge

Drewsteignton Cottages

Widecombe at Dusk

Widecombe in the Moor

1759 John Smeaton completes the third lighthouse on Eddystone Rock.

1760 Ramillies frigate wrecked off Bolt Head with loss of 500 lives.

Special Places to Visit...

Becky Falls.
50-acre estate of woodland, rivers and waterfalls plus nature reserve and walking trails with special interest to woodland ecology; mosses and lichens. Visitors in the past have included Bronze Age man, and the writers Rupert Brooke and Virginia Woolf. Café. Open daily 24 Mar-4 Nov 10-5. (K7) 01647 221259 www.beckyfalls.com

Castle Drogo
(NT). Granite castle built by Lutyens between 1910 and 1930 for Julius Drewe, the founder of Home and Colonial Stores. Varied collection of furniture and paintings. Terraced gardens and croquet lawn. Superb views over the Teign Gorge. Open daily Apr-Oct except F 11-5.30. Reduced charge for garden and grounds. Restaurant and shop. (H2) 01647 433306 www.nationaltrust.org

Dartmoor Prison Museum, Princetown.
Contains part of the famous prison built between 1805 and 1808. Discover the lives of the French and American prisoners of war held here. Open Tu-Sa, Nov-Mar 9.30-12.30 & 1.30-4.30. Apr-Oct 9.30-430. (A10) 01822 890305

Gidleigh Castle.
Ruined Norman keep, with church adjoining. Not open but visible from the road. (E3)

Higher Fingle Farm.
Soil Association approved farm breeding poultry; geese, ducks, turkeys and chickens. See website for details. (J1) 01647 281281 www.exmoor-organic.co.uk

Little Ash Farm, Whiddon Down. Organic farm produce; Ruby Red beef, free range eggs from ducks, geese and chickens, vegetables, pies and puddings. (F2) 01647 231130 www.littleashfarm.com

Powder Mill Pottery, Nr Postbridge. Hand-made, glazed pots using the local clays found on Dartmoor. Shop selling Dartmoor arts and crafts. Cream teas. Open daily. (C8) 01822 880263 www.powdermillspottery.com

Stone Circle, Merrivale

The Miniature Pony Stud & Farm. Interact with miniature mares and their foals, tiny donkeys and a whole host of other friendly animals. Play areas, miniature farm, shops, restaurants and walks. Open East-1st Nov 10.30-Dusk. (H5) 01647 432400

Dartmoor Attractions...

Bowerman's Nose.
The word is a corruption of bowman, archer or huntsman. So the legend goes that Bowerman was a might hunter afraid of no man or beast and dismissive of crones. One day he disturbed a group of witches/crones, and in their disgust they turned him to stone. Access is via a short ascent from the road. Climbing is forbidden. (J7)

Standing Stone, Hemsworthy Gate

Castle Drogo ss/nt

Cranbrook Castle, Prestonbury Castle & Wooston Castle.
These three Iron Age forts near Drewsteignton were designed to protect families and their livestock from raiding parties. (J3/J4/K2)

Cranmere Pool. The first Letterbox site set up by James Perrott of Chagford in 1854. It can be a bleak, wet and boggy place. Quite a challenge in foul weather. Easier access now the Military road is open. (B4)

Dartmeet Bridge. Remains of C13 clapper bridge. A popular picnic spot, best avoided on bank holidays, and former gathering site for gypsies. Tea rooms at Badgers Holt. (E10)

Fingle Bridge. A popular beauty spot beside the River Teign. Waymarked walks lead off in all directions. There's a pub/tearoom to assuage your thirst, if need be. Steep lane descends from Drewsteignton, so beware of other traffic. (J2)

Haytor Rocks. The most visited rock formation on Dartmoor. It is easily accessed with car parking close to, but best seen at dawn or sunset when the molten granite appears to change colour and shape. At 1,499 feet with two granitee outcrops, it has been classified as an "Avenue Tor" due to the erosion of the central section. (J8)

Postbridge Clapper Bridge

Scorhill Circle

Grey Wethers Stone Circle. Two granite circles excavated in 1898, and restored in 1909. The northern circle has 20 stones and is 107 ft diameter, the southern has 29 with a diameter of approximately 115 feet. All the stones are about 4.5 feet. (D6)

Grimspound. Bronze Age village hut circle overlooked by Hookney Tor. A walled enclosure of about 4-acres, and it's situation is not strategically sound was most probably a farm. (G7)

Postbridge Clapper Bridge. One of Dartmoor's most visited beauty spots built in the C13 and C14. (D8)

Scorhill Circle. A Bronze Age circle with about 35 stones remaining from the original 70. Local legend has it that horses cannot be ridden through the circle. Try it. Waymarked access via Batworthy or Gidleigh. (E3)

Hound Tor.
Associated with the legend of Bowerman's Nose, for his hounds were too, turned to stone by the witches, and here they lie, scattered and forlorn. It also inspired Conan Doyle's *The Hound of the Baskervilles*. Some refuse to visit believing it is haunted and a dangerous place. It can be. In 1995, a 500-ton boulder came crashing down. Popular with rock climbers. (J8)

Wistman's Wood dp

1769 William Cookworthy set up the first British porcelain factory in Plymouth.

1786 Final meeting of the tinners Great Court held at Dunnabridge.

Wistman's Wood. According to legend, planted some 600 years ago by Isabella de Fortibus, Countess of Devon. What remains is a unique collection of stunted, gnarled and weatherbeaten oaks curiously interspersed amongst granite boulders. A sacred place populated by adders. A 40-minute walk beside the wall from Two Bridges. Not to be undertaken in mist, or fog. (B9)

The Drewe Arms

Pubs Serving Food…

Cleave Inn, Lustleigh.
C15 thatched pub with inglenook fireplaces and thick cob walls. Cosy and comfortable. Daily specials. Fine ales. Dogs and children welcome. (L6) 01647 277223

Drewe Arms, Drewsteignton.
Lovely old tables, simple decor and wholesome food. Formerly run by Mabel Mudge for 75 years, retiring at 99 in 1996. Her memory lives on. Children and dogs welcome. Accommodation. 01647 281224. (J2)

Rock Inn, Haytor Vale. A long-standing favourite. Never know who you might sit next to; Ex-Cabinet Ministers or a UN Ambassador. Friendly atmosphere and good, honest food. Log fires. Large garden. Accommodation. 01364 61305. (K9) www.rock-inn.co.uk

Warren House Inn, Nr Postbridge. Welcome site on a bleak and blustery day. Third highest Inn in England. Home cooked fare. Simple decor suits the Dartmoor landscape. (F6) 01822 880208

Special Places to Stay…

Bovey Castle.
Recently refurbished to exude the luxury, elegance and excitement of the 1920s. With castle staterooms, health and beauty spa, sporting activities including golf and 24 miles of trout and salmon fishing, cocktail bars, Art Deco dining and facilities for children. (H5) 01647 445016 www.boveycastle.com

Lydgate House, Postbridge.
Set in the heart of Dartmoor. Ideal for walking, pony trekking and golf. Home-cooked evening meal using local produce. Bedrooms have luxurious goose down duvets and pillows. Dogs welcome. No children under 12. (E8) 01822 880209 www.lydgatehouse.co.uk

Gidleigh Park ss

Haytor Rocks at Dawn

Gidleigh Park.
Recently refurbished interiors but the gastronomic delights will continue to spellbind you. Treat yourself and taste a morsel of Michael Caine's reputation. 15 rooms. Open for Lunch and Dinner. 01647 432367. (F3) www.gidleigh.com

Edgemoor Country House Hotel, Haytor Road.
Set in beautiful gardens on the edge of Dartmoor. The owners claim "Elegance without Pretension", and provide clean and neat decor. (M8) 01626 832466 www.edgemoor.co.uk

Mill End.
Comfortable old-style charm and superb restaurant. Fine walking and sportsman's base from which to explore the National Park. Private salmon and trout fishing. Dogs welcome. (G3) 01647 432282 www.millendhotel.com

Prince Hall Hotel, Two Bridges.
In the heart of Dartmoor and fine centre for walking, fishing, touring, relaxing. French style cuisine using local produce. Bedrooms with all facilities. Dogs welcome. (C10) 01822 890403 www.princehall.co.uk

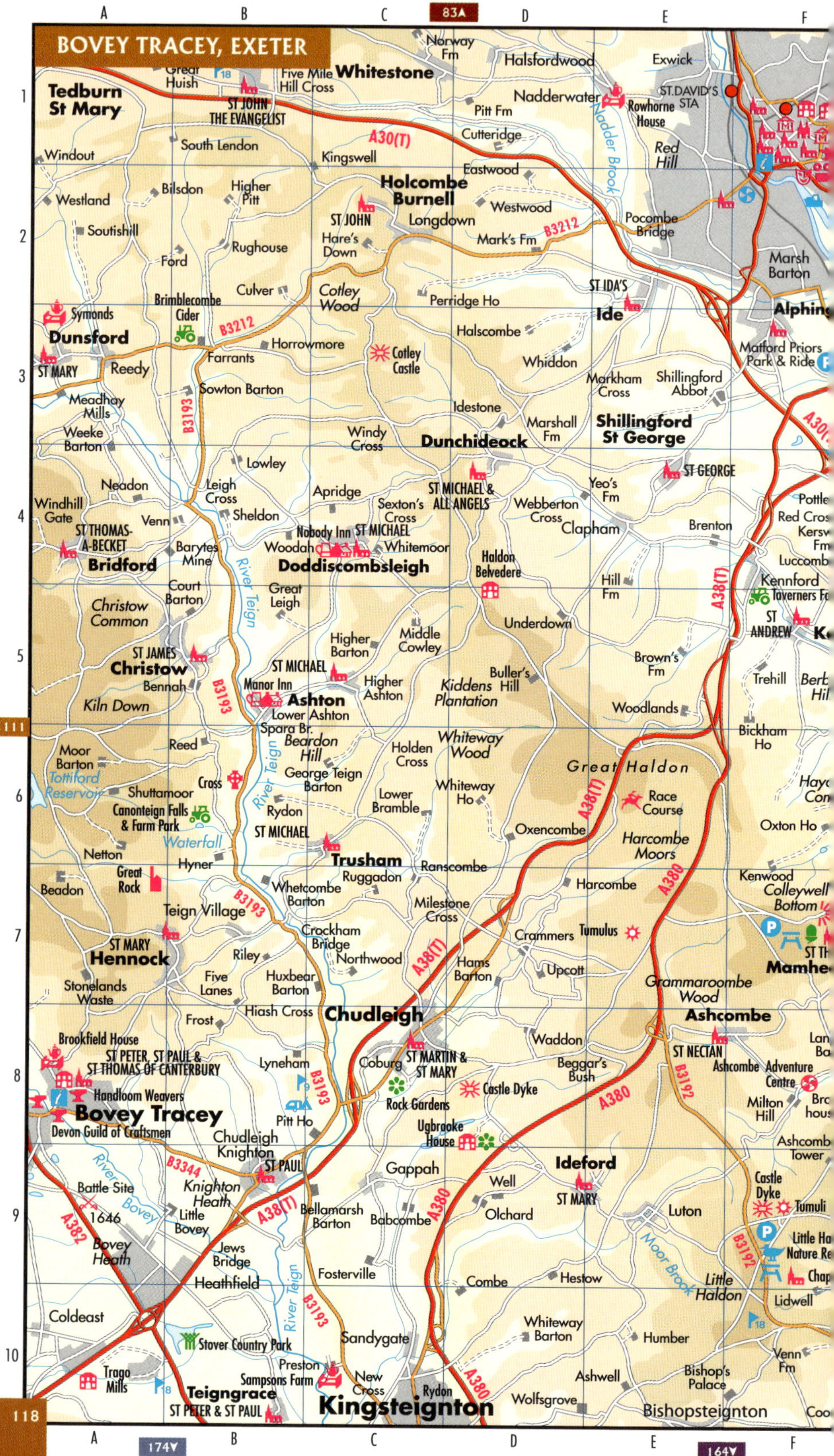
BOVEY TRACEY, EXETER
83
A
B
C
D
E
F
1
2
3
4
5
6
7
8
9
10
111
174
164
Tedburn St Mary
Great Huish
Five Mile Hill Cross
Whitestone
Norway Fm
Halsfordwood
Exwick
ST JOHN THE EVANGELIST
Nadderwater
Rowhorne House
ST.DAVID'S STA
Pitt Fm
Cutteridge
A30(T)
Nadder Brook
Red Hill
South Lendon
Windout
Kingswell
Eastwood
Bilsdon
Higher Pitt
Holcombe Burnell
Westland
Westwood
Pocombe Bridge
ST JOHN
Longdown
Soutishill
Hare's Down
Mark's Fm
B3212
Marsh Barton
Rughouse
Ford
Culver
Cotley Wood
ST IDA'S
Brimblecombe Cider
Perridge Ho
Ide
Alphing
Symonds
Dunsford
B3212
Horrowmore
Halscombe
Matford Priors Park & Ride
ST MARY
Reedy
Farrants
Cotley Castle
Whiddon
Markham Cross
Shillingford Abbot
Sowton Barton
Meadhay Mills
B3193
Idestone
Weeke Barton
Windy Cross
Dunchideock
Marshall Fm
Shillingford St George
Lowley
ST GEORGE
Neadon
Leigh Cross
Apridge
ST MICHAEL & ALL ANGELS
Yeo's Fm
Windhill Gate
Sexton's Cross
Webberton Cross
Pottle
Sheldon
Red Cros
Venn
Clapham
Brenton
ST THOMAS-A-BECKET
Nobody Inn
ST MICHAEL
Kersv Fm
Barytes Mine
Woodah
Whitemoor
Bridford
Doddiscombsleigh
Haldon Belvedere
Luccomb
A38(T)
Kennford
Court Barton
River Teign
Great Leigh
Hill Fm
Taverners Fa
Christow Common
Underdown
ST ANDREW
Middle Cowley
Higher Barton
ST JAMES
Brown's Fm
Christow
ST MICHAEL
Buller's Hill
Trehill
Bennah
B3193
Manor Inn
Higher Ashton
Kiddens Plantation
Ashton
Kiln Down
Lower Ashton
Woodlands
Spara Br.
Bickham Ho
Beardon Hill
Whiteway Wood
Moor Barton
Reed
Holden Cross
Great Haldon
Tottiford Reservoir
Cross
George Teign Barton
Whiteway Ho
Race Course
Shuttamoor
River Teign
Lower Bramble
A38(T)
Canonteign Falls & Farm Park
Rydon
Oxencombe
Oxton Ho
Harcombe Moors
Waterfall
ST MICHAEL
Netton
Hyner
Trusham
Great Rock
Ranscombe
Ruggadon
Kenwood
Beadon
Whetcombe Barton
Harcombe
A380
Colleywell Bottom
B3193
Teign Village
Milestone Cross
Crockham Bridge
Crammers
Tumulus
ST MARY
Hennock
Riley
Northwood
A38(T)
Hams Barton
Upcott
Mamhe
Five Lanes
Huxbear Barton
Stonelands Waste
Grammaroombe Wood
Frost
Hiash Cross
Chudleigh
Ashcombe
Brookfield House
Waddon
ST NECTAN
ST PETER, ST PAUL & ST THOMAS OF CANTERBURY
Lyneham
ST MARTIN & ST MARY
Coburg
Beggar's Bush
Ashcombe Adventure Centre
B3192
Handloom Weavers
B3193
Castle Dyke
Rock Gardens
Milton Hill
A380
Bovey Tracey
Devon Guild of Craftsmen
Pitt Ho
Ugbrooke House
Chudleigh Knighton
Ashcomb Tower
B3344
River Bovey
ST PAUL
Gappah
Ideford
Castle Dyke
Battle Site
Knighton Heath
Well
Tumuli
1646
A38(T)
Bellamarsh Barton
ST MARY
A380
Luton
Little Bovey
Olchard
Babcombe
A382
Bovey Heath
Moor Brook
Little Ha Nature Re
Jews Bridge
B3192
Fosterville
Chap
Heathfield
Combe
Hestow
Little Haldon
River Teign
Lidwell
Coldeast
B3193
Whiteway Barton
Sandygate
Stover Country Park
Humber
Venn Fm
Preston
Trago Mills
New Cross
Ashwell
Bishop's Palace
Sampsons Farm
Rydon
Teigngrace
A380
Wolfsgrove
ST PETER & ST PAUL
Kingsteignton
Bishopsteignton
Coo

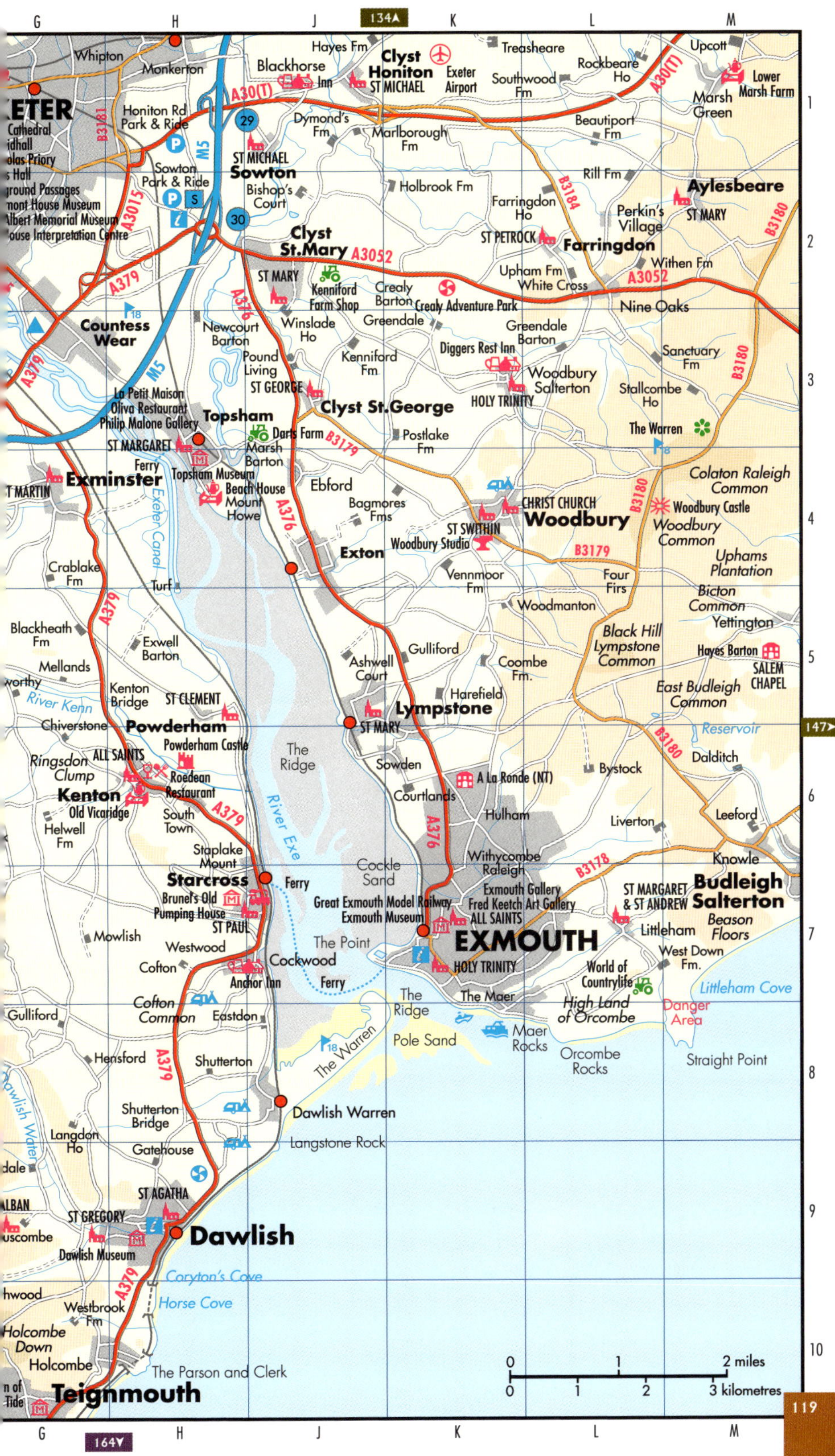
134
164
147
Exeter Airport
Clyst Honiton
Sowton
Clyst St.Mary
Aylesbeare
Farringdon
Countess Wear
Topsham
Clyst St.George
Woodbury Salterton
Exminster
Woodbury
Exton
Lympstone
Powderham
Kenton
Starcross
Cockwood
Dawlish Warren
EXMOUTH
Budleigh Salterton
Littleham
Dawlish
Teignmouth
River Exe
Exeter Canal
River Kenn
Pole Sand
Cockle Sand
The Ridge
The Point
The Warren
Langstone Rock
Orcombe Rocks
Maer Rocks
Straight Point
Littleham Cove
Coryton's Cove
Horse Cove
The Parson and Clerk
A La Ronde (NT)
Crealy Adventure Park
Powderham Castle
Woodbury Castle
Colaton Raleigh Common
Woodbury Common
East Budleigh Common
Lympstone Common
A30(T)
A3052
A379
A376
B3179
B3180
B3184
B3178
A3015
B3181
M5
0 1 2 miles
0 1 2 3 kilometres

EXETER

The great Cathedral city and county town of Devon, has been a strategic settlement since the Romans came here in 55 AD. Later, developed by Alfred the Great, and followed by the Normans who strengthened the town with City Walls. The magnificent Cathedral can be seen from the M5, where it dominates the view. There are medieval churches and the City Walls to discover, a circuit will take one-and-a-half hours. The City centre was badly damaged during the Second World War but luckily most of the ancient buildings escaped, including the Guildhall, St Nicholas Priory and Tucker's Hall. The city had a busy time of it during the Civil War, changing sides on numerous occasions. Outside the City walls, on the east side, the gracious avenue of C18 buildings, Southernhay, was where hangings took place, and agitators aired their views. John Wesley preached here. It is today the home of lawyers and estate agents, and a convenient place to park if visiting the Cathedral.

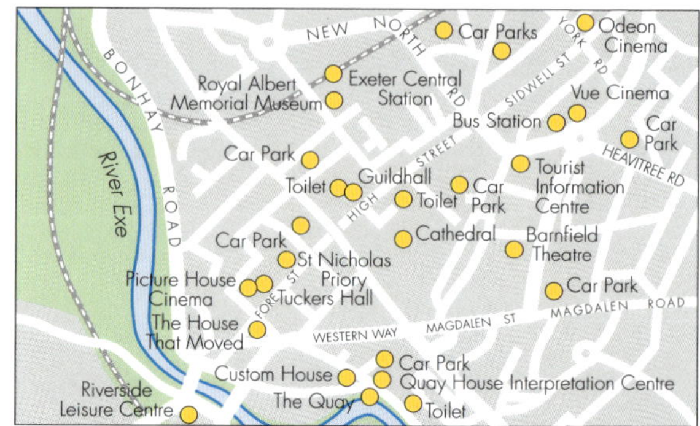

Exeter

The House That Moved

The Guildhall

When the celebrated traveller Celia Fiennes visited Exeter in 1698 she noted that for twenty miles around, all the villages, farms and country folk were in some way involved in the production of serge cloth. Exeter made more money in a week than any other town in England. This all halted during the Napoleonic Wars, and production moved north to Yorkshire and Lancashire.

The new buildings replacing those destroyed in the Second World War have not had a good press. The High Street has been described as dull. This will hopefully change, as the City fathers and planners are undergoing a massive reconstruction programme, and are aware that the City's heritage must stand out against the new, too.

The visitor will naturally first progress to the Cathedral and its spacious Close where there are restaurants, cafes and smart shops. Then, onto the Quay, where you can also eat and drink well, and take up some exercise by foot, cycle or paddle, and if this is not to your pleasure, aimlessly visit the many antique and bric-a-brac emporia.

Church detail

For more retail therapy, a short distance north-west from the Quay you will come to shopping outlets represented by TK Maxx and others.

The Devon County show is in May, and the Exeter Festival from May-June. (G1)

1792 Fashionable houses built on the beacon in Exmouth.

1793 Jan 11. The radical Tom Paine's effigy burnt in Exeter.

Custom House

What to Visit in Exeter; Historic Buildings & Museums…

Custom House, Quayside. Earliest surviving brick building in Exeter, used by HM Customs until 1989. Only open to Red Coat Guided Tours. (F2)

Guildhall, High St. One of the oldest municipal buildings in England dating back to 1330. (F1) 01392 265500

Quay House Visitor Centre, 46 The Quay. Exhibits an audio-visual presentation, "Exeter – 2,000 Years of History", highlighting Exeter, from Roman times to the present day. Open daily Apr-Oct 10-5, Nov-Mar W/Es only 11-4. (F1) 01392 271611 www.exeter.gov.uk/visiting

Royal Albert Memorial Museum, Queen St. Largest Museum in South West; Prehistory and Roman Gallery, natural history, archaeology, Exeter silver, clocks and watches, pottery, world cultures and paintings by British artists, especially of Devon. Cafe. Gift shop. Open M-Sa 10-5. Free. (F1) 01392 665 858 www.exeter.gov.uk/museums

Royal Albert Memorial Museum

Mol's Coffee House, Cathedral Close

The Quayside Exeter. Apart from the Cathedral and its surrounds, this is where the action takes place in Exeter. Wander down from the Cathedral (and car park) and admire the boats and swans, the old warehouse buildings. There are many cafes, tearooms, a couple of pubs, Antique emporia, nightclubs, craft shops, the Custom House and Quay House Visitor Centre. If you fancy a cycle or a paddle on the river, visit Saddles & Paddles, and next door, so claimed, the finest coffee in town at Mangos. (F1)

Tuckers Hall, Fore St. C15 Medieval Guildhall with unique roof. Open Tu & Th 10.30-12. (F1) 01392 412348

Underground Passages, c/o Tourist Information Centre, Dix's Field. Guide tours of medieval vaulted passageways stretching under the City's streets. New Visitor Centre opening in September 2007. (F1) 01392 665887

University Gardens. 300 acres of grounds, award winning landscaped gardens, sculptures. Open daily, free admission. (G1) 01392 215566

St Nicholas Priory, The Mint. Founded in 1087. 900-year old guest wing of former Benedictine Priory. Open East-Oct, Guided tours 2, 2.30, 3 & 3.30 pm. (F1) 01392 665858

Underground Passages ss

Cathedral Church of St Peter. One of the finest English cathedrals, and Devon's most magnificent building. Statuesque with twin Norman Towers. Bishop Marshall in the C13 started this great project. However, it was Bishop John Grandisson, 1327-1365, in the C14 who moved the construction forward with greater panache and fortitude, greatly encouraged by Pope John XX11. He organised the construction up to the Nave, largely his own creation. The truly magnificent (and it is difficult not to be over awed by this) rib-vaulting of the Nave extends to over 300 feet, and is quite unique. The carved misericords, 1230-1270, were the first in England. But surely what strikes the visitor, time and again, is the great West Front.

West Front

Sit outside in the Close with your coffee and admire the frontage. The large window filled with intricate tracery, Grandisson's work, and the lower wall, filled with sculptured images, eighty-eight in all, of warriors, angels, kings and saints. The effect is unforgettable, truly astounding. In recent years, some have crumbled and have been restored. Defoe claimed it took four hundred years to build, and yet it appears as one whole. No patchwork lines to spy. The interior has more to succour; colourful roof bosses, C14 Choir screen and Bishop's Throne, Lady Chapel, East Window with medieval glass. The C14 Window with modern glass. Sir John Speke's C16 Chantry, The C15 Astronomical Clock and Minstrel's Gallery.

One can't not mention Herbert Read, who did so much to restore the Cathedral following the bombing of 1942. We must give thanks to his memory, for his tireless and patient work. Open M-F 9.30am-5.30pm, Sa 9am-5pm, Su 7.30am-5pm. (F1)

Hugh Oldham

The Nave

1799 Spinning (yarn) mill started by Thomas Fox at Uffculme.

1801 The population of Devon recorded as 340,308 in the first national census.

123. The Resurrection Mural

The Assumption Mural

The East Window

Walter Bronescombe

Edmund Stafford

The Astronomical Clock

The Carew Tomb

Lady Doderidge

The Courtenay Tomb

1808	Dartmoor Prison founded at Princetown for French and American prisoners of war. Converted to present use in 1850.
1809	First publication of Ordnance Survey's map of Devonshire.

What to see in Exeter; Art, Cinema, Crafts, Music...

Bill Douglas Centre, University Campus. Museum housing a unique collection of items relating to cinema history, tracing its roots in earlier forms of entertainment. Explore the Victorian world of animated toys, dioramas, panoramas and magic lanterns, or follow British and Hollywood cinema through the C20. Guided tours. Open daily M-F 10-4. (G1) 01392 264321 www.exeter.ac.uk/bill douglas

Spacex Gallery, 45 Preston St. Large contemporary gallery devoted to the visual arts, film, poetry and workshops. Open Tu-Sa 10-5. (F1) www.spacex.co.uk

What to do in Exeter; Sail, Tour, Canoe, Cycle...

Carrie of Camaret, Crisping House. Sailing trips aboard 90 ft Schooner. Help set the sails or just relax and enjoy. No sailing experience necessary. (F2) www.carriecruising.co.uk

Saddles & Paddles, The Quay. Single and double kayacks (with child seats) or Canadian canoes hired out to explore the wildlife beside the River Exe and canal. Drop in on the two pubs on route. Buoyancy aids provided. Or on bikes explore 7 miles of flat, easy traffic-free routes. Large selection of mountain bikes and hybrids, plus child seats and trailers for under-5s. 01392 424241 www.sadpad.com

Exeter Canal

The Boatyard, The Quay

Exeter Red Coat Guided Tours, c/o Civic Centre, Dix's Field. Free entertaining guided walking tours revealing Exeter's fascinating history and hidden treasures. No booking required and choice of 16 tours. Open daily, all year. See Notice Board for Start Times. (F1) 01392 265203

Exeter Phoenix, Gandy St. Arts and media centre with daily programme of events; music, drama, dance, film, visual arts. A centre of student life in Exeter. Cafe/Bar. Open M-Sa from 10 til 11 pm. (G1) Box Office: 01392 667080 www.exeterphoenix.org.uk

Polka Dot Gallery, 67 South Street. Attractive gallery just down from the Cathedral brimming with ceramics, glass, jewellery, paintings, photography, sculpture and textiles. Open daily M-Sa. 01392 276330 www.polkadotgallery.com

Bill Douglas Centre ss

Where to Eat, Drink & Be Merry in Exeter...

Abode Exeter, Royal Clarence Hotel, Cathedral Yard. Understated contemporary design married with luxurious bedrooms and great food supplied by Michelin Star chef Michael Caines' Restaurant. Prices from £125 per room. For the more laid back, the Cafe Bar, next door. (F1) 01392 319955 www.abodehotels.co.uk

Medieval Door, The Close

And next door...

Michael Caines at the Royal Clarence Hotel, Cathedral Yard. Exeter's premier restaurant whose vision is Service with Style. His two Michelin Stars and other accolades have made this a destination for great food and wine. Also, a Champagne Bar. Lunch M-Sa 12-14.30, Dinner M-Sa 19.00-22.00. (G1)01392 223638 www.michaelcaines.com

1810 Construction of the Grand Western Canal.

1812 Plymouth breakwater begun by Rennie.

Michael Caine's Restaurant ss

St Olaves Hotel & Treasury Restaurant, Mary Arches St. Set in the heart of the city close to the cathedral. Intimate C19 Georgian house with stunning Spiral Staircase. Walled garden or Conservatory for light lunches and teas. Fine restaurant. 01392 217736. (F1) www.olaves.co.uk

Conservatory, 18 North Street. Small restaurant on three levels that is amassing a loyal clientele in Exeter. Fresh fish specials daily (£14.95-£19.95) and Two Course Lunch for £11.95. Open Tu-Sa from 12.00 pm. (E1) 01392 273858

Effings, 74 Queen Street. Food hall and restaurant where its pleasant to sit and sip a coffee or glass of wine, enjoy a carefree lunch, and watch the "Foodies" enjoying themselves. (G1) 01392 211888 www.effings.co.uk

Firestone Exeter, 10-12 Palace Gate. Just down from the Cathedral. Spacious bar and seating area downstairs with restaurant upstairs serving pizzas, burgers, steaks and pasta. Open all week. (G1) 10-12, Palace Gate 01392 252525 www.millhouseinns.co.uk

Hotel Barcelona, Magdalen St. A feast of chic, bright, modern design in the former Eye Hospital. A great place to meet friends, chat and have coffee, and admire the artworks. Cocktail bar, Kino. Cafe Paradiso for lunch and dinner. (F1) 01392 281000 www.aliashotels.com

Hour Glass Inn, 21 Melbourne Street. Just up from the Quay. This is a proper pub with atmosphere and real ales (Doom Bar, Otter and Adnams), an assortment of old chairs, newspapers, books, wooden panelling and dark red paintwork. The food is good, pub grub. Basement restaurant. (F1) 01392 258722

Plant Cafe, 1 Cathedral Yard. Child friendly cafe-deli has a full range of organic, free trade, vegetarian and children's food. Sit inside or out overlooking Cathedral Green. Open daily 9-6. (F1) 01392 428144

Westgate Festival Mural

Café Paradiso, Hotel Barcelona ss

1812 Shelley honeymooned in Lynmouth.

1814 The Devon prophetess Joanna Southcott claims to be pregnant with Shiloh, the second Messiah.

BOVEY TRACEY

A quiet, elongated town noted for its exquisite church (and Beckett associations) and the Devon Guild of Craftsmen, the finest craft gallery in Devon. The town's wealth was built from china clay deposits, or Bovey Clay, established in 1772. The results can be seen on Bottle Road, statuesque, old kilns. In the C18 and C19, Haytor quarries carried granite on tramways to Bovey for onward transport to Teignmouth. These were used in the construction of London Bridge and the pillars for the British Museum. In the Second World War lignite (peat and coal mix) was mined for a short time. Park beside the bridge and the Information Centre, following the road over the bridge takes you to the little High Street. (A8)

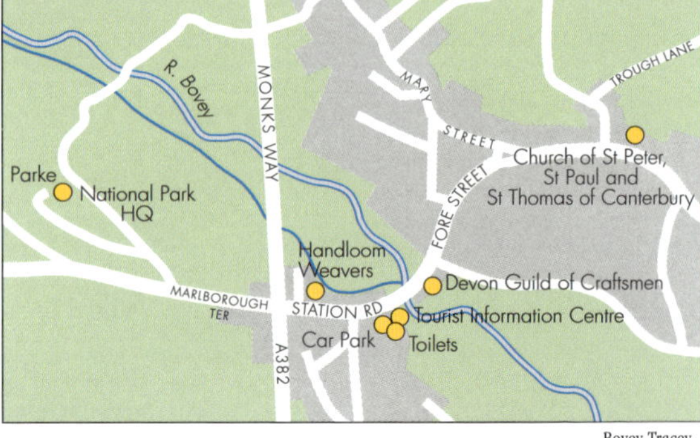

Bovey Tracey

Special Places to Visit...

Cardew Pottery. Newton Rd. 10 acres of woodland, train rides, paint your own pots. Open daily. (A8) 01626 832172 www.TheCardewTeapottery.com

Devon Guild of Craftsmen. The largest contemporary craft centre in the South West exhibiting work by artists of national and international renown, in the converted grade 11 listed Riverside Mill, in a beautiful location. Refurbished with new Jubilee Gallery, extended Craft Shop and The Terrace café with rooftop seating. Open daily 10-5.30. (A8) 01626 832223 www.crafts.org.uk

Handloom Weavers, 1 Station Road. For 70-years, and two generations, they have produced tweeds, ties, scarves and throws from soft, pure new wool, in exclusive designs. View the production process in the workshop. Shop stocks sheepskin products and classic knitwear. Shop opens M-Sa 9-5. (EC W). Workshop mid-May to Oct, times vary. (A8) 01626 833424

Handloom Weavers ss

Heritage Trust. The Trust is a registered charity which researches and preserves the history of the town and area. Open May-Sept Tu W & Sa. (A8) TIC 01626 832047

Parish Church of St Peter, St Paul & Thomas of Canterbury. Catholic guilt hath no bounds with William de Tracey, one of the four knights who carried out Henry 11's dastardly command "Who will rid me of this meddlesome priest"? Hacking to death Thomas a Beckett on the High Altar of Canterbury Cathedral, in 1170. For his penance, he built this church. Later additions in the C14, and a C15 Tower with pinnacled battlements and the C15 rood screen, considered the town's greatest treasure, and one of Devon's finest, has an exquisite panel of carved sculptures of the 31 apostles. And a medieval stone, carved pulpit and old wood bosses. (A8)

Devon Guild of Craftsmen ss/jp

House of Marbles, Pottery Rd. Museum of glass, games, marbles, and Bovey Pottery. Coffee shop. Open M-Sa 9-5, Su 10-5. (A8) 01626 835285 www.houseofmarbles.com

Special Places to Stay...

Brookfield House, Challabrook Lane. Imposing red brick Edwardian pile on the edge of Dartmoor. Big beds, rich decor and sumptuous breakfasts using local farm produce and home made breads and preserves. Secluded tranquillity, yet within walking distance of Bovey Tracey's centre for pubs and restaurants. ££. Closed Dec & Jan. (A8) 01626 836181 www.brookfield-house.com

1815 August 7th.Napoleon moored off Berry Head before transportation in the Northumberland to St Helena, exile and death.

1816 John Heathcoat, inventor of the bobbin machine, sets up lace manufacture in Tiverton.

DAWLISH

A modest resort compared to its neighbours. Yet recognised in literature as the birthplace of Dicken's *Nicholas Nickleby*, and as a pleasing place in Jane Austen's *Sense and Sensibility*. IK Brunel's railway cut a swathe through the red cliffs, a brilliant feat of Victorian engineering. Troubled today by heavy seas and an eroding coastline. To the north of the town, a row of pretty cottages, then onto Dawlish Warren, a naturalist's feast. (H9)

Places to Visit...

Dawlish Museum, The Knowle. Victorian rooms, military and railway with unique collection of photos of Dawlish. Open daily May-Sept M-Sa 10.30-5, Su 2-5. (H9) 01626 888667 www.devonmuseums.net/dawlish

Dawlish Warren. A spit of land at the mouth of the Exe Estuary, its shape, best appreciated from a bird's eye. On the seaward side, an extensive beach noted for shells. Inland, the mudflats are teeming with birdlife, especially autumn and winter migrants. The botanist will be excited with the Rare Crocus in spring, and the Ladies Tresses Orchid, in summer. Guided walks. (J8)

Special Places to Visit...

Brimblecombe's Devon Farmhouse Cider. Traditional cider made at Farrant's Farm for over 400 years. Sample the range of ciders. Original 450 year old press, display of agricultural hand tools. Cider and honey on sale. Open daily East-Oct, 10-6. (B3) 01647 252783

Canonteign Falls. Dramatic waterfalls, featuring the highest in England, lakes and ancient woodland, in private 100-acre park. Assault course, children's play areas. Restaurant/Tea room. Open daily mid-March to Nov 10-dusk. (B6) www.canonteignfalls.com

Haldon Belvedere. A monument to Major General Stringer Lawrence built in 1788. Superb viewpoint. Also called Lawrence Castle. Open daily May-Sept 2.30-6. Oct-Apr W/Es pm. (D4)

Powderham Castle. Built in 1390 by Sir Philip Courtenay whose descendants, the Earls of Devon, have lived here ever since. Restored and altered in C18 and C19. Fine interiors including music room by Wyatt. Furniture, paintings, tapestries, china and plasterwork. Newly restored C18 Woodland Garden. Formal garden and well stocked deer park with fine views. Open daily Apr-Oct except Sa 10-5.30. (H6) 01626 890243 www.powderham.co.uk

Civil War Re-enactment, Powderham Castle ss

Powderham Country Store. Produce from the estate; with butchery, bakery, delicatessen and food hall. A great day out. Open M-Sa 9-5, Su 10-4. (H6) P 01626 891883 www.powderham.co.uk/pcshop

Rock Gardens, Station Hill. 8 acres of wild garden with ponds, rare trees and shrubs set in the old Palace Quarry. Plant sales. Open daily 9-5. (C8) 01626 852134 www.therockgardens.co.uk

Taverner's Farm. Makers of Orange Elephant ice cream named after the herds of Devon cattle (of long ago) because of their enormous size. 18 different flavours to savour. (F4) 01392 833766

Ugbrooke House. Medieval House redesigned by Robert Adam. Home of the Clifford family. Fine furniture and paintings, embroideries, uniforms and costumes. Library. Marble Catholic chapel of 1830. Cardinal's 4-poster bed. Gardens and grounds by Capability Brown. Open mid-July to early Sept Tu, W, Th & Su. Guided tours at 2 & 3.45. Cafe open 1-5.30 for teas. (D8) 01626 852179 www.ugbrooke.co.uk

Pubs Serving Food...

Anchor Inn, Cockwood. C16 Inn with superb estuary views. Fine range of beers. Bar and restaurant menu. Dog/child friendly. (J7) 01626 890203 www.anchorinncockwood.com

Canonteign Falls

Manor Inn, Lower Ashton. Fine country pub loaded with ambience. Range of fine ales. Large portions. No children under 14. Open Tu-Su. (B5) 01647 252304

Nobody Inn, Doddiscombseigh. C16 Inn provides jolly atmosphere and supreme service. Serious wine and whisky list. Local ales. Accommodation. (C4) 01803 558279 www.nobodyinn.co.uk

1817 North Walk cut into cliffs from Lynton to Valley of Rocks. 1818 John Keats spends winter in Teignmouth preparing Endymion for publication.

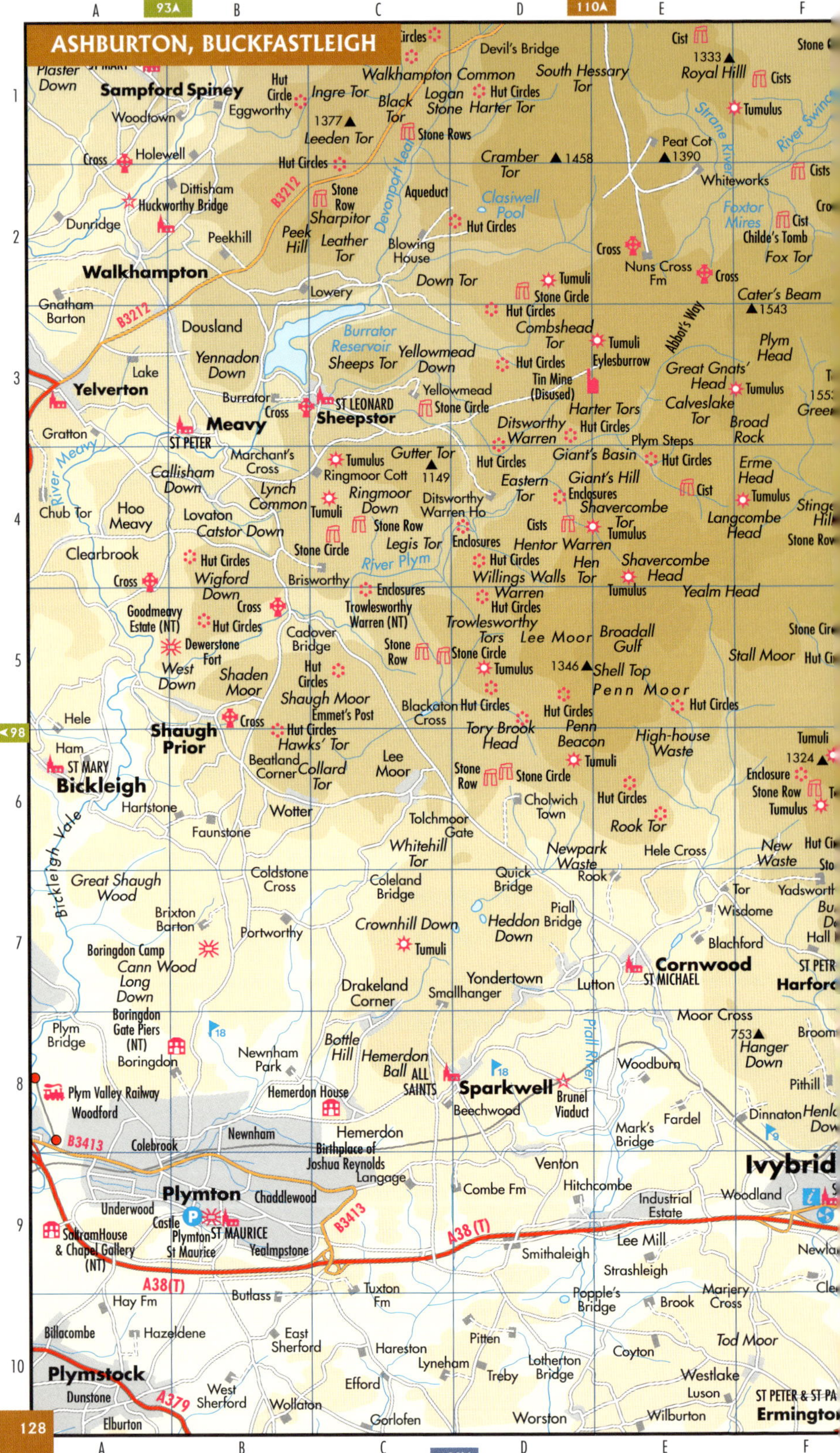

Sampford Spiney
Walkhampton
Yelverton
Meavy
Sheepstor
Shaugh Prior
Bickleigh
Cornwood
Sparkwell
Plympton
Plymstock
Ivybridge
Burrator Reservoir
River Plym
Lee Moor
Penn Moor
Down Tor
Cramber Tor
Nuns Cross Fm
Plym Valley Railway
Saltram House & Chapel Gallery (NT)
A38(T)
B3212
B3413
A379

111▲

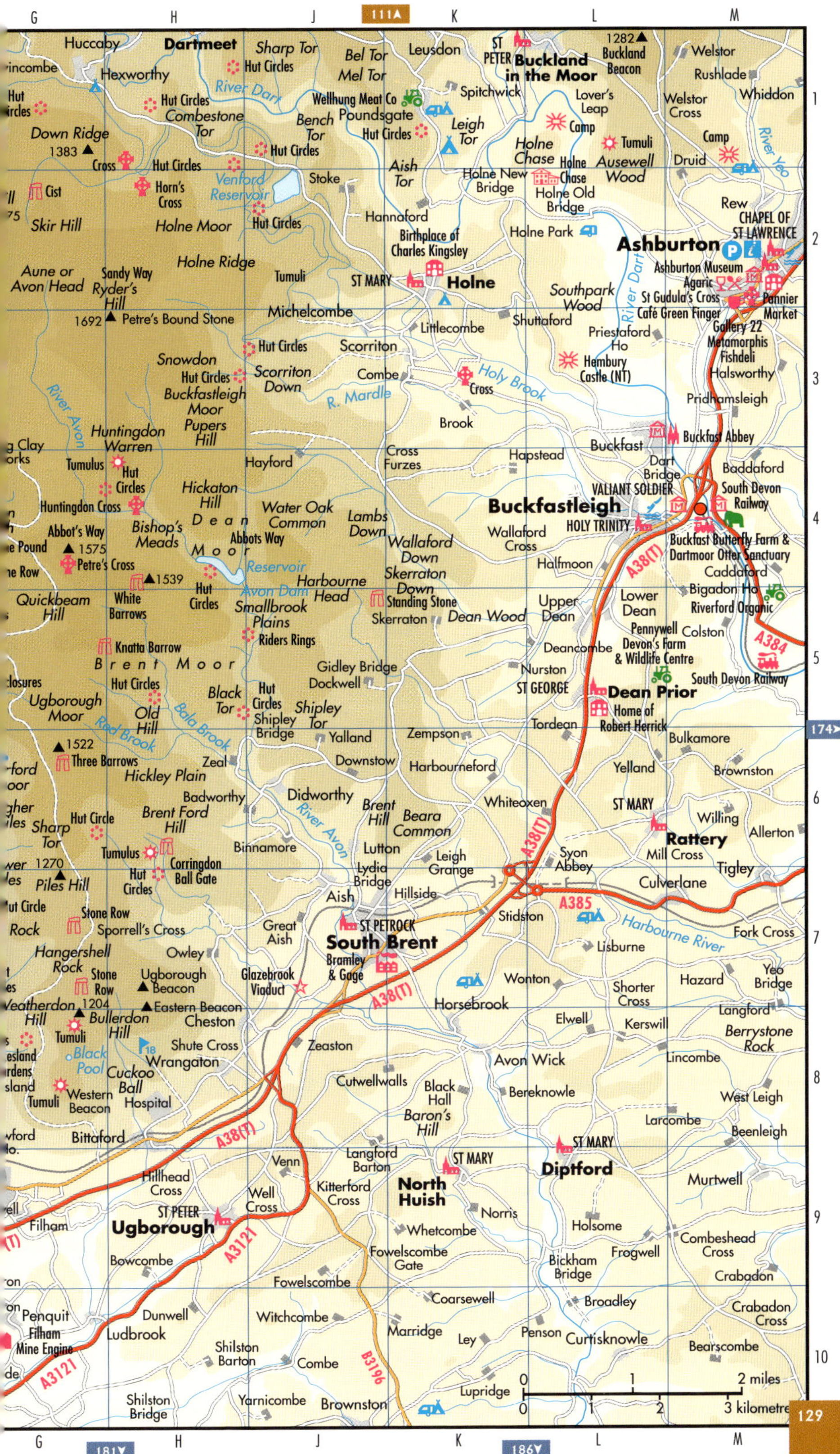

174▶

181▼
186▼

ASHBURTON

A charming town just off the A38, and well placed to explore Dartmoor and the South Hams. An ancient borough and "Stannary Town" considered by Anthony Trollope, to be the fairest corner of England. There is a gracious air and steady civility here, and pleasing architecture of slate carved roofs and oriel windows. Now a centre for good eating. It also has everything an outdoors person requires; a bookshop, outdoor equipment retailer, deli, and just outside town on the industrial estate, Big Peaks, bike and surf shop. (M2)

Ashburton Museum, 1 West St. History and geology of Dartmoor. Tin and woollen industries. Red Indian collection. Open mid-May to end Sept Tu, Th, F & Sa 2.30-5. (M2) 01364 653595

Gallery 22, North St. Contemporary paintings, prints, sculpture, ceramics, glass, wood & jewellery. Open daily M-Sa. (M2)01364 652046

Metamorphis, 29 East St. Contemporary art, original furniture and decorative items. Interior design. Open M-Sa from 11. (M2) 01364 653943 www.metamorphisart.co.uk

Parish Church of St Andrew. C15 creation with cradle roof and fine bosses. Herbert Read's sculptures fill three niches over the west door. (M2)

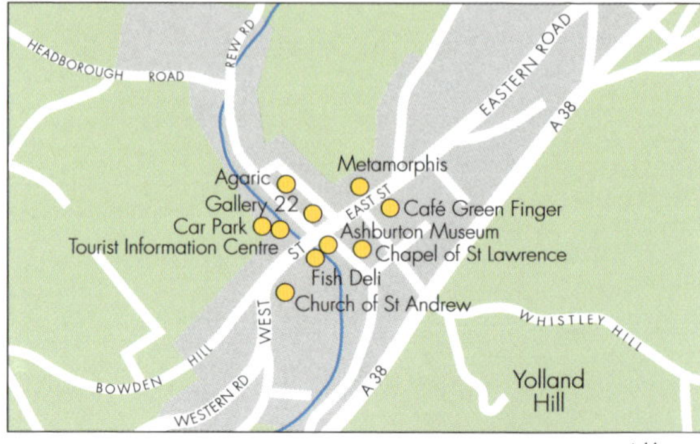

Ashburton

Where to Eat, Drink & Be Merry...

Agaric, 30 North St. A real treat. East Dartmoor's answer to epicurean delights. Local produce and a loyal following. Lunch and Dinner. Open W-Sa (Su lunch). Accommodation. (M2) 01364 654478 www.agaricrestaurant.co.uk

Cafe Green Finger, 26 East St. A real find; spacious elegant rooms to enjoy home produced food, all day. Soups, light lunches, cream teas. Garden. (M2) 01364 653939

The Fish Deli, 9 West Street. Fresh fish sourced from local boats, and Isles of Scilly lobster. Fish cooked on premises for home consumption. Deli. (M2) 01364 654833 www.thefishdeli.co.uk

Agaric ss

Buckfast Abbey. Benedictine Abbey church built by personal labour of the community of monks during the years 1903-38, on site of the former medieval Cistercian abbey. Finely decorated interior. Chapel of the Blessed Sacrament added in 1966 with the colourful mosaic window. Exhibition of monastic history, vestments and plate in C15 Guest Hall. The community produce honey, wine and other artefacts for sale. These, they sell onto the visitors who come in charabancs and coaches, in their teeming hundreds. Their commercial acumen has had the locals decrying the place as "Fastbuckleigh." Restaurant/café. Open daily; church and grounds 5.30-19.00. Visitors from 9 (10 in winter). (L3) www.buckfast.org.uk

Buckfast Butterfly & Otter Sanctuary. Butterflies from all over the world in tropical landscaped garden. Otters in underwater viewing areas. Open daily Mar-Oct 10-5.30 (dusk). 01364 642916 www.ottersandbutterflies.co.uk

The Fish Deli

1820 Haytor Granite Railway opened.

1823 Jul 19. The first cholera case reported in Exeter in an epidemic in which 440 were to die.

South Devon Railway. Seven-mile Great Western heritage steam railway from Buckfastleigh to Totnes beside the picturesque River Dart. Buckfastleigh Station, with free car parking, beside the A38 Devon Expressway. Totnes Station beside Mainline Station. (M4) 01364 642338/0845 3451420 www.southdevonrailway.org

BUCKFASTLEIGH
Worth a detour to visit this pretty, well-groomed village with a one-way High Street. Swimming pool and museum, below. (L4)

The Valiant Soldier, 79 Fore Street. A village inn for two centuries, now a museum showing furniture, pub artefacts of the 40s and 50s. Open Apr-Oct M-Sa 10.30-4.30. Sundays before BHs 12.30-4.30. (L4) 01364 644522

Buckfast Abbey

Special Places to Visit...

Dean Prior, Church of St George. For all lovers of English poetry, and considered by some scholars to be our finest poet, the home of Robert Herrick, Cavalier Poet and acolyte to Ben Johnson. It was here he wrote his great Hesperides, a lengthy manuscript on Celibacy, Marriage, Ritual and Sexual Politics. Appointed vicar by Charles 1 in 1629, he took a long, long time to understand his flock, eventually to be driven out by Puritans, to return fifteen years later after the Restoration. It is a little church, on a fast road, with parking. The east window is his Memorial. He lies outside in an unmarked grave. (L5)

Hemerdon House. Georgian family house. Collection of West Country paintings and prints, furniture and library. Open May & Aug BHs 2-5.30 and occasional days May-Sept. (B8) 01752 337350

Lukesland Gardens ss

Lukesland Gardens, Harford Road. 24 acres of flowering shrubs, trees and wild flowers by a Dartmoor stream. Open Apr to mid-June Su W & BH Ms 2-6, also Sa in May, & mid-Oct to mid-Nov Su & W, 11-4. (F8) 01752 691749 www.lukesland.co.uk

Pennywell Farm & Wildlife Centre. 80 acres to roam, with activities every half-hour. Farm & British wild animals. Owl and Falconry Centre. Pets corners. Open Feb half term for lambing special, then daily East-Oct 10-5.30. (L5) 01364 642023 www.pennywellfarmcentre.co.uk

Rattery. Village with one of the oldest inns in Christendom, and Devon, if you believe the tall stories told here in the Church House Inn. C13-C15 church beside the village green with Norman font and C15 oak screen restored in the C20. Rambling old mill with leadened windows. (L6)

Ermington Metalcraft. Unit 13, Ermington Workshops. Wrought ironwork, weather vanes, gates tables and chairs. (F10) 01548 831040

Riverford Organic, Wash Barn. Organic vegetables from the farm to table. Riverford vegetable box scheme allows you to choose from a range of box sizes, the contents of the box will be different each week. (M5) 01803 762720 www.riverford.co.uk

Well Hung Meat Company, Cordonford Farm. A wonderful selection of pork sausages, from the garlicky Toulouse taster to the softer Breakfast type, also with organic apples. 01364 631595 www.wellhungmeat.com

Dartmoor Special Places of Interest...

Childe's Tomb. A stone cross marks the site of the tragedy of the Lord of the Manor of Plymstock. Caught in a blizzard, he killed his horse and climbed inside to keep warm but still froze to death. He left a Will leaving his estate to those who would find and bury him. The monks of Tavistock did so, and thus, claimed his land. (F2)

Dewerstone Rocks. Granite outcrop 300 feet high, packed with legend and known as the Devil's stone. Fine views to be had over Goodameavy, the River Meavy and beyond. (B5)

Holne Bridge. Another beauty spot; a fine old bridge. (L2)

Special Places to Stay...

Higher Beneknowle, Diptford. 01364 649209 www.higherbeneknowle.co.uk

Holne Chase. Former hunting lodge for the Abbots of Buckfast Abbey set amidst a nature reserve. A leading Sporting hotel specialises in fly fishing, riding and shooting. Fresh local produce served in the restaurant. Dogs welcome. (L2) 01364 631471 www.holne-chase.co.uk

Kilbury Manor. Colston Road. 01364 644079 www.kilbury.co.uk

Sampford Manor. Sampford Spiney 01822 853442 www.sampford-spiney.fsnet.co.uk

To the east of the Exe is a stretch of coastline where for the most part sand gives place to shingle interspersed with high cliffs; Devon Red to start with, but changing to White Chalk towards the Dorset border.

Along the coast, the busy port of Exmouth, the genteel town of Budleigh Salterton, the elegant Regency buildings of Sidmouth, and Seaton with its attractive neighbouring village of Beer. Inland, the market town of Honiton, renowned for lace, and Ottery St Mary, with its magnificent church. All around is a beautiful landscape of patchwork fields and rolling hills, where Devon meets Somerset. It is a countryside worthy of exploration and best suited to those with time on their hands. Best to leave the A-roads and to wander aimlessly from village to village.

Explore the Farway Valley and you may imagine you are lost in time, or if you are lost on a foreign shore, dreaming of England's green pastures and smooth hillsides. It is this valley that may come to mind; a bowl of aching beauty, bidden with villages of thatch and little churches. Climb out of this valley, and you will find yourself on a plateau with stupendous views, to west and east.

But if architecture, or to be more specific, church art and craftsmanship, interests you, then this corner of England will hold your attention for hours. You will be entranced by the magnificent churches of Broadclyst, Colyton, Cullompton and Ottery St Mary, and the smaller, no less charming ones, of Branscombe, East Budleigh, Northleigh, Shute, Southleigh and Uplyme … the list goes on.

131. Broadhembury Church

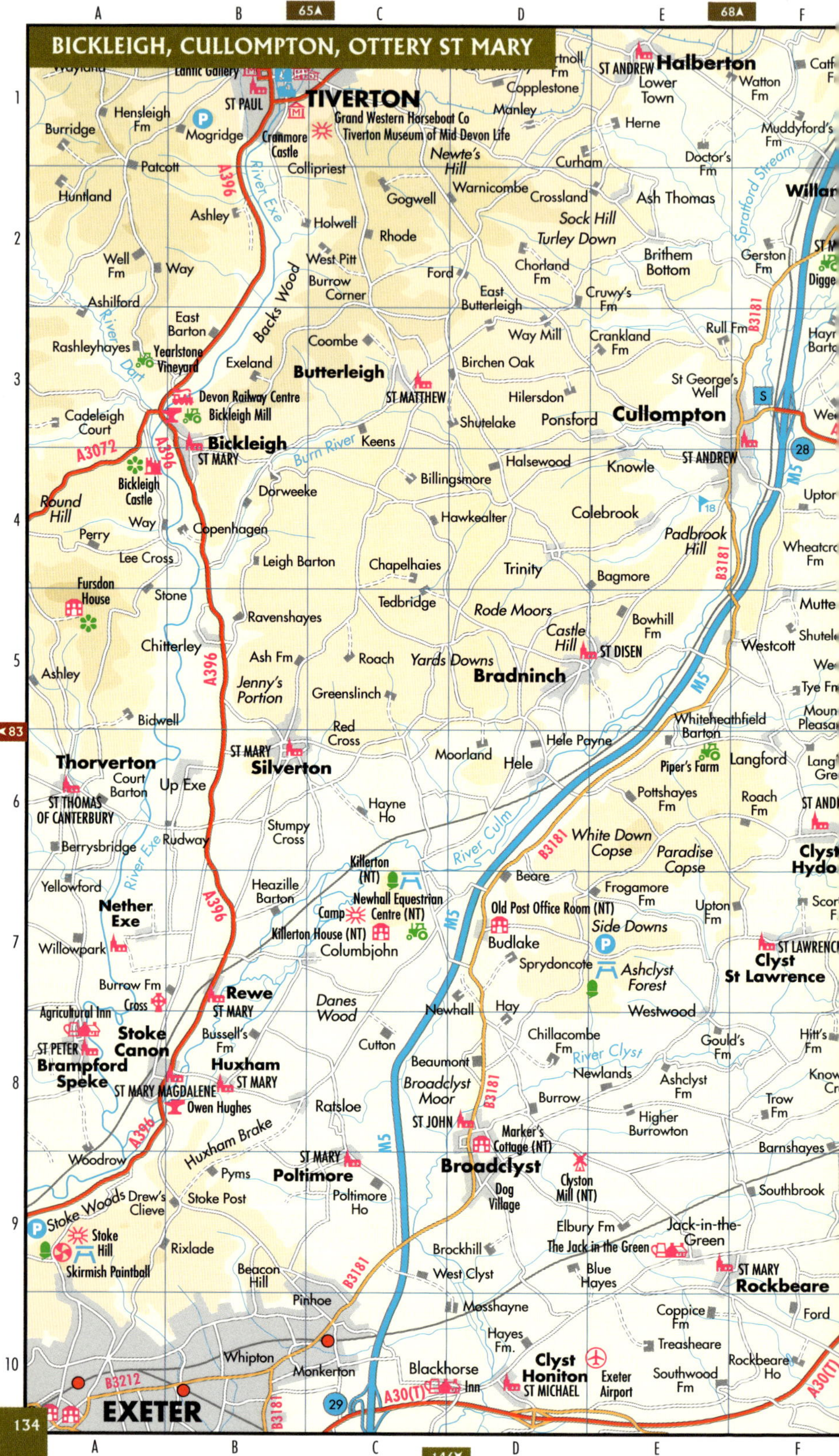
65
68
TIVERTON
Halberton
Cullompton
Butterleigh
Bickleigh
Bradninch
Silverton
Thorverton
Nether Exe
Rewe
Stoke Canon
Brampford Speke
Huxham
Poltimore
Broadclyst
Clyst Honiton
Clyst St Lawrence
Rockbeare
EXETER
Exeter Airport
Killerton (NT)
Killerton House (NT)
Devon Railway Centre
Bickleigh Mill
Bickleigh Castle
Yearlstone Vineyard
Grand Western Horseboat Co
Tiverton Museum of Mid Devon Life
Cranmore Castle
Newhall Equestrian Centre (NT)
Old Post Office Room (NT)
Marker's Cottage (NT)
Clyston Mill (NT)
Stoke Hill
Skirmish Paintball
Agricultural Inn
Owen Hughes
Piper's Farm
Ashclyst Forest
Fursdon House
M5
A396
A3072
B3181
B3212
A30(T)
River Exe
River Culm
River Clyst
River Dart
Burn River
Spratford Stream
83
146

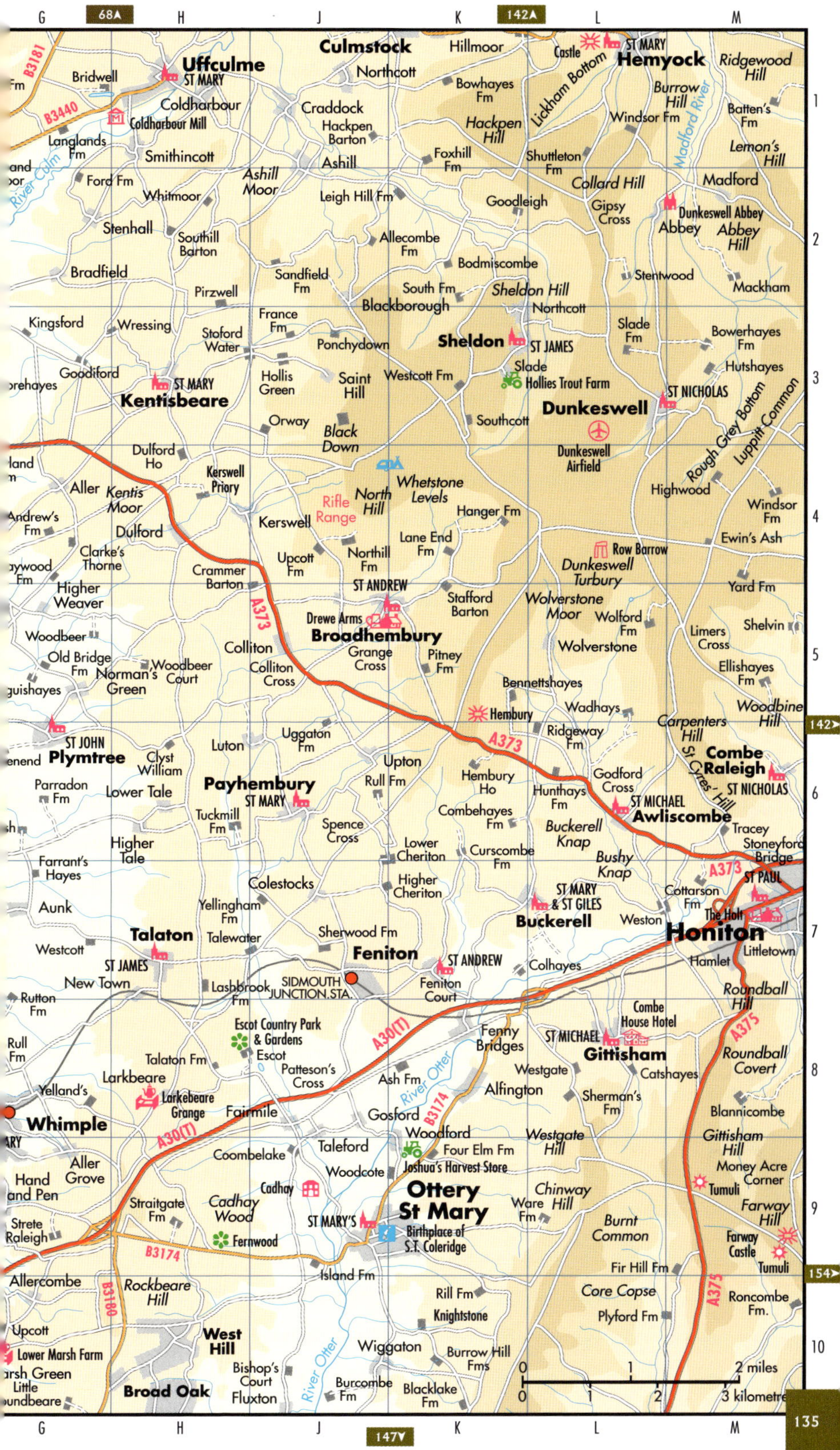
Culmstock
Hillmoor
Hemyock
Uffculme
Northcott
Bowhayes Fm
Craddock
Coldharbour
Coldharbour Mill
Hackpen Barton
Hackpen Hill
Ashill
Ashill Moor
Smithincott
Langlands Fm
Ford Fm
Whitmoor
Leigh Hill Fm
Goodleigh
Collard Hill
Madford
Dunkeswell Abbey
Abbey Hill
Stenhall
Southill Barton
Allecombe Fm
Bradfield
Sandfield Fm
Bodmiscombe
Pirzwell
Sheldon Hill
Stentwood
Mackham
Blackborough
Kingsford
Wressing
Stoford Water
France Fm
Sheldon
Ponchydown
Goodiford
Kentisbeare
Hollis Green
Saint Hill
Westcott Fm
Hollies Trout Farm
Dunkeswell
Dunkeswell Airfield
Orway
Black Down
Southcott
Whetstone Levels
North Hill
Rifle Range
Kerswell
Kerswell Priory
Dulford
Aller
Kentis Moor
Hanger Fm
Row Barrow
Dunkeswell Turbury
Broadhembury
Drewe Arms
Stafford Barton
Wolverstone Moor
Wolverstone
Plymtree
Clyst William
Payhembury
Upton
Hembury
Combe Raleigh
Awliscombe
Buckerell
Honiton
Talaton
Feniton
SIDMOUTH JUNCTION STA.
Escot Country Park & Gardens
Fenny Bridges
Gittisham
Combe House Hotel
Whimple
Larkbeare Grange
Fairmile
Alfington
Ottery St Mary
Birthplace of S.T. Coleridge
Cadhay
Fernwood
Joshua's Harvest Store
West Hill
Broad Oak
Wiggaton
Burnt Common
Farway Castle
A373
A30(T)
A375
B3174
B3180
B3181
B3440
River Otter
River Culm
0 1 2 miles
0 1 2 3 kilometres

Bickleigh Bridge

BICKLEIGH

Pretty village beside the Rive Exe with fine bridge and fisherman's cottages. You can sit in the garden of the Inn and admire the pastoral scene. (B3)

Places to Visit...

Bickleigh Castle. Royalist stronghold spanning 900 years of history. C11 Chapel, Armoury, Guardroom, Great Hall and Tudor bedroom. Picturesque moated garden. Open W and Su afternoons from Easter Su-Sept 2-5. (A4) 01884 855363

Bickleigh Mill. Extensive shopping with crafts, gallery, ladies' & gentlemen's fashions, interiors, furnishings and a Farm shop. Licensed restaurant and coffee shop. Waterside tea garden. Working pottery studio. Open daily from 10. (B3) 01884 855419

Devon Railway Centre. Train rides on two lines with 10 working model layouts and over 30 trains in motion. Museum. Shop. Cafe. Open Easter & BHs, June-Sept 11-5. (B3) 01884 855671 www.devonrailwaycentre.co.uk

Yearlstone Vineyard. Devon's oldest vineyard producing wines for almost thirty years. Terrace café-Wine Bar serves light meals from Slow, local producers. Open daily in summer, other times see below. (A3) 01884 855700 wwww.yearlstone.co.uk

OTTERY ST MARY

Famous as the birthplace in 1772 of Samuel Taylor Coleridge; poet, philosopher, naturalist, and son to the Vicar of the parish. Set in the valley of the River Otter, the town is a friendly and pleasing place to visit. The surrounding, pastoral landscape, is distinguished by a web of narrow lanes, these join little farms and hamlets. Map reading requires concentration, or you can just let the road take you hither and thither, and explore the rich, red earthy lanes. The Blackdown Hills rise to the north, and to the East, the Jurassic Coast of East Devon. The church is not to be overlooked, and is plainly, a feast for the churchophile. (K9)

Broadhembury

1827 Teignmouth to Shaldon bridge built at length of 1671 feet.

1830 Plymouth Brethren formed.

136.

St Mary's

Memorial Figure

St Mary's, Ottery St Mary. One of the great churches of Devon. Largely built in the C14 but later modelled on Exeter Cathedral with its fine transeptal towers. The Dorset Aisle from 1520, is an exquisite example of fan faulting perhaps only matched by Gloucester Cathedral. Fine Grandisson tomb. Unusual 600-year old clock. The father of the great Romantic poet, Samuel Taylor Coleridge was vicar here from 1760-81. A studious and simple man, he read the bible in Hebrew to his parishioners; country folk and farm workers! (J9)

Fan Vaulting, Dorset Aisle

The Nave

The Clock

Samuel Taylor Coleridge

1839 Fire destroyed 260 homes in Cullompton.

1839 Dec 25. 8,000,000 tons of soil slipped into the sea near Axmouth.

Marker's Cottage, Broadclyst

Special Paces to Visit...

Broadclyst – Marker's Cottage (NT). A thatched medieval cob house with an interesting interior containing a screen decorated with "grotesque" work, and a landscape scene of St Andrew. Cob summerhouse in garden. Open Apr-Oct M, Tu & Su, 2-5. (D8)

Budlake – Old Post Office Room (NT). A charming thatched cottage in 1950s style that housed the village post office. Outside the washhouse, double-seated privy, pigsty and chicken house. Half an acre of vegetable garden. Open Apr-Oct M, Tu & Su, 2-5. (D7)

Cadhay
Built in 1550 on the site of an earlier house to incorporate its Great Hall with a fine, timbered roof. Elizabethan Long Gallery and some Georgian work. Splendid Courtyard with statues of Henry V111 and his children. Maritime paintings and ancient fishponds. House is available to rent for house parties. House and gardens open F May-Sept, also Spring & Aug Su & M BHs 2-5.30. (J9)

Killerton House & Garden

Clyston Mill (NT).
C19 water-powered grain mill lovingly restored to its former glory, and now producing top quality flour. Set beside the River Clyst surrounded by farmland and orchards, an idyllic spot. Open Apr-Oct, M, Tu & Su, 2-5. (D9)

Coldharbour Mill. 200 year old working woollen mill. Giant water wheel. Special Events; Steam Up Days and Autumn Country Fair. Mill shop and waterside gardens. Picnics. Open daily Feb-Xmas 10.30-5. (H1) 01884 840960 www.coldharbourmill.org.uk

Diggerland. Children (and adults) can drive real JCBs and construction machinery. Fully trained instructors on hand. Open daily from 10. (F2) 08700 344437

Fursdon House. The Fursdons have lived here for 700 years. The guided tour takes you through the medieval, Jacobean, Georgian and Regency periods. Family portraits, furniture and paintings to view. Open June-Aug Su & W (also BH W/Es, from 2-5, tours at 2.30 & 3.30 pm. (A5) 01392 860860 www.fursdon.co.uk

Killerton House & Garden (NT). Home of the Acland Family for over three hundred years, and rebuilt in 1778. Downstairs rooms furnished in different periods. Upstairs the Pauline de Bush Costume Collection. 15 acres of superb gardens developed through many generations. Victorian laundry. Ice House. Restaurant and NT shop. Garden & Park open all year 10.30-7. House open daily mid-Mar to 4 Nov & 8-23 Dec 11-5 except Tu (& M in Oct), daily in Aug. (C7)

Skirmish Paintball. Set in 100 acres of Stoke Woods, close to Exeter city centre. Trenches, bridges, ravines, jungles and swamps. Catering & sheltered rest areas. (A9) 01548 580025 www.skirmishpaintball.co.uk

Elizabeth 1's Statue, Cadhay

1839 The ship Tory departs Plymouth bound for New Zealand with the first pioneer colonists.

1840 Braunton Great Field is recorded as having 448 strips, 46 landowners and 62 cultivators.

The Wagon Roof

The West Tower

St Andrew's Church, Cullompton. The great West Tower added in 1545-1549 dominates the town's skyline, and is exceptional. It measures 100 feet and the pinnacles are nearly 20 feet higher. One of the great wagon roof and rood screens of Devon. Fan vaulting in the Lane Aisle with stained glass window by Burne-Jones on south side. Carved heraldic shields of the Moore family on the parclose screen. C15 Golgotha carving on west side. (F3)

The Rood Screen

Stained Glass Window

The Golgotha Carving

Fan Vaulting, Lane Aisle

Coldharbour Mill

Countryside Interests...

Joshua's Harvest Store, Gosford Road. One of the leading specialist food shops in Devon. It celebrates local, fresh, organic and specialist food and drink, and sells gifts and greeting cards. The cafe serves beautifully presented platters allowing you to sample the food sold in store. Open M-Sa 9-6, Su 10.30-4.30. (K9) 01404 815473 www.joshuaharveststore.co.uk

Newhall Equestrian Centre. Historic thoroughbred stud visitor centre on the National Trust Killerton Estate. Tearooms, Saddler and gift shop. Rocking Horse workshop. Open East to end Oct 10.30-5.30. (C7) 01392 462453

Pipers Farm. They support a community of local family farms producing red meats, poultry, and sausages and burgers of the highest quality. Visit their shop in Exeter at the Magdelan Road shopping parade. (E6) 01392 881380 www.pipersfarm.com

Hollies Trout Farm, Slade Lane. Supplies many local pubs and restaurants with their award-winning fish. Try catching your own with rod and line. B & B available. (K3) 01404 841428 www.holliestroutfarm.co.uk

Churches of Interest...

St John the Baptist, Broadclyst. A magnificent church in the Perpendicular style; the tower is 100 feet and decorated in the style of Somerset tracery with eight pinnacles of Beer stone. This is the fourth church on this site, and forms the second largest parish in Devonshire. The roof was restored with iron tiles by I K Brunel. There are four elaborate tombs and some beautiful, and sad stained glass; the Ellen Acland window commemorates the ten year old killed in a cycling accident. Up high, some fine bosses, the Green Man and the Three Rabbits. In the churchyard, a board remembers the Veitch family of gardeners, of Killerton. (D8)

St George Window, Broadclyst Church

Where to Eat, Drink & Be Merry...

Agricultural Inn, Brampford Speke. Centre of village facing a cobbled courtyard. Log fires in winter. Specially brewed Speakeasy Ale and Adnams. Good honest food; casseroles and fishcakes. (A8) 01392 841591 www.theagriculturalinn.co.uk

Drewe Arms, Broadhembury. Open fires for winter nights. Fresh fish, quality wines and real ale. Put simply- Your hosts the Burges are true professionals of their craft. (K5) 01404 841267

The Jack in the Green, Rockbeare. One of the first gastro-pubs in Devon started fifteen years ago that has become more a restaurant than a pub. It has won countless awards and accolades from food writers and built up a loyal clientele. Seasonal menus. The one drawback, the large, open space lacks intimacy. (E9) 01404 822240 www.jackinthegreen.uk.com

Broadclyst Cottages

1844 May 1. The first steam locomotive reaches Exeter from Bristol.

1846 Braunton Tower built to commemorate the abolition of the Corn Laws.

Combe House Hotel

This is one of the great Country House Hotels and Restaurants of England, forever gaining prestigious awards. They provide luxury, old style elegance, and an ambience where you can relax and feel totally at ease. Unstuffy, the staff are discreetly on hand for your every need, but never, in your space. This could indeed be your Country Retreat, (your Elizabethan manor, hidden away in a Devon combe, a valley of 3,500 acres, your's without the trauma of upkeep) for you will have the tranquillity, the blissful comfort and Two Master chefs on hand to create superb cuisine. You, too, can walk in the surrounding parkland and join footpaths, or explore Gittisham with its pretty thatched cottages – once described by Prince Charles as the ideal English Village. There is also the World Heritage Coastline from Sidmouth to Lyme Regis, just 20 minutes away.

For complete discretion, a cottage in the grounds is available. A Land Rover is on hand to collect and return you. Non-residents are welcome at Combe House and it is a wonderful place to stop for lunch and coffee. Combe House Hotel, Gittisham, Nr Honiton. (L8) 01404 540400 www.thishotel.com

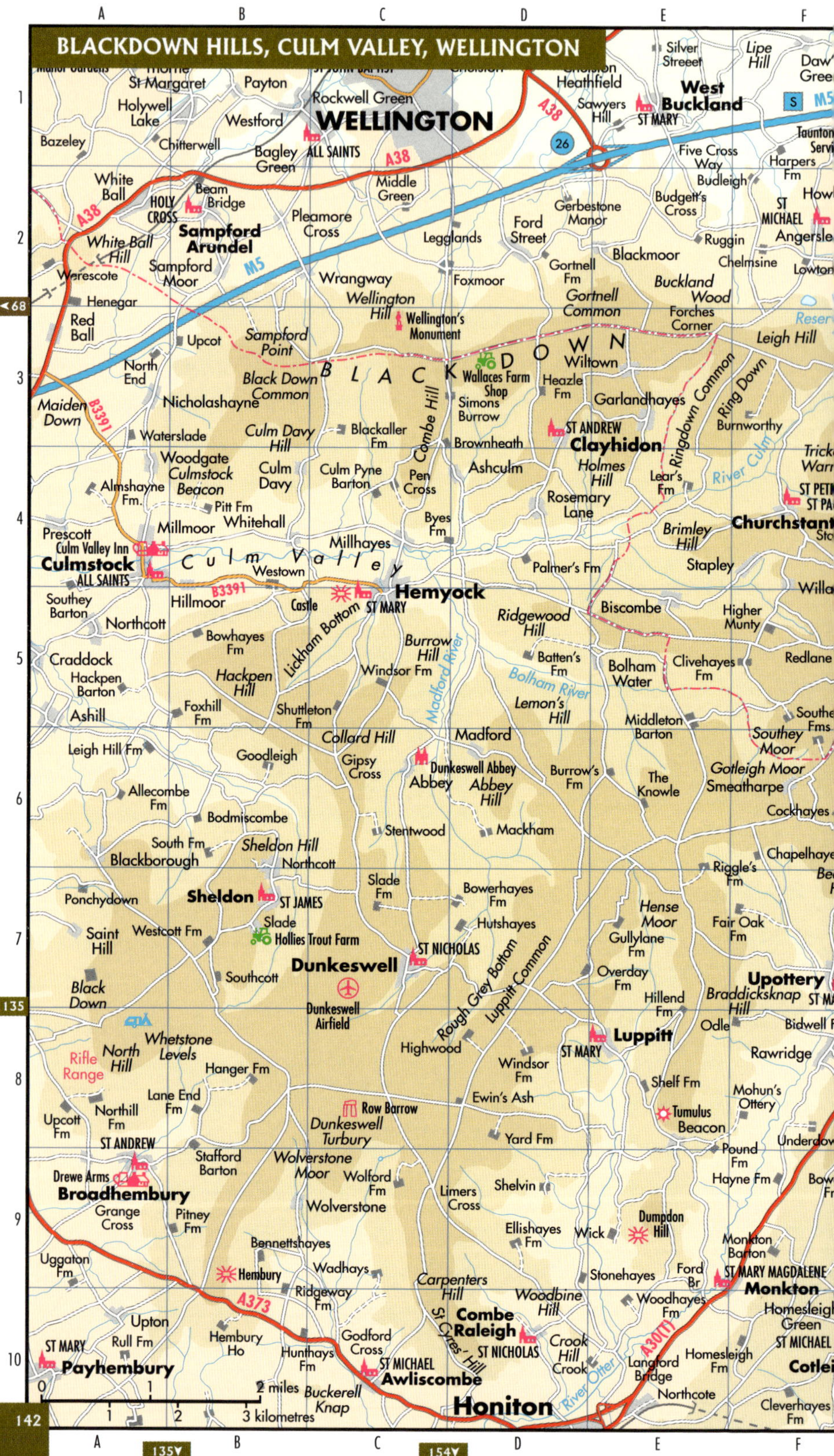
A
B
C
D
E
F
St Margaret
Payton
Holywell Lake
Rockwell Green
WELLINGTON
Westford
Bazeley
Chitterwell
Bagley Green
ALL SAINTS
A38
Middle Green
Heathfield
Sawyers Hill
West Buckland
ST MARY
Silver Street
Lipe Hill
M5
26
Five Cross Way
Budleigh
Harpers Fm
Budgett's Cross
ST MICHAEL
Angersleigh
Ruggin
Chelmsine
Lowton
White Ball
HOLY CROSS
Beam Bridge
Sampford Arundel
Pleamore Cross
Legglands
Ford Street
Gerbestone Manor
Blackmoor
White Ball Hill
Sampford Moor
Wrangway
Foxmoor
Gortnell Fm
Gortnell Common
Buckland Wood
Forches Corner
Wrescote
Henegar
Red Ball
Wellington Hill
Wellington's Monument
Upcot
Sampford Point
Leigh Hill
North End
Black Down Common
B L A C K D O W N
Wallaces Farm Shop
Wiltown
Heazle Fm
Simons Burrow
Garlandhayes
Ringdown Common
Ring Down
Burnworthy
Maiden Down
B3391
Nicholashayne
Combe Hill
Blackaller Fm
Brownheath
ST ANDREW
Clayhidon
Waterslade
Culm Davy Hill
Woodgate
Culmstock Beacon
Culm Davy
Culm Pyne Barton
Pen Cross
Ashculm
Holmes Hill
Lear's Fm
River Culm
Almshayne Fm.
Pitt Fm
Rosemary Lane
ST PETER
ST PAUL
Churchstanton
Prescott
Culm Valley Inn
Culmstock
ALL SAINTS
Millmoor
Whitehall
Byes Fm
Brimley Hill
Culm Valley
Millhayes
Westown
Palmer's Fm
Stapley
Hillmoor
Castle
Hemyock
ST MARY
Willand
Southey Barton
Northcott
Lickham Bottom
Ridgewood Hill
Biscombe
Higher Munty
Bowhayes Fm
Burrow Hill
Madford River
Craddock
Hackpen Barton
Hackpen Hill
Windsor Fm
Batten's Fm
Bolham River
Bolham Water
Clivehayes Fm
Redlane
Ashill
Foxhill Fm
Shuttleton Fm
Lemon's Hill
Middleton Barton
Southey Moor
Leigh Hill Fm
Collard Hill
Madford
Goodleigh
Gipsy Cross
Dunkeswell Abbey
Abbey
Abbey Hill
Burrow's Fm
The Knowle
Gotleigh Moor
Smeatharpe
Allecombe Fm
Bodmiscombe
Stentwood
Mackham
Cockhayes
South Fm
Blackborough
Sheldon Hill
Northcott
Riggle's Fm
Chapelhayes
Ponchydown
Sheldon
ST JAMES
Slade Fm
Bowerhayes Fm
Hense Moor
Fair Oak Fm
Saint Hill
Westcott Fm
Slade
Hollies Trout Farm
Hutshayes
Gullylane Fm
ST NICHOLAS
Dunkeswell
Rough Grey Bottom
Luppitt Common
Overday Fm
Upottery
Braddicksknap Hill
Black Down
Southcott
Dunkeswell Airfield
Hillend Fm
Odle
Bidwell
Luppitt
ST MARY
Whetstone Levels
Rifle Range
North Hill
Highwood
Windsor Fm
Rawridge
Hanger Fm
Shelf Fm
Mohun's Ottery
Lane End Fm
Ewin's Ash
Upcott Fm
Northill Fm
Row Barrow
Dunkeswell Turbury
Tumulus
Beacon
ST ANDREW
Yard Fm
Pound Fm
Stafford Barton
Wolverstone Moor
Wolford Fm
Drewe Arms
Broadhembury
Limers Cross
Shelvin
Hayne Fm
Grange Cross
Pitney Fm
Wolverstone
Ellishayes Fm
Wick
Dumpdon Hill
Bennettshayes
Monkton Barton
Uggaton Fm
Hembury
Wadhays
Carpenters Hill
Stonehayes
Ford Br
ST MARY MAGDALENE
Monkton
A373
Ridgeway Fm
Woodbine Hill
Woodhayes Fm
Homesleigh Green
Upton
Combe Raleigh
ST MICHAEL
Hembury Ho
Rull Fm
Godford Cross
St Cyres' Hill
ST NICHOLAS
Crook Hill
Crook
A30(T)
ST MARY
Payhembury
Hunthays Fm
ST MICHAEL
Awliscombe
River Otter
Langford Bridge
Homesleigh Fm
Cotleigh
Buckerell Knap
Northcote
Cleverhayes Fm
Honiton
0
1
2 miles
2
3 kilometres
68
135
135
154

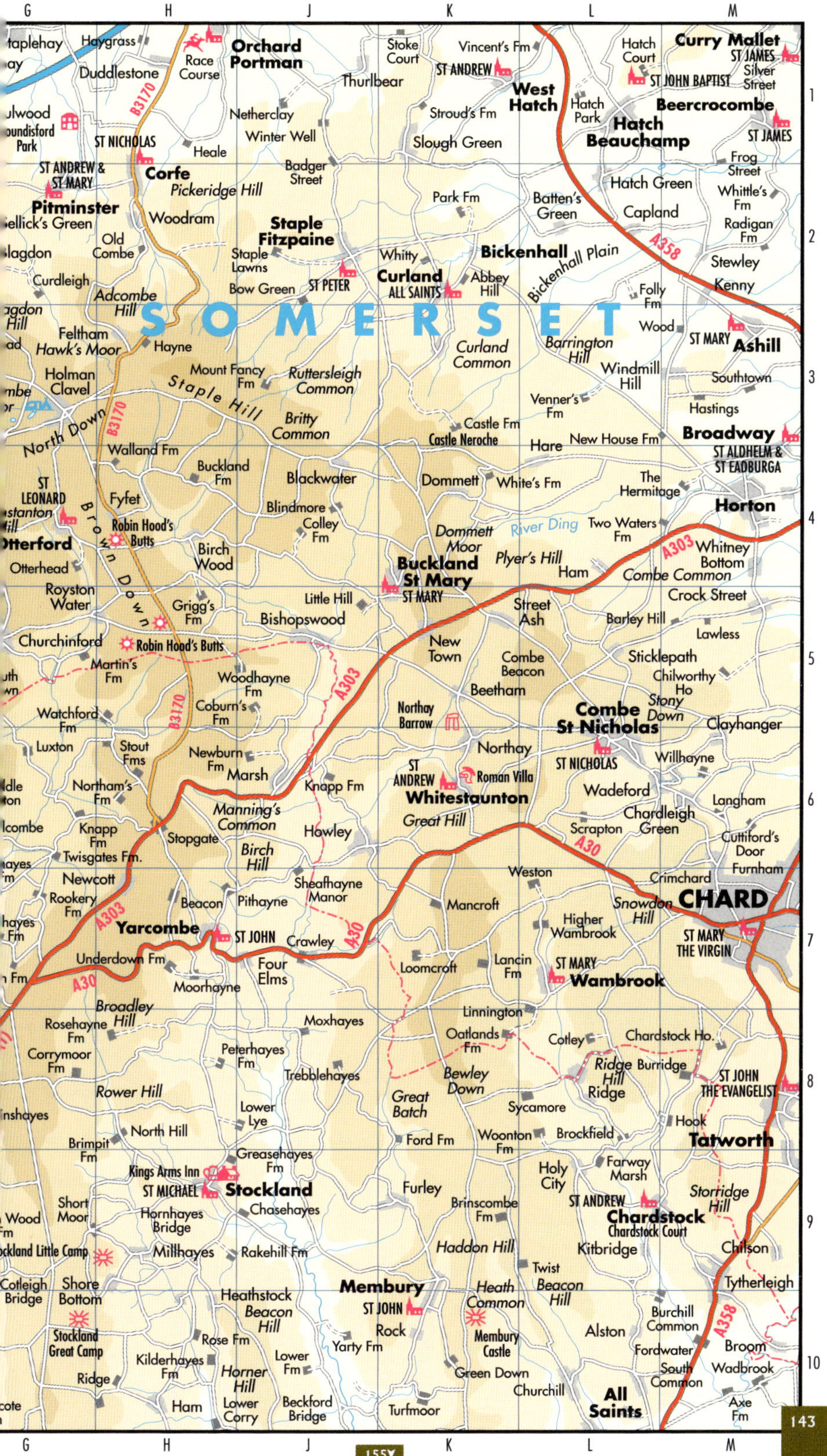

G
H
J
K
L
M
SOMERSET
Orchard Portman
Race Course
Haygrass
Duddlestone
Stoke Court
Thurlbear
Vincent's Fm
ST ANDREW
West Hatch
Hatch Court
Curry Mallet
ST JAMES
Silver Street
ST JOHN BAPTIST
Beercrocombe
ST JAMES
Hatch Park
Hatch Beauchamp
Netherclay
Winter Well
Stroud's Fm
Slough Green
ST NICHOLAS
Heale
Corfe
Pickeridge Hill
Badger Street
ST ANDREW & ST MARY
Pitminster
Woodram
Staple Fitzpaine
Park Fm
Batten's Green
Hatch Green
Capland
Frog Street
Whittle's Fm
Radigan Fm
Old Combe
Staple Lawns
Bow Green
ST PETER
Whitty
Curland
ALL SAINTS
Abbey Hill
Bickenhall
Bickenhall Plain
A358
Stewley
Kenny
Curdleigh
Adcombe Hill
Folly Fm
Wood
ST MARY
Ashill
Feltham
Hawk's Moor
Hayne
Curland Common
Barrington Hill
Windmill Hill
Southtown
Holman Clavel
Mount Fancy Fm
Ruttersleigh Common
Staple Hill
Venner's Fm
Hastings
B3170
Britty Common
Castle Fm
Castle Neroche
Hare
New House Fm
Broadway
ST ALDHELM & ST EADBURGA
North Down
Walland Fm
Buckland Fm
Blackwater
Dommett
White's Fm
The Hermitage
Horton
ST LEONARD
Fyfet
Blindmore
Colley Fm
Dommett Moor
River Ding
Two Waters Fm
Brown Down
Robin Hood's Butts
Otterford
Birch Wood
Buckland St Mary
ST MARY
Plyer's Hill
Ham
A303
Whitney Bottom
Combe Common
Otterhead
Royston Water
Grigg's Fm
Little Hill
Bishopswood
Street Ash
Crock Street
Barley Hill
Lawless
Churchinford
Robin Hood's Butts
New Town
Combe Beacon
Sticklepath
Chilworthy Ho
Martin's Fm
Woodhayne Fm
Beetham
Stony Down
Watchford Fm
Coburn's Fm
B3170
Northay Barrow
Combe St Nicholas
Clayhanger
Luxton
Stout Fms
Newburn Fm
Marsh
Northay
ST NICHOLAS
Willhayne
Northam's Fm
Knapp Fm
ST ANDREW
Roman Villa
Whitestaunton
Wadeford
Langham
Manning's Common
Great Hill
Chardleigh Green
Knapp Fm
Stopgate
Howley
Scrapton
A30
Cuttiford's Door
Twisgates Fm.
Birch Hill
Furnham
Newcott
Sheafhayne Manor
Weston
Crimchard
Rookery Fm
Beacon
Pithayne
Mancroft
Snowdon Hill
CHARD
Yarcombe
ST JOHN
Crawley
Higher Wambrook
ST MARY THE VIRGIN
Underdown Fm
Four Elms
Loomcroft
Lancin Fm
ST MARY
Wambrook
Moorhayne
Broadley Hill
Rosehayne Fm
Moxhayes
Linnington
Oatlands Fm
Cotley
Chardstock Ho.
Corrymoor Fm
Peterhayes Fm
Trebblehayes
Bewley Down
Ridge Hill
Burridge
Ridge
ST JOHN THE EVANGELIST
Rower Hill
Great Batch
Sycamore
Lower Lye
Hook
Brimpit Fm
North Hill
Ford Fm
Woonton Fm
Brockfield
Tatworth
Greasehayes Fm
Holy City
Farway Marsh
Kings Arms Inn
ST MICHAEL
Stockland
Furley
Brinscombe Fm
ST ANDREW
Chardstock
Chardstock Court
Storridge Hill
Short Moor
Hornhayes Bridge
Chasehayes
Millhayes
Rakehill Fm
Haddon Hill
Kitbridge
Chilson
Twist
Shore Bottom
Membury
Heath Common
Beacon Hill
Tytherleigh
Cotleigh Bridge
Heathstock
Beacon Hill
ST JOHN
Rock
Burchill Common
Alston
A358
Stockland Great Camp
Rose Fm
Yarty Fm
Membury Castle
Fordwater
Broom
Kilderhayes Fm
Lower Fm
Horner Hill
Green Down
South Common
Wadbrook
Ridge
Churchill
Ham
Lower Corry
Beckford Bridge
Turfmoor
All Saints
Axe Fm
155

Wellington Monument

BLACKDOWN HILLS
Fine bit of country on the Somerset/Devon border. Get off the A303 and turn right following the B3170, after three miles, take a left at the North Down junction to follow a straight road beneath a tree lined avenue, towards Clayhidon. Follow to Culmstock turn off. Wonderful. (D3)

CULM VALLEY
An enchanting valley fed by the rivers Culm, Bolham and Madford. Culmstock has a fine pub (described) and Hemyock is an ancient village with castle and church. (C4)

WELLINGTON
Old established centre of the woollen trade. Fine Georgian houses. The Duke of Wellington took his title from here, and is commemorated in monument on the hilltop three miles south. Small museum. E/C W. (C1)

Wellington Monument. A notable landmark, 175 feet high on the Blackdown Hills. The first stone was laid in 1817, and completed in 1892. Arthur Wellesley took his title from Wellington, although it is claimed he only visited the area once in 1819. He did own land hereabouts. (C3)

Where to Eat, Drink & Be Merry...

Culm Valley Inn. Looks a bit scruffy from the outside but when you enter you are awarded with a warm welcome and a proper old fashioned bar leading off to a chic

Approaching the Monument from the West

1848 The railway reaches Torquay.

1849 Apr 2. The South Devon Railway completed to Plymouth.

restaurant with artwork hanging from the walls. The proprietor is your host and chef, and great friend to Lurchers who may be asleep in a corner. Real Ales. (A4) 01884 840354

The Kings Arms Inn, Stockland. Former C16 coaching Inn is the hub of this pretty village and has gained a deserved reputation for serving fine cuisine. Whether its Monkfish, sirloin steaks or (plain) Beef Roulade, it will be delicious. Live Music every Sunday. B & B. (H9) 01404 881361

Garage Remains, Stockland

Hemyock Church

Wallace's Farm Shop & Restaurant, Hill Farm. Breeds Highland cattle, Red Deer and Bison. Sells venison and dry cured bacon. Licensed restaurant. Cream teas. Open daily 9.30-5. (D3) 01823 680307 www.welcometowallaces.com

B&B's...

Greenham Hall, Greenham
01823 672603
www.greenhamhall.co.uk

Old Vicarage, Yarcombe.
01404 861594

Dunkeswell Abbey Ruins

Churchinford

134▲
Brampford Speke
Stoke Canon
Huxham
Upton Pyne
Poltimore
Broadclyst
Exeter
EXETER
Exeter Cathedral
The Guidhall
St Nicholas Priory
Tuckers Hall
Underground Passages
Rougemont House Museum
Royal Albert Memorial Museum
Quay House Interpretation Centre
University Of Exeter
Sowton
Clyst Honiton
Exeter Airport
Clyst St.Mary
Farringdon
Alphington
Countess Wear
Topsham
Topsham Museum
Clyst St.George
Exminster
Woodbury
Woodbury Salterton
Exton
Kenn
Kenford
Powderham
Powderham Castle
Kenton
Lympstone
A La Ronde (Nt)
Starcross
Brunel's Old Pumping House
EXMOUTH
Great Exmouth Model Railway
Exmouth Museum
Exmouth Gallery
Fred Keetch Art Gallery
Mamhead
Ashcombe
Cockwood
River Exe
Exeter Canal
River Kenn
River Clyst
M5
A30(T)
A379
A376
A3015
A3052
A396
A377
A38(T)
B3212
B3181
B3184
B3179
B3123
119▼
◄83
◄118

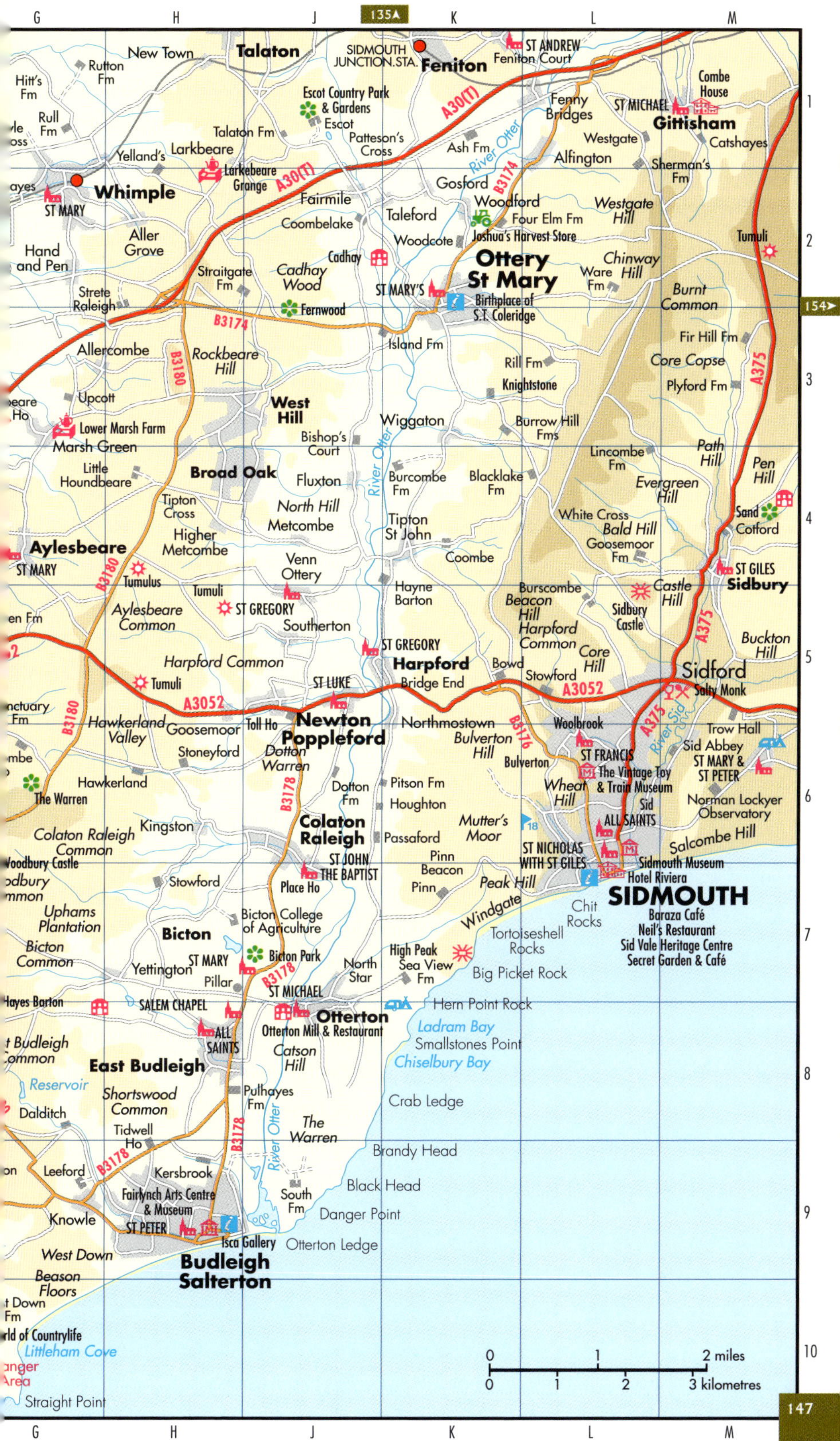

Talaton
New Town
Rutton Fm
Hitt's Fm
Rull Fm
SIDMOUTH JUNCTION.STA.
Feniton
ST ANDREW
Feniton Court
Escot Country Park & Gardens
Escot
Talaton Fm
Patteson's Cross
Fenny Bridges
ST MICHAEL
Combe House
Gittisham
Catshayes
Westgate
Alfington
Sherman's Fm
Ash Fm
River Otter
Yelland's
Larkbeare
Larkbeare Grange
A30(T)
Whimple
ST MARY
Gosford
B3174
Woodford
Four Elm Fm
Joshua's Harvest Store
Westgate Hill
Fairmile
Coombelake
Taleford
Woodcote
Aller Grove
Hand and Pen
Cadhay
Ottery St Mary
Chinway Hill
Ware Fm
Tumuli
Straitgate Fm
Cadhay Wood
ST MARY'S
Birthplace of S.T. Coleridge
Burnt Common
Strete Raleigh
Fernwood
B3174
Island Fm
Fir Hill Fm
Allercombe
Rockbeare Hill
B3180
Rill Fm
Core Copse
A375
Plyford Fm
Knightstone
Upcott
West Hill
Wiggaton
Burrow Hill Fms
Lower Marsh Farm
Marsh Green
Bishop's Court
Lincombe Fm
Path Hill
Pen Hill
Little Houndbeare
Broad Oak
Fluxton
Burcombe Fm
Blacklake Fm
Evergreen Hill
Tipton Cross
North Hill
Metcombe
Tipton St John
White Cross
Bald Hill
Sand
Cotford
Higher Metcombe
Goosemoor Fm
Aylesbeare
ST MARY
Coombe
Venn Ottery
ST GILES
Sidbury
Tumulus
Tumuli
Hayne Barton
Burscombe
Castle Hill
Beacon Hill
Sidbury Castle
Aylesbeare Common
ST GREGORY
Southerton
Harpford Common
Buckton Hill
ST GREGORY
Harpford
Core Hill
A375
Harpford Common
Bowd
Sidford
Stowford
Bridge End
Tumuli
ST LUKE
A3052
Salty Monk
A3052
Newton Poppleford
Northmostown
Woolbrook
Trow Hall
Hawkerland Valley
Goosemoor
Toll Ho
Bulverton Hill
B3176
Sid Abbey
Stoneyford
Dotton Warren
Bulverton
ST FRANCIS
River Sid
ST MARY & ST PETER
The Vintage Toy & Train Museum
Hawkerland
Dotton Fm
Pitson Fm
Wheat Hill
The Warren
B3178
Houghton
Sid
Norman Lockyer Observatory
Kingston
Colaton Raleigh
Mutter's Moor
ALL SAINTS
Colaton Raleigh Common
Passaford
Salcombe Hill
Woodbury Castle
ST JOHN THE BAPTIST
Pinn Beacon
ST NICHOLAS WITH ST GILES
Sidmouth Museum
Stowford
Hotel Riviera
Place Ho
Pinn
Peak Hill
SIDMOUTH
Uphams Plantation
Bicton College of Agriculture
Windgate
Chit Rocks
Baraza Café
Neil's Restaurant
Bicton
Tortoiseshell Rocks
Sid Vale Heritage Centre
Bicton Common
High Peak
Secret Garden & Café
ST MARY
Bicton Park
North Star
Sea View Fm
Yettington
Pillar
B3178
Big Picket Rock
Hayes Barton
SALEM CHAPEL
ST MICHAEL
Hern Point Rock
Otterton
Otterton Mill & Restaurant
Ladram Bay
ALL SAINTS
Smallstones Point
Catson Hill
Chiselbury Bay
East Budleigh
Reservoir
Shortswood Common
Pulhayes Fm
Crab Ledge
Dalditch
Tidwell Ho
B3178
The Warren
River Otter
Brandy Head
Leeford
B3178
Kersbrook
Fairlynch Arts Centre & Museum
Black Head
South Fm
Knowle
ST PETER
Danger Point
Isca Gallery
Otterton Ledge
West Down
Budleigh Salterton
Beason Floors
Littleham Cove
Straight Point
0
1
2 miles
0
1
2
3 kilometres

154

BUDLEIGH SALTERTON

A genteel town favoured by the retired, especially elderly ladies of means. The shelving, oval pebbled beach does not attract day visitors or families, like nearby Exmouth and Sidmouth. The High Street is lacklustre and uninviting. The climate; mild, sheltered and well suited for the frail and weary. The high point of one's visit may be the conversation. The wisdom gained from meeting a lonely soul. It is possible to strike up an easy conversation with the residents who are often blessed with too much charm and manners, but they will frankly inform you that they would prefer to keep the town to themselves, than be overrun by outsiders.

There are some attractive, little Regency and Georgian houses. Sir John Millais lived here and painted "The Boyhood of Raleigh". The Fairlynch Museum is an interesting building. Of more interest, East Budleigh to the north with its fine church, and monuments to Sir Walter Raleigh. Also, Otterton Mill and the gardens of Bicton. (H9)

Fairlynch Arts Centre

Fairlynch Arts Centre & Museum, 27 Fore St.
Interestingly shaped building designed in 1811 with costumes, geology and lace making exhibits plus demonstrations. Open daily East-Oct & Christmas, 2-4 (11-1 mid-July to Aug). (H9)

ISCA Gallery, 3 Chapel Street.
Small gallery established in 1993 displays a diverse range of contemporary paintings by West Country artists. Some driftwood sculptures, too. (H9) 01395 444193 www.iscagallery.co.uk

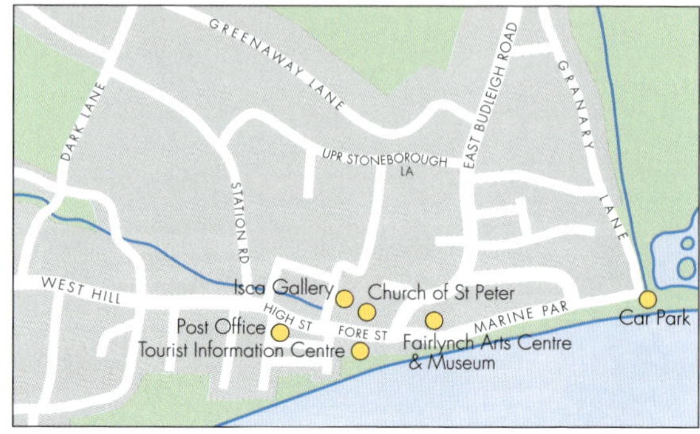

Budleigh Salterton

EXMOUTH

The oldest seaside resort in Devon, and the fourth largest town, in population, in Devon. It is a town with two sides; on the one, the commercial port and new marina development, and on the other eastern side, the sweeping sands of the seaside resort meet the cliff wall of the World Heritage Site.

Sir Walter Raleigh, East Budleigh

The town's beaches developed as a recreation area for Exeter folk in the early C18 before the upper classes came here during the Napoleonic Wars barred from Continental travel. Thus, the demand for civilised housing was acute which prompted the building of The Beacon in 1792, a fine Regency Terrace and the finest piece of architecture in the town. The numbers 6 and 19, were to become homes for the widows of Nelson and Byron.

There are a number of recreational activities to be gained from visiting Exmouth; deep sea fishing, donkey rides, and a fine cricket ground used for Minor County and Devon Youth Cricket. The new Marina is an interesting spot to while away the time. Just to the north of the town, the fascinating property, A La Ronde. (E10)

Exmouth Gallery, 46 Exeter Rd.
Hundreds of original paintings with West Country theme, sculpture garden and framing service. Open daily. (E10) 46 Exeter Rd 01395 273155 www.exmouthgallery.co.uk

Hayes Barton (Raleigh's Birthplace)

1855 Oct 20. The North Devon Railway opened from Bideford to Barnstaple.

1857 June. School Examination system set up in Exeter by Sir Thomas Acland.

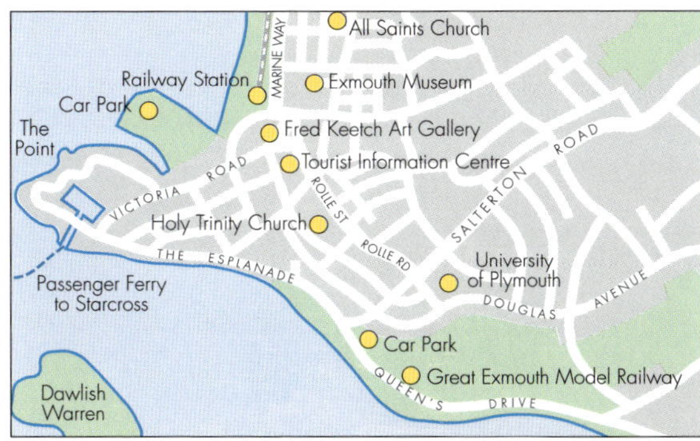

Exmouth

Bicton College Gardens, via Sidmouth Lodge. Monkey puzzle avenue, walled garden, herbaceous borders, rock garden and arboretum. Open Daily, 10-4.30. (H7) 01395 562353 www.bicton.ac.uk

Bicton Park. 60 acres of glorious gardens and parkland. Specialist greenhouses. Tropical & Palm House. Bird Garden, childrens fun world, 'Fabulous Forest'indoor activity for under teens. Restaurant, gift and plant shop. Disabled facilities. Open daily 10-6 (-5 winter). (J7) 01395 568465 www.bictongardens.co.uk

Fred Keetch Art Gallery, 46 The Strand. Exhibs by local artists in courtyard-style gallery. Open Tu-Sa 10-5. (E10)

Great Exmouth Model Railway, Queens Drive. The world's largest 00 gauge railway with over 7,500 ft of track. Open daily Apr-Oct 10.30-5.30. (E9) 01395 278383

World of Country Life. All weather family attraction with falconry displays (except Sa). Playgrounds and Pets Centre. Vintage cars. 'Victorian' street. Open daily from 10. (G10) 01395 274533

Exmouth Marina

A La Ronde ss/nt

Special Places to Visit...

A La Ronde (NT), Summer Lane. Unique 16-sided house designed in 1795 by two ladies on returning from the 'Grand Tour' combining the features of a rustic cottage with the style of the Basilica at Ravenna. Inside are Gothic grottoes, the Shell Gallery, and the Feather Frieze and Dado. 12 acres of parkland with fine views. Open daily Apr-Oct except F & Sa 11-5.30. (E8) 01395 265514

Crealy Adventure Park, Sidmouth Road. Animal and working dairy farm with viewing galleries, milk a cow - hands on adventures for children. Restaurant. Open daily from 10, all year except Nov-Mar W-Su. (E5) 01395 233200 www.crealy.co.uk

Darts Farm. Award-winning farm shop and independent gift retailer with food hall, restaurant (child friendly), bakers/deli, fish shed, plant centre, Aga, Fired Earth, Cotswold Outdoor, contemporary art and much, much more. Open daily. (D6) 01392 878200 www.dartsfarm.co.uk

Escot Fantasy Gardens & Woodland. Birds of Prey & Falconry displays, otter, squirrels & wild boar, tropical fish, coach house restaurant, arts & crafts, wetlands & waterfowl. (J1) 01404 822188 www.escot-devon.co.uk

Fernwood, Toadspit Lane's off B3174. 2 acre woodland garden. Flowering shrubs, conifers, bulbs, rhododendrons, azaleas. Open Apr-May by appointment. (J2)

Kenniford Farm Shop, Clyst St Mary. Succulant produce from their free range herd of pigs; ideal for hog roast baps, bacon and pork joints. (D5) 01395 273004 www.kennifordfarm.com

Otterton Mill. Centuries old working water mill, bakery and shop selling local produce, restaurant and art and crafts gallery. Live music most Th eves. Open daily 10-5. (J8) 01395 568521 www.ottertonmill.com

Woodbury Studio Gallery. Tim Andrew's raku ceramics, and pieces by other well-known contemporary ceramicists. Annual Ceramics Exhibition in mid September. Open M-F 10-6, Sa 10-1. (F7) Please phone out of season to check times. 01395 233475

Bicton Park bc

Special Places to Stay...

Beach House, The Strand, Topsham. In sensational position overlooking the sea, at the bottom of the High Street. (C6) 01392 876456

Woodbury Studio Gallery ss

Darts Farm

Larkbeare Grange. Set in idyllic countryside close to Exeter and Ottery St Mary. The beds are Vi-Spring, the bathrooms are luxurious. All mod cons are provided for our Laptop Age; wireless broadband and direct dial telephones. (H2) 01404 822069 www.larkbeare.net

Lower Marsh Farm. Charming former C16 manor house set in five acres of spacious grounds affording countryside views. Your hosts are like their house, full of old world charm and character. All bedrooms with bathroom and fine bed linen. Library and lounge with log fires in winter. (G3) 01404 822432 www.lowermarshdevon.co.uk

1860 Great Consols mine above the Tamar is the largest copper mine in the world, and by 1869, half the world's output.

1860s. Farm rents are high and farm workers wages are 70% of the national average resulting in a mass exodus of 126,000 folk leaving England.

SIDMOUTH

One of Devon's earliest, and most elegant, of seaside resorts developed in the late C18 and C19s.

First patronised by the Prince of Wales (later George 111) who came here to escape his creditors, and childhood home of Queen Victoria, who narrowly escaped being shot by a neighbouring child.

The town is positioned within a narrow valley beset by high, sandstone cliffs, and bisected by the River Sid rising from the hills to the north.

A town of distinction and character, with no less than 484 "Listed" buildings. Many of who belong to the Blue Plaque Scheme.

The town has an open and relaxed air about it. The sun reflects brilliantly on many of the Regency buildings painted in their creams and whites. Often mirrored by the cricketers standing about on the turf laid down in 1820.

Surely one of the country's most attractive town grounds, where I have had the good fortune to play, for The Boffins, these past twenty years.

There are energetic coastal walks to be had, to the west and east, but if architecture holds your attention, then spend a few hours wandering around with the Blue Plaque Guide. I was at a loss to find a guide detailing the entire, 484 "listed" buildings. You may have more luck.

The town comes alive during the Folk Festival in August, and while I was there in November surfers were riding a Slow Break. It has youth in numbers, and unlike nearby Budleigh, it likes to party. We have seen nothing yet. (L7)

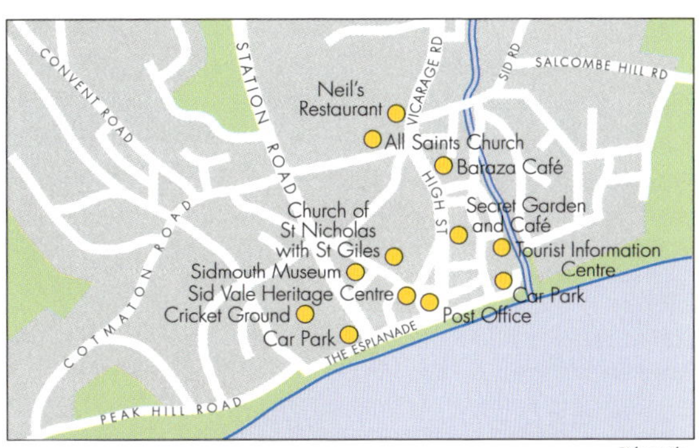

Sidmouth

Beach House, Sidmouth

Special Places to Visit...

Sid Vale Heritage Centre, Church St. Local lace, costumes, geology, archaeology, prints, photographs etc. Open daily mid-Apr to Oct 2-4.30 (& Tu-Sa 10-12.30 BHs & Summer). (L6)

Where to Eat, Drink & Be Merry...

Baraza, 128 High Street. Friendly cafe serving breakfasts from 9.00 am and lunches. Themed Nights with live music. Outside catering service. (L6) 01395 577553

Neil's Restaurant, Radway Place. Chef Neil Harding has 25 years experience, so be prepared to be spoilt and indulge yourself in the English Channel's rich larder, for fish is his speciality. Booking advised. Open Tu-Sa from 6.30 pm. Lunch and business parties by arrangement. (L6) 01395 519494 www.neilsrestaurant.com

Salty Monk, Church Street, Sidford. Award-winning restaurant with rooms. All food is prepared on the premises. Accomodation includes spa baths, hydro massage showers and king-size beds. (M5) 01395 513174 www.saltymonk.co.uk

Secret Garden & Cafe, 4-6 The Parade. To reach the cafe upstairs you must first walk through a pot-pourri of gifts and perfumes, then the aroma of fresh coffee. A glamorous cafe serving light lunches and homemade fare. The best Devon cream teas. Organic farm shop, too. Open daily. (L6) 01395 579449

TOPSHAM

One of South Devon's most attractive little towns, and a popular "Eating Out" destination for Exeter folk. The nearby Darts Farm has multiplied the visitors of late. The long, narrow High Street is fronted with many old houses in the "Dutch" style dating from the C17 and C18. Continue past the many restaurants, pubs, two excellent tearooms, and museum, and you come to the small harbour and antique emporium. The former port of Exeter, hence its evident heritage of past wealth. (C6)

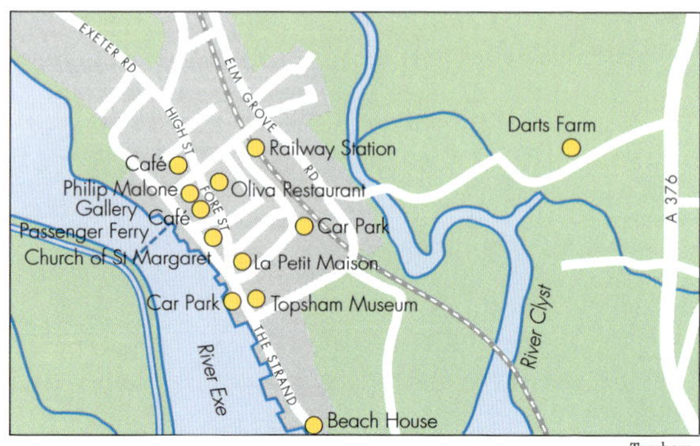

Topsham

Where to Eat, Drink & Be Merry…

La Petite Maison, 35 Fore Street. As the name suggests, an intimate restaurant that has won garlands galore, and rightly so. You won't be disappointed. Fish off the local boats, pork from Somerset and Exmoor lamb, all cooked with a flourish. Booking advised. Open Tu-Sa. (C6) 01392 873660 www.lapetitemaison.co.uk

Oliva Restaurant, 6-7 Fore Street. Family run restaurant; Dad out front, son in kitchen, producing mediterranean style food with a twist of the Latin. Paellas a speciality. (C6) 01392 877878 www.olivarestaurant.co.uk

The Estuary at Dusk, Topsham

La Petite Maison ss

Special Places to Visit…

Topsham Museum, 25 The Strand. Late C17 merchant's house with attractive period rooms, sail loft, gardens. Shipbuilding, maritime trade, the Exe Estuary. Honiton Lace and Vivien Leigh. Teas. Shop. Open Feb-Nov M, W & Sa 2-5 (Su in Aug & Sept). (C6) 01392 873244

The Philip Malone Gallery, 76 Fore St. Co-operative of eight artists and craftsmen who hold regular exhibitions of their work; paintings, glass, sculpture and ceramics. The gallery is open intermittently, and as locally advertised. (C6) 01392 874 311 www.philipmalonegallery.co.uk

Pubs Serving Food - Where to Eat, Drink & Be Merry…

Black Horse, Old Honiton Road, Sowton. Large inn serving all manner of food. Very popular with local businessman, and the Retired with time on their hands. (D3) www.blackhorseinnexeter.co.uk

Diggers Rest Inn. Child friendly pub serves pasta and fishnchips, and free ice cream. Beer garden. Food from 12-2, 7-9.30 pm. (F5) 01395 232375

Otterton Mill Restaurant. Cosy little restaurant serving home-made soups and dishes of the day. Fabulous bread and cakes from the Bakery next door. Fresh coffee and newspapers, what more do you need? Open daily. (J8) 01395 567041 www.ottertonmill.com

1864 Vitifer Mine, near Warren House produces 154 tons of tin, reducing to 22 tons in 1907.

1864 Kents Cavern systematically explored.

Beaches...

Exmouth. Wide sandy beach with rocks. Water sports. D/LG/R/WC. Also, a sandy beach at the east end beneath Orcombe Cliffs. (E10)

Budleigh Salterton. Steeply shelving with oval pebbles. D/R/WC. (H9)

The Quay, Topsham

Orcombe Cliffs, Exmouth

Rock Pooling, Sidmouth

Ladram Bay. Pebble beach with high cliffs. Short walk from P. D/R/WC. (K8)

Sidmouth. Sand at low tide. "Jacobs Ladder" leads down to western beach with rock pools, pebbles and shingle. Main beach below promenade has pebbles. Water sports. Surfing is unusual. D/R/WC. (L7)

Below Salcombe Hill, Sidmouth

Coastal Footpath...

Exmouth to Budleigh Salterton; 6 miles. The first 2 miles are along Exmouth Promenade, followed by an ascent to the 'High Land of Orcombe' (NT). Then a descent to Littleham Cove and a steep climb to 'The Floors', where the undercliff is noted for birdlife, and a gradual descent into the town.

Budleigh Salterton to Sidmouth; 8 miles. A detour is needed to cross the Otter a mile upstream. Returning to the coast the path ascends the red sandstone cliffs and provides a fairly level walk with fine views. Ladram Bay is noted for its curious rock formations and bird life. The final section involves a steep climb over Peak Hill

Ladram Rocks sh

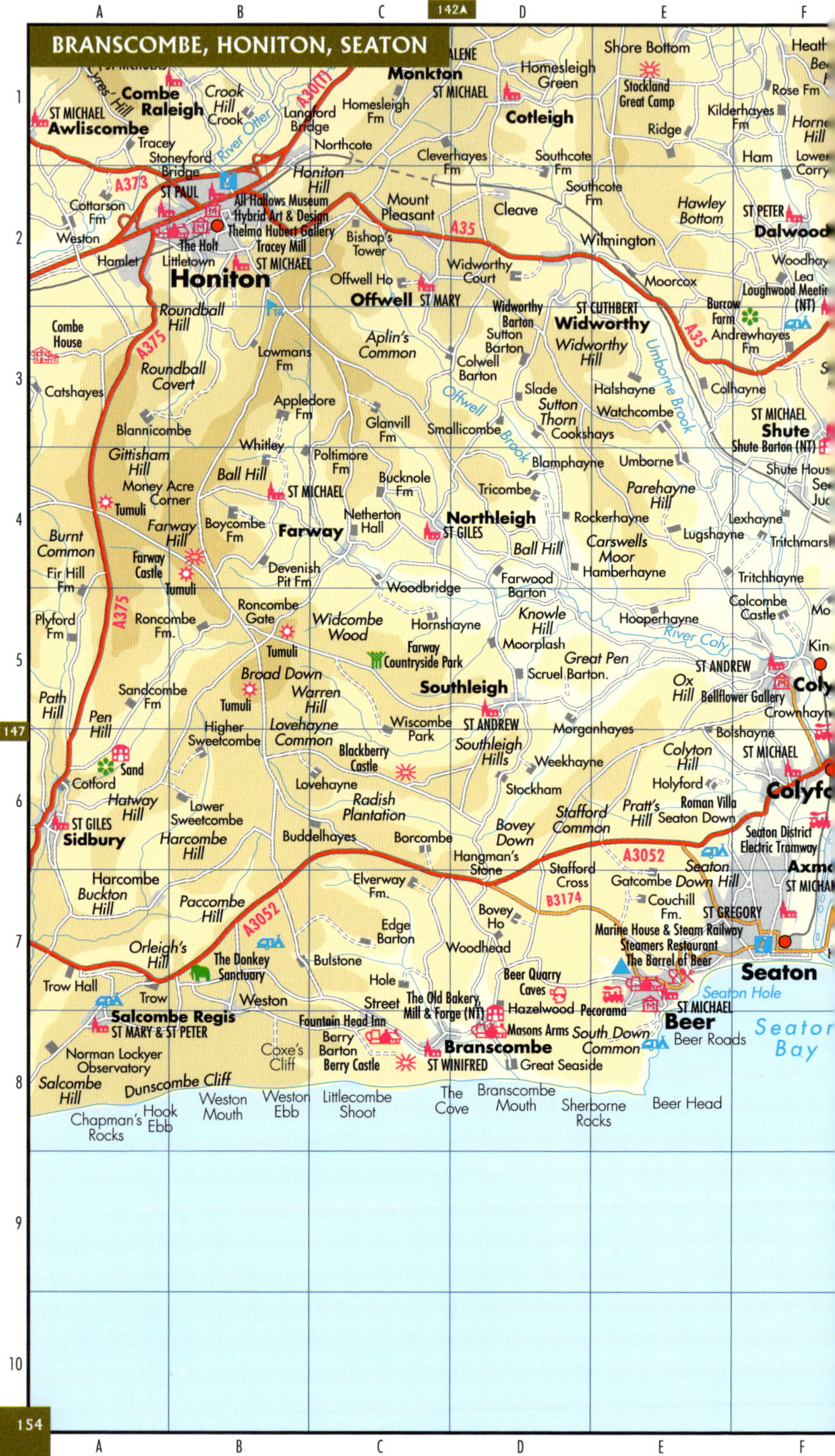
BRANSCOMBE, HONITON, SEATON
142A
A
B
C
D
E
F
1
2
3
4
5
6
7
8
9
10
◄147
Monkton
ST MICHAEL
Homesleigh Green
Shore Bottom
Stockland Great Camp
Rose Fm
Combe Raleigh
Crook Hill
Crook
ST MICHAEL
Awliscombe
Tracey
Stoneyford Bridge
River Otter
A30(T)
Langford Bridge
Homesleigh Fm
Northcote
Cotleigh
Ridge
Kilderhayes Fm
Ham
Cleverhayes Fm
Southcote Fm
A373
ST PAUL
Honiton Hill
Cottarson Fm
Weston
All Hallows Museum
Hybrid Art & Design
Thelma Hulbert Gallery
The Holt
Tracey Mill
Mount Pleasant
Cleave
Southcote Fm
Hawley Bottom
ST PETER
Dalwood
A35
Bishop's Tower
Wilmington
Hamlet
Littletown
ST MICHAEL
Honiton
Widworthy Court
Offwell Ho
Offwell
ST MARY
Moorcox
Burrow Farm
Loughwood Meeting (NT)
Andrewhayes Fm
Roundball Hill
Widworthy Barton
Sutton Barton
ST CUTHBERT
Widworthy
Widworthy Hill
Combe House
A375
Aplin's Common
Colwell Barton
Umborne Brook
Roundball Covert
Lowmans Fm
Catshayes
Colhayne
Offwell Brook
Slade
Sutton Thorn
Halshayne
Watchcombe
Appledore Fm
Glanvill Fm
Smallicombe
Cookshays
ST MICHAEL
Shute
Shute Barton (NT)
Blannicombe
Whitley
Gittisham Hill
Poltimore Fm
Blamphayne
Umborne
Shute House
Money Acre Corner
Ball Hill
ST MICHAEL
Bucknole Fm
Tricombe
Parehayne Hill
Tumuli
Farway Hill
Boycombe Fm
Farway
Netherton Hall
Northleigh
ST GILES
Rockerhayne
Lexhayne
Burnt Common
Lugshayne
Tritchmarsh
Ball Hill
Carswells Moor
Hamberhayne
Farway Castle
Tumuli
Devenish Pit Fm
Fir Hill Fm
Woodbridge
Farwood Barton
Tritchhayne
Roncombe Gate
Colcombe Castle
Plyford Fm
Roncombe Fm.
Widcombe Wood
Hornshayne
Knowle Hill
Hooperhayne
River Coly
Moorplash
Tumuli
Farway Countryside Park
Great Pen
Scruel Barton.
ST ANDREW
Broad Down
Southleigh
Ox Hill
Bellflower Gallery
Sandcombe Fm
Warren Hill
Path Hill
Tumuli
Crownhayne
Pen Hill
Higher Sweetcombe
Lovehayne Common
Wiscombe Park
ST ANDREW
Morganhayes
Bolshayne
Blackberry Castle
Southleigh Hills
Weekhayne
Colyton Hill
ST MICHAEL
Sand
Cotford
Lovehayne
Holyford
Stockham
Hatway Hill
Radish Plantation
Roman Villa
Lower Sweetcombe
Stafford Common
Pratt's Hill
Seaton Down
ST GILES
Sidbury
Harcombe Hill
Buddelhayes
Borcombe
Bovey Down
Seaton District Electric Tramway
Hangman's Stone
A3052
Harcombe
Elverway Fm.
Stafford Cross
Seaton Down Hill
Buckton Hill
Paccombe Hill
Gatcombe
Couchill Fm.
ST GREGORY
B3174
Bovey Ho
A3052
Edge Barton
Marine House & Steam Railway
Orleigh's Hill
Woodhead
Steamers Restaurant
The Barrel of Beer
The Donkey Sanctuary
Bulstone
Seaton
Trow Hall
Beer Quarry Caves
Hole
Seaton Hole
Trow
Weston
Street
The Old Bakery, Mill & Forge (NT)
Hazelwood
Pecorama
ST MICHAEL
Salcombe Regis
ST MARY & ST PETER
Fountain Head Inn
Masons Arms
South Down Common
Beer
Seaton Bay
Berry Barton
Beer Roads
Norman Lockyer Observatory
Coxe's Cliff
Berry Castle
Branscombe
ST WINIFRED
Great Seaside
Salcombe Hill
Dunscombe Cliff
Weston Mouth
Weston Ebb
Littlecombe Shoot
The Cove
Branscombe Mouth
Sherborne Rocks
Beer Head
Chapman's Rocks
Hook Ebb

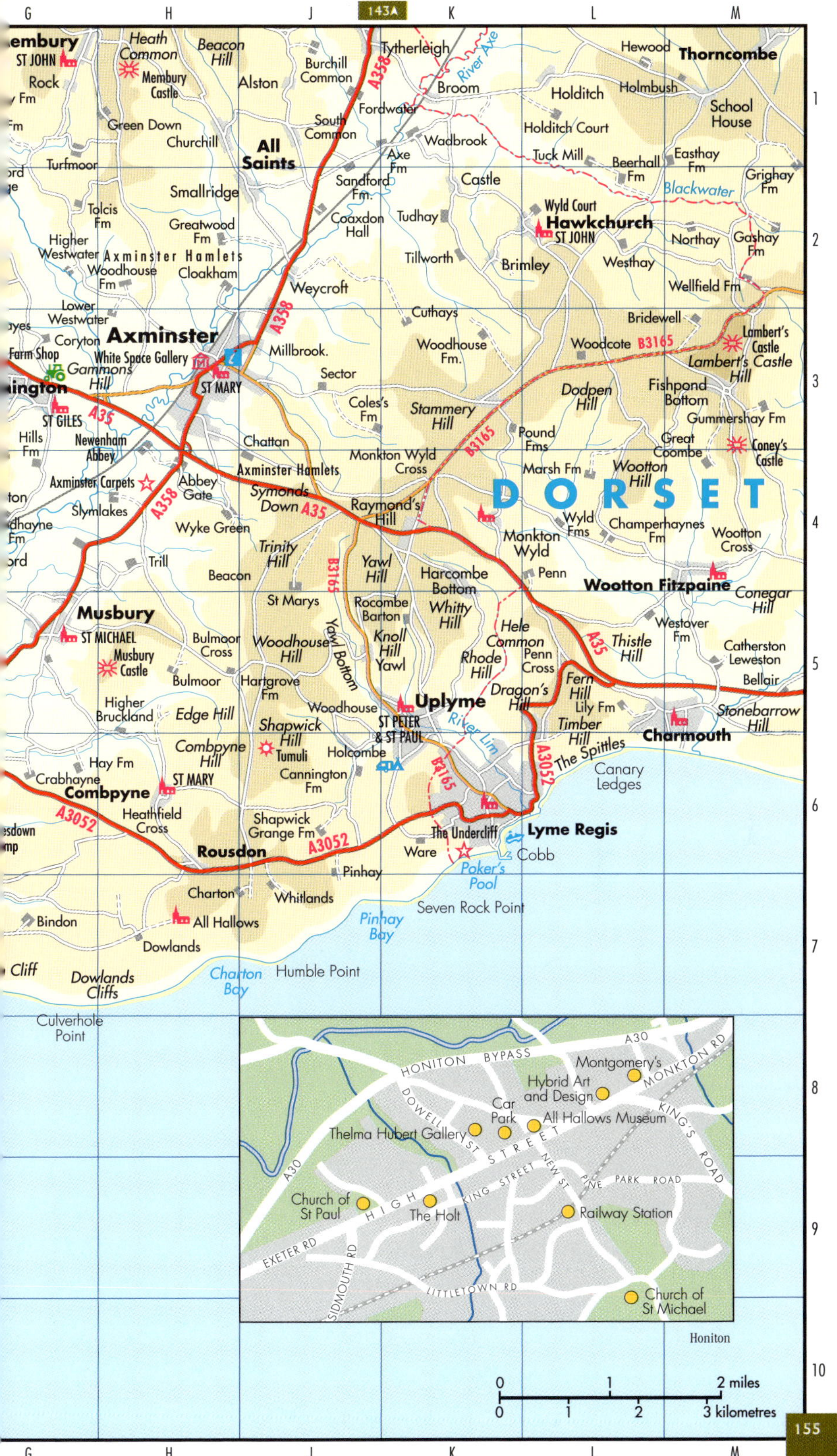

G H J K L M
1 2 3 4 5 6 7 8 9 10
DORSET
Axminster
Thorncombe
Hawkchurch
All Saints
Musbury
Combpyne
Rousdon
Uplyme
Lyme Regis
Charmouth
Wootton Fitzpaine
Monkton Wyld
Tytherleigh
Broom
Holditch
Holditch Court
Hewood
Holmbush
School House
Burchill Common
Beacon Hill
Heath Common
Membury Castle
Alston
Fordwater
South Common
Wadbrook
Green Down
Churchill
Turfmoor
Smallridge
Sandford Fm.
Axe Fm
Castle
Tuck Mill
Beerhall Fm
Easthay Fm
Grighay Fm
Blackwater
River Axe
Wyld Court
Northay
Gashay Fm
Westhay
Wellfield Fm
Brimley
Tillworth
Tudhay
Coaxdon Hall
Greatwood Fm
Tolcis Fm
Higher Westwater
Axminster Hamlets
Woodhouse Fm
Cloakham
Weycroft
Cuthays
Lower Westwater
Coryton
Farm Shop
White Space Gallery
Gammons Hill
ST MARY
Millbrook.
Sector
Woodhouse Fm.
Woodcote
B3165
Bridewell
Lambert's Castle
Lambert's Castle Hill
Fishpond Bottom
Dodpen Hill
Stammery Hill
Coles's Fm
Gummershay Fm
ST GILES
A35
Hills Fm
Newenham Abbey
Chattan
Monkton Wyld Cross
Pound Fms
Great Coombe
Coney's Castle
Marsh Fm
Wootton Hill
Axminster Carpets
Abbey Gate
Symonds Down
Raymond's Hill
Slymlakes
A358
Wyke Green
Trinity Hill
Wyld Fms
Champerhaynes Fm
Wootton Cross
Trill
Beacon
Yawl Hill
Harcombe Bottom
Penn
Conegar Hill
St Marys
Rocombe Barton
Whitty Hill
Hele Common
Westover Fm
ST MICHAEL
Musbury Castle
Bulmoor Cross
Woodhouse Hill
Yawl Bottom
Knoll Hill
Yawl
Rhode Hill
Penn Cross
Thistle Hill
Catherston Leweston
Bulmoor
Hartgrove Fm
Fern Hill
Bellair
Higher Bruckland
Edge Hill
Woodhouse
ST PETER & ST PAUL
Dragon's Hill
Lily Fm
Stonebarrow Hill
Shapwick Hill
Tumuli
River Lim
Timber Hill
Combpyne Hill
Holcombe
The Spittles
Hay Fm
Cannington Fm
A3052
Canary Ledges
Crabhayne
Heathfield Cross
Shapwick Grange Fm
The Undercliff
Ware
Cobb
Pinhay
Poker's Pool
Charton
Whitlands
Seven Rock Point
Bindon
All Hallows
Pinhay Bay
Dowlands
Cliff
Dowlands Cliffs
Charton Bay
Humble Point
Culverhole Point
Honiton
HONITON BYPASS
A30
MONKTON RD
Montgomery's
Hybrid Art and Design
Car Park
All Hallows Museum
KING'S ROAD
DOWELL ST
Thelma Hubert Gallery
STREET
NEW ST
PINE PARK ROAD
Church of St Paul
HIGH
The Holt
KING STREET
Railway Station
EXETER RD
SIDMOUTH RD
LITTLETOWN RD
Church of St Michael
0 1 2 miles
0 1 2 3 kilometres

AXMINSTER

Well situated to be an ancient and quiet market town on a slight contour above the River Axe. The Roman Fosse Way passed close by. King Athelstan, the first King of All England fought a victorious battle against the Danes in 937 nearby on Brunanburgh field, and in celebration he founded a College, now completely vanished. The Royalist troops occupied in 1644 during the Siege of Lyme Regis. Later, Axminster Carpets were in business from 1755-1835, later to be revived in 1937 by Harry Dutfield.

Mud Flats, Axmouth

The Arts Café, Axminster

Just off the central square, the little Bookshop, The Arts Café, a crafts shop, open M-F 10-3 and weekends displaying outdoor sculpture. Next door, the little museum opens from May to September, from 10. The chic bar, The Swan, on the corner, is a bistro during the day, and in the evenings a restaurant. For a traditional pub and pint, the George Hotel, a friendly local and host to Oliver Cromwell during his siege of Lyme Regis. (H3)

Special Places to Visit…

Axminster Carpets. Factory showroom with small museum and video of production, from fleece to floor. Open daily. (H4)

White Space Gallery, West St. Co-operative of 4-artists selling and displaying their work; paintings, mixed media, sculptured ceramics. Open M-Sa 10-5. 01297 35807 (H3)

Axminster Church, St Mary. Cruciform in shape with Norman dooray. Fine E window in Chancel, exceptional N & S windows, sedilia and piscina. Effigy of headless priest. Finely carved C17 pulpit. On his travels in 1740 Daniel Defoe saw the Monuments of the Saxon Bishop of Sherburne and two Dukes slain at the Battle of Brunanburh, yet nothing in evidence today. (H3)

The Arts Café, Axminster

AXMOUTH

Before this village silted up in the C17 it held a large harbour. Now the silted mud flats are a haven for birdlife, an ornithologists delight. Large campsite. Two fine inns, the Harbour Inn is a popular dining pub, authentic in design and purpose. (F7)

Axmouth Church, St Michael. Norman c. 1140 with additions in 1330. A perpendicular stair-turret tower. Three Italianate wall paintings. (F7)

BEER

The major coastal attraction in this part of East Devon. An old fishing and smuggling village made notorious by the published diaries of one Jack Rattenbury in 1837 who later lived the life of a gentleman. Lace making was a major occupation; Queen Victoria's wedding dress was woven here, and Beer Stone was quarried here, first in Long Galleries, then as open caste, supplying the stone for Exeter Cathedral.

The fishing boats are shelved on the beach and you can buy fresh fish (usually sole or flounders) from the fisherman's hut above the beach. A dashing stream runs beside the high street and plunges over a cliff into the pebbles. Gift and craft shops, tearooms and inns, aplenty all serving freshly caught fish.

The coastal path rises 400 feet to Beer Head, the most southerly chalk cliffs in England that run down from Flamborough Head in Yorkshire. Below are cliffs, "riddled with caverns and rent with spires", made useful by smugglers past. (E7)

Wall Paintings, St Michael's, Axmouth

1869 Closure of the Grand Western Canal.

1870s Plymouth becomes a great liner port with over 500 visits per year.

Gutting the Day's Catch, Beer

Special Places to Visit...

Beer Quarry Caves. A 2,000-year old history of quarrying stone from the Romans until the last century. Tour of awe-inspiring caves like a vast underground cathedral. Also formerly used to hide persecuted Catholics and for storing contraband. Open daily East-Sept 10-5, & Oct 11-4. (D7) 01297 680282 www.beerquarrycaves.fsnet.co.uk

Marine House & Steam Gallery, Fore Street. Established gallery representing a fine collection of painters, sculptors, ceramicists and jewellers. One of Devon's best. (E7) 01297 625257 www.marinehouseatbeer.co.uk

Pecorama. Miniature steam railway, PECO Model railway exhibition, children's safety surfaced activity area, all surrounded by manicured gardens with fine sea views. Restaurant. Open early East-Oct M-F 10-5.30, Sa 10-1, Su East to early Sept, 10-5.30. (E7) 01297 21542 www.peco-uk.com

Where to Eat, Drink & Be Merry...

Steamers Restaurant, Fore Street. Bright and colourful eatery serving local fish, duck and pasta dishes. Sunday lunch specials. Open Tu-Sa 12-2.30 & 6.30-9.30. (E7) 01297 22922 www.steamersrestaurant.co.uk

Branscombe

The Barrel O' Beer, Fore Street. Dining pub specialises in seafood dishes where your chef has earned his stripes in some top class restaurants across the globe. Real ales. (E7) 01297 20099 www.barrelobeer.co.uk

Pecorama ss

BRANSCOMBE

One of the most romantic and picturesque villages in Devon set amidst a series of deep, narrow, tortuous combes. Three hamlets, or nests of houses make up the village. Notable church, forge (NT) and baker. Many of the cottages (some thatch) and houses are built of local Beer stone. Legend has it that a Spanish galleon foundered here in the C17, whence the sailors wed the local girls, and dark haired and brown eyed folk have "melted into the flaxen-haired Saxon fold". The ladies would sit at their cottage doors with cushion and bobbin darning the lace.

At Branscombe Mouth (parking charge) there is a fine stretch of chalk cliff, broken by landslips and noted for fossils. There's also a cafe/beach restaurant serving locally caught fish. Shingle beach. (D8)

1870 Every parish to have their own school. 1872 Repeal of the Corn Laws.

Joan Tregarthen's Tomb, Branscombe

The Forge, Branscombe

Special Places to Visit...

Branscombe Church, St Winifred. Magnificent and stately for a small, isolated village with Norman tower, gallery, 3-decker pulpit and tomb of Joan Tregarthen d. 1583, mother of twenty children, fathered by her two husbands who stand opposite each other. Turn R out of the entrance descending to a footpath that leads along the valley, zig-zagging to Branscombe Mouth. (C8)

The Old Bakery, Manor Mill & Forge (NT). Now thankfully restored to working order after the closure of the business in 1987. The baking equipment has been preserved and the building is used as a tearoom. The Manor Mill supplied the flour for the bakery, and the forge is open daily, all year, where the blacksmith sells the ironwork he produces, and takes commissions. Old Bakery Open Apr-Oct W-Su, 11-5. Manor Mill open Su (& W July-Aug), 2-5. (D8)

Where to Eat, Drink & Be Merry...

Masons Arms. "Here Ye Toil Not" but enjoy the fine ales and food; lobster and crab dishes, a speciality. Fireplaces and exposed walls. Summer beer festival. Restaurant. Bar food. Sit outside and idly watch passes-by. Accommodation. (D8) 01297 680300 ww.masonsarms.co.uk

Fountain Head Inn. On the western edge of the village. An intimate and popular little pub serving fresh meals and real ales. Small seating area outside. (C8)

St Andrew's, Colyton

COLYFORD

Former site of Roman villa on t he western edge of the Rive Axe, and probable fort beside the Fosse Way. Wide water meadows beside the river strike northwards towards Colyton. (F6)

COLYTON

A pretty village noted for its sumptuous church, village square and highly rated Grammar School. In the C15 one of the wealthiest wool towns in Devon that took advantage of exporting its goods through nearby Seaton. Saxon traditions still prevail in the town, for the Town Councillors

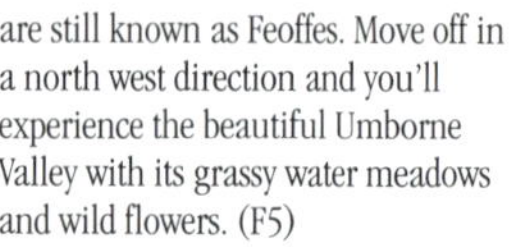

are still known as Feoffes. Move off in a north west direction and you'll experience the beautiful Umborne Valley with its grassy water meadows and wild flowers. (F5)

Special Places to Visit...

Colyton Church, St Andrew. Fine, impressive building with central tower. Memorials to Margaret, Countess of Devon, granddaughter of John of Gaunt. Her tomb was smashed up by the Parliamentarian troops in Civil War. Also monuments to Sir John Pole and his wife Elizabeth who lived at nearby, Shute. (F5)

Bellflower Gallery, Market Place. Contemporary fine art. Open Tu-Sa 10-5. (F5)

HONITON

One gets the feeling that Honiton is undergoing a revival of good fortune. New restaurants, new coffee shops and galleries...there's a buzz about the place. The long, wide High Street with Georgian buildings is always busy and bustling. I counted half a dozen antique-bric-a-brac-emporia shops at the west end, and more at the top, east end. At the east end, the earthy Honeybee coffee shop, and at the west end, next to a wine bar, the Boston Tea Party with art gallery and garden.

A deep connection with lace and glove making, as illustrated in the little museum. The almshouse was the former leper hospital, St Margaret's. July Fair, Agricultural show in August, Carnival in September. (B2)

1872 Devon County Agricultural Association formed.

1874 United Services College founded at Westward Ho! Alma Mater to Rudyard Kipling (and appears in Stalky & Co).

All Hallows Museum of Lace

Worcester parson. The bridge crossing the Rive Axe was opened in April 1877 and became the first concrete toll in England, until September 1907. Bass are caught off the bridge. The Axe is also known to favour salmon and sea trout. (F7)

Special Places of Interest...

Seaton Tramway Co., Harbour Road. An unforgettable three mile ride; Seaton-Colyford-Colyton. Unique open top and enclosed single deck trams giving superb views of the beautiful Axe valley, noted for its wading river birds. Open daily East-Oct. (F6) 01297 20375

Special Places to Visit...

AllHallows Museum of Lace & Antiquities, High Street. Local history and world famous lace with demos. Open East-Oct M-F 9.30-4.30, Sa 9.30-1. (B2) 01404 44966

Hybrid Art & Design, 51 High Street. Art gallery and shop selling original and hand-crafted work. Also, a Design Consultancy. (B2) 01404 43201 www.hybrid-devon.co.uk

Thelma Hulbert Gallery, Dowell Street. East Devon's only public art gallery shows an exciting programme of contemporary art and crafts. Open W-Sa 10-4. (B2) 01404 45006 www.thelmahulbert.com

Where to Eat, Drink & Be Merry...

The Holt, 178 High Street. New bar and restaurant set up by the local Otter Brewery is quickly establishing a reputation. Artworks line the walls. Film nights every second Su. (B2) 01404 47707

Montgomery's, 21 High Street. Coffee shop and cafe offering home made cakes and soups, lunch specials in a friendly environment. (B2) 01404 44666

The Medieval Bells, Northleigh Church

Seaton Harbour

SEATON

Small resort with pebble beach not noted for it's architecture like nearby Sidmouth but there are attractive Georgian buildings in the centre of town. The small harbour is of interest, also the coastal path to Downland Cliffs. The cliffs rise to either side of the town affording sweeping views from the coastal footpath. There are precious stones to be found on the beach; jaspers and garnets.

In former times the Romans used the Fosse Way and the harbour here as a conduit to ship out Cotswold and Mendip wool back to their Republic. A Roman pavement was found here in 1921 measuring 16 feet square with a twisted pattern, now in Exeter Museum. Much later in the C19 coal was exported off the beach, sometimes beside patients seeking the calm waters of Seaton Spa! A fact noted in Francis Kilvert's diaries, the

Special Places to Visit...

Burrow Farm Gardens.
4 acre woodland garden created since 1966. Rhododendrons, azaleas, primulas. Planned for foliage effect. Bog garden. Open daily Apr-Sept 10-7. Cream teas Su, W & BHs. (F3) Dalewood 01404 831285 www.burrowfarmgardens.co.uk

Church of St Giles, Northleigh.
A fine Norman doorway with intricate carvings of animal heads. C16 fan-vaulted screen with colourful vine leaves, and so claimed, the oldest stained glass in Devon; figures of St Peter and St Paul. (C4)

Farway Countryside Park.
100 acre nature reserve. Friendly animals and pets to feed and handle. Trailer rides. Indoor childrens play area. Pony rides. Restaurant. Open daily Mar-Nov 10-5.30, W/Es in winter 11-5. Open all school hols in winter. (C5) 01404 871367

1881 4,000 miners at work in Devon.

1882 Lord Manners married to Constance Hamlyn of Clovelly trains and rides the Grand National winner, Seaman.

Hawkesdown Camp. An oblong earthwork consisting of two banks with a fosse between. (G6)

Lyme Bay Winery. A specialist producer of country wines, ciders and liqueurs, all on sale from M-F 9-5, Sa 10-4, Su 11-4. 01297 551355 www.lymebaywinery.co.uk

Miller's Farm Shop, Kilmington. Established 26 years ago, it's a successful combination of a French deli (with imports from Miller's Normandy farm) and an English farm shop. (G3) 01297 35390

Shute Barton

Sand. Elizabethan manor house in the Huyshe family for over 50 years. Medieval hall and period features in Guided Tour. 6 acres of varied garden. Teas. House open East, Spring & Aug BHs, Garden Su, M & Tu Apr-Sept, 2-6 (A6) 01395 597230 www.sandsidbury.co.uk

Shute Barton (NT). Impressive entrance to medieval manor house built in 1380 with later additions in the C18. The Pole family lived here until the fire, leaving just the gatehouse and one wing. Open Apr-Oct W & Sa 2-5.30, Oct 2-5.

Sir William Pole, St Michael's Church

The C13 Church of St Michael, just up the hill, is cruciform, and has fine memorials to the Poles, see Sir William Pole d.1741, Master of Queen Anne's household. (F3)

Tracey Mill & Trout Farm, Tracey Road. Restored C17 working water mill on the River Otter produces flour, and power, and is also the site of a thriving trout farm. Shop selling many goodies. Open M-Sa 9-5. (B2) 01404 45114 www.traceymill.co.uk

Villages of Interest...

Lyme Regis.
Although just over the border in Dorset, if you are touring this area you can't exclude this fascinating little town from your itinerary. Its literary and film connections are endless; from Jane Austen to John Fowles. Who can forget the French Lieutenant's Woman (Meryl Streep) standing isolated on the Cobb, almost being washed asunder by the crashing waves until rescued by the dashing Jeremy Irons in the film of the same name? There are two parts of the village, the High Street area, and the Cobb (harbour). The High Street has a number of galleries, fossil emporia and places to eat plus the excellent local museum, to visit. A walk along the promenade connects to the Cobb where you can watch the fishing boats come and go, and sit on the little beach. A small aquarium is open in season, and there are a number of pubs, cafes and gift shops. (L6)

Musbury.
Birthplace in 1650 of John Churchill, the first Duke of Marlborough. The Musbury Monument erected in 1611 commemorates the Drake family. A pleasant walk is to be had leading away from the Musbury Castle earthwork, an Iron Age hillfort along the old packhorse route to Combpyne via Higher Bruckland farm. (G5)

Uplyme.
Attractive village to the north west of Lyme Regis just across from the Dorset border. Set amidst quaint, sheltered valleys. An early Saxon and Roman settlement connected to the fort at Seaton. (K5)

Churches...

Uplyme Church, St Peter & St Paul. Pretty little church with Gallery and wagon roof painted with clear blue and embellished with gold stars. (K5)

Ammonite Fossil, Lyme Regis

Coastal Footpath...

Sidmouth to Seaton
11 miles. One of the toughest sections of the path with cliffs up to 450 ft and intervening valleys. Much of this stretch is National Trust land. The red sandstone gradually changes to chalk and there is some difficult going in places. The path descends to sea level at Branscombe Mouth, and again at Beer.

Seaton to Lyme Regis
8 miles. After crossing the Axe there is a steep climb and the path enters the 'Landslip', an area of broken ground caused by a major earth movement in 1839. Here again there is some difficult ground but there is much to interest the naturalist and geologist. Shortly before reaching Lyme, the path crosses into Dorset.

Beaches...

Branscombe. Steep pebble beach. Interesting rocks at LT. P Charge. R/WC. (D8)

Beer. Steep shingle and pebble beach with rocks. Boating pool. Short walk from P. D/R/WC. (E7)

Seaton. Shelving pebbles. Sand at LT. D/R/WC. (F7)

1884 John Babbacombe Lee unsuccessfully hanged three times for the murder of Mrs Keyes.

1887 Sep 5. Theatre Royal, Exeter, destroyed by fire with loss of 160 lives.

St Giles, Northleigh

This is the "Glorious Devon" of the old railway posters. Centred on the wide bay made popular in Napoleonic times as an important naval base. The mild climate and fine coastal scenery attracted the naval officers to set up their domestic quarters, the foundation of present-day Torquay.

Around the Bay, the three contrasting towns of Torquay, Paignton and Brixham, providing amenities for differing tastes; Torquay with its fine situation, imposing buildings and lush semi-tropical vegetation, the wide beaches and traditional seaside diversions of Paignton, and the old-world charm of the fishing port of Brixham.

To the north, beside the beautiful Teign Estuary lie the smaller resorts of Shaldon and Teignmouth, set just to the south of the bright red sandstone cliffs so characteristic of this part of Devon. Brunel's Great Western Railway hugs the coast, perhaps forming a barrier to local visitors but providing a magnificent introduction to Devon for generations of rail travellers.

Living Coasts, Torquay fh

BRIXHAM, NEWTON ABBOT, PAIGNTON, TORQUAY

BRIXHAM

One of the oldest fishing ports in Britain manages to combine the balance of a busy fishing industry with the demands of modern tourism. Colour-washed cottages on the hillside front narrow, winding streets that overlook the harbour and rows of colourful craft. The prettiest of the three Torbay towns, popular with artists and writers. Robert Graves, Flora Thompson and Francis Brett Young, all made Brixham their home, for a short while.Prominent in the war against the Spanish Armada, and later, the landing place of William of Orange, for his rebellion to rid England of the Stuart dynasty and Catholicism, although he had the indignity of being piggy-backed off his stranded ship by a local fisherman.

Church of All Saints' vicar Henry Lyte wrote the hymn "Abide With Me' which rings out daily at 18.00 hours. Annual Trawler Race in June. (D9)

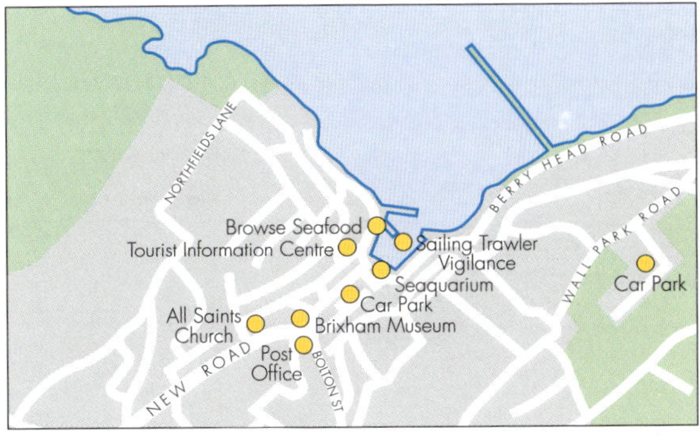

Brixham

Brixham Harbour fh

Fishing Boats, Brixham fh

Special Places to Visit...

Berry Head Country Park. Within a half-hour walk of Brixham; an old Napoleonic fort on the headland with lighthouse, café and Visitor Centre open Apr-Sept. Live TV link to bird colonies below. Park open all year. (E9)

Browse Seafood, The Quay. Wholesale crab business with wet fish shop, crab sandwiches and cafe. Supplies top hotels in Devon. (D9)

Brixham Museum, Bolton Cross. Local maritime and social history, boat building and navigation. Scale model of Brixham Station as in 1947. Open East-Oct M-F 10-5, Sa 10-1 (C9) 01803 856267

Brixham Sailing Trawler, Vigilance. One of the last four in existence available for charter and afternoon/evening trips. Restored 78 foot sailing ketch built for strength and speed, made them unique in British waters. They were able to tow heavy trawl gear and be capable of getting fish to market on time. Sailings from Easter. (E9) 07764 845353 www.vigilanceofbrixham.co.uk

Perils of the Deep, The Quay. Shipwrecks, treasures and the perils of the sea. Open daily East-Oct 10.30-4.30. (C9)

Seaquarium, 12 The Quay. All specimens found in British waters, including octopus, sharks, conger eels. Pictures and models of old sailing trawlers. Open daily East-Sept 10.30-4. (D9) 01803 882204

Strand Art Gallery, 2 The Strand. Working studio and large gallery of original paintings. Open daily 10-5. 2 The Strand 01803 854762/ 854892 www.strandartgallery.com

NEWTON ABBOT

Busy market town dating back to Roman times. The Great Western Railway moved their locomotive and carriage repairs here in the 1800s. C17 Forde House, now Council Offices, and one-mile to the south, Bradley Manor. Racecourse open from April to early September for Flat racing. Air Fusion Festival. Merrymaker's Day in May. Cheese and Onion Fair in September. E/C Th. (A2)

1889 Jan 24. Meeting of the provisional Devon County Council.

1890 Lynton-Lynmouth Cliff Railway opened by Sir George Newnes.

Special Places to Visit…

Orchid Paradise, Forches Cross. Rare & exotic orchids. Open daily 10-4. (A1) 01626 352233 www.orchids.uk.com

Plant World, St Marychurch Rd. Outstanding collection of rare and exotic plants from around the world. 4 acres of landscaped gardens. Large cottage garden. Mediterranean garden. Seeds from rare plants are offered for sale through mail order catalogue. Open daily, Apr-Oct 9.30-5. (A2) 01803 872939 www.plantworld-devon.co.uk

Town & GWR Museum, 2a St Paul's Road. History of the GWR and the people who operated it. Working signal box, Aller Vale Art Pottery Collection, John Lethbridge's diving machine automaton. Open Jan-Sept M-Th 10-4, F 10-12, Sa 2-4. (A2) 01626 201121

Tuckers Maltings, Teign Rd. Traditional working malthouse open to the public. Speciality Bottled Beer Shop. Open Gd Fr-Oct Mon-Sat 10am, open Su in July & Aug. (A2) 01626 334734 www.tuckersmaltings.com

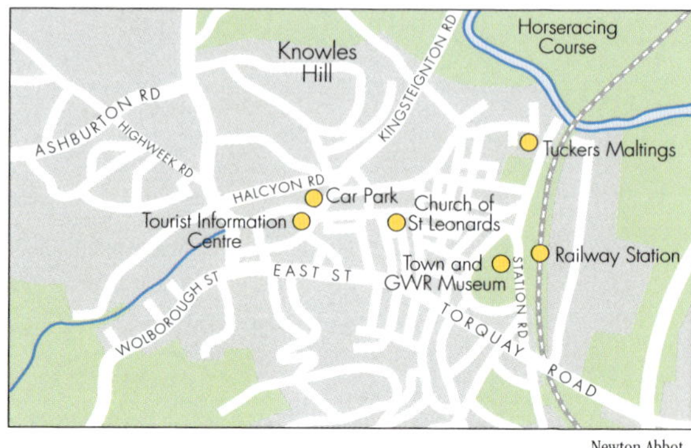

Newton Abbot

PAIGNTON

Often overlooked given its proximity to Torquay, and as a family resort has had to struggle against the cheap Mediterranean resorts. It has a little harbour, a flat, extensive beach and a number of interesting attractions described below. Affordable place to live for those who work and socialise in nearby Totnes and Torquay. Theatre and cinema. June carnival. E/C W. (B7)

Special Places to Visit…

Indigo Blue Gallery, 294 Torquay Road, Preston. Stylish new gallery selling all manner of art; from sculpture to ceramics, to paintings in all forms. (B6) 01803 551347 www.indigoblue4art.com

Kirkham House (EH), Kirkham St. Small C14 merchant's house somewhat hidden among back streets. Display of furniture, pottery, and fabrics. Open BH Ms Good F-Aug, & all Su July/Aug 2-5. (B7) 01803 522775 www.english-heritage.org.uk

Occombe Farm, Preston Down Rd. Here you are invited to engage in the whole organic process; the food, farming and wildlife (as well as butchers and bakers). (B6) 01803 520022 www.occombe.org.uk

Oldway Mansion, Torquay Rd. Building planned by Isaac Singer (of Singer sewing machines) in 1873. Remodelled 1904. Marble staircase, ballroom, ornamented painted ceilings and extensive gardens. Open M-Sa 10-5, also Su in summer 2-5. Grounds open daily. No charge. Cafe open in summer. (B6) 01803 201201

Paignton

Goodrington Sands, Paignton

1892 May 20. The final broad gauge railways in Devon converted to standard gauge over this weekend.

1892 Aug 15. Torquay granted royal charter for incorporation as a municipal borough.

Dart Valley Railway ss

Dart Valley Railway.
Relive the 'Great Age of Steam' on the Nations Holiday Line along the spectacular Torbay coastline to Kingswear for Dartmouth and the fascinating River Dart Estuary. Steam trains run East BH, selected days in Apr, May & Oct. Daily June-Sept. Santa Specials in Dec. 01803 555872 www.paignton-steamrailway.co.uk

Paignton Pier.
£1,000,000 rebuild of part of pier. Pier head includes trampolines, mega slide & kiddies cars. Open Mar-Oct 9-late. Nov-Feb 10-6/8. (C6) 01803 522139 www.paigntonpier.co.uk

Paignton Zoo, Totnes Road.
Elephants, giraffes, lions, tigers, gibbon islands. Birds flying freely. Tropical plants. Rhino House. Family activity centre. Miniature railway (East-Sept). Open daily summer 10-6, winter 10-5. (B7) 01803 697500 www.paigntonzoo.org.uk

Quaywest, Goodrington Sands.
Outdoor waterpark with 8 slides and pool, go-karts, bumper boats, shops etc open late May to early Sept 11-5 (July-Aug 10-6). (B7) 01803 550034 www.quaywest.co.uk

SHALDON

A seafaring community of long standing that has made their livelihood from fishing, boat trips and water sports. Connected since the C13 by foot ferry to Teignmouth. A thriving village with an immaculate village green used for the game of Bowls. Georgian and earlier buildings. Five pubs. June Festival attracts world-class musicians. (D2)

Paignton Pier fh

Special Places to Visit…

Shaldon Wildlife Trust, Ness Drive. Collection of small, rare, and unusual mammals, birds reptiles and invertebrates in woodland setting. Open daily East-Sept 10-6.30, winter 11-4. (D2) 01626 872234

Where to Eat, Drink & Be Merry…

Ode Restaurant, 21 Fore Street. World-travelled Tim Bouget brings his vast experience of working at Michelin Star restaurants to this Georgian house. Open W-Sa 7-10.30 pm. (D2) 01626 873977 www.timbouget.com

Shaldon Coffee Rush, 27 Fore Street. Friendly, comfortable café sells home made cakes, pastries and delish hot chocs and coffees. Photography exhibitions. Open daily. (D2)

Net Fishermen, Shaldon

TEIGNMOUTH

A seaside resort of long standing, trying to reinvent itself. The harbour and estuary side is always a busy and attractive with fine views across to Shaldon. The town centre needs a lot of paint and tlc. The Den, an area of open space and early C19 buildings overlooks the sea front. Sea and river excursions. August carnival and regatta. (E1)

Special Places to Visit….

Brodequin Shoemakers, 42 Teign Street. Handmade shoes, boots, sandals & other leather goods. Open M-Sa 10.30-4. (D1) 01626 776341 www.handcraftedshoes.co.uk

1896 New county boundary adds the villages of Stockland, Chardstock and Hawkchurch to Devon.

1899 First motor car driven in Exeter.

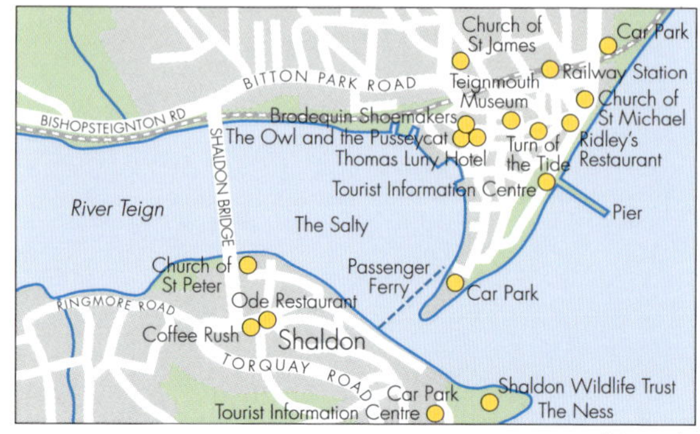

Teignmouth

Teignmouth Ferry

Teignmouth & Shaldon Museum, 27 French Street. The story of sea and land, war and peace, of interactions with far off places and developments of domestic industries. Open May-Oct M-Sa 10-4.30. (E1) 01626 777041

Turn of the Tide, 7 The Triangle. Gallery selling ceramics, stained glass, woodcarvings, sculpture, paintings and glass by major local artists. Open M-Sa 10-5, Su June-Oct. (E1) 01626 777455 www.theoldpassagegallery.co.uk

Torquay Marina fh

Where to Eat, Drink & Be Merry...

Ridley's Restaurant & Patisserie, 9-10 Regents Street. Award-winning Master pastry chef Darren Ridley, Teignmouth born, goes to extreme lengths to provide that extra something. Book now! 0845 241 0790 (D1)

The Owl and Pussycat Restaurant, 3 Teign Street. You will dance to the light of the moon after sampling this fine Devon cuisine and friendly service. Live Jazz on Mondays. Open M-F 10-2.30, 6-9.30, Sa 10-2.30, 6-10. (D1) 01626 775321 www.theowlandthepussycat.co.uk

Where to Stay...

Thomas Luny House, Teign St. Elegant Georgian house behind a walled courtyard. Spacious Drawing Room, Breakfast room and individually decorated bedrooms. No Dinner, pets or children under 12. (E1) 01626 772976 www.thomas-luny-house.co.uk

Brodequin Shoemaker ss

1901 Devon population recorded at 660,000.

1904 Motor cars first registered in Exeter.

TORQUAY

Devon's "Queen of Resorts" occupying a magnificent natural setting on the north side of Tor Bay where the mild climate encourages sub-tropical vegetation and all-year-round visitors. There are twenty-two miles of attractive cliff paths stretching around to Babbacombe, and beyond. Well provided with a comprehensive shopping centre, numerous hotels, entertainments and a thriving nightlife.

Torquay

Living Coasts, Torquay fh

There was an early Premonstratension house at Torre Abbey in the C12 but it was not until the Napoleonic Wars that Torquay expanded so. During the C17 and C18s the Navy would seek shelter here from all but the East and South Easterly winds. More often in preference to Plymouth Sound. The Napoleonic Wars attracted the wives and families of the Naval officers to Torquay, to be near their loved ones. The difficulties of travel on the Continent also brought new visitors, and physicians would recommend their consumptive patients to come here for the clear skies and sea air for towns and cities were often ridden with smog and damp conditions. The C19 saw an explosion of new villas and terraces set amidst woodland drives. Much in evidence today.

It can best be described as a genteel resort that has had to change some of its old-fashioned ways to meet the demands of today. Some of the larger hotels have realised they must improve their interior design, service and cuisine, and to return Up-Market, and return to their origins. One wonders who fills all the beds in the other mediocre hotels and guesthouses. It can't all be coach parties and businessmen attending the numerous conferences held in the Riviera Centre. A name taken from the marketing men's slogan, "The English Riviera". A poor cousin when compared to the original, and a misleading description. Better to wax lyrical about the mild, temperate climate, the shimmering sea, the miles of footpaths leading up and down to numerous beaches, the English civility, the fine terraces and tree-lined avenues. And, if you should tire of this oasis, and wish for action and company, strike to the harbour, a haven of coffee shops, bars and restaurants, and if you still have your sea legs, take a boat trip to Brixham, or further afield, to Dartmouth and Totnes, pleasing towns very different from your hostess. (C5)

Torquay Seafront ab

Special Places to Visit...

Haddon Galleries, 107 Teignmouth Rd. Prints and originals from internationally renowned artists. Open M-F 9-5.30, Sa 9-5. (C5) 01803 313133 www.haddongalleries.co.uk

Kents Caverns, Ilsham Road. Two million years in the making. Let your imagination and senses be challenged as you travel back to the realm of bears, cavemen and beyond. New Visitor Centre, Rock & Fossil shop. Open all year from 10. (D5) 01803 215136 www.kents-cavern.co.uk

1905 The Royal Naval College (Brittania) built at Dartmouth. 1907 Buckfast Abbey built (again).

Living Coasts, Beacon Quay. Aquatic visitor attraction; penguins, seals, puffins. Reconstructed beaches, cliff-faces and an estuary. Gift shop. Café serving child-size portions. Open daily 10-dusk. (D6) 01803 202470 www.livingcoasts.org.uk

Rainbow Fun House, Torwood Gardens Rd. 13,000 sq ft of indoor adventure play area. Open daily 10-6:30. 01803 296926 www.rainbowfunhouse.co.uk

Cockington

The Gallery, Torbay Hospital. Contemporary (professionally run) art gallery with paintings, textiles and photos by local artists. Open daily 24hrs. (C5) 01803 655744 www.sdhct.nhs.uk

Torbay Quad Centre, Moles Lane. Bikes for all ages 5yrs+, beginners welcome, supervised instruction track. Open 9:30-5:30 Sa, Su & Schl Hols. (C5) 01803 615660 www.torbayquadcentre.co.uk

Torquay Museum, Babbacombe Rd. Animal remains from Kent's Cavern. Pictorial records, Victoriana, rural Devon, pottery, archaeology, Agatha Christie, world jewellery and adornment. Open M-F 10-4.45 all year, East-Oct Sa 10-4.45, Su 1.30-4.45. (C5)

Torre Abbey & Gallery, Kings Drive. Torquay's oldest historic building. Art gallery specialising in maritime paintings, landscapes, genre & works by local artists. Devon miniatures, antiques, Torquay terracotta & sculpture. Open M-Sa 10-5.30. (C5) 01803 293593 www.torre-abbey.org.uk

Waves Leisure Pool, Riviera Centre. Giant inflatable, paddling pool, sloping beach, indoor soft play area, gym, sun beds, sauna, steam room & jacuzzi, beauty suite & aerobics. Cafe diner. (C5) 01803 299992 www.rivieracentre.co.uk

Where to Eat, Drink & Be Merry...

Cafe Mambo, Harbourside. Overlooks the sea front and a cool place to be in Torquay. Open daily. (C5) 01803 291112

Elephant Bar & Restaurant, 3-4 Beacon Terrace. Award-winning restaurant considered one of the most stylish places to eat in the South West. Michelin Star. Open M-Sa for lunch and dinner. 01803 200044 www.elephantrestaurant.co.uk

No 7 Fish Bistro, 7 Beacon Terrace. Simply cooked fish just off the boats. Specials; lobster, Dover sole, oysters. Warm and efficient service. 01803 295055 www.no7-fish.com

Ocean Brasserie, 3 Croft Road. Family-run business building a positive reputation. The seafood orientated restaurant is a relaxed and attractive place to hang out. Open all week except Monday lunchtime. 01803 292359 www.oceanbrasserie.com

Bath and Boathouse, Greenway ss/nt

Special Places to Visit...

Babbacombe Model Village, Hampton Avenue. 5 acres of gardens with miniature landscapes and buildings to scale of 1 inch to 1 foot. Model railway. Open daily. (D4) 01803 315315

Bishopsteignton Museum of Rural Life, Shute Hill. Displays ranging through geology, occupations, dress, village and school life. Open East-Sept Su & BHs 2.30-4.30. (C1) 01626 775308 www.devonmuseums.net

Bygones, St Marychurch. Nostalgic look at a life size Victorian Street of shops. Giant Model Railway and Railwayana Collection. Open daily all year. (C4) 01803 326108 www.bygones.co.uk

Cockington Court. Green Fig Award for 7th year running. Set amidst traditional Devon material village. Organic Kitchen garden. Craft studios. 01803 606035 www.countryside-trust.org.uk

Cockington Court Pottery. Working studio producing wheel thrown fine tableware, giftware, unusal table lamps, house nameplates. Open 10-4. 01803 607773

Compton Castle (NT). C14 manor. Great hall, Solar, Chapel, Rose Garden and kitchen. Open Apr-Oct M W and Th 10-12.15, 2-5. 01803 875740 www.nationaltrust.org

Greenway (NT). Birthplace of Sir Humphrey Gilbert in 1539. The beautiful woodland garden slopes down to the River Dart. Now famous as the former home of Agatha Christie with new features about her

1914 The three towns amalgamated into Plymouth.

1917 During the U-boat blockade, 100 merchant ships were sunk around the coasts of Devon and Cornwall.

life. Unique bath and boathouse. Café. Try visiting by river transport aboard the Greenway ferry from Dartmouth. The NT operates a traffic management system. Open Mar to early Oct W-Sa 10.30-5. (A9) 01803 842382 www.nationaltrust.org.uk

Special Places to Stay...

Orestone Manor, Rockhouse Lane. Mix of the Mediterranean and English Country House style pervades this well appointed manor. Spacious rooms. Fine cuisine. 01803 328098. (D3) www.orestone.co.uk

Preston - Sampsons Farm Medieval thatched farmhouse. 01626 354913 www.sampsonsfarm.com

Pubs Serving Food...

Church House Inn, Village Road, Marldon. Large C14 inn, popular with locals. Flagstone floors and fireplaces. Fine ales and honest fare. Dogs and children welcome. (A5) 01803 558279

Beaches

St Mary's Bay, Brixham. Sand and shingle. Safe bathing. Access tricky at the bottom of cliffs. Panoramic views from the coast path above. Dogs permitted. P. (D9)

Churston Cove, Brixham. Sand and shingle. Safe bathing. Dogs permitted. P. (D8)

Fishcombe Cove, Churston Ferrers. Sand and shingle. Safe bathing. Dogs permitted. P/R/WC. (C8)

Elberry Cove, Churston Ferrers. Shingle. Safe bathing. Dogs permitted. P. (C8)

Preston, Paignton. Popular sandy beach lined with colourful beach huts. Restricted parking. Deckchairs. (B6)

Goodrington Sands, Paignton. Expansive, wide beach with red sand. Safe bathing. Rock pools at LT. Deckchairs. Disabled access. Dogs permitted in restricted areas. P/R/WC. (B7)

Central Paignton, Paignton. Extensive, flat sands attract young families wishing to paddle, and water sports. Pedaloes/boats for hire. D/R/WC. (B6)

Corbyn Head Beach, Torquay. Shingly sand and rocky pools. Beach huts. Disabled facilities. Boating pool. No dogs in summer. D/R. (C6)

Torre Abbey Sands, Torquay. Main beach for Torquay and traditional family beach with flat sand. No dogs in summer. D/R. (C5)

Beacon Cove, Torquay. Sheltered position makes for a warm, sunny spot. Pebbles and rocks. Short walk from the harbour. D/R/WC. (C5)

Meadfoot, Torquay. Shingle. Safe bathing. Beach huts. Paddle boats. Café. Dogs permitted in restrictive areas. P/R/WC. (D6)

Maidencombe, Babbacombe Bay. Sand and rocks. Short hike from parking, steep in places. Café. D/R/WC. (D3)

Shaldon, Babbacombe Bay. Sand and cliffs. Cliff access. D/WC. (D2)

Coastal Footpath...

Kingswear to Brixham; 10 miles. A fairly arduous stretch with some fine scenery. The first few miles traverse National Trust land. The path gives access to sandy beaches at Scabbacombe and Man Sands, later rounding Sharkham Point and Berry Head.

Brixham to Godrington Sands; 5 Miles. An easy semi-urbanised stretch passing some pleasant beaches. From Godrington the route passes through Paignton and Torquay, and there is no path as such.

Meadfoot Beach to Teignmouth; 10 miles. The route follows the Marine Drive past Thatcher Point and round Hope Nose. The path branches off at Hope Cove and runs for the most part close to the cliff edge with a series of ups and downs. Beyond Maidencombe, sea views tend to be obstructed by thick hedges. After passing Ness Headland, Teignmouth is reached by ferry from Shaldon.

Babbacombe Beach ab

Ansteys Cove, Torquay. Shingle and rocks. Set between high cliffs and wooded hillside. Steep path leads down from P. D/R/WC. (D5)

Babbacombe, Babbacombe Bay. Sand and shingle with safe bathing. Local sailing club. Steep walk down, or take the short railway ride. Spectacular views from above. Dogs permitted. P/R/WC. (D4)

Oddicombe, Babbacombe Bay. Shingly sand. Steep path descends to beach or take the cliff lift. Café. Paddle boats. Disabled facilities. D/R/WC. (D4)

Watcombe, Babbacombe Bay. Sand. Short, difficult access from parking down steep path. Café. D/WC. (D4)

Stretching from Plymouth to Salcombe and Start Point, and up the eastern coastline to Dartmouth. This curiously named area, based on the old English name "Hamme" meaning enclosed or sheltered place, is one of rocky coasts and beaches broken up by the tidal estuaries of the Yealm, Erme and Avon, and the lovely stretch of water below Kingsbridge with its quiet creeks delving far inland.

High cliffs mostly dominate the coastline, but here and there are attractive little villages of thatched cottages; Wembury, Bigbury, Inner and Outer Hope. Inland is a pastoral landscape of rolling hills and red-earthed fields bisected by twisty roads beneath high hedges - not a place for the traveller in a hurry.

Arriving from the north of the county one first descends on Totnes, the Jewel of the South Hams, which is bordered to the north eastern edge by the enchanting Dart Estuary and the well-tended villages on its shoreline; Cornworthy, Dittisham and Tuckenhay, all are worth a leisurely visit.

Bantham Boathouse

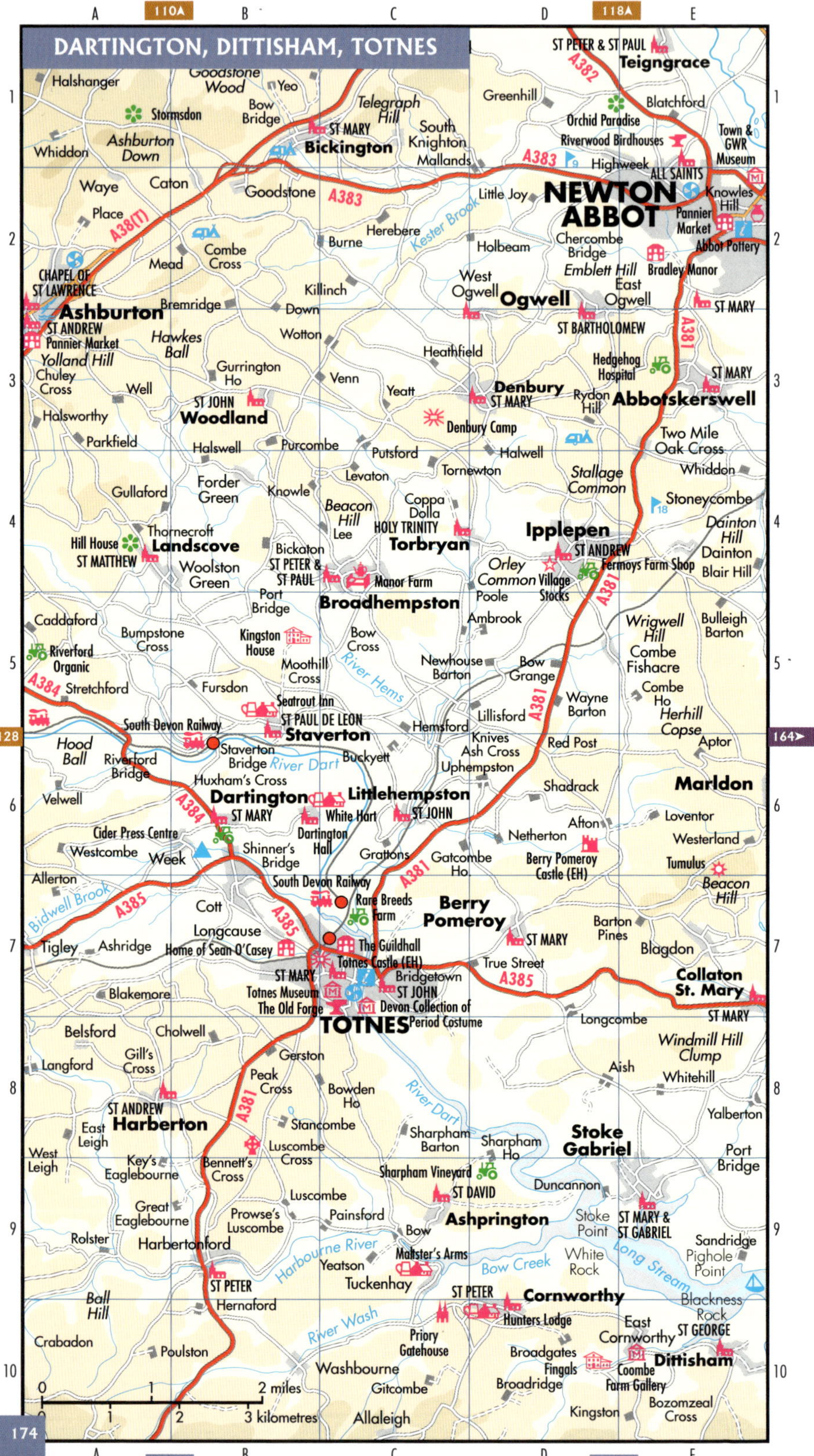
DARTINGTON, DITTISHAM, TOTNES
110A
118A
A
B
C
D
E
128
164
186
187
Halshanger
Goodstone Wood
Yeo
Stormsdon
Bow Bridge
Telegraph Hill
ST MARY
Bickington
South Knighton
Mallands
Greenhill
ST PETER & ST PAUL
Teigngrace
A382
Blatchford
Orchid Paradise
Riverwood Birdhouses
Town & GWR Museum
Whiddon
Ashburton Down
A383
Highweek
ALL SAINTS
Waye
Caton
Goodstone
Little Joy
NEWTON ABBOT
Knowles Hill
Place
A38(T)
Herebere
Kester Brook
Pannier Market
Combe Cross
Burne
Holbeam
Chercombe Bridge
Abbot Pottery
Mead
Emblett Hill
Bradley Manor
CHAPEL OF ST LAWRENCE
Killinch
West Ogwell
Ogwell
East Ogwell
ST MARY
Ashburton
Bremridge
Down
ST BARTHOLOMEW
ST ANDREW
Pannier Market
Hawkes Ball
Wotton
A381
Yolland Hill
Heathfield
Hedgehog Hospital
Chuley Cross
Gurrington Ho
Venn
ST MARY
Well
ST JOHN
Yeatt
Denbury
ST MARY
Rydon Hill
Abbotskerswell
Woodland
Halsworthy
Denbury Camp
Two Mile Oak Cross
Parkfield
Halswell
Purcombe
Putsford
Halwell
Whiddon
Levaton
Tornewton
Stallage Common
Gullaford
Forder Green
Knowle
Coppa Dolla
Beacon Hill
Stoneycombe
Lee
HOLY TRINITY
Torbryan
Ipplepen
Dainton Hill
Thornecroft
Dainton
Hill House
Landscove
Bickaton
ST ANDREW
ST MATTHEW
Woolston Green
ST PETER & ST PAUL
Manor Farm
Orley Common
Village Stocks
Fermoys Farm Shop
Blair Hill
Port Bridge
Broadhempston
Poole
Caddaford
Ambrook
Wrigwell Hill
Bulleigh Barton
Bumpstone Cross
Kingston House
Bow Cross
Riverford Organic
Combe Fishacre
Moothill Cross
Newhouse Barton
Bow Grange
River Hems
A384
Stretchford
Fursdon
Combe Ho
Seatrout Inn
Wayne Barton
Herhill Copse
ST PAUL DE LEON
Lillisford
South Devon Railway
Staverton
Hemsford
Aptor
Hood Ball
Staverton Bridge
Knives Ash Cross
Red Post
Riverford Bridge
River Dart
Buckyett
Uphempston
Huxham's Cross
Shadrack
Marldon
Velwell
Dartington
Littlehempston
ST MARY
White Hart
ST JOHN
Loventor
Cider Press Centre
Dartington Hall
Afton
Netherton
Westerland
Westcombe
Week
Shinner's Bridge
Grattons
Gatcombe Ho
Berry Pomeroy Castle (EH)
Tumulus
Allerton
South Devon Railway
Beacon Hill
Bidwell Brook
A385
Cott
Rare Breeds Farm
Berry Pomeroy
Barton Pines
Longcause
ST MARY
Tigley
Ashridge
Home of Sean O'Casey
The Guildhall
Blagdon
Totnes Castle (EH)
True Street
Collaton St. Mary
ST MARY
Bridgetown
ST JOHN
Blakemore
Totnes Museum
The Old Forge
Devon Collection of Period Costume
ST MARY
TOTNES
Longcombe
Belsford
Cholwell
Windmill Hill Clump
Gill's Cross
Gerston
Langford
Peak Cross
Aish
Whitehill
Bowden Ho
River Dart
ST ANDREW
Harberton
Yalberton
East Leigh
Stancombe
Sharpham Barton
Sharpham Ho
Stoke Gabriel
Port Bridge
West Leigh
Key's Eaglebourne
Bennett's Cross
Luscombe Cross
Sharpham Vineyard
Duncannon
ST DAVID
Luscombe
Great Eaglebourne
Prowse's Luscombe
Painsford
Ashprington
Stoke Point
ST MARY & ST GABRIEL
Sandridge
Rolster
Bow
Harbertonford
Harbourne River
White Rock
Pighole Point
Long Stream
Maltster's Arms
Yeatson
Bow Creek
ST PETER
Tuckenhay
Ball Hill
Hernaford
ST PETER
Cornworthy
Blackness Rock
Hunters Lodge
River Wash
Priory Gatehouse
East Cornworthy
ST GEORGE
Crabadon
Poulston
Broadgates
Fingals
Coombe Farm Gallery
Dittisham
Washbourne
Broadridge
Gitcombe
Bozomzeal Cross
Kingston
Allaleigh
0
1
2 miles
1
2
3 kilometres

TOTNES

"The Jewel of the South Hams", so they say, and who would argue with them. If music be the food of your love, and art your divine mistress, then Totnes is the town for you. The close proximity to Dartington and the well-heeled villages of the Dart Estuary has given Totnes an artiness and comfort level rarely seen outside London. It is the "Boho" Look, mix of bohemian and affluence, you see here. The many health shops, cafes and restaurants, busy all year, lend the town, an affluence, unique to Devon. It is a colourful place to People Watch, best seated from the many cafes above East Gate, the medieval arch. The shops are unusual and independent, festooned with colour, a welcome release from the samey, dull, dreariness of many British High Streets.

East Gate

The town is split into two parts connected by the ascending Fore Street. The lower end, beside the River Dart, has open spaces and riverside walks overlooked by yacht marinas and former warehouses converted into prestigious flats. It is here you can hop on a boat to Dartmouth. The ascending Fore Street which becomes the High Street above the medieval arch is one of Devon's and England's most historic and interesting thoroughfares leading to the Castle and Guildhall, passing by Elizabethan and Jacobean houses fronted by more modern exteriors.

According to legend, Totnes was discovered by Aeneas (Brutus),

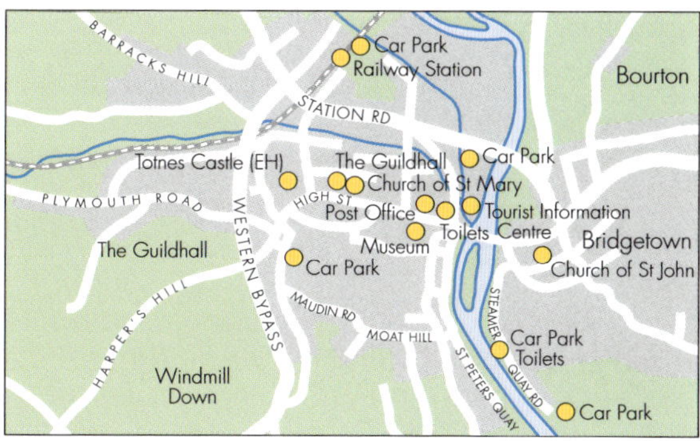

Totnes

who had left Troy encouraged by a prophecy from the Goddess Diana. He sailed up the Dart, landing here, to discover Albion. He rid the land of giants and serpents, and created The Britons. The Brutus stone on Fore Street commemorates this unlikely tale.

Totnes is the second oldest borough in England, minted coins in 979, and was granted a Charter by King John in 1206, authorising the Merchant's Guild. The export of tin and wool enriched the town's medieval merchants who also imported wines from France. Defoe noted that in 1740 "the town has more gentleman in it than tradesmen of note". A truism of today? The history of the town can be discovered in the castle, church and museums.

And when next you climb the draughty High Street think of William Wills, born 1834 in Totnes, the first white man to cross Australia, south to north (Melbourne to the Gulf of Carpentaria), who finally succumbed to starvation at Cooper's Creek in 1861, missing out on the £2,000 prize money. (C7)

Special Places to Visit...

Costume Museum, 43 High St. Tudor merchant's house. Costume from mid-C18 onwards. New themed exhibition each year. Open Spring BH-Sept M-F 11-5. 01803 862857

Guildhall, Ramparts Walk. Originally the Rectory of 1088 Benedictine Priory. Rebuilt as meeting place of Merchant Guild in 1553. From 1624-1974 used as Magistrates Court and Town Gaol until 1887. Now Mayor's Parlour with historic prints, documents and artefacts. Open Apr-Oct M-F 10-1, 2-5. 01803 862147

Image Bank, Information Centre, Town Mill. Photographic archive of the town. View 1,000s of photographs on a computer database. Heritage exhibition describing the history of Totnes. Open Tu & F 10-1, 2-4. (Totnes Tourist Information Centre) (C7) 01803 863168

Rare Breeds Farm. View the rare breeds, cuddle and fuss the friendly animals, walk and brush the donkeys, see the owls. Refreshments. Open daily 10-5. Totnes 01803 840387

Totnes Castle. Norman motte and bailey castle probably built about 1100. Open daily Apr-Sept 10-6, Oct daily 10-5, Nov-Mar W-Su 10-4, closed 1-2 in winter. Castle Street 01803 864406 www.english-heritage.org.uk

The Guidhall, Totnes

1919 May 31. First Transatlantic Flight of American seaplane N.C. 4.

1921 March. Henry Williamson moves to live in Georgeham, arriving on his 499 cc long-stroke Norton motorcycle and rents Skirr Cottage for £5 a year.

Rood Screen, The Parish Church

But, if it's an old fashioned tea party you're after, look no further than Greys Dining Room at 96 High Street.

Effings, 50 Fore St.
Popular, intimate restaurant/deli with a South European angle believing food should be fun and joyous. Lunch and snacks. Child friendly. Recommended. (B7) 01803 863435 www.effings.co.uk

Wills Restaurant, 3 The Plains.
Birthplace of explorer William Wills. Relaxed and intimate rooms. Cafe and restaurant. Open daily from 10. 01803 865192 www.willsrestaurant.co.uk

Totnes Museum, 70 Fore St.
Period furniture, toys, exhibition on Charles Babbage and computing. Artisans Kitchen and grocer's shop. Open Apr-Oct, M-F 10.30-5. (B7) 01803 863821

Whitespace Contemporary Art, 72 Fore Street.
Exhibits emerging British contemporary artists at affordable prices. Situated just before the Clock Tower. Open daily.(B7) 01803 864088 www.whitespaceart.com

Where to Eat, Drink & Be Merry…

Totnes is spoilt for choice. Apart from the two featured below, herewith a tour of what's on offer. Ascend Fore Street through the East Gate arch,

Dart Quilters, Parish Church

Coombe Farm Gallery, Ditttisham

and on your left is the wine bar, Rumours, recently decorated, a convivial and laid back eatery, always popular. A few yards on, La Fourchette Brasserie, French in style, English in ingredients, also recommended. As you pass the bookshop on your left, look across the road to a couple of cafes, and a health food shop with tasty sandwiches. Keep going, rounding the corner, Woods Bistro, getting hungry? And, across on the other side of the road, Willows Vegetarian restaurant.

Special Places to Visit…

Berry Pomeroy Castle.
Late C15 stone quadrangular fortress and stone Elizabethan mansion. Open daily Apr-Oct from 10. 01803 866618

Bradley Manor (NT).
Small roughcast C15 manor house. Great Hall, screens passage, buttery. Perp. chapel. Medieval stencils and paintings. One of the oldest inhabited houses in Devon. Open Apr-Sept W 2-5 and some Th in Apr/Sept. 01626 54513

1921 Sir Ernest Shackleton's ship, Quest, bound for the south seas on her final voyage, puts in at Plymouth.

1922 University College of the South West of England established.

Tuckenhay

Coombe Farm Gallery, Dittisham. Ceramics, sculpture, watercolours and oils, collages, jewellery, papier-mache, mirrors, glass, turned wood, prints, sconces and furniture. Open M-Sa 10-5. Su by appoint. 01803 722352 www.coombegallery.com

Gorse Blossom Miniature Railway. 1/4" guage steam railway running over 3/4 mile through woodland. Walks. Children's play area. Open East to first Su in Oct 10-5. (C1) 01626 821361 www.gorseblossom.com

Hedgehog Hospital & Prickly Ball Farm, Dentbury Road. Cares for sick and injured hedgehogs, rears baby hoglets. Also an open farm - lots of "hands on" fun. Cafe. Open daily Mar-Sept from 10-5. (D3) 01626 362319 www.hedgehog.org.uk

Hill House Nursery & Garden. Construction of over 18,000 sq ft of glass-houses, open to the public with a large range of plants for sale. You are invited to relax in the Garden. Tea Room (Mar-Sept) over looking water garden. Open daily, all year 11-5. (A4) 01803 762273 www.hillhousenursery.co.uk

Sharpham Vineyard & Cheese Dairy. Farm set in 500 acres of vineyard, meadows & wooded slopes. Vineyard & riverside trails. Shop offers full range of wines & cheeses. Open Mar to 24 Dec M-Sa, Su June-Aug, 10.30-5.30. (C8) 01803 732203 www.sharpham.com

Spencer Larcombe, Brewery Cottages, Old Rd. Forged metalwork designs; chairs and candlelabra. Commissions. Open M-F 9-5. 01803 732254

Bow Creek, River Dart

Special Places to Stay...

Fingals. A complete one-off, in style and attitude. Richard Johnston has created a refuge from our mad, mad world where you can relax, meet old and make new friends in a laid back, comfortable environment. Art is ubiquitous. Fleet of wooden boats moored nearby. (D9) www.fingals.co.uk

Hooks Cottage, Bickington. (B1) 01626 821312

Kingston House. Rare survivor of C18 architecture. Lovingly restored to former glory with fabrics and furniture true to period. Magnificent 4-poster beds. Candlelit gourmet dinners. Self-catering cottages. (B5) 01803 762235 www.kingston-estate.co.uk

Dartington Hall Trust. 1,000-acre estate bought in the 1920s by Leonard Elmhirst and his wife, American heiress, Dorothy Whitney as a base to try new methods of farming and forestry, and rural construction. It has developed into an international centre for the generation and application of new ideas in the arts, ecology and social justice. C14 mediaeval courtyard. Music and Literature Festivals. International summer school. Small hotel. One of the great independent institutions in Britain. (B6) 01803 847147/ 847100 www.dartingtonhall.com

Special Attractions at Dartington...

Cider Press Centre. A complex of twelve shops and two restaurants in a picturesque cluster of C16/C17 stone buildings; bookshop (arts and crafts), Dartington Crystal, jewellery, pottery, farm foods, toys, kitchenware. Open daily M-Sa 9.30-5.30, & Su East-Xmas 10.30-5.30. 01803 847500

High Cross House. A superb Modernist 1930s house with period furniture. Art exhibited (Ben Nicholson and Christopher Wood) and material derived from The Dartington Hall Trust and its beginnings. Open May-Oct, Tu-F 2-4.30. (B6)01803 864114

1927 October. Henry Williamson's "Tarka the Otter" is published.

1941 Mar 20. The Plymouth blitz at its worst. 336 civilians killed on 20 and 21 March.

Totnes

Lone

Fingals ss

Sea Trout Inn. 400-year old inn. Many bars. Restaurant. Mix of cosy and spacious rooms. Accommodation. (B5) 01803 762274 www.seatroutinn.co.uk

B & Bs...

Avenue Cottage, Ashprington. 01803 732769

Crowdy Mill. 01803 732340 www.crowdymill.co.uk

Manor Farm, Broadhempston. 01803 813260

More Cafe Restaurant. Within the Cider Press Centre, serves breakfast, brunch and lunch, and Devon cream teas. Why not try the Dartington Mushroom burgers? Open M-Sa 9.30-5.30, Su 10.30-5.30. (B6) 01803 847524 www.dartingtonciderpress.co.uk

White Hart Inn, Dartington Hall. Great value food. Extremely popular with the locals. Relaxed attitude and booking advised. (B6) 01803 847111.

River Dart, Dartington Estate

Pubs Serving Food...

Hunters Lodge Inn, Cornworthy. Popular local offering a fine range of ales. Fish and shellfish feature strongly. Children and dogs welcome. (D9) 01803 732204 www.hunterslodgeinn.com

Maltsters' Arms, Bow Creek. C18 inn accessed via boat, car or foot with many small, bright rooms. Serious selection of ales and wines, cider too. Wholesome food. Child friendly. Accommodation. 01803 732350. (C9) www.tuckenhay.com

Dittisham Church

High Cross House, Dartington

Merlewood Cottage, Tristford Road. 01803 864261 www.merlewoodcottage.co.uk

Parliament House, Longcombe. 01803 840288

Penpark, Bickington. 01626 821314 www.penpark.co.uk

Red Slipper. Stoke Gabriel. 01803 782315 www.redslipper.co.uk

The Old Forge, Seymour Place. 600 year old building offfering cosy, cottage-style comfort. Dogs in cars. 01803 862174 www.oldforgetotnes.com

The White House, Manor Street, Dittisham. 01803 722355

A
98A
B
C
D
128A
E
F
Cattedown
Oreston
Pomphlett
Cattewater
Summerskill Brewery
Turnchapel
Plymstock
ST MARY & ALL SAINTS
Dunstone
Hooe
ST JOHN
Goosewell
Elburton
Halwell
East Sherford
West Sherford
A379
Hareston
Pitten
Popple's Bridge
Lyneham
Lotherton Bridge
Treby
Efford
Gorlofen
Worston
Wollaton
Brixton
ST MARY
Stonycross
Yealmbridge
Yealmpton
ALL SAINTS
Fort Staddon
Combe
Spriddlestone
Winston
Kitley
Kitley Caves & Country Park
Torr
Staddon Heights
Staddiscombe
Bovisland Lodge
Bovisand Bay
Spriddlestone Ho
Puslinch Bridge
Warren Point
Raneleigh
Down Thomas
Wrescombe
Creacombe
Luson
Andurn Point
Knighton
Hele Almshouses
Cofflete Creek
River Yealm
B3186
Collaton
Heybrook Bay
Wembury Mill (NT)
Wembury Ho
Brownston
Renney Rocks
Wembury
ST WERBURGH
Newton Ferrers
Claricombe
Preston
Battisborough Cross
HOLY CROSS
Membland
Wembury Point
Blackstone Rocks
Season Point
Pool
Wembury Bay
Warren Point
Ship Inn
ST PETER
Bridgend
Mouthstone Point
Noss Mayo
Rowden
Lambside
St Anchorite's Rock
Great Mew Stone
Worswell
The Warren
Beacon Hill
Blackaterry Point
Butcher's Cove
Gara Point
Stoke Ho
Netton
Cunnimall
Battisborough Island
Blackstone Point
Hillsea Point
Netton Island
Stoke Pont
1
2
3
4
5
6
7
8
9
10
0
1
2 miles
0
1
2
3 kilometres

G
H
J
K
L
M
Keaton
Penquit
Filham
Mine Engine
Dunwell
Ludbrook
Witchcombe
Coarsewell
Marridge
Ley
Penson
Tod Moor
Thornham
Strode
Shilston
Barton
Combe
B3196
Gara
Bridge
Lupridge
A3121
ST PETER & ST PAUL
Ermington
Hollowcombe
Shilston
Bridge
Yarnicombe
CHAPEL
California Cross
Brownston
Coldharbour
Cross
Hazelwood
Plantation House
Hotel
Sheepham
Mill
Mary
Cross
A379
Modbury
Brownstone
Gallery
West
Leigh
East
Leigh
Churchland
Green
Blackdown
Rings
Sequer's
Bridge
Goutsford
Bridge
ST GEORGE
Battle site
(A.D.1643)
Babland
Heathfield
Wizaller
Wigford
Hole
Flete
Little
Orcheton
Little
Modbury
Harraton
Woolston
Holbeton
ALL SAINTS
Ashridge
Fishleigh
Chillaton
Combe
River Erme
Great Orcheton
Whympston
Ho.
A379
Lixton
Efford
Ho
Oldaport
Ley
B3196
B3392
Wakeham
Earthwork
Shearlangstone
Ham
Langston
Seven Stones
Cross
Hingston
Borough
Chantry
Mike's Smokehouse
Torr
Down
Duffland
Ashford
Yanston
Flete
South
Langston
Challon's
Cross
ST MICHAEL
Loddiswell
Weeke
ST JAMES
St Ann's
Chapel
ST ANDREW
Aveton
Gifford
Kingston
New
Bridge
Rake
Malthouse
Point
Chapel
Holy Well
Waterhead
Oyster Shack
Marwell
Hatch
Scobbiscombe
Houghton
Bridge
End
Venn
Sorley
Bigbury
Court
ST LAWRENCE
Fernycombe
Beach
Merrifield
Hoist
Point
ALL HALLOWS
Ringmore
Bigbury
River Avon
A379
ST MARY
Combe
Royal
Stadbury
Meddrick
Rocks
Aymer Cove
Churchstow
Toby's Point
Elston
Norton
Challaborough
Henley Hotel
Mount
Folly
Worthy
Kingsbridge
Warren Point
B3392
Aunemouth
Bigbury-on-Sea
Venus Café
Clanacombe
May ne Gallery
Whitley
Huxton
Cross
B3197
ALL SAINTS
Pilchard Inn
Murray's
Rock
Burgh Island
Sloop Inn
Upton
Burgh Island Hotel
Bantham
Buckland
West
Alvington
ALL SAINTS
Prestons
Butter
Cove
ALL
SAINTS
Thurlestone
South
Milton
Easton
Village Inn
Thurlestone Hotel
Auton
Yarmouth Sand
Horswell
Ho
Sutton
Collapit Bridge
Warren Point
A381
Woolston
Bigbury
Bay
The
Books
South
Huish
Southdown
Thurlestone
Rock
Bagton
Blanksmill
Bridge
Great
Ledge
Beacon Point
Burleigh
Alston
Woolman Point
Galmpton
Hope Cove
All Saints
Yarde
Ilton
Thatched Village
BOLT TAIL
Hope
A381
Redrot Cove
Promontory
Fort
Malborough
Collaton
Hope
Barton
Bolberry
Whitechurch
Salcombe
Fennybolt Point
Slippery Point
Southdown
Rew
Combe
Catholе
Cliff
Soar
Lantern Rock
Soar Mill Cove Hotel
Stink Cove
Overbeck Museum
& Garden (NT)
Ham Stone
Steeple Cove
Off Cove
BOLT HEAD
1
2
3
4
5
6
7
8
9
10
186

MODBURY

A hilltop town set in a deep hollow surrounded by the rolling, undulating hills, of the South Hams. The drive descending the High Street draws you to smart slate-hung houses built in the C18 and C19s. In the Middle Ages the fortunes of the town was derived from wool. The affluent clothiers decorated the C14 church, and built some fine houses burnt down by the Parliamentarians in the Civil War battles of 1642 and 1643. Birthplace of Thomas Savery, business partner to Thomas Newcomen. St George's Fair. Today, there are teashops, art galleries, antique shops and a fine fish deli. (J2)

Special Places to Visit…

Brownston Gallery, 36 Church Street. Lively little gallery with an ever-changing venue for new and established artists, sculptures and ceramicists. Open daily. (J2) 01548 831338 www.thebrownstongallery.co.uk

Parish Church of St George. Tall, lofty medieval spire is unusual for a C14 church. Tombs of the Crusaders. Prideaux Arms. Carved pulpit. Jacobean chair. (J2)

SALCOMBE

No visitor can come to the South Hams without visiting Salcombe. The setting of the town beside the estuary with the pastoral backdrop of emerald green fields is simply, stunning. Its sheltered position, and mild climate, encourages the growth of sub-tropical plants and flowers. The pockets of golden sand on either side of the estuary make for ideal family holidays. It is also a busy and popular location for learning to sail dinghies, and a favourite Port-of-Call for yachtsmen. In July and August the visitors outnumber the locals by 10 to 1. The abundance of second homes is a sore issue for those Salcombe born and bred, who now have to look far and wide for affordable housing. The busy High Street and the narrow streets off it are brimming with yachtie-designer shops, restaurants and gift shops. There is a wide choice

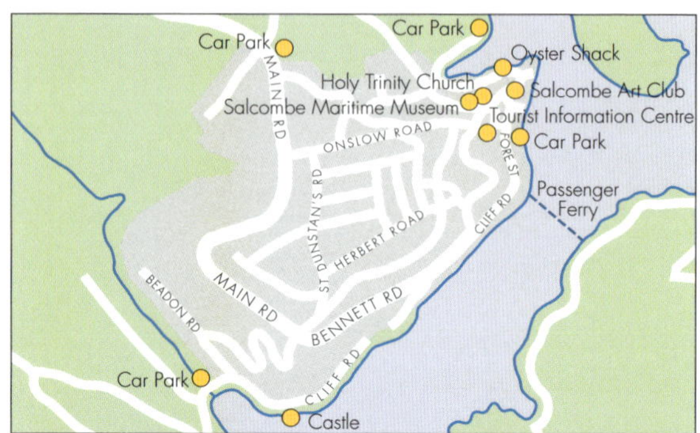

Salcombe

Entering Salcombe Harbour

Spring Blossom, Overbecks Garden

1943 Evacuation of the South Hams for invasion exercises.

1944 June 6. American and British troops leave Devon ports for D-Day landings on Normady.

Salcombe Maritime Museum

Oyster Shack, Hannaford's Landing, 10-13 Island Street. If they can make this business work in the middle of nowhere (near Bigbury), why not in sunny Salcombe? Just opened. Expect the same fresh delivery of crustacea and locally caught seafood. Open daily. (M8) 01548 843956 www.oystershack.co.uk

Restaurant 42, 42 Fore Street. Restaurant, bar and brasserie's terrace overlooks the beautiful estuary. Simple, elegant and unfussy describes the style of cuisine, ingredients for one of Devon's finest. (M8) 01548 843408 www.restaurant42.co.uk

of eateries and a number of boat hirers, too. The RNLI Lifeboat is one establishment that has no seasonal shortfall, and for all seafarers, the RNLI Museum, opposite the Victoria Inn, is a worthy Port-of-Call. (M8)

East Portlemouth

Special Places to Visit…

Coves Quay Gallery, 6 Coves Quay. One of Salcombe's great attractions not to be missed; a bright and attractive gallery with a wide range of paintings and decorative art in all forms. Open daily. (M8) 01548 842666

ICC Activity, 10 Island Street. Watersports, sailing centre; courses (residential and non-residential) and daily boat hire. (M8) 01548 531176. www.icc-salcombe.co.uk

Overbecks Museum & Gardens (NT). Elegant Edwardian house containing local photos, model boats, animals, birds and eggs, moths and butterflies, dolls and toys. Special interest for children. Museum open daily Apr-Oct 11.30-5.30. (M9) 01548 842893 www.nationaltrust.org

Rosie Smith, Russell Court. Contemporary and abstract art, ceramics and textiles. Open Th F & W/Es, in summer M-Sa. (M8) 01548 844600

Salcombe Art Club, Victoria Quay. Paintings, drawings and ceramics by local artists in large studio overlooking the Estuary. Open East to early Oct M-Sa 10-1, 2-4.30 - also most Su. Victoria Quay. (M8)

Salcombe Chocolate Factory, Orchard Court, Shadycombe Road. Viewing area with video link to the Chocolatier. Factory shop. Open daily. M8) 01548 842260 www.choc-factory.com

Salcombe Maritime Museum, Market St. Unique collection of antique paintings. Trading schooners. Shipwrecks, fishing and shipbuilding. Open daily Apr-Oct 10.30-12.30, 2.30-4.30. (M8)

Tucker's Boat Hire, Victoria Quay. Self drive hire in 14-19ft boats. Fishing trips. (M8) 01548 842840

Where to Eat, Drink & Be Merry…

Catch 55, 55 Fore St. Popular, unpretentious, hardworking bistro offering simple recipes; steaks, tuna, hand-made burgers. Big portions. Open M-Sa. (M8) 01548 842646

Salcombe Coffee Co, 73 Fore St. Friendly little diner in centre of village. All day breakfast, high teas and supper. Open all year. (M8) 01548 842319 www.salcombe.co.uk

Ship to Shore, 45 Church St. Finest of modern English cuisine using fresh local produce, meat and seafood. Non-smoking. Open Tu-Sa (Su in Aug). (M8) 01548 8540 www.ship-to-shore.co.uk

Victoria Inn, Fore St. Traditional village Inn in the heart of the village. Home-made dishes, fish off the local boats. (M8) 01548 842604 www.victoriainnsalcombe.co.uk

RNLI Museum, Salcombe

1951 Oct 30. Dartmoor designated a National Park.

1952 Aug 16. River Lyn floods and drowns 31 people in Lynmouth.

Special Places to Visit…

Flete. Grade 1 listed building. Originally a Tudor manor house with C18 and C19 additions. Redesigned in late 1800s by Norman Shaw. Private residence with self-contained apartments. Public rooms & gardens open May-Sept W & Th 2-4. (G2)

Kitley Caves & Country Park. Come rain or shine, one can explore these famous South Devon caves with all the family. Open daily Good F-Oct 10-5.30. (E2) 01752 880885

Special Places to Stay…

Burgh Island Hotel.
Art Deco meets Agatha Christie. A one-off in a sensational position on a private island overlooking Bigbury Bay. Evening Dress is the norm for Dinner, more casual dining on beachside terrace or in Ganges room at lunch. (H6) 01548 810514 www.burghisland.com

Henley Hotel, Folly Hill.
Edwardian seaside villa with magical views over Bigbury Bay. Beautifully prepared food. Six bedrooms. (J5) 01548 810240 www.thehenleyhotel.co.uk

Plantation House Hotel, Totnes Rd. Highly rated Matisee Restaurant has won much praise from foodie writers. An elegant dining experience. Accommodation. (H2) 01548 831100. www.plantationhousehotel.com

Thurlestone Hotel. Luxurious family hotel set beside the unspoilt and spectacular South Devon Coast. There are many leisure, sports and spa facilities including a 9-hole golf course and the Dolphin Children's Club. Award-winning restaurant. For more informality, the Village Inn, next door. (K6) 01548 560382 www.thurlestone.co.uk

B & Bs – a selection

Ermington, Goutsford
01548 831299(H1)

Palm Cross Green, Orchard Cottage, Back St.
01548 830633 (J2)

Ringmore, Aymer House
01548 810391 (H5)
www.ayrmerhouse.org

Pubs Serving Food…

Pilchard Inn, Burgh Island.
A glorious watering hole (since 1336) on a sunny day made famous by Tom Crocker whose ghost still haunts it. Fine ales and bar food. Cross via Sea tractor (cut off twice daily). (H6) 01548 810514 www.burghisland.com

Ship Inn, Noss Mayo. Light, airy and nautical. Fresh fish, Devon lamb and salmon. Log fires and newspapers. (C4) 01752 872387 www.nossmayo.com

Sloop Inn, Bantham.
Former smugglers inn offering fine fresh fish and shell fish. Accommodation. (J6) 01548 560489.

Village Inn, Thurlestone.
C16 Inn belonging to the Grove family for over 100 years. Free house serving real ales and fresh seasonal food, seafood a speciality. Themed nights. Live music. Children and dogs welcome. Open daily from 11.30 for coffee and pastries. (K6) 01548 563525 www.thurlestone.co.uk

Newton Ferrers

Thurlestone Sands

1954 Exmoor designated a National Park.

1955 University of Exeter receives royal charter.

Bantham Boathouse

Sharp Tor the path comes down past Overbecks Gardens to join the road to Salcombe.

Beaches & Surfing...

Bovisand.
Sand and rocks. R/WC. (A3))

Wembury. Sand and rocks. R. (B4)

Stoke. Pebbly sand and rocks 1/4 mile hike from P. (D5)

Mothecombe. Sand and low cliffs. 1/4 mile hike from P/WC/R. (G4)

Where to Eat, Drink & Be Merry...

Old Mill Cafe, Wembury (NT). Mill house on beach. Open Apr-Oct 10.30-5. (B3)01752 862314

Oyster Shack, Milburn Orchard Farm. Seafood bistro; local oysters and fresh fish al fresco. Open for breakfast and lunch Tu-Su. (K4) 01548 810876 www.oystershack.co.uk

Rose & Crown, and Seafood Restaurant, Yealmpton. Two new, separate restaurants, opposite each other, are fast gaining deserved reputations for delivering the goods. (E2) 01752 880223/01752 880502. www.theroseandcrown.co.uk

Venus Cafe, Bigbury On Sea. Environmental award-winning cafe in stunning beach location. Breakfast, lunch and ice creams. Open daily East-Oct & winter W/Es. (J6) 01548 810141 www.venuscompany.co.uk

Coastal Footpath...

Yealm Estuary to Erme Mouth; 11 miles. From the far side of the ferry the path follows the left bank of the Yealm and rounds Gara Point, continuing along Revelstoke Drive, a scenic C19 carriageway. Up to Blackstone Point the coastline is owned by the National Trust. The path keeps close to the clifftops and there is access to a number of secluded coves. After Stoke Point comes the ascent of Beacon Hill and a succession of further climbs and descents. Approaching Mothercombe the route turns inland and there is a short stretch of road leading to the beach at the mouth of the Erme. There is no ferry and the water can only be crossed one hour either side of low tide - otherwise a long detour is necessary.

River Erme, Sequers Bridge

Erme Mouth to Bigbury; 5 miles. The path continues near the cliff edge with fairly strenuous ups and downs. Bigbury is a small resort with modest amenities, from which Burgh Island can be visited.

Bigbury to Hope Cove; 7 miles. There is a ferry across the Avon on a limited summer schedule, but the river can also be crossed on foot at low tide. From Bantham is an easy cliffside walk skirting the golf course to Thurlestone Sands and along the shore to Hope Cove, an attractive fishing harbour.

Hope Cove to Salcombe; 9 miles. One of the most spectacular sections of the path - the whole stretch is owned by the National Trust. After ascending Bolt Tail, the route follows the cliff top all the way, with steep descents to Soar Mill Cove and Starehole Bay. After ascending

Bigbury-on-Sea. Fine sandy beach popular with young families. Rock pools. One of Britain's best locations for windsurfing, canoeing and coastal walks. Beach cleaned daily in summer. Lifeguards May-Sept. Burgh Island and the Pilchard Inn accessible by the unique tractor, or by foot, at low tide. Check tractor times if looking to spend a day on the island. No dogs, May-Sept. Café/gift shops. (H6)

Bantham. Sand and safe bathing. Dogs in restricted areas. P/R/WC. (J6)

Thurlestone. Sand and safe bathing. Disabled access. Dogs permitted. P/R/WC. (K7)

Hope Cove. Sand and safe bathing. Popular with young families. Shop. Inn. P/R/WC. (K8)

Salcombe South Sands. Fine golden sand. Safe bathing. Beach shop. Café and bar. Parking limited but can be accessed by ferry from Salcombe. R/WC. (M9)

Salcombe North Sands. Sand and safe bathing. Limited disabled access. Dogs permitted. P/R/WC. (M9)

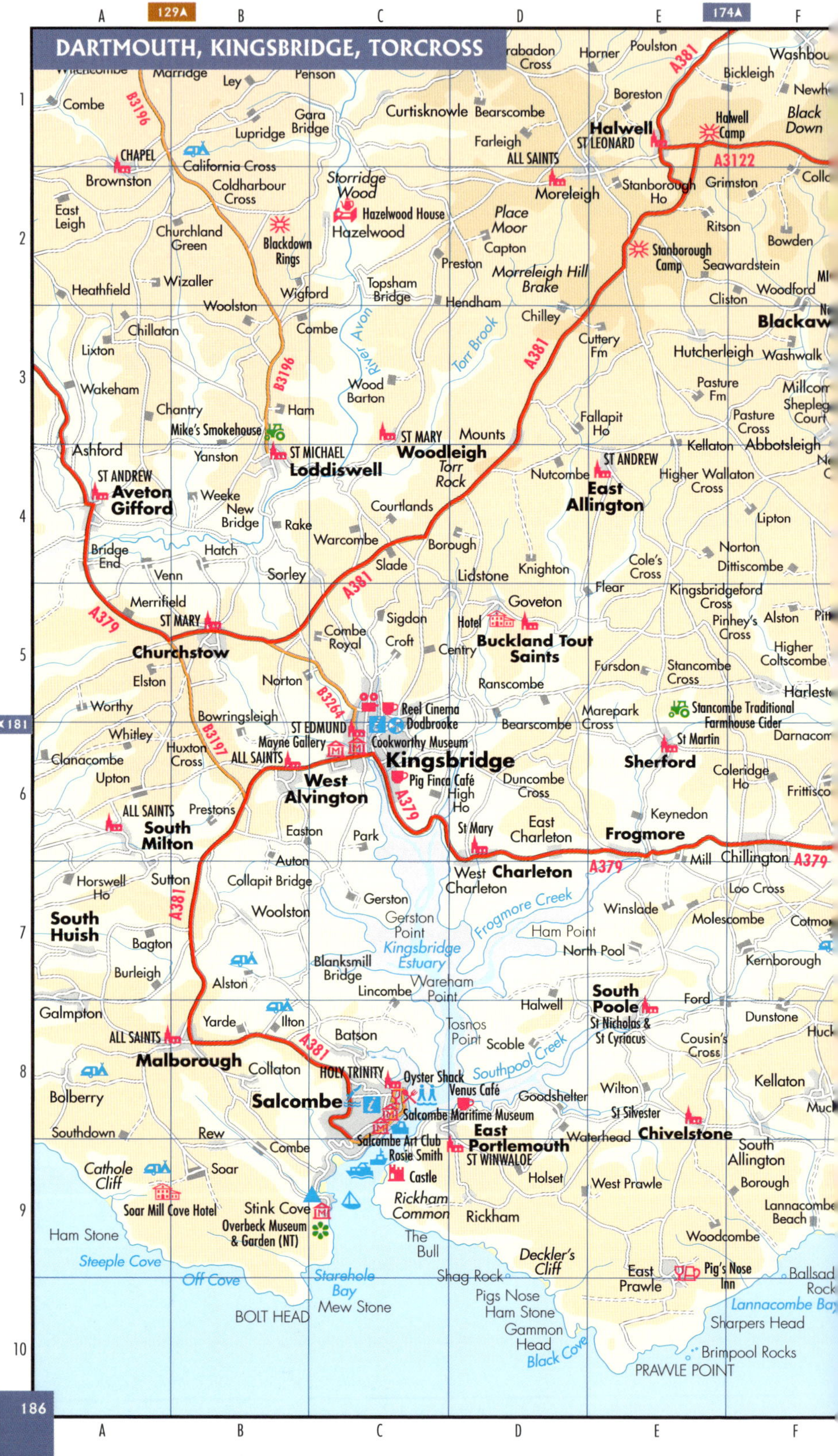

DARTMOUTH, KINGSBRIDGE, TORCROSS
129A
174A
181
186
A
B
C
D
E
F
1
2
3
4
5
6
7
8
9
10
Marridge
Ley
Penson
Horner
Poulston
Washbou
Combe
B3196
Gara Bridge
Curtisknowle
Bearscombe
A381
Boreston
Bickleigh
Newh
Lupridge
Farleigh
Halwell
ST LEONARD
Halwell Camp
Black Down
CHAPEL
Brownston
California Cross
ALL SAINTS
A3122
Coldharbour Cross
Storridge Wood
Moreleigh
Stanborough Ho
Grimston
East Leigh
Hazelwood House
Hazelwood
Place Moor
Ritson
Churchland Green
Blackdown Rings
Capton
Bowden
Stanborough Camp
Seawardstein
Preston
Morreleigh Hill Brake
Heathfield
Wizaller
Wigford
Topsham Bridge
Hendham
Woodford
Clifton
Woolston
Chilley
Blackaw
Chillaton
Combe
River Avon
Torr Brook
Cuttery Fm
Lixton
Hutcherleigh
Washwalk
A381
B3196
Wood Barton
Pasture Fm
Millcom
Wakeham
Shepleg Court
Chantry
Ham
Pasture Cross
Fallapit Ho
Mike's Smokehouse
ST MARY
Mounts
Kellaton
Abbotsleigh
Ashford
ST MICHAEL
Woodleigh
Yanston
Loddiswell
Torr Rock
ST ANDREW
ST ANDREW
Nutcombe
Higher Wallaton Cross
Aveton Gifford
Weeke
East Allington
New Bridge
Courtlands
Lipton
Rake
Warcombe
Borough
Norton
Bridge End
Hatch
Ditiscombe
Slade
Cole's Cross
Venn
Sorley
Lidstone
Knighton
Flear
A381
Kingsbridgeford Cross
Merrifield
Goveton
A379
Sigdon
Pinhey's Cross
Alston
ST MARY
Hotel
Combe Royal
Buckland Tout Saints
Croft
Higher Coltscombe
Churchstow
Centry
Fursdon
Stancombe Cross
Elston
Norton
Ranscombe
B3264
Harlest
Worthy
Reel Cinema
Marepark Cross
Stancombe Traditional Farmhouse Cider
Bowringsleigh
Dodbrooke
Bearscombe
Whitley
ST EDMUND
Cookworthy Museum
St Martin
Darnacom
B3197
Mayne Gallery
Huxton Cross
Clanacombe
ALL SAINTS
Kingsbridge
Sherford
Upton
West Alvington
Pig Finca Café
Duncombe Cross
Coleridge Ho
High Ho
A379
Frittisco
ALL SAINTS
Prestons
Keynedon
South Milton
East Charleton
Easton
St Mary
Park
Frogmore
Auton
Mill
Chillington
A379
Horswell Ho
Sutton
West Charleton
Charleton
A379
Collapit Bridge
Loo Cross
A381
Gerston
Frogmore Creek
Winslade
South Huish
Woolston
Gerston Point
Molescombe
Ham Point
Cotmor
Bagton
Kingsbridge Estuary
North Pool
Blanksmill Bridge
Kernborough
Burleigh
Wareham Point
Alston
Lincombe
South Poole
Ford
Galmpton
Halwell
Tosnos Point
Dunstone
Yarde
Ilton
St Nicholas & St Cyriacus
ALL SAINTS
Batson
Scoble
Huck
Cousin's Cross
A381
Southpool Creek
Malborough
Collaton
HOLY TRINITY
Oyster Shack
Kellaton
Venus Café
Goodshelter
Wilton
Bolberry
Salcombe
Salcombe Maritime Museum
St Silvester
Much
East Portlemouth
Southdown
Rew
Waterhead
Chivelstone
Salcombe Art Club
South Allington
Combe
ST WINWALOE
Rosie Smith
Catholé Cliff
Soar
Castle
Holset
West Prawle
Borough
Rickham Common
Soar Mill Cove Hotel
Stink Cove
Rickham
Lannacombe Beach
Overbeck Museum & Garden (NT)
Ham Stone
The Bull
Woodcombe
Deckler's Cliff
Steeple Cove
East Prawle
Pig's Nose Inn
Ballsad Rock
Off Cove
Starehole Bay
Shag Rock
Pigs Nose
Lannacombe Bay
Mew Stone
Ham Stone
BOLT HEAD
Sharpers Head
Gammon Head
Black Cove
Brimpool Rocks
PRAWLE POINT

Fingals
ST GEORGE
Dittisham
Home of Agatha Christie
Greenway House
Maypool
A379
Higher Brixham
ST MARY
Brixham
Broadridge
Bozomzeal Cross
Fire Beacon Hill
RIVER DART
Guzzle Down
Southdown
Kingston
Hillhead Fm
Hillhead
Woolcombe
Bosomzeal
A379
Man Sands
Capton
Downton
B3205
Dinnicombe
Hole
Noss Points
River Link
Woodhuish
Bruckton
BRITANNIA HALT
Old Mill Creek
Rough Hole Point
Hoodown
Nethway Ho
Long Sands
Chipton
Hemborough Post
Hemborough
A3122
Royal Naval College
Boohay
Scabbacombe Sands
Lower Norton
Old Mill
Wadstray
ST CLEMENT
ST SAVIOUR
Dartmouth
Norton
Kingston
Hillfield
A3122
Agincourt House
Henley Museum
ST THOMAS
Kingswear
Coleton Fishacre (NT)
Dartmouth Town Museum
Woodbury Camp
Ivy Cove
Newcomen Engine House
Kingswear Castle
Royal Castle Hotel
Pudcombe Cove
Greenswood Ash
ST PETROX
Dartmouth Castle (EH)
Day Mark Column
Kelly's Cove
Worden
B3205
Fast Rabbit Farm
Blackstone Point
Outer Forward Point
Eastdown
Bowden
A379
Inner Forward Point
Mew Stone
Compass Cove
Stoke Fleming
Little Dartmouth
Combe
Combe
Meg Rocks
Combe Point
Fuge
Blackpool Gardens
ST PETER
Blackpool
Redlap Cove
Dancing Beggars
Mill
Venus Café
Hansel
Blackpool Sands
Landcombe
Strete
ST MICHAEL
Merrifield
Forest Cove
Loworthy
Asherne
A379
Pilchard Cove
Homelands
Lower Green Cross
Strete Gate
Slapton
Slapton Ley Field Studies Centre
ST JAMES
Slapton Ley
Slapton Sands
Slapton Nature Reserve
Lower Ley
Raised Beach
A379
Start Bay Inn
Torcross
Fuchsia Ceramics
Limpet Rocks
Sunnydale
Beesands
Tinsey Head
Greenstraight
Hallsands
Shoelodge Reef
Start
Nestley Point
START POINT
Ravens Cove
Black Stone
Peartree Point
0 1 2 miles
0 1 2 3 kilometres
1 2 3 4 5 6 7 8 9 10

DARTMOUTH

A rare gem. Magnificently situated harbour in deep water, sheltered by steep hillsides and a conduit for trade and pleasure boats sailing up and down the River Dart to Totnes. Few towns in Devon, or England, have had such an influence on the course of England's rich past. In the C12, the assemblage point for the second and third Crusades. The Elizabethan Age encouraged Devon men to explore the globe; to seek the North West Passage, the Straits of Magellan and the piratical waters of the Far East.

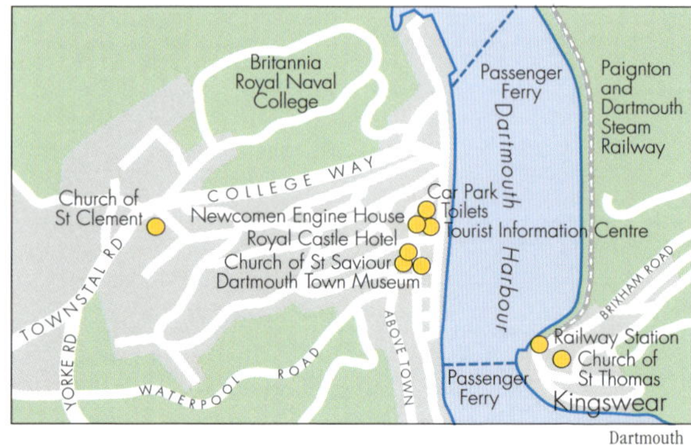

Dartmouth

Painting of Bayards Cove, Dartmouth Museum

Their boundless exploits on the High Seas, in the good name of Queen Elizabeth 1, and England, brought maritime supremacy and great bounty to this corner of England. Whether these men; Drake, Raleigh, Hawkins and Davis, be seen as adventurers, privateers or Her Majesty's Most Loyal Subjects, is open to debate. By the time of the Spanish Armada, Dartmouth was to be superseded by Plymouth as Devon's busiest port. The old warships would dock at Warfleet Creek, the smaller craft, largely smugglers, at Bayards Cove, now overlooked by some splendid C18 houses. Notably, the Custom House.

The town has great character and activity. Always a medley of locals and visitors. There is much to see; the finest building, The Butterwalk, enriched with eleven stone pillars. But take the riverside walk to the Castle and St Petrock's church, and look out across the water to smiling Kingswear, a feast of pastel-coloured houses, and junction for the Paignton Steam Railway, a marvellous site when in full steam charging up beside the river.

Behind, dominating the hillside stands the Brittania Royal Naval College, designed by Sir Aston Webb, architect of the V & A Museum. Opened by Edward V11, it is a most impressive building overlooking the Estuary, and the beckoning sea.

Always a popular port-of-call for yachtsmen, the Estuary has two marinas, and many cruisers plying their trade to show you the enchanting River Dart. The town has become something of a food and arts centre. Witness below the many arts and craft galleries, and the bountiful eating out emporia. Regatta time is a rewarding time to visit, the Estuary ablaze with sail and colour, and good times. (K2)

Arts & Crafts...

Ainscough Contemporary Art, 16 Foss Street. London gallery's south-west outpost has ever-changing exhibitions on West Country themes. Open daily. (K2) 01803 832160 www.acag.co.uk

Andras Kaldor Gallery, 15 Newcomen Rd. Drawings and paintings of architectural subjects. Originals and prints. Open daily. (K2) www.kaldor.com

Baxters, 12 Foss St. New enthusiastic owner displays contemporary art, crafts and jewellery. Open M-Sa 10-5, Su 11-4 (Apr-Dec) (closed W). (K2) 01803 839000 www.baxtersgallery.co.uk

Baxters ss

Simon Drew Gallery ss

1961 Tamar Bridge opened to traffic.

1966 Francis Chichester sets sail in Gypsy Moth IV on a solo one-stop global navigation, to be knighted the following year at Greenwich.

Painting of Brittania and Dartmouth, Dartmouth Museum

Blown Studio Glass Gallery, 2 Smith Street. Beautiful glass pieces in all shapes and sizes, and in multi-colours. Studio open by appointment. Gallery open daily. (K2) 01803 835123

Combe Gallery, 20 Foss St. Exhibits some of the finest artists and craftsmen in the West Country with regular quarterly shows. Open daily (K2) 01803 833833

D'Art Gallery, 4 Lower St. Paintings with a broad range of styles. Quarterly exhibitions display 70 + new works. Open daily 10-5 except Tu. (K2) 01803 834923 www.dart-gallery.com

Facets, 14 Broadstone. Specialises in a broad selection of affordable jewellery in gold, silver, metals, acrylics and ceramics. Displays over 70 designers. Open daily. (K2) 01803 833534 www.facets.co.uk

Higher Street Gallery, 1 High St. Fine arts and crafts; pottery, textiles, ceramic sculpture, jewellery, and oils and watercolours. Open M-Sa 9.30-5, Su 11-4. (K2)

Imago, 22 Fairfax Place. Gallery of contemporary jewellery displaying over 30 designers. Open M-Sa 10-5. (K2)

River D'Art Gallery, 7 Anzac St. Environmental project selling artworks linked to the River Dart. Open daily. (K2) www.riverdart.net

Dartmouth Castle

St Saviour's Church

Simon Drew Gallery, 13 Foss St. Studio ceramics, oils and watercolours, and Drew's illustrations. Open M-Sa 9.30-5. (K2) 01803 832832 www.simondrew.co.uk

Stewart Gallery, 3 The Old Market Place. Watch artist at work on his oils and acrylics from portraits to landscapes. Open daily. (K2) www.stewartgallery.co.uk

White Sails, 1 St Georges Square. Contemporary, modern and traditional art, in originals and limited editions. Many local artists. Open daily. (K2)

Special Places to Visit...

Brittania Museum, Royal Naval College. The Royal Navy's Officer Training Establishment since 1905. Fine works of naval art. Museum with historic naval artefacts. Fully escorted tours East-Oct in term time, W & Sa pm; see Dartmouth TIC on 01803 834224. 01803 677787. (K2)

Dartmouth Castle (EH), Castle Road. Castle dating back to the late C15, stands guard over the Dart Estuary. Features include hands-on exhibitions and displays. Open daily Apr-Sept 10-5, Oct-Mar Th-M 10-4. 01803 833588 (K2)

Dartmouth Museum, The Butterwalk. Housed in a group of C17 merchants' houses with fine panelled rooms. Notable ship models, paintings and rare books. Open all year, Mar-Oct 11-5, Nov-Feb 12-3. 01803 832923 (K2)

Newcomen Engine House, Mayors Avenue. Atmospheric beam engine on the unusual mechanical principle developed by Thomas Newcomen, a native of the town, in 1725. Now electrically worked. Open Apr-Oct M-Sa 9.30-5.30, Su 10-4. Nov-Mar M-Sa 10-4. (K2) 01803 834224 www.dartmouthtourism.org.uk

Parish Church of St Saviour. In the centre of the town and worth a visit just for seeing its magnificent C15 rood and parclose screen. Multi-coloured Jacobean pulpit in stone. Fine ironwork to South doorway. (K2)

St Petrock's Church. Set within the Castle grounds and the last sacred site sailors would spy as they sailed off to new horizons. Rebuilt in the Gothic style. Fine brasses to wealthy merchants. Pulpit and Royal Arms. Norman font. (K2)

The Flavel Arts Centre, Flavel Place. Multi-purpose arts and entertainment centre housing cinema, theatre and live music. Children's programmes, too. Café and bar. (K2) 01803 839530 www.theflavel.org.uk

The Quay, Dartmouth

Boating & River Interests...

Dartmouth Boat Hire Centre, North Embankment. Self-drive cabin and open boats. Comprehensive safety brief. Competitive rates include, fuel, life jackets, river charts and info pack. Skippered boat trips available. (K2) 01803 722367

Devon Angling, Orchard Meadow. Regular charter deep sea and coastal trips from Dartmouth. Summer opening M-Sa 8-5, Su 8-10. (K2) 01548 580888 www.anglingcentre.net

River Explore. Pleasure cruises to and from Dartmouth and Totnes. 1 hour Dartmouth Harbour sightseeing cruises. (K2) 07768 846605

River Link, 5 Lower Street. Cruises on the beautiful River Dart departing from Dartmouth and Totnes. Bar, commentary, toilets. Day time and evening cruises from Apr-Oct, Nov-Mar by arrangement. Daily circular cruises from Dartmouth except M & F. (K2) 01803 834488 www.riverlink.co.uk

Special Places to Stay...

Browns Hotel, 27-29 Victoria Road. Classy boutique hotel a short stroll from the harbour. Restaurant specialises in tapas, but this should not exclude their culinary credentials, for the proprietor organises the local food festival. (K2) 01803 832572 www.brownshoteldartmouth.co.uk

Royal Castle Hotel, The Quay. Former C17 Coaching Inn within the heart of Dartmouth. Four-poster beds and jacuzzis. Bargain Breaks. (K2) 01803 833033 www.royalcastle.co.uk

Where to Eat, Drink & Be Merry...

Anzac Street Bistro & Guesthouse, 2 Anzac Street. Bright, wood panelled restaurant serving locally caught seafood complimented with their home grown herbs and fruit. Contemporary, comfy double bedrooms. (K2) www.anzacstreetbistro.co.uk

Cafe Alf Resco, Lower Street. Busy with a lively buzz. All-day breakfast. Coffees. Live music. A great place to meet up. Open 7-2. (K2) 01803 835880

Dart Marina, Sandquay Road. The Wildfire Bar & Restaurant is a relaxed and informal place to eat and drink with fabulous river views; Try Sushi or grilled fish for lunch, or more formal Dinner. Close to Health Spa, Yacht Harbour, hotel and apartments. (K2) 01803 832580 www.dartmarina.com

Jan & Freddies Brasseries, 10 Fairfax Place. The cooking is simply done, the interior design is minimalist and contemporary. Both fuse to present a memorable and relaxed occasion. (K2) 01803 832491 www.janandfreddiesbrassrie.co.uk

New Angel, 2 South Embankment. TV chef, John Burton Race's new venture is already a massive success. A rich mix of Devon produce and French flair produces mouthwatering dishes from the kitchen, in full view. Accommodation on Victoria Road. Open Tu-Sa from 9am-11am, 12-2.30pm, 6.30-10pm. Su brunch & lunch only. (K2) 01803 839425 www.thenewangel.co.uk

Ruby Red Devon

Spice Bazaar, St Saviours Square. Simple style and relaxed atmosphere offering a fusion of authentic Indian cuisine suited to English tastes. Open 12-2, 6-11.30. (K2) 01803 832285.

Taylor's Restaurant, 8 The Quay. A more traditional restaurant affording spectacular views over the harbour. (K2) 01803 832748 www.taylorsrestaurant.co.uk

1985 Plymouth Dome designed.

1987 North Devon link road opened.

KINGSBRIDGE

Old established port at the head of a wide, landlocked estuary, now largely silted up but still active with small craft. The High Street ascends away from the river and is fronted by some attractive C18 and C19 buildings. The Shambles (or Market Arcade) extends over the pavement with Elizabethan piers. Birthplace of William Cookworthy, discoverer of china clay. A centre for the "South Hams" district. St Edmund's church is C13 with C15 additions. Cruises to Salcombe and around the coast. E/C Th. (C6)

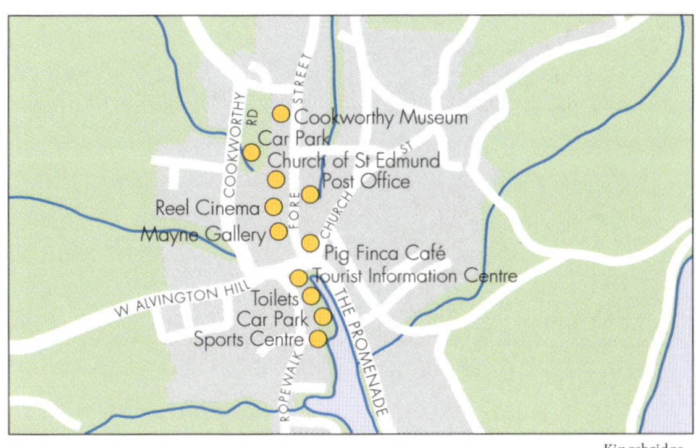

Kingsbridge

Special Places to Visit...

Cookworthy Museum, 108 Fore Street. Toys and dolls, farmhouse kitchen, rural trades, costumes, and local photos. Craft exhibs. "The Story of Kingsbridge". Conservation in farm gallery. Open Apr-Oct 10.30-5. (C6) 01548 853235

Mayne Gallery, 14 Fore St. Sculptures, etchings, watercolours of local artists. Open M-Sa 9-5. (C6) 01548 853848 www.maynegallery.com

Rivermaid, Rivermaid Boatyard, Embankment Road. Kingsbridge to Salcombe ferry cruises, scenic creeks & coastal excursions, evening cruises. Light refreshments. May-Sept. (C6) 01548 853525/853607

Pig Finca Café

Where to Eat, Drink & Be Merry...

Pig Finca Cafe, Opposite The Quay. Breakfast, lunch, dinner - it's organic. Wacky decor of Moorish-Iberian influence. Cazy loos. (C6) 01548 855777 www.pigfinca.co.uk

The Reel Cinema, Fore St. Cafe/bar. For cinema addicts; twice nightly and Sa matinees. All-inclusive meal deals. (C6) 01548 856636

Special Places to Visit...

Blackpool Gardens. Newly restored C19 sub-tropical garden. Open daily East-Oct. (J4) 01803 770606 www.blackpoolsands.co.uk

Coleton Fishacre (NT). Sheltered 18 acre garden in stream-fed valley. Uncommon trees and exotic shrubs. New plantings for year-round colour and interest. Set amid spectacular coastal scenery. Associations with D'Oyly Carte family. Tearoom. Gardens open W/Es in Mar, and House Apr-Oct W-Su & BHs 10.30-5.30. (M3) 01803 752466 www.nationaltrust.org.uk

Coleton Fishacre

1992 University of Plymouth receives charter.

1998 Local government re-organisation. Plymouth and Torbay become unitary authorities.

Mike's Smokehouse, 3 The Butts, Robins Park, Loddiswell. Fish, duck and chicken are smoked over New Zealand manuka woodchip, giving a unique flavour. Complete range of products available. (B4) 01548 559333 www.mikes-smokehouse.co.uk

Fast Rabbit Farm. 12 acres set in a sheltered valley with a natural stream. Ponds and lakes. Native and exotic plants. Walks through 30 acres of woodland. Open Su & BH Ms Mar-Jul 11-5. (H3) 01803 712437 www.fastrabbitfarm.co.uk

Fuchsia Ceramics, Torcross. Hand thrown stoneware. Fuchsia decorated Pottery. Open 10-5.30, closed Su (& M in winter). (G7) 01548 580390

Rosemary Moser Painter, East Prawle. Located at Rosemary Cottage. She's a painter of land and seascapes in oil, watercolour, mixed media and handmade prints. Open to pot luck. (E9) 01548 511318

Stancombe Traditional Farmhouse Cider. Traditional West Country brew made on premises, and for sale. Open all year 10-5. (E5) 01548 531634

Start Point Lighthouse. Set on Devon's most southerly peninsula. Climb the Tower, hear of shipwrecks and lighthouse living. Open Apr-July, Sept-Nov, W Th Su & BHs 12-5. July-Aug daily 11-5 (12 on M), 26th Dec-1st Jan 12-dusk. (H9) 01803 770606 www.lighthouse-visits.co.uk

Woodlands Leisure Park. A unique combination; indoor and outdoor attractions and family rides from Watercoasters, Toboggan Run, Arctic Gliders to playzones for all ages. Awesome Avalanche, Polar Pilots, Dizzy Dune Buggies, Falconry centre. Huge indoor venture zone, five floors of rides and slides. New Big Fun Farm. Award-winning camping site. Open daily mid-Mar to early Nov, winter W/Es & school hols, 9.30-5. (G2) 01803 712598 www.woodlandspark.com

Special Places to Stay…

Buckland-Touts-Saints. Magnificent C17 manor house set within romantic gardens. Luxury, peace and solitude, the by-word. Fine wines, local and international cuisine. Conference & Wedding facilities. (D5) 01548 853055 www.tout-saints.co.uk

Hazelwood House, Nr Loddiswell. Early Victorian country house set in a 67 acre estate of woodland, meadows and riverbanks. 5 self-catering cottages. Regular Concerts, Cultural Events and Courses. (C2) 01548 821232

Soar Mill Cove Hotel. In superb position overlooking one of England's prettiest coves. Unusual in that the hotel is on one level. All the necessities to unwind; saunas, indoor and outdoor pools. West Country produce supplies the kitchen. (A9) 01548 561566 www.soarmillcove.co.uk

Pubs Serving Food…

Normandy Arms, Blackawton. More restaurant with bar, than village inn, hence the later opening at 7pm. Gaining something of a reputation in South Hams for their "Modern British" menu. Open W-Su 12-2, Tu-Sa 7-9. (F3) 01803 712884

Pig's Nose Inn, East Prawle. Jolly atmosphere and fine hostelry for walkers and birdwatchers. Children and dogs welcome. Tempting ales. (E9) 01548 511209

Start Bay Inn, Torcross. C14 thatched inn noted for its wealth of seafood; John Dorey, Bass, skate, cod, sole (Dover and lemon) caught off the beach. Dog/child friendly. (G7) 01548 580553

Woodlands Leisure Park

Tower Inn, Slapton ss

Tower Inn, Slapton. C14 coaching inn hidden away beside the Chantry Tower. Fresh local produce prepared for lunch and dinner. (G5) 01548 580216

Where to Eat, Drink & Be Merry…

Venus Cafe, Blackpool Sands Beach. Alfresco dining; breakfast lunch and ice creams. Organic foods. Open daily from 10am. (J4) 01803 770209 www.venuscompany.co.uk

The Venus Cafe, Ferry Steps, East Portlemouth. Overlooks Salcombe's best beaches. Specialises in organic and local produce. Open daily East-Oct. (C8) 01548 843558 www.venuscompany.co.uk

Pig's Nose Inn, East Prawle

B & Bs – a selection…

Blackawton - Woodside Cottage 01803 898164 www.woodsidedartmouth.co.uk (F2)

Dartmouth - Hill View House, 76 Victoria Road. 01803 839372 www.hillviewdartmouth.co.uk (K2)

East Allington - Lower Norton Farmhouse, Coles Cross. 01548 521246 (E4)

Kingsbridge - Galleons Reach, Embankment Road. 01548 853419 (C6)

2001 Foot and Mouth epidemic in Devon.

2005 Feb. Foxhunting, deer-hunting and hare-coursing banned in England and Wales.

Slapton Sands

Kingsbridge - Washbrook Barn, Washbrook Lane. 01548 856901 www.washbrookbarn.co.uk (C6)

Kingswear - Nonsuch House, Church Hill. 01803 752829 www.nonsuch-house.co.uk (K2)

Coastal Footpath...

Salcombe to Start Point; 9 miles. There is a frequent ferry service to East Portlemouth throughout the year. The path traverses National Trust land for the first 5 miles and continues along an increasingly rugged coast, with some isolated beaches, and spectacular views around Prawle Point. Walking is moderately strenuous. Start Point has witnessed many wrecks over the years. The lighthouse can be visited and the area is noted for birds and butterflies.

Start Point to Torcross; 5 miles. After the descent to Hallsands the path follows an almost level shore.

Torcross to Dartmouth; 10 miles. For the first 6 miles the path follows the main road alongside Slapton Ley and on to Stoke Fleming. At the NT car park a mile beyond the village the path diverges round the coast and commands some fine views. The road is regained after Dartmouth Castle.

Beaches...

Mill Bay. Fine golden sands and rock pools. Limited parking. Access is via the ferry from Salcombe, or on foot from East Portlemouth. (C8)

East Portlemouth. Fine golden sand and rock pools popular with young families. Dogs permitted. Dinghy sailing centre. (C8)

Lannacombe.
Small sandy beach accessed via the Coast Path. (F10)

Beesands.
Shingle. Safe bathing. Boating pool. Disabled access. Dogs permitted. P/R/WC. (G8)

Torcross.
Sand and shingle. Disabled access. Dogs permitted. P/R/WC. (G7)

Blackpool Sands.
The most popular family beach on this stretch of coastline. Set in a sheltered cove. The sands are cleaned daily in summer. Lifeguards on duty May-Sept. Fine location for water sports, swimming, sailing and scuba diving. No dogs permitted. Café. Shop. Parking charge. WC. (J4)

Blackpool Sands

Spinster's Rock, Drewsteignton

Devon history starts with the discovery of Early Man in the caves of Torquay (Kent's Cavern) and Brixham. He lived off reindeer and hunted with weapons sharpened from flint. Their successors, the long-headed Iberians settled on Dartmoor living in circular stone huts topped with thatched.

At first they buried their dead in the crouch position. They later burnt them to store their ashes in clay pots. A stone chest was erected around the body or pot and covered with earth. At around 2,500 BC bronze was discovered and Dartmoor streams were washed for tin. In 1,000 BC a Celtic invasion from Ireland subdued the Iberians. With a second Celtic invasion around 500 BC came the knowledge of Iron and a new language with the Brythons. Some words continue in use to this day:- dun – hill, dur – water, combe – hill side valley, pen – head or end, and avon – river. The Celts later gave way to the Romans. But, it is important to understand the countless Neolithic and Bronze Age terms and their original uses.

Burial Chambers (Dolmens/Cromlech)

Originally built as family mausoleums made up of several large stones with a capstone, or two across the top. Inside, the unburned body was placed, then filled over with earth. The finest example is "Spinster Rock" at Shilstone Farm, Drewsteignton. You can park beside the road and walk into the field where it remains in fine condition. A more sophisticated development of this design, the chambered tumulus, is to be found at Carnac, Brittany, Belas Knap, Gloucestershire and in Wiltshire. Small burial chambers (Kistvaens) were scattered all over Dartmoor. There is little evidence of these today, all desecrated long ago. You would have seen a heap of stones with ashes placed in a pot. The normal construction would take a surround of stone circles. Examples to be seen at Merrivale Bridge, Postbridge or Lake Head Hill, Hound Tor.

Stone Circles

These are to be found all over Dartmoor. The stones were set upright in a diameter of between 60-100 feet but often larger. Marked with a small stone (burial chamber) in the centre. A ditch or bank may border the site. The best examples to be seen at Scorhill near Chagford, Greywethers near Fernworthy, and at Langstone Moor near Peter Tavy. Their original purpose is not clear. Some scholars believe they were used for tribal meetings; judicial, religious, sepulchral. Large charcoal remains in the centre suggest great fires or rituals; sacrificial burials, or mass burials following disease or pestilence.

Stone Rows or Stone Avenues

(single or double rows). These have long been associated with funeral rites. At the head of the row, a tumuli or burial chamber and at the end, a blocking stone. Each stone would have represented a household, or family of the tribe, and would have been placed in honour of their chief. Fifty plus such sites have been counted on Dartmoor. The best are to be seen at Drizzlecombe, Down Tor, Merrivale Bridge and Watern Hill.

Standing Stones (Monoliths/Menhirs)

These are prehistoric memorials, remnants of stone that have survived the elements; wind and rain, and archaeological interference. The Christian Celts sculpted crosses out of the granite blocks, and more recently the Romans and others drew inscriptions. The finest survivors, Caratacus Stone, Winsford Hill and Toreus Stone in Yealmpton churchyard.

Ancient Villages (Hut Circles)

There are literally hundreds of these scattered across Dartmoor. The original smallholding, a basic hut with enclosure to protect their animals from preying beasts. Occupied by late Neolithic and Bronze Age Man. The village would be located in a dry, well drained position close to pure water stocked with abundant fish, and on open ground, easily protected against wild beasts and away from the hostile valleys and wild swamps. As time moved on into the Bronze Age, Man learnt to exploit the streams working for tin, later to trade and export to the Continent through the mouths of the rivers Otter, Axe, Dart and Exe. Early trade routes have been traced from Wray Barton in Moretonhampstead, by Berry Road to Merripit, via Postbridge and on to Mis Tor. A Roman route runs south from Okehampton from 100 BC to 100AD.

The Roman Period

The Romans didn't venture much beyond their garrison at Exeter beside the River Exe although satellite warning forts have been discovered at Countisbury on the North Coast and they would have reached this remote spot via sea, sailing down from Gloucester (Glevum). Evidence of the Roman Occupation has been excavated at Seaton and Uplyme. A Roman road through Honiton and south to Axminster (and Axmouth) connects the Fosse Way.

The Celtic Period

Once the Romans left, Britain was ripe for invasion. In the early C5 the Irish Celts invaded North Devon and Cornwall, and the west became the Kingdom of Dumnovia, to be Christianised by Irish missionaries. They gave firm resistance to the Saxon invaders. Later in the C6 and C7 the mystical King Arthur was born. In the C9 and C10, Kings Egbert and Athelstan pushed to forge a united Kingdom. Thereafter the Saxons settled into the valleys within their enclosures to raise their crops and domestic animals. Peace was interrupted by the invading Danes in the C9 who ravaged the coast. It was not until the Norman Conquest of the C11 that life took on a modicum of stability for the Saxon peasant.

William I

William divided the Saxon lands amongst his favourite Norman knights. The great Lords of Devon became the Earl of Mortain, Earl Hugo, Baldwin the Sherrif, Judhael de Totnes, William de Mohun and Ralph de Pomeroy. Many of the Saxon manors were passed to the churches (Abbeys) in Normandy. Exeter Castle was put to siege and most of the county barring Dartmoor and Exmoor was disafforested and given over to agriculture.

West Front, Exeter Cathedral

The Tudor monarchs

With Henry V11, Henry V111 and Edward V1, life in Devon was full of strife and difficulty. In 1497, the men of Devon and Cornwall rose up against the burden of taxation, and took to arms under Lord Audley. They were defeated at Blackheath. Later that year the Pretender Perkin Warbeck collected followers from Devon and Cornwall and besieged Exeter to be beaten back by the Earl of Devon. The Dissolution of the Monasteries under Henry V111 kept unrest on the boil. But, things took a turn for the worse under Edward V1 when he introduced changes to the Common Book of Prayer (the following turn of events incomprehensible today). A rebellion started at Sampford Peverel, and quickly spread. Headed by Sir Thomas Pomeroy, they marched to Exeter, occupied the town and set up fortifications at St Mary Clyst. To be soundly defeated by German mercenaries under the command of Lord Russell. The ringleaders were summarily executed; hung, drawn and quartered. So ended the Devon Rebellion.

Elizabeth 1

Devon men took patriotism (and self-interest) to all corners of the globe. Under a galaxy of famous sea captains; Raleigh, Drake, Gilbert and the Hawkins. Their devotion to England and her cause (or Queen) could not be questioned?

The Civil War

The gentry and countryside were Royalist, whilst the towns largely followed the Parliamentarians (Cromwell). The Queen, Henrietta Maria, inspected Prince Rupert's army at Crediton. Plymouth and Dartmouth withstood sieges, and Exeter was garrisoned by the Parliamentarians. Tavistock became a Royalist stronghold in 1643. Tiverton changed hands many times. Torrington was the scene of one of the bloodiest battles when Fairfax defeated the Royalists under Lord Hopton in 1646. The irony was that the Parliamentarian General Monk, a Torrington man, became the main force behind the Restoration (return of Charles 11).

Agriculture

The Devon man was soon to become shaped by his social and economic circumstances. Those living beside, or close to, the sea made a living from it, either as sailors in the Navy, or as fishermen. Devon had long held a tradition of trade well before the Roman Occupation. The development of shipbuilding in the ports of Bideford and Barnstaple, Brixham, Dartmouth and Plymouth, enlivened the entrepreneurial skills of merchants who took to trading on a global scale. The landscape was shaped by the Devon peasant. The small fields, or enclosures were cleared of rock and stones, to shape either drystone walls evident on Dartmoor, or the tall, thick hedges that look soft and inviting as you drive past in the summer but beware they have an underbelly of rock and solid earth. The same earth, mixed with straw and stones, made the mixture known as cob. The vernacular building material to be topped with thatch. The substance of the soil moulded the variations in Agriculture. The rich, red soil of South Hams encouraged cream and cider production, the district of Holsworthy was noted for horses, today it's the Ruby Red Devon cattle. The Tamar Valley took to strawberries. Dartmoor was overlooked for cereal production but the ruggedness suited sheep farming. The North Devon soil produced clay.

Industry

The major industry of the time was developed from the metals, tin and copper. The two western counties, Devon and Cornwall were the sole suppliers of tin up until about 1700. Obtained either as stream-tin or mined-tin (from alluvial deposits). The governance of tin came under the auspices of the Courts of Stannary set up under a Charter by Edward 1. The Court was held at Crockern Tor, an isolated location in the middle of Dartmoor Forest, often attended by 300 gentlemen on horseback. They fixed the price and production.

The purchase and distribution of tin was organised through the four Stannary towns; Ashburton, Tavistock, Plympton and Chagford. The manufacture of woollen cloth was an important Devon industry through the Middle Ages and up to the C19. Crediton and later Exeter were the centres, second to only Leeds in the C18. Tiverton and Cullompton were also centres. But by 1825 the trade had declined. Lace production in the towns of Honiton, Bampton, Uffculme, Cullompton, Ottery St Mary compensated for the loss of the woollen industry and the outlying villages were responsible for much of the labour but this was short-lived. The construction of the Grand Western Canal was a hoped-for saviour to connect Topsham with the River Tone at Taunton.

Exeter however continued to grow as a City. The Napoleonic Wars restricted European travel so the gentry were forced to seek out new places to relax. Exmouth became the first watering-place, soon followed by Sidmouth, Budleigh Salterton, Teignmouth and Torquay. So began the great tourist industry. New roads made the sojourn easier, and so the transformation from horse-borne to horse-drawn began along the new road from London to Exeter via Amesbury (A303 today). Later the Golden Age of the Railways brought much needed affluence, and the development of more coastal towns; Ilfracombe, Minehead, Dawlish and Totnes.

The C20 brought prosperity to the county through the increase in tourism. Small companies moved to the region to provide a higher standard of living for their employees, and the ever-present pensioner looked to the South West Coast as a pleasing place to end their days. The great naval dockyard at Devonport flourished in the two World Wars, and continues to this day, maintaining our fleet of nuclear submarines. The fishing fleets of Brixham and Plymouth provide seafood for the many restaurants of the Southwest, and beyond. Shipbuilding has had a similarly precarious time of it. It is difficult to keep up to date with their news.

The results of a recent poll in a national newspaper concluded that Devon would be the first choice county to live in the UK. It is host to the same number of visitors as Cornwall per year.

Sir Francis Drake

Sir John Hawkins, 1532-1595

Adventurer, Privateer, Slave Trader. Son of Plymouth privateer William Hawkins. He was one of the first to capture slaves in Sierra Leone and to sell them on to the Spanish settlers in the Caribbean. Voyages backed by Elizabeth 1 and the Earls of Leicester and Pembroke. Knighted for his role in defeating the Spanish Armada. Later made Treasurer of the Navy. Foiled plot to assassinate Queen Elizabeth 1.

Sir Humphrey Gilbert, 1539-1583

Explorer, MP, Navigator, Soldier. Born at Greenway, lived at Compton Castle. Educated at Eton and Oxford where he studied Navigation and the Art of War. Later called to the Bar at the Inns of Chancery. Half-brother to Sir Walter Raleigh. Military career in Ireland and the Netherlands. Obsessed with the Elizabethan Quest to find the North West Passage. He sailed to America and discovered Newfoundland in 1583, but generally his sea voyages achieved very little and ended disastrously.

Sir Francis Drake, 1541-1596

Explorer, Pirate, Privateer, Slave Trader and the Queen's Favourite. Beckoned to the sea aged 13, to learn his trade in the North Sea. Later, aged 23, he made his first voyage to the New World as a slave trader (first started by the Spanish). His dislike of the Spanish endeared him to Queen Elizabeth who encouraged his raiding of Spanish and Portugese shipping. His successful circumnavigation of the world between 1577-1580 on the Golden Hind was his greatest achievement. He was second-in-command during the Armada campaign and Mayor of Plymouth. He died of dysentery off the coast of Panama.

John Davis, 1550-1606

Arctic Explorer, Cartographer, Inventor, Scientist. Writer on Seamanship. Born at Sandridge Park near Stoke Gabriel beside the River Dart. He made three unsuccessful voyages in search of the North West Passage. He did, however, map the coastlines of Greenland, Baffin Island and Labrador. The Davis Strait was named after him. He identified the cod fishing banks off Newfoundland, and his famous "Traverse Book" became a model for the ships' log books. Inventor of the navigational device, the backstaff and double quadrant (Davis Quadrant). Commanded the Black Dog against the Spanish Armada. Discovered the Falkland Islands in 1592 aboard the Desire, having earlier failed to pass through the Straits of Magellan. His crew killed 14,000 penguins for homeward bound food, but the meat went foul on reaching the Tropics, and only 14 out of a crew of 76 men survived. Assassinated by Japanese pirates off the coast of Malaysia.

Sir Walter Raleigh, 1554-1618

Explorer, Seafarer, Pirate, Poet and Politician (who came to a sticky end – beheaded for Treason on James 1's ruling). Born at Hayes Barton, East Budleigh. His exploits at sea came to the notice of Queen Elizabeth 1 where he became one of her favourites. Posted to the Captain of the Guard, he foiled the "Babington" plot whose purpose was to replace Elizabeth with Mary, Queen of Scots. His trips to the New World, and discovery of tobacco, originally thought of as a cure for coughing, brought him great wealth. He later built Sherborne Castle in Dorset.

Sir Walter Raleigh

Sir Richard Hawkins, 1562-1622
Adventurer, Seafarer, Mayor of Plymouth. Son of Sir John Hawkins. Sailed with Drake in 1585 to the Caribbean, to attack Spanish shipping. Later, distinguishing himself commanding The Swallow against the Spanish Armada. Sailed through the Straits of Magellan, attacked Valparaiso (Chile), to be held captive by the Spanish for ten years. Vice Admiral of Devon. Knighted in 1603 by James 1.

John Churchill,
1st Duke of Marlborough, 1650-1722. Soldier, Statesman. Born Ashe. The greatest European General of his generation. Served with distinction in Ireland and Flanders, later during The War of the Spanish Succession, 1701-1714 where on the fields of Blenheim (Hochstadt), Ramillies and Oudenarde, his place in history was assured. His wife, Sarah Jennings, was a confidant and friend to Queen Anne whose gift was Blenheim Palace after his victory over Louis XIV at Blenheim halted Louis ambitions to capture Vienna, and dominate Europe.

Thomas Newcomen, 1663-1729
Inventor. "Father of the Industrial Revolution". Born in Dartmouth. A humble, Ironmonger by profession and Baptist Lay Preacher. He invented the Atmospheric Steam Engine around 1710, and with the help of Thomas Savery, and his patents, one hundred engines were operating in Britain and Europe by the time of his death. His designs were later improved by James Watt who arranged for the steam to be condensed in a separate condenser.

John Lethbridge, 1675-1759
Inventor. Wool Merchant. Based in Newton Abbot, and as a father of seventeen children he sort wealth to feed them. He invented the one-man, enclosed diving suit with glass porthole for viewing and two watertight armholes with sleeves. The suit was made up of reinforced leather over an airtight oak barrel. His salvage work brought him great wealth.

John Gay, 1685-1732
Countryman, Dramatist, Journalist, Poet, Satirist, Wit. Born in Barnstaple, and educated at the local Grammar School. Apprenticed to a London silk merchant. He was friend to Pope and Swift, and William Congreve. His patrons were the Duke and Duchess of Queensberry, and the Earl of Burlington. This man loved to party, he loved good food, good company and blue ribbons. He was an early chronicler of country life. His breakthrough came with the play *The Beggar's Opera* in 1728, a satirical play about highwayman and the corrupt governing class. The two main characters, Captain Macheath and Polly Peacham, have entered the Hall of Fame. The basis for Kurt Weil and Bertolt Brecht's Threepenny Opera. Financially ruined by the South Sea Bubble. He lies in Poet's Corner, Westminster Abbey. On his tombstone, Pope wrote this epitaph: "Life is a jest, and all things show it, I thought so once, and now I know it".

Sir Joshua Reynolds, 1723-1792
English Painter. Born in Plympton and son of a clergyman. Studied in Rome 1749-52. The most influential of C18 English Painters specialising in portraits and promoting the "Grand Style". First President of the Royal Academy. Friend to Dr Johnson, Oliver Goldsmith, Edmund Burke and David Garrett. In his lifetime, 3,000 portraits commissioned. Buried in St Paul's Cathedral.

Charles Kingsley

Samuel Taylor Coleridge, 1772-1834
Poet, Philosopher and Womaniser. Born in Ottery St Mary and educated at Jesus College, Cambridge. He's considered one of the great Romantic poets (and philosophers). Shakespeare scholar, and friend to the Wordsworth's, Southey and Lord Byron. He and Southey married the Fricker sisters of Clevedon. His poem *The Rhyme of the Ancient Mariner* is listed on many school syllabuses.

The Reverend John (Jack) Russell, 1795-1883
Dog Breeder, Huntsman, "The Sporting Parson". Born in Dartmouth. Educated at Blundell's and Oxford where he spotted a terrier bitch called Trump owned by the local milkman. His ambition was to develop a hardy breed of terrier that could flush out the fox. He became a founder member of the Kennel Club, and friend of King Edward VII, who as the Prince of Wales, commissioned a portrait of Trump. Buried in Swimbridge churchyard, opposite the Jack Russell Inn.

Charles Kingsley, 1819-1875
Chartist, Clergyman, Novelist, Poet, Political Activist, Social Reformer, Wit, Writer. Born at Holne. Educated at Kings College, London and Magdalene College,

Sir Humphrey Gilbert nt

Cambridge. Brought up around Clovelly. He has the unique legacy of having a town named after his novel, *Westward Ho!* which in due course inspired the construction of the Appledore-Bideford Railway. Witnessing the Bristol Riots of 1831 formed his social and political outlook. His parish was Eversley in Hampshire.

Sir Richard Burton, 1821-1890
Adventurer, Diplomat, Explorer, Fencer, Linguist, Orientalist, Soldier, Translator. Born in Torquay. He was thrown out of Oxford and continued to undermine authority for much of his life. He had a natural empathy with languages and as a master of disguise managed to enter the Forbidden Cities of Harar, Mecca and Medina. He co-discovered Lake Tanganyika searching for the source of the Nile. He translated the Arabian Nights, and the Kama Sutra, and introduced the words Pyjama and Safari to the English language. Served in India. Diplomat in Equatorial Guinea, and Brazil. Knighted by Queen Victoria. He died in Trieste.

Sabine Baring-Gould, 1834-1924
Hymn-Writer, Novelist, Scholar, Squire & Parson. Born in Exeter, lived for 40 years at Lewtrenchard Manor where he fathered 15 children with Grace, a Yorkshire mill girl, and his wife for 48 years, who on meeting and then marrying her sent her off to be educated for two years. Wrote Onward Christian Soldiers and 200 published works. His output was immense, not least his enthusiasm for West Country folk songs resulting in the collection "Songs of the West".

Captain Robert Falcon Scott, 1868-1912
Antarctic Explorer, Royal Naval Officer and father of Peter Scott; Founder of the Wildfowl and Wetlands Trust, and the World Wide Fund for Nature. Born at Outlands, Stoke Damerel. He led two expeditions backed by the Royal Geographical Society; The Discovery Expedition of 1901-1904 was the first attempt at reaching the South Pole. They turned back 450 miles from their objective. This included Ernest Shackleton in the party. The second, and final attempt, the Terra Nova Expedition of 1910-1913, "The Race to the South Pole" failed. Beaten by the Norwegian, Raold Amundsen, by a month. On their return journey to base camp all four of his party died of exposure and hunger eleven miles from their fuel and food depot.

Agatha Christie, 1890-1976
Born and brought up in Torquay, later to live with her archaeologist husband, Max Mallowan, at Greenway on the banks of the River Dart. Known as the Queen of Crime, and inventor of crime's two famous sleuths; Hercule Poirot and Miss Marple. Two billion copies of her books have been sold world-wide.

Sir Francis Chichester, 1901-1972
Aviator, Navigator, Solo Sailor, Map Publisher and Writer. Born in Barnstaple, emigrated to New Zealand aged 18 where he set up a lumber and property business. An interest in flying fostered a passion for navigation. He was to write the official Navigation Manual for the Air Ministry. Best remembered for his epic single-handed circumnavigation of the globe in 1966, from West to East, with one stop in Sydney. Knighted by Queen Elizabeth 11 using Sir Francis Drake's sword.

Robert Herrick, 1591-1674
Cavalier Poet, Country Parson. Born in Cheapside, London. Apprenticed to a Goldsmith. Educated at St John's College, Cambridge. He was a friend of the poets Dryden and Marvel, and one of the "Sons of Ben", the

Cavalier Poets who idolized Ben Jonson, meeting regularly in the London tavern, the Devil's Head. In 1629, he was appointed by Charles 1 to be Vicar of Dean Prior. At first, country life bored him. Country people misunderstood him. He was to write his greatest poems in "dull Devonshire". Still hankering for the fleshpots of London. The puritans sent him packing back to London in 1647. In 1648, *Hesperides* was published, a mighty tome of 1,200 poems. He continued to live well, patronised by the Earls of Buckingham, Pembroke and Westmorland where his poems were read at Court. The Restoration of Charles 11 in 1660 returned him to Devon where he died a bachelor dreaming of fair Julia and Dianeme.

"Gather ye rosebuds while ye may,
Old time is still a flying
And this same flower that smiles today
Tomorrow will be dying"
To the Virgins to make Much of Time

Charles Babbage, 1792-1871
Computer Genius, Inventor, Mathematician. Born in London, moved to Devon, aged 8. Educated in Totnes and at Cambridge where he founded the Analytical Society in 1872 to combat poor learning methods. Designed the first mechanical computer, later the Analytic Engine, a complex machine, and the first mathematical machine to use punch cards (previously used on textile machines).

R. D. Blackmore, 1825-1900
Classicist, Horticulturalist, Literary Pioneer, Naturalist, Poet. Born in Oxfordshire, but his roots and ancestry lay in Devon. Educated at Blundell's and Oxford. His early life was spent at Culmstock and Ashford, then later on Exmoor beside Badgworthy Water. The setting for much of his classic novel, *Lorna Doone.* Called to the Bar in 1852, he was later advised by his Doctor (on account of his epilepsy) to live a calmer life. So he settled for teaching Classics in Teddington, Middlesex. By all accounts a lovely man, reclusive after his adoring wife's death. He started a Market Garden specialising in fruit. Fellow of the RHS.

Henry Williamson, 1895-1977
Broadcaster, Farmer, Naturalist, Soldier, Writer. Born in Brockley, South London. He fought on the Western Front during the First World War, at the Battles of the Somme, and Passchendale. Wounded, he returned home to speak out against the horrors of the trenches. Belittled, ignored, he found solace in the writings of Richard Jeffries, WH Hudson, Francis Thompson and the music of Delius, and Richard Wagner. On the publication of his first book, *The Beautiful Years*, he was thrown out of home, so rode his Norton 500 Motorcycle down to his beloved North Devon, and Skir Cottage, Georgeham. Remembered for the magnificent *Tarka the Otter*, Winner of the Hawthornden Prize in 1928, *Salar the Salmon*, and his tetrology *The Flax of Dreams*, and his fifteen-book work of Edwardian life, *The Chronicle of Ancient Sunlight.* He was largely ignored, shunned, ostracised by the British establishment due to his misguided dalliance with Mosleyism in the 1930s. His death coincided, to the day, with David Cobham's filming of Tarka's death scene in the film of the book.

Ted Hughes, 1930-1998
Children's Author, Farmer, Fly Fisherman, Naturalist, OM, Poet Laureate. Born in Mytholmroyd, West Yorkshire and raised on the surrounding farms. He entered Pembroke College, Cambridge to read English but switched to Archaeology and Anthropology. He married the American poet and feminist, Sylvia Plath 1956-63, who committed suicide, aged 30. His second great love, Assia Wevill, gassed herself and their four-year old daughter, Shura six years after Plath's death. He lived at Court Green, North Tawton and fished the River Torridge being a great encourager to fellow children's author, Michael Morpurgo. His last marriage to Carol Orchard, nurse, lasted until his early death from cancer.

Michael Morpurgo, Born 1943
Children's Author and Laureate, Countryman, Farmer, Fly Fisherman. Born in St Albans, he has lived in Mid Devon for thirty years. Good friend of Ted Hughes, who offered kind encouragement in his early days as a writer. With his wife, he founded the charity, Farms for City Children, in 1976. At the last count, more than 50,000 children have spent at least a week staying in one of their three farms. He has written over 90 books winning countless awards. Now a father and grandfather. He is the current Children's Laureate.

Samuel Taylor Coleridge

For specific dates please contact the local Tourist/Visitor Information Centre (see next page)

March

Easter Egg Hunt, Buckland Abbey
Exeter Vibraphonic Festival
Minehead – West Somerset Railway Diesel Gala

April

Dartmoor Hunt Point to Point, Flete Estate
Dartmouth Gig Regatta
North Devon & Exmoor Walking and Cycling Festival
Stokenham Garden Society Spring Show,

May

Appledore Visual Arts Festival
Blackawton Worm Charming Festival
Bluebell Spectacular; Parkham to Buck's Mill walk
Brendon Folk Festival
Brixham Heritage Festival
Combe Martin – Hunting of the Earl of Rone
Cornwood Spring Show, Cadleigh
Dart Music Festival
Devon County Show, Westpoint, Exeter
Exmoor Folk Festival
Exeter - Great West Run
Great Torrington Carnival
Great Torrington May Fair
Ivybridge Horse Show and Family Dog Show
Lord Mayor's Day, Plymouth
Lyme Regis Fossil Festival
Mayor's Sunday Parade, Dartmouth
Minehead & Dunster Hobby Horse Fair
Modbury Fair Week
Modbury Harriers, Point to Point, Flete Estate
Porlock Village Gardens, open
Potwalloping Festival, Westward Ho!
Prawle Fair
Quantock Food Festival
Saltram House Park Fair and Dog Show
Torquy Maritime Festival
Westward Ho! Potwalloping Festival

June

Allerford Spring Fair
Axe Vale Festival
Bigbury Fun Run
Bovey Tracey – Devon Guild Arts Fair
Brixham Trawler Race
Cornish Pilot Gig Regatta, Salcombe
Croyde Ocean Fest
Dartmouth Carnival
Dunster Castle – Grand Western Archery Competition
Ermington Fair
Holesworthy Carnival
Hot Penny Day, East Devon.
Lynton Music Festival
North Devon Festival
Ottery St Mary Pixie Day
Salcombe Festival.
Salcombe Regis Country Fayre.
South Brent Carnival Week.
Vintage Bus Rally, Seaton Tramway
West Country Garden Festival, Westpoint, Exeter
West Somerset Railway – Father's Day Special
Westward Ho! Carnival

July

Branscombe Air Day
Braunton Wheels Extravaganza
Budleigh Salterton Flower Show
Dartington International Summer School & Festival of Music
Dartington Literary Festival
Dunsford Show
Exeter Air Day. Teignmouth Regatta.
Exmouth Regatta
Exmouth Summer Fun Time
Filham Fun Day, Filham Park, Ivybridge
Holsworthy Show
Honiton Glove Fair
Honiton Hot Pennies Day
Killerton Open Air Concerts
Kingsbridge Bandstand Concert
Kingsbridge Fair week
Lyme Regis Lifeboat Week
Malborough Fayre
Marldon Apple Pie Fair
Merlin Rocket Week, Salcombe.
Mid Devon Show, Tiverton.
Midsummer Respect Festival, Exeter
Minehead Arts Festival
Porlock Pantomine
Port of Plymouth Regatta
River Yealm Regatta Rowing Finals
Saltram Jazz Picnic
Sidmouth International Folk Festival
Sidmouth Secluded Gardens Week
Sidmouth Society of Artists Annual Exhibition
Tavistock Food Festival
Teignmouth Regatta
Teignmouth Summer Carnival
Torbay Carnival
Totnes & District Agricultural Show
Ugborough Village Day Fair
West Somerset Folk Festival
Wiscombe Hill Climb
World Powerboat Champs British Grand Prix, Plymouth.
Yealmpton Show

August

Allerford Summer Fair
Beer Regatta
Bideford Folk Festival
Braunton Fair
Brendon Show
Brixham Fish Market Open Day.
Brixham Regatta.
Chagford Craft Fair
Combe Martin Fair
Dartington International Music Festival
Dartington West Country Storytelling Festival
Dartmouth Royal Regatta
Dawlish Carnival
Dawlish Regatta
Dunster Bat Hunt
Dunster Show
Exford Show
Emoor Mountain Bike Marathon
Honiton Show
Ilfracombe Carnival
Ilfracombe Fair
Lustleigh Show
Newton Abbot Antique Fair, The Racecourse
Newton Abbot Cheese & Onion Fayre
North Devon Show, Great Torrington
Okehampton Show
Paignton - Torbay Childrens' Weeks
Paignton Regatta.
Salcombe Regatta

Shaldon Regatta Week
Shaldon Water Festival
Sidmouth Folk Festival
South Devon Railway Fair
South Molton Sheep Fair
South Zeal – Dartmoor Folk Festival
Teignmouth National and World Fireball Sailing
Teignmouth Regatta.
Torbay Fortnight
Torbay Royal Regatta
Torbay Steam Fair
Totnes Carnival.
Woolacombe Creation Festival

September
Agatha Christie Week
Barnstaple Carnival
Barnstaple Regatta
Bideford Regatta
Colyford Goose Fair
Porlock Festival
Torbay Sea Angling Festival
Wellington Carnival
Widecombe-in-the-Moor Fair

October
Beer Rhythm And Blues Festival.
Dartmouth Fishing Festival
Devon Food Festival
Devon Hedge Week
Dulverton Carnival
Exeter Cathedral Trafalgar Day Service
Exeter Off The Wall Comedy Festival
Exmoor Food Festival
Exmouth Illuminated Winter Carnival.
Ivybridge Vintage Club Crank-Up
Tavistock Goosy Fair
Two Moors Festival

November
Ashburton Winter Carnival
Dunster By Candlelight
Dunster Festival Fireworks
Exeter Autumn Festival
Kingsbridge Christmas Extravaganza
Lynton & Lynmouth Festivities
Minehead – Winter Steam Festival
Okehampton Farmers Market
Ottery St Mary – Flaming Tar Barrels
Porlock Fireworks
Shebbear – Turning the Devil's Stone
South Brent Winter Carnival

Monthly Farmer's Markets
Bideford First Wednesday
Buckfastleigh Every Thursday
Cullompton Second Saturday
Crediton First Saturday
Exeter Last Wednesday
Kingsbridge First Saturday
Minehead Third Friday
Okehampton Third Saturday
Plymouth Second Saturday

All Year Markets
Barnstaple Pannier Market
Monday-Saturday
Local produce; Tuesday, Friday & Saturday
Local crafts; Monday & Thursday
Antiiques, collectables; Wednesday

Bideford
Tuesday – Pannier and Cattle Market
Wednesday – Seasonal Open Air Market
Saturday – Pannier Market

Great Torrington
Tuesday – General Market
Thursday – Pannier Market
Friday – Craft Market
Saturday – Collectors and Flea Market

Holsworthy
Wednesday – Open Air and Cattle Market

Tourist/Visitor Information Centres & National Park HQs
Ashburton – 01364 653426
Axminster – 01297 34386
Barnstaple – 01271 375000
Bideford – 01237 477676
Bovey Tracey – 01626 832047
Braunton – 01271 816400
Brixham & Paignton – 0870 70 70 010
Buckfastleigh - -1364 644522
Bude – 01288 354240
Budleigh Salterton – 01364 445275
Combe Martin – 01271 883319
County Gate – 01598 741321
Crediton – 01363 772006
Dartmoor National Park – 01626 832093
Dartmouth – 01803 834224
Dawlish – 01626 215665
Dulverton – 01398 323841
Dunster – 01643 821836
Exeter – 01392 265700
Exmoor National Park – 01398 323665
Exmouth – 01395 222299
Great Torrington – 01805 626140
Holsworthy – 01409 254185
Honiton – 01404 43716
Ilfracombe – 01271 863001
Ivybridge – 01752 897035
Kingsbridge – 01548 853195
Lyme Regis – 01297 442138
Minehead – 01643 702624
Modbury – 01548 830159
Lynton & Lynmouth – 01598 752225
Newton Abbot – 01626 67494
Ottery St Mary – 01404 813964
Plymouth – 01752 306330
Princetown - 01822 890414
Salcombe – 01548 843927
Seaton – 01297 21660
Shaldon – 01626 873723
Sidmouth – 01395 516441
South Molton – 01769 574122
Tavistock – 01822 612938
Teignmouth – 01626 215666
Tiverton – 01884 255827
Torquay – 0870 70 70 010
Totnes – 01803 863168
Woolacombe 01271 870553

The Map Reference Numbers follow the description.